MW00831631

THE PERILS OF NORMALCY

George L. Mosse Series in Modern European Cultural and Intellectual History

Series Editors

STEVEN E. ASCHHEIM, STANLEY G. PAYNE,
MARY LOUISE ROBERTS, AND DAVID J. SORKIN

Advisory Board

ANNETTE BECKER
Université Paris X–Nanterre

CHRISTOPHER BROWNING
University of North Carolina at Chapel Hill

NATALIE ZEMON DAVIS
University of Toronto

SAUL FRIEDLÄNDER
University of California, Los Angeles

EMILIO GENTILE
Università di Roma "La Sapienza"

YUVAL HARARI
Hebrew University Jerusalem

ANSON RABINBACH
Princeton University

JOHN S. TORTORICE
University of Wisconsin–Madison

JOAN WALLACH SCOTT
Institute for Advanced Study

JAY WINTER
Yale University

The Perils of Normalcy

George L. Mosse and the
Remaking of Cultural History

KAREL PLESSINI

THE UNIVERSITY OF WISCONSIN PRESS

Publication of this volume has been made possible, in part, through support from
the George L. Mosse Program at the University of Wisconsin–Madison.

The University of Wisconsin Press
1930 Monroe Street, 3rd Floor
Madison, Wisconsin 53711-2059
uwpress.wisc.edu

3 Henrietta Street
London wc2e 8lu, England
eurospanbookstore.com

Copyright © 2014
The Board of Regents of the University of Wisconsin System
All rights reserved. No part of this publication may be reproduced, stored in a
retrieval system, or transmitted, in any format or by any means, digital, electronic,
mechanical, photocopying, recording, or otherwise, or conveyed via the Internet
or a website without written permission of the University of Wisconsin Press,
except in the case of brief quotations embedded in critical articles and reviews.

Printed in the United States of America

Library of Congress Cataloging-in-Publication Data

Plessini, Karel, author.
The perils of normalcy : George L. Mosse and the remaking of cultural history /
Karel Plessini.
pages   cm — (George L. Mosse series in modern European cultural and
intellectual history)
Includes bibliographical references and index.
isbn 978-0-299-29634-6 (pbk. : alk. paper) — isbn 978-0-299-29633-9 (e-book)
1. Mosse, George L. (George Lachmann), 1918–1999. 2. Historians—
United States—Biography. I. Title. II. Series: George L. Mosse series in
modern European cultural and intellectual history.
D15.M668P55   2014
907.2′02—dc23
[B]
2013015053

To my parents

The wise man does not discriminate;
he gathers together all the shreds of light,
from wherever they may come.

—UMBERTO ECO

CONTENTS

ACKNOWLEDGMENTS

A large number of people have helped me along the way toward this paper. My deepest gratitude goes to Marina Cattaruzza, whom I would like to thank for the constant encouragement in this work on both a professional and a personal level, and for the help, the support, and the invaluable criticism she offered me over these years. My sincerest thanks go also to John Tortorice, Mosse's life partner, who has made possible, and greatly facilitated, my research in Madison, and who took the time to answer myriad questions and to provide me with hard-to-find materials: his friendship and his generous help have been inestimable for the completion of this work. Special thanks are also due to Emilio Gentile, who has supported this research from the beginning, and whose insightful writings on George Mosse have represented for me a constant source of inspiration as well as of confrontation. I owe a particular debt of gratitude to Stanley Payne for the numerous and pleasant conversations we have had about Mosse, history, and much else. I wish to record my gratitude as well to Raphael Kadushin, who has patiently encouraged and supported the publication of this study.

I gratefully acknowledge helpful discussions with Steven Aschheim, Jean-Jacques Becker, Paul Breines, Christopher Browning, Seymour Drescher, Modris Eksteins, Roger Griffin, the late Robert Kingdon, Dieter Langewiesche, Anson Rabinbach, Johann Sommerville, David Sorkin, Klaus Vondung, and Jay Winter, all of whom helped me gain new insights into Mosse's work and personality and enriched my perspectives with precious suggestions. Obviously any errors or inadequacies are my own.

This research was supported by several grants from associations and institutions to which I am most grateful: the Mosse Program in Cultural and

Intellectual History at the University of Wisconsin–Madison (directed by John Tortorice); the Friends of the University of Wisconsin–Madison Library (here in particular I wish to thank Tom Garver); the Fondazione Luigi Einaudi in Turin, Italy (which has generously allowed for the final completion of the manuscript); the Institut für Europäische Geschichte in Mainz, Germany (my thanks are due to Heinz Duchhardt and to the whole staff, who have made my stay there most fruitful and pleasant); the Josephine-de-Kármán-Stiftung and the Paul und Gertrud Hofer-Wild-Stiftung in Bern, Switzerland, which have supported the final stages of my PhD research.

I am greatly indebted to George Mosse, whom I unfortunately never met in person, but whose teachings and beliefs as expressed by his writings have nonetheless managed to change the course of my studies, and of my life. He belongs to those who have taught me what history means.

Furthermore, I wish to thank my parents, without whom this book would not have been at all possible in the first place. A special thanks also to Aleksija (who has tolerantly followed the maturation of this book, bearing considerable part of the burden), Gabriella (and her dreams), Mitja, Marco, Luca, Gio, Alessio, Toma and Didi, Justin, Jack Brisko, Sebastian, and Karl-Heinz Riesling. Last but not least, I am grateful to Marco Cimmino, Donatello Aramini, Merel Leeman, Simon Levis Sullam, Ethan Katz, Lorenzo Benadusi, Luciano Zani, and Giorgio Caravale for many enriching conversations about George Mosse and his work.

THE PERILS OF NORMALCY

Introduction

The Serpent and the Dove

The problem involved is to keep the balance between the Serpent and the Dove, so that neither obliterates the other: for the victory of the Dove can lead to unbridled idealism, and the ignoring of secular realities; while the victory of the Serpent means the total acceptance of what the sixteenth century called "Machiavellism."

—GEORGE L. MOSSE

Without the modern state there couldn't have been a holocaust.

—GEORGE L. MOSSE

George Mosse was a rebel who, along with many other pioneers of cultural history, fought against the so-called traditional historical concerns of politics, society, and economics. His cause, which he shared with so many of his generation, was that of liberty in the face of conformity and totalitarianism. Rebellion and cause went hand in hand, as the historian also rebelled against conformity by bolstering the cause of cultural history as a tool for a social and intellectual deliverance. Mosse was a double outsider, to use his own definition that embraced both his Jewishness and his homosexuality: he poured this outsiderdom into the historical discipline, becoming himself an outsider even in the historiographical landscape of his century, a greatly unfashionable, unorthodox, and unconventional historian who pioneered cultural history by brushing against the grain of "respectable" historiography.

History, in his view, had to transcend the boundaries of the plain narrative of events, or of strict analyses of class or economic structures: it pointed to the investigation of problems rather than chronologies, using a multidisciplinary approach that sought to complement "traditional" kinds of history with

3

perspectives taken from anthropology, psychology, literature, and the arts. This approach, which lies at the basis of cultural history as we know it in the early twenty-first century, charged historiography with a civic mission: the study of history was, in his scheme of things, necessary to make well-informed life choices on a political as well as on a personal level, which in his view fully coincided. Indeed, he viewed life and history as a totality, and this implied a pervasiveness of politics in all private matters, and a pervasiveness of all private matters in history. The cultural history he performed embraced all aspects of life, from sexuality to manners and morals, from art to literature, from emotions to hopes and aspirations: he delved into their political meaning, coming to also view politics as a totality encompassing all aspects of life. To separate the political from other aspects of life he regarded as a retreat from reality, a method of social control that inhibited social change and encouraged the status quo. His was a cultural history of politics, originating from the conviction that nothing can be left outside the political realm.

Mosse's stand for individual liberty constitutes the "continuity of interests" in his work, as he defined it.[1] Parallel to this runs a "continuity of intents" constituted by his belief that history must necessarily be a pedagogical endeavor. He regarded the historical profession as more than a detached study of the past: history, in his view, "must needs be present politics."[2] Politics is a totality that encompasses the whole of existence, and therefore it is impossible to be apolitical, since any act of ours, be it of commission or of omission, has a direct political relevance: hence, his "fundamental moral indignation against the aspiration to the apolitical."[3] For him, writing history was an essentially political act, and as a consequence, what the historian does must necessarily spring from his own beliefs, ideals, and convictions; what motivates him to investigate the past must be some internal relation he has with it. Like Benedetto Croce, whom he greatly admired, Mosse believed that there is always a direct connection between the mind of the historian and his object of study. Like Croce's, Mosse's history was intended to be ethical-political, to promote a message, to defend values that were supposed to have political implications.[4] Thus history becomes a faith imbued with a sense of mission. Mosse argued that "historical diagnosis based upon the unrelenting use of the critical mind should be combined with a certain vision";[5] he himself drew a picture of his own vision when he stated, at the end of a lecture course, that "I believe with Romain Rolland that it is the primary duty of the intellectual to keep the torch of freedom alive in an age of iron."[6] In a 1967 letter to Professor Merle Curti, Mosse expressed his views explicitly, praising his colleague's works and stating that his history was a "history with a purpose, not for its own sake alone." Curti, he wrote, embraced a "concept of history as the projection of values"; he sought to combine history "with those liberal values which must be ours. . . . If the present task is to humanize the world or perish then you have pointed history in the right direction and made intellectual history the pioneer in this task."[7] These passionate views, mostly expressed in the early phase of his career, did not change substantially over the years.

From these premises, in line with Croce's belief that history must perform an ethical-political goal, Mosse developed an "ethical-political historiography" of his own, well attuned to the restless mood that had pervaded the American historiographical scene since the first decades of the twentieth century. The "noble dream," that is, the attainment of objectivity in the writing of history, was besieged under the impact of relativism in historiography, anthropology, arts, literature, and the new physics.[8] Moreover, the great political upheavals following the First World War and the age of totalitarianism called for a reconsideration of the dominant Rankean parameters in historiography, which preached "objective" analyses without the personal involvement of the historian. Such a view could hardly withstand the urge, felt by many, to make a stand for democracy and liberty as against the mounting wave of authoritarianism. History viewed as contemporary thought about the past—as past actuality, as Croce would have it—was necessarily related to the personal interests and preoccupations of the historian, who performed an "act of faith"[9] when writing it; and yet the relativism inevitably implied by such a conviction could coexist with the historian's deepest convictions. Indeed, Mosse championed a deeply autobiographical (and therefore relativistic) historiography that was firmly hinged around his belief in the liberty and dignity of the individual as opposed to totalitarian mass politics. No history can ever be "objective," he told his students, and his own personal way of writing history touched upon his double outsiderdom: as a Jew he was an exile from Nazi Germany; as a homosexual, his personal liberty inevitably clashed against the strictures imposed by bourgeois society. Thus history became for him a means to penetrate the roots of his own discrimination.

The "Eternal Emigrant"

Born Gerhard Lachmann Mosse in Berlin on September 20, 1918, to a wealthy and influential Jewish family, the life he experienced as a child was anything but ordinary. The Mosses had made a name for themselves in the late nineteenth century thanks to the entrepreneurial skills of Rudolf Mosse (1843–1920),

founder of the Annoncen-Expedition Rudolf Mosse (1867), the most important and innovative advertising agency in late-nineteenth-century Germany and
soon to become the publishing house of several influential newspapers, including the *Berliner Tageblatt* (1872) and the *Berliner Morgenzeitung* (1889).[10] As
exponents of the values of the German liberal elite, the Mosses embodied the
liberalism of Jewish emancipation. After the Great War they were closely linked
to the Deutsche Demokratische Partei (a leftist, social-liberal party committed
to the defense of the institutions of the Weimar Republic). Theodor Wolff
(1868–1943), the editor in chief of the *Berliner Tageblatt* (from 1906 to 1933),
was a liberal who lined up against any kind of extremism, be it rightist or leftist, and sought to represent democratic values and to defend the newly born
Weimar Republic against its opponents.[11] The family had been engaged for
decades in the process of Jewish integration and assimilation. Rudolf Mosse
had represented the Jewish community of Berlin at the turn of the century and
then also the German Jewish Reform Congregation, one of the strongest
organs of Jewish life, which aimed at full assimilation in the German context.

The rise of National Socialism put an end to this world, and in 1933 the
entire family immigrated first to Switzerland, and then to France. The young
Gerhard, grandson of Rudolf Mosse, experienced a traumatic change in his life
circumstances. Until then, he had been a spoiled and rebellious boy raised in
an opulent and luxurious environment. Despite the luxuries that surrounded
him, he was a lonely boy and had few friends. Moreover, his parents were rarely
present, and he felt much closer to his governesses and servants.[12] His search
for intimate bonds and for constant attention contributed to the shaping of a
rebellious nature. After primary school, he had been sent to the famous Berlin
Mommsen Gymnasium, but he chafed at the strict discipline required by the
school, and his father decided to send him to the Schule Schloss Salem, a well-
known boarding school on lake Constance (the Mosse family had been major
financial supporters of this progressive school founded after World War I by
Kurt Hahn). Character building was the essential mission of the school, and
this was the educational legacy Mosse brought into exile when, on March 31,
1933, he managed to take the ferry to Switzerland minutes before a law that
restricted Jewish emigration took effect (his parents had departed Germany
the day after Hitler was appointed chancellor in January 1933, leaving young
Gerhard to finish the semester at Salem so that his education would not be dis-
rupted; they may have felt that Hitler would not long retain power in Germany).
From Switzerland and France, he moved to England in 1934, where he first
attended the Quaker Bootham School in York. In 1937 he entered Cambridge

University. Here Gerhard, who had by then become George,[13] decided to study history. In York he had been fascinated by reading George M. Trevelyan's *History of England*, which Leslie Gilbert, his history teacher, had assigned to him: "Reading it, I was on the way to find my vocation," Mosse wrote in his memoir.[14] Gilbert may have played a role in his decision, and yet Mosse himself admits that at the time he was unsure where he should specialize, and chose history also because that was "the course of study my English friends took at Cambridge when they did not know what they really wanted—a 'gentleman's' subject—and I too drifted into it, rather than, at first, regarding it as a firm choice."[15]

In August 1939, not long before his twenty-first birthday, he went to the United States on his father's visa to visit his sister Hilde, who was studying medicine in New York. He had a British reentry permit and firmly intended to get back and settle in England, where he now felt he had found a home. But during his stay in the United States, the outbreak of the Second World War changed everything, making it "extremely risky to take advantage of my reentry permit into England because, as a former German citizen, I could now be considered an enemy alien."[16] As a result, he had no choice but to remain in the United States, with very little money and few contacts. Luckily, because of his affiliation with Bootham and a concern by Quaker institutions for the plight of refugees, he was accepted at a Quaker school, Haverford College, where he continued his studies. At Haverford he initially meant to major in English literature, but he changed to history and earned his Bachelor of Science degree in 1941. It was at Haverford, he recalled, that he was "truly initiated into scholarship as a lifelong preoccupation."[17] Mosse then went to Harvard University, where he received his doctorate in 1946 under the supervision of Charles Howard McIlwain, with a thesis on the idea of sovereignty in early modern England.[18] In 1944 he was already lecturing at the University of Iowa, where he would remain until 1955. Here Mosse first lectured within the Army Specialized Training Program,[19] and then, in 1946, he was hired as an assistant professor, moving quickly to the rank of associate professor. He taught large classes of postwar veterans, and taught the large beginning classes in Western civilization. He also pursued his scholarship and at a young age became an expert in early modern history, first on English constitutional history, and then on the period of the Reformation. He was recognized at Iowa as a brilliant teacher who often was asked to participate in statewide radio broadcasts and commencement ceremonies, where he was in demand as a defender of the liberalism that had only recently been under intense threat. He also published his first books and got involved in American political life.[20]

In 1955 Mosse moved to the University of Wisconsin–Madison, under the proviso that he specialize in modern European history, and he taught there until his retirement from the University of Wisconsin in 1987. To be sure, he always continued to travel extensively both for research and teaching, and from 1969 to 1985 he also taught at the Hebrew University of Jerusalem, where he spent a semester a year, and after his official retirement from Madison, he taught at many other universities throughout Europe and America until his death in 1999. Yet, although he had found a home in Madison, he always felt like an "eternal emigrant."[21] In Madison, Mosse reached his maturity as a historian. The shift to modern history meant, in his case, a turn to the study of National Socialism. He continued to publish books and articles in early modern history for some years, but he shifted his attention toward a subject that was much closer to his personal and research interests. As he writes in his memoir, he had by then attained full integration into American society, and he felt freer to explore new fields of research that touched him more closely than those he had been dealing with in the 1940s and 1950s. He himself defines his previous works as

respectable, indeed core subjects at the time. . . . That they were also far removed from my own origins may have played an unconscious role as I tried to dive into my new Anglo-Saxon environment. But even at that time I was already looking ahead and starting to investigate National Socialism, a subject which I had avoided, perhaps because it touched me so closely. Nearly two decades had now passed since I had arrived in the United States and there was no more need to immerse myself in a respectable Anglo-Saxon subject in order to distance myself from my past as an outsider. I have no good explanation for my switch to modern history, which occurred even before my position at Wisconsin locked me in place as a modern historian. Surely my interest in the more recent period had always existed, but my graduate training had been entirely in the earlier periods of European history.[22]

From then on, Mosse would focus his attention on the study of fascism and National Socialism, making vital contributions to their interpretation through a series of innovative and groundbreaking works. In 1966 he also founded (with Walter Laqueur) the *Journal of Contemporary History*, which was to "become the leading journal published in English in the field of twentieth-century European history."[23]

His contribution, however, did not remain confined to the analysis of fascism. Mosse contributed to the revolution in what was commonly understood as cultural history, widening the scope of the discipline, anticipating many trends that would emerge only in later years, and opening new perspectives into what were then neglected fields of research such as the history of sexuality and of the body. His original approach greatly contributed to an understanding of modern mass movements, but it also shed light on how the mechanisms of mass society function. His interest in the history of sexuality was admittedly connected with the other side of his outsiderdom, his homosexuality. Just as his Jewishness had urged him to investigate the roots of National Socialism and anti-Semitism, the homosexuality he had to repress for decades (until the sexual revolution of the 1960s and 1970s brought about greater liberty and tolerance) turned his attention to the history of bourgeois respectability and masculinity. These two concerns were, in his mind, part of one problem: the liberty and dignity of the individual in mass society, a liberty that he saw as permanently threatened by cohesive forces such as nationalism or respectability.

Mosse authored several groundbreaking books throughout his long career as a historian, among them *The Crisis of German Ideology: Intellectual Origins of the Third Reich* (1964), a study of *völkisch* ideology in pre-Nazi Germany. Then, in the second half of the 1960s, he began his investigation into visual means of expression, such as architecture and physical stereotypes, including in his methodology anthropological categories and the analysis of myths and symbols. This anthropological and visual turn laid the foundations for his most original and innovative works, notably *The Nationalization of the Masses* (1975), *Toward the Final Solution* (1978), *Nationalism and Sexuality* (1985), *Fallen Soldiers* (1990), and *The Image of Man* (1996). He coined the term "new politics" to define the new liturgical style of mass politics born at the time of the French Revolution; he set the Holocaust at the center of European culture, helping to unmask its links with Enlightenment rationalism; he then highlighted the connections between bourgeois respectability, sexuality, and nationalism (and, extensively, fascism), opening new and controversial vistas on the history of fascism; he eventually analyzed the Great War and the process of brutalization of the individual in mass culture and politics it brought about, seeing in what he called the myth of the war experience and in the cult of the fallen soldiers a further point of contact between nationalism and Christianity. After having already interpreted nationalism and fascism as religious phenomena, he put his vast knowledge of early modern religious history at the service of his understanding of modern politics, drawing a further line along the secularization process he had begun to analyze in his works on reason of state and Christian ethics.

Why an Intellectual Biography of George L. Mosse?

In his memoir Mosse wrote that "an encounter with my own history might be instructive to myself as to others, illuminating a very personal corner of recent times."[24] Mosse's intellectual biography provides us with an encounter with his history and his historiography that can illuminate more than a "personal" corner of recent times: it is a voyage into the birth of cultural history as we know it. Moreover, the problems he addressed are very much alive and topical today in the twenty-first century, and in all likelihood will be for many years to come. As Jay Winter put it, Mosse's books can be important to understand Europe today, with its contradictory relationship between liberalism and antiliberal, nationalistic tendencies to exclude outsiders: "People keep dying today because this contradiction hasn't been solved. This history is our history, and George Mosse has done more than others to point it out, in his implacable and unsettling way."[25] His work, which Emilio Gentile has defined as "a historical anthropology of modern man,"[26] can still serve as a precious guide in a society in search of a definite identity, in a multicultural world dominated by mass politics where nationalism and racism surface again with renewed strength, where the confrontation with the other, as the great Polish journalist Ryszard Kapuściński put it, seems to be the "challenge of the twenty-first century."[27] Indeed, Mosse's work was not only a cogent critique of fascism, nationalism, and racism: it also addressed the dangers inherent in modern democracies, notably conformity through respectability, political and cultural polarization, the dismissal of opposing opinion, and the trivializing power of mass media. In the face of all this, he sent a message fraught with hope; a convinced historical pessimist, his writing and teachings had a "bright side": they advocated the positive potentials of communitarian identities, patriotism, and political symbolism. He chastised irrationality, and yet he deemed it necessary to maintain a much-needed balance with reason. He believed irrationality to be a fundamental outlet for men and women, as long as emotion remains "tempered by reason." His can be called a "philosophy of the balance," to which he clung all his life. In his dialectic view of history, myth confronts reality, ethics confronts reason of state, irrationality confronts reason: in this scheme of things, as he argued in one of his most important books, "the problem involved is to keep the balance between the Serpent and the Dove, so that neither obliterates the other: for the victory of the Dove can lead to unbridled idealism, and the ignoring of secular realities; while the victory of the Serpent means the total acceptance of what the sixteenth century called 'Machiavellism.'"[28]

Much has been written on George Mosse, and yet no attempt has been made to write an intellectual biography that seeks to offer a wide and organic perspective on his work, focusing on its inner development from his earliest writings on the early modern age to the more recent studies on the nineteenth and twentieth centuries. A large number of analytical articles focus on either particular aspects of his work or its more general significance.[29] The Italian historian Emilio Gentile has recently published an excellent analysis of Mosse's historiography that is not, however, an intellectual biography: as the author clearly states, it is rather an attempt to "analytically piece together the genesis and development of his interpretation of fascism and of the catastrophe of modern man as manifestations of 'powerful and gloomy forces that threaten to swamp, and have recently swamped, the European humanity.'"[30] This is a first attempt to write an intellectual biography of Mosse, relying not only on his published writings, but also on the unpublished materials that are now at the biographer's disposal. The George L. Mosse Archive at the Memorial Library, University of Wisconsin–Madison, and the George L. Mosse Collection at the Leo Baeck Institute of New York contain unpublished articles, lectures, and speaking engagements, as well as Mosse's vast correspondence with students, colleagues, and friends. These materials shed new light on the historian's work and, when integrated with his published writings, offer new and precious insights into the development of his thought. The purpose of this book is then that of drawing a picture of Mosse's historiography from the point of view of its inner development, highlighting the main methodological turns and the thematic shifts, and seeking to link them with the events of his life.

There are a number of aspects of Mosse's work that have not received the attention they deserve. The intellectual roots of the anthropological and visual turn (the major methodological turn in his historiography), the development of his concept of myth, his interpretation of the Enlightenment, the crucial role of the 1960s student movement in his intellectual biography,[31] the influence of Judaism on his interpretation of nationalism, his view of fascism as a nationalist revolution, the historicist foundation of his cultural history, and the role played by the Annales in his interpretation of the Great War are all areas of his work that require investigation. Also, his perhaps most controversial statement, that is, that the new man of National Socialism was the ideal bourgeois, is an assertion whose complex origins require careful examination.

Through his teaching methods and his focus on the power of the myths we live by, Mosse shattered many common assumptions about fascism and bourgeois society that in its economic essence and ability to surreptitiously impose systems of behavior seems ever more potent and powerful. He believed irrationality to be an inextricable part of human nature: as Jeffrey Herf recalls, "in often successful efforts to provoke, stimulate, and entertain his audience, he would say something like, 'you all think these ideas are so preposterous. Well, don't you know that preposterous ideas are very important. Or are you so naive as to think that history is made only by nice, logical Kantian ethics?'"[32] It has been observed that Mosse became a historian of modern irrationalism; in the effort to grasp the appeal of National Socialism, he focused on the historical relevance of irrational myths and of ideologies that sprang not from the "high" thought of noted intellectuals, but rather from the often obscure second- or third-rate thinkers who were much closer to popular piety and feelings. He defined his history as one of perceptions, and "perceptions" seem to represent today one underlying interpretive category of most cultural history, and here too he was a pioneer as he extensively adopted the term in the early 1980s, relying on an implicit theoretical substratum he had been building for over twenty years.

Mosse was also instrumental in constructing a bridge between history and the social sciences in the study of fascism, bringing a historicist attitude into a personal concept of cultural history, in line with other pioneering efforts in the same direction that were being made at the time.[33] However, since his historiography lacked a theoretical apparatus intended as a methodological backbone to his works, it is difficult to trace the origins of his ideas, or to reconstruct the influences that played a role in his intellectual development. Sometimes he directly mentioned them, sometimes they can be found in footnotes, and sometimes any effort at discovering them is necessarily tentative. In this respect, this book is intended as the first attempt to put them together, as far as Mosse's usual evasiveness toward his sources of inspiration allows us to do.

Against this solid humanistic and pedagogical background, Mosse's work underwent crucial thematic and methodological shifts, moving from early modern to modern history, analyzing a great variety of political phenomena from a number of different perspectives, considerably modifying his methodology in the process. He read the nineteenth and twentieth centuries as a "visual age," in which the need of society for cohesion was expressed through the construction of stereotypes that draw boundaries between the normal and the abnormal, the moral and the immoral. Society defines itself, and in the process it creates a type that corresponds to the accepted values and morality, as well as an anti-type that represents its antithesis. Here historiography and politics were not far from each other in Mosse's mind: his critique of the political, social, and academic establishment since the 1960s was precisely aimed at its effort to preserve conformity. As he said during a lecture in the early 1970s, there is one real question: "Is it dangerous to see in non conformity and long hair something that has to be suppressed?" People, Mosse said, seek law and order, freedom and the preservation of the status quo: "This is the future," he sadly stated. The great danger in this, Mosse warned, is that "everyone depends for his comforts and livelihood on the working of an integrated and complex system," and the individual has become a "plaything of complex society. . . . That is partly what the revolt of youth is about, that is partly what law and order is about: to keep this system intact. That is why individualism, an essential basis of freedom, is in some danger." He believed that law, order, and the technocrats had become the new Gods, and although he did not think that fascism could repeat itself, he was convinced that "freedom will suffer once more."[34] Mosse's preoccupation with the danger inherent in society's self-definition, with conformism, with the balance between the rights of the individual and national security, or with the relationship between ethics and politics led him to tackle recurrent problems that are still at issue today.[35] His moral and historiographical legacy can therefore be of great value; it can provide cultural tools for historical analysis that can offer deep insights into the workings of modern society and politics.[36]

The Link between Life and Work

In *Beyond Good and Evil*, Friedrich Nietzsche wrote: "It has gradually become clear to me what every great philosophy up till now has consisted of—namely, the confession of its originator, and a species of involuntary and unconscious auto-biography; and moreover that the moral (or immoral) purpose in every philosophy has constituted the true vital germ out of which the entire plant has always grown."[37] If applied to history, the same principle stands for Mosse's work. He was a historian whose personal experience (his double outsiderdom) and whose work intermingled to the point that they cannot be separated without losing sight of the sense, and the significance, of his accomplishments. He could not really hide his Jewishness, but he "did not have to parade it in a society which discriminated against Jews"; as to his homosexuality, this had to be kept hidden to avoid persecution and exclusion, which would have prevented him from attaining a "respectable position in society or in any profession." Society's "pressure for conformity—he recalled—could not be resisted."[38] If it is not surprising that he, like many other German Jewish émigré historians, turned to the study of National Socialism and of the Holocaust and made them the core of his work, the fact that he, beyond this, delved deeply into the moral and sexual dimension of Nazism and, more generally, into the workings of modern mass society, with its processes of stereotyping, inclusion, and exclusion, certainly represents an element of great originality. Steven Aschheim, a former student, colleague, and friend of Mosse's, has written about the "experiential roots" of his studies; Renato Moro has argued that "as always, perhaps, the best interpreter of the persecutor can be the victim," and Emilio Gentile, stressing the "intertwining of autobiography and historiography" in Mosse, has referred to the "fascination of the persecutor," an expression that fits the latter's attitude toward National Socialism.[39] Indeed, Mosse believed empathy to be one of the most effective tools in the hands of the historian, and he made full use of it. He was fully aware of what the "fascination of the persecutor" meant: as a young boy in Germany, he had run away from home to go to see a Hitler rally, and many years later he still recalled how this had been an "experience," how he got "carried away" by the feeling of belonging to the mass of people, seduced by Hitler's charisma.[40] At Salem he had found himself immersed in an environment that gave him the savor of nationalism through the linkage of history, literature, and the landscape: the school gave him "a first taste of nationalism, which at the time I found congenial; there was a danger that it might provide the belief system I so sadly lacked. . . . When as a historian much later I wrote about German nationalism, I did have an insight into its truly seductive nature."[41] In Israel he admittedly felt drawn to Zionism. He knew full well that he was far from immune to the appeal of emotion, and it is not surprising that he set irrationality at the center of his works on mass movements.

As a homosexual, in order to be accepted in society and, above all, in the academic world, Mosse had to suppress his sexual character; he did so sublimating it "into work and fantasy life."[42] Only in the 1960s, when the "sexual revolution" opened the window to more tolerant views toward homosexuality, his slow "coming out" could begin through a very active and enjoyable sexual life in Europe, a perhaps understandable response to years of repression, and to the continued need to protect his teaching career in the United States. Yet, although he initiated a long-term relationship with a man in Israel in 1972, it was only in 1982 that he first participated in a conference on sexuality in Amsterdam as an openly gay man. His experience of exile and repression obviously left a mark on his personality. His "anger" was to be reflected in his historiography when he turned to the study of racism, bourgeois morality, and sexuality, thus becoming a historian of that very respectability that had so much affected his life.[43] He did so, however, not through an indiscriminate attack on bourgeois society and values but, rather, through serious and well-documented historical analysis, opening new and often unorthodox perspectives on the history of fascism and, more extensively, of modern Western society.

It must be said from the outset that Mosse never considered his "double outsiderdom" a handicap: rather, he saw it as a privileged point of observation, as an opportunity. From that perspective, he could look at society from the outside while at the same time he could observe it from within, being himself a member who had attained integration through respectability. In this light, it is not surprising that he admittedly felt "perversely a kind of gratitude" for his Jewishness, in that exile changed his life and made him a historian.[44] His criticism of bourgeois society was simply meant to be constructive, in line with the "bright side" of his work: through deliberate provocation, his assault on the workings of bourgeois society and mass politics was meant to "break taboos" to "get people to think."[45] A balance then needs to be drawn, when analyzing Mosse's historiography, between provocation and autobiography, and this is not always an easy task.

Machiavellism and the Holocaust

One of Mosse's earliest books, *The Holy Pretence* (1957), has generally been disregarded by his critics. However, as Mosse firmly believed, it should be considered a central work in his intellectual biography.[46] The book dealt with the assimilation of the idea of reason of state into the Christian framework of ethics in the sixteenth century, describing how Puritan Divines had attempted to find a balance between the Serpent and the Dove, that is, between Machiavellism and Christian ethics. In a similar way, Mosse advocated the necessity to find a balance between reason and irrationality, to develop a "new Casuistry" capable of integrating myths and symbols into the rationalistic modern parliamentary politics born of Enlightenment liberalism.

Mosse's writings on Renaissance Europe rested on two pillars that would support all his subsequent writings. The first was the already mentioned preoccupation with the liberty of the individual when confronted with the modern state; the second was the question of political morality. Both themes sprang from his concern with the reception of the thought of Machiavelli in Europe. His investigation into the relationship between these two themes led him to trace the origins of the Holocaust back to the assumptions laid by Machiavelli's political philosophy, embodied by the separation of ethics and politics that it, in Mosse's view, entailed. If the first of these two tenets has often been connected with Mosse's subsequent interest in totalitarianism, the connection of the second with his other central interest, the Holocaust, has never been highlighted. Machiavelli, in Mosse's interpretation, represented the beginning of a new politics, of a "conscious acceptance of politics as a struggle for power in which almost all means are justified" to reach the end goal, the good of the commonwealth.[47] Speaking of the age of the Renaissance, Mosse said that it was "at that point where modern politics first [began] to intrude upon the moral sphere," where the public started its invasion of the private that was to culminate in the triumph of public morality with nationalism and fascism, where morality was directed by the state.[48]

The Holocaust can thus be depicted as the triumph of the Serpent over the Dove, the point of arrival of Mosse's inquiry into his own past, which was so tightly connected to the heart of twentieth-century European history. Obviously, Mosse never drew a direct line between the reception of the thought of Machiavelli and the "Jewish catastrophe" of his time; neither did he see any inevitability, or predestination, in European history that could make one envisage its apex of violence and brutality at the hands of the Nazis: concrete, historical causes brought Germany into the hands of Hitler. And yet Mosse's intellectual biography can be read as an attempt to comprehend that long and winding visionary road that led from Machiavellism to totalitarianism, from Machiavellism to the Holocaust.

The Great Provocateur

Mosse's work can be seen as a "continuum" of his main preoccupations, where the threads woven through one work surface in another, observed from a different perspective. He generously drew from many authors who inspired him, and yet he assimilated in a very personal way only the ideas he found useful, in order to support the themes he was conceiving, giving them new directions, opening unexplored avenues and giving birth to a highly original historiography. To be sure, his approach was not devoid of problems and contradictions. Within a widespread appreciation and recognition of his groundbreaking achievements, many critics have highlighted several weaknesses and discrepancies involved in his methodology. This is certainly due to the fact that, as James Wald put it, Mosse was a "scout rather than a settler," and to the "general nature" of his work.[49] Indeed, he unrelentingly explored new fields of research well into his old age, opening new scenarios only to immediately follow new insights and new problems that fascinated him; he always lacked the patience to linger on a specific topic long enough to fully explore all the possible variations and contradictions raised by his research. This he gladly left to other, more disciplined, historians. In a letter to Christopher Browning, he wrote that "it is so easy to get bogged down in the details . . . and to overlook the more general and important historical implications": here he was referring specifically to the Holocaust, but these remarks undoubtedly have a more general significance.[50] As Gerhard L. Weinberg, reviewing *The Crisis of German Ideology*, pointed out, "this book tells us much, but we need to know more."[51] This apparently obvious observation takes on a special meaning when applied to Mosse's work. Indeed, he seldom sought to provide systematic treatment for any of the topics he dealt with. This was certainly one risk involved in his penchant for long periodizations, for analyses that covered, in most cases, one or two centuries of history. The result was, at times, overt generalizations or simplifications at the service of a central thesis. *The Crisis of German Ideology* put excessive emphasis on anti-Semitism in *völkisch* ideology, according to reviewers such as Peter Pulzer or A. J. Nicholls;[52] in Walter Laqueur's words, "sometimes Professor Mosse casts his net too wide" in analyzing the *völkisch* phenomenon;[53] his view of the variegated groups that constituted the *völkisch* landscape was often too homogeneous.[54] In *The Nationalization of the Masses*, Mosse surely took "a great deal for granted in his analytic use of terms like 'religion,' 'myth' and 'symbol' which conceal as much as they explain,"[55] and the same can be held true for his usage of such terms as "middle classes" or "bourgeoisie." Mosse's work often lacks more rigorous quantitative analysis, and, referring to *Nationalism and Sexuality*, critics have commented on the "unanchored quality of many of the trends discussed. These ideals float, and while they were undoubtedly authored they are not clearly assessed as to representativeness or impact."[56] Similar observations, as it will emerge in this study, can be made with regard to many aspects of the Madison historian's work, along with the accusation of writing teleological history, which is, however, only partly true, as Mosse himself admitted: National Socialism and the Holocaust are doubtlessly the point of arrival (and often of departure) of his analyses, but he never supported historical determinism. There is little doubt that he was (understandably) very sensitive toward those forces, anti-Semitism and respectability above all, which had crudely shaped his existence: and yet he always sought to keep his emotions in check. Whether and to what extent he succeeded or not is for the reader to decide, as even opinions from his close friends and colleagues do not always coincide.

All this must be kept in mind during the attempt to take stock of Mosse's work and figure, which cannot be judged exclusively by the various problems involved in his methodology and in the deep personal commitment of his historiographical efforts. Such an approach would lead to a misunderstanding of his ethical goal and of his accomplishments. More often than not, the criticisms directed toward his work went hand in hand with high praise for his innovative contributions. Mosse's "disdain of a grand seigneur vis-à-vis dates in history" pointed out by Walter Laqueur holds true also for "academic abstractions, power structures, social structures and so on," as Mosse himself acknowledged.[57] When confronted with such criticism, he would have stressed that only a provocative, innovative, startling thesis can get people to think, to look beyond prejudice, and to take nothing for granted. One day, in a conversation among Jay Winter, Steven Aschheim, and Mosse, Winter reproached Mosse for using the term "myth" in a vague and unscholarly way; to which Mosse replied that it did not really matter: what he wanted to do was to convey a message to the people.[58] His entire work should be seen also from this perspective: it must be conceived as an ethical-radical effort at breaking historical as well as personal conventions through deliberate provocation. And yet the great demystifier of respectability, of communities, of nationalism, of the symbolism of mass politics, was himself a highly respectable person, a creator of communities based on intellectual friendships, an advocate of the positive potentials of patriotism, and eventually a supporter of the symbolic in parliamentary politics.

1

From Machiavellism
to Totalitarianism

From Machiavellism to Nationalism—this could be described as the
theme of the whole sinister development of which we have tried to
clarify the earlier stages.

—FRIEDRICH MEINECKE

My work in early modern history set forth some themes which
were followed up later in my work on fascism and National Socialism
and which have influenced most of my writings on a wide variety of
subjects.

—GEORGE L. MOSSE

There is no doubt that George Mosse's fame as a historian is due to his
major works on fascism, National Socialism, racism, nationalism, and
sexuality. His efforts in early modern history, despite some success,
have certainly had a less momentous impact on the history of historiography,
and therefore have often been neglected by his critics.[1] In the late 1940s and
early 1950s Mosse was an exile at the beginning of his career, had just been nat-
uralized as an American citizen, and was still struggling to be fully accepted in
his new environment. This is the reason, as he pointed out in his autobiography, he focused on issues that seemed so far from his personal experience of
exile: he was in search of respectability within the academic establishment.[2]
He apparently did so to the point that a colleague at the University of Iowa once
asked him how he could be so interesting while his books were so dull.[3] However, such a view of his work would be profoundly misleading. Despite their
apparent detachment, his early works originate from his life experiences in a
remarkable way, though the themes he dealt with were far removed from the
events that had shaped his own destiny.

Mosse's life as a refugee from totalitarianism, his involvement in the anti-fascist movement in the 1930s, and his belief in liberalism informed his constant struggle "against the encroachments of absolute power upon the liberties of the subject" that characterizes the indissoluble link between his life and his work.[4] Strongly influenced by Benedetto Croce's belief that all history is contemporary history in that it necessarily pertains to the historian's interest in the life of the present, Mosse came to the view that in early modern European history, and particularly in the birth of the nation-state and in the development of the idea of reason of state, were the origins of the twentieth-century totalitarianism he would soon begin to analyze directly. It can be said that the issues he dealt with throughout his career remained, in a sense, the same, and this explains what he meant when he spoke of a "continuity of interests" informing his writings over the decades.[5] Indeed, two guiding concerns run through the whole of his work: the relationship between the liberty of the individual and the power of the state, and a related question of the relationship between ethics and politics. The crucial methodological changes that occurred in Mosse's historiography in the 1950s and 1960s never affected this continuity, which can be regarded as the central tenet of his work.

The Holy Pretence (1957), one of Mosse's most neglected books and yet a milestone in his intellectual biography, dealt with the assimilation of the idea of reason of state (in Machiavelli's formulation) within the Christian framework of ethics, and represented the flowering of many years of reflection over what Mosse called "the most modern of problems," the question of religion and political morality, which he regarded as "a central one in our Civilization."[6] Moreover, the idea of reason of state implies the problem of power and the state, and is therefore directly connected to the relationship between the individual and the state, and thus acts as a common denominator for both thematic guidelines of Mosse's continuity of interests. This continuity, epitomized by the idea of reason of state, was expressed in its most revealing connotations by Mosse himself in 1963, when he defined totalitarianism as the "stretching of the old idea of raison d'état."[7] Here lies the connection between Machiavellism and totalitarianism.[8] From this perspective, his work appears as a whole, as an organic body whose backbone is represented by the concern with the liberty of the individual when confronted by the state.

If Croce with his belief in the contemporaneity of all history had been an important influence on a methodological level, the German historian Friedrich Meinecke was equally important as a source of inspiration on a thematic plane. Meinecke wrote his *Machiavellism: The Doctrine of Raison d'Etat and Its Place in*

Modern History in the shadow of the First World War (the book was published in 1924), with the catastrophe caused by European nationalism vivid before his eyes. In his view, power and reason of state are needed by every community in order to survive: taken in itself, power is not an evil force; rather, it is a necessity. However, those who hold power can easily abuse it and trespass the limits of morals and of right: here, the politics of power degenerate into excess, and the irrational suffocates the rational. The problem involved in the doctrine of reason of state, that is, the fragility of the balance between politics and morals, was highlighted by the Great War, and Meinecke could claim to have followed, in his book, the main stages of the sinister development leading from Machiavellism to nationalism.[9] And yet the Second World War brought about another catastrophe, and Meinecke stretched that "sinister development," adding a further stage in the history of reason of state when he defined National Socialism as "mass Machiavellism."[10] It can be said that Mosse followed a somewhat similar route, concluding that the process set in motion by the reception of Machiavelli's ideas had laid the basis for the totalitarian state of the twentieth century. Reason of state can be compared to a Pandora's box that, once opened, unleashes powerful and uncontrollable forces that characterize the development of European civilization from the sixteenth century onward (i.e., of all modernity in its wider meaning). Mosse regarded European history as the history of the progressive limitation of the freedom of the individual.

The influence of Meinecke's thought on Mosse, however, cannot be confined to the relationship between reason of state and National Socialism. The historian's reflections crossed the German boundaries in the attempt to establish a philosophical pattern for the whole of modernity. Here the connections with Mosse's work are equally powerful and suggestive. Meinecke attributed the "German catastrophe" to the loss of balance between rationality and irrationalism in favor of the former, through an excessive mechanization of life brought about by industrialism that suffocated human feelings and fantasy. Reason, in Meinecke's view, "should dominate the whole surging play of the mind. But reason itself, to reach its highest and best, must also nourish itself upon irrational forces," he argued.[11] Feelings are the source of morality and religion, and therefore they must be integrated into a "psychological equilibrium between the rational and the irrational" because "any one-sided development of either the rational or the irrational forces threatens to unbalance the whole, and can eventually, if carried further and further, lead to catastrophes for the individual and for the masses, even for a whole nation, if the storm of events drives the nation in a dangerous direction."[12] Moreover, Meinecke believed Machiavellism and reason of state to be "general and eternal human phenomena."[13] Such an argument is fully reflected in Mosse's convictions, expressed throughout the 1950s, that reason of state is a "constant and continuing historical problem,"[14] and that a balance between Christian ethics and reason of state, between faith and practical life, is necessary for living a moral life.

Mosse's moral concerns were directly related to the problem posed by Machiavelli: how a good man can survive in an evil world. He was fully aware of the potential contradiction raised by reason of state: how to reconcile individual freedom and practical realities such as national security? Such questions are, in turn, directly related to Mosse's committed involvement in politics. Both in England and in America, he actively participated in political life, first as an antifascist at the time of the Spanish Civil War, then as an American citizen committed to the preservation of liberal, individual rights against the mounting wave of McCarthyism. These commitments are crucial for understanding the political implications of his works, which can be, as far as his early modern writings are concerned, divided into two separate and yet intertwined phases. The first includes the years between 1946 (Mosse's doctoral dissertation) and 1950 (*The Struggle for Sovereignty in England*), when Mosse, under the influence of Charles Howard McIlwain (his thesis advisor), wrote about English constitutional history, facing the problem of sovereignty and its relation to the liberty of the individual; the second can be set between 1950 and 1957 (*The Holy Pretence*), when he delved into the question of religion and political morality. Mosse's political concerns offer a point of observation from which his historical work can be viewed from a more comprehensive perspective.

Political Concerns

One of the major elements of continuity in Mosse's work is certainly the deeply political character of his view of history. Barely escaped from totalitarian persecution and a certain death at the hands of the Nazi regime, the "eternal emigrant" brought with him a psychological heritage that was to give his writings their peculiar political bend. As a victim of political events, he regarded politics as a central element in everyone's life: to be politically conscious and responsible was, in his view, a duty no one had the right to give away. "No one has a right to be ignorant about his social, moral and intellectual origins," he clearly stated in a speech delivered in 1946;[15] such a belief scarcely concealed, as it has been put, his "fundamental moral indignation against the aspiration to the apolitical."[16] His whole life and work were therefore devoted to the promotion of an ideal of history as a profession that ought not to confine itself to a detached,

impersonal analysis of events: on the contrary, history must be the means
through which the historian, without losing his impartiality before the facts,
must deliver an ethical message. As Ze'ev Mankovitz once put it, Mosse had
taught his students "the art of passionate detachment."[17]

The moral fervor concerning the fate of the individual when confronted by
the state incontestably originated from Mosse's experience as an exile, a young
refugee whose earliest political experiences were marked by a lively opposition
to fascism. The feeling of bewilderment induced by being a stateless outcast
was enhanced by the political reality of the times. In the 1930s, he wrote in his
memoirs, "one seemed to live at the edge of catastrophe."[18] This feeling of fear
and insecurity left a deep mark on both Mosse the man and Mosse the historian. The link between life and work emerges here with even greater impetus
in the historian's biography. His political awakening originated in the Spanish
Civil War, which, in his own words, "aroused our passions and engaged our
emotions, determining our political attitudes for a long time to come."[19] The
period he spent between York, Cambridge, and Paris saw an increasing involvement in the antifascist movement, which entailed his leaning toward left
liberal positions, toward a kind of social democracy that aimed at preserving
"liberal ideas of freedom and parliamentary government."[20] Contradictorily
enough, at the same time as he was defending individuality and parliamentarism, in the wave of the antifascist opposition to the Spanish Civil War the
young Mosse came very close to a pro-Soviet stance that it would take a long
time to shake.[21]

In those years he came to appreciate the work and ideas of the English
thinker Harold Laski. As Mosse recalled in his autobiography, Laski became "a
role model for both me and many others in the [antifascist] movement," and
through his synthesis of intellectualism and active political involvement as well
as his attempt to balance Marxism and liberalism, had "a great influence on my
thought."[22] In both his doctoral thesis and in his first book, *The Struggle for Sovereignty in England,* Mosse referred to Laski's feeling of insecurity about the
efficacy of constitutional systems to withstand major crises. It is hardly surprising that he felt in tune with such preoccupations, which are reflected in his
writings and speeches from as early as his time as an undergraduate student.
In a 1940 paper, Mosse wrote that "democratic insecurity brings conditions to
such a point that we will grovel before any commanding power of the will. That
this assumption is true, was proved in Germany in 1933."[23] The downfall of the
Weimar Republic and the manifest inability of democratic institutions (supported by his family) to thwart the rise of National Socialism left a scar that

could still be seen in the years to come. Giving various lectures and speeches in Iowa City and in Madison, Mosse insisted upon the danger that fear and insecurity presented to liberty. Education was, in his view, the only possible solution, since "learning means understanding, and such an understanding in turn means dignity and a rational attitude in times of adversity."[24] When scared and insecure, people would "retreat behind the protective skirts of the State: a putting down of all opinion which might bring about any kind of change."[25] Fascism and National Socialism, Mosse said, had fed on this insecurity, which challenged liberty and paved the way for an increase of the power of government and an "endangering of individual liberty": "insecurity and fear of the future bring nations closer to the police state," he concluded.[26] Reflecting on the role played by scholars of common law in contrasting Hobbes's absolutist theories in early modern England, Mosse praised their attempt to preserve an individual sphere of freedom that the state could not touch. And yet he was aware that times of crisis posed a serious challenge that could not be escaped, thus finding himself seeking a possible balance between liberty and authority in his own thought.[27] He quickly imbued his early modern writings with the spirit of his stormy times, establishing a connection in his mind between the birth of the modern state and the rise of fascism in twentieth-century Europe. If he had become a historian almost by chance, he then approached the object of his studies from an intensely personal point of view. The United States, his new home, came to represent a bulwark of liberalism, a safe haven against the totalitarian shadow that had enveloped Europe: his "feel for America" stood as the firm counterpart to his "fear of authority . . . the worst legacy of [his] German education."[28]

Living "at the edge of catastrophe" and "experiencing stormy times" relevantly determined the political goal of Mosse's work. When he moved to the United States and began teaching at the University of Iowa, his political views intertwined with his profession, and he devoted a considerable amount of time to political engagement. He did so both through "didactic" speeches about freedom, which he defined as "motivational" speeches, and through direct involvement in American politics.[29] The postwar years saw Mosse cling to a left-liberal position, definitely inclined toward the left and utterly opposed to McCarthyism. Liberalism was his main concern, which he expressed on several occasions in unfolding his opposition to militarism. Liberalism "will not last if it comes in on bayonets," he argued referring to American policies in Europe: education rather than militarization was the answer, he claimed on another occasion.[30] Indeed, as a visiting expert on behalf of the United States High

Commission in Germany in the early 1950s, he lectured to inform the Germans about American foreign policy and the country's educational system, in order to make the Germans aware of what American reality and policies were so that they might understand democracy before Germany was rearmed, an eventuality he strongly opposed over the years.[31] Mosse complained about the decline of liberalism, asserting that democracy needed true liberals if a balance between national security and individual freedom were to be found.[32] He emotionally embraced the cause of liberalism, as it forcefully emerges from a passionate speech by the title "What Price Freedom?" he gave during the Iowa period:

> Armed with this true Liberalism let us stand before the world, convinced of the righteousness of our cause as were the Puritans of old; say with Blake's hymn that we will build Jerusalem on our green and pleasant land, and unashamedly invite all to imitation. Thus armed we are better prepared to meet those who oppose our ideals than with ten atom bombs which all can make. Our ideals are, once again, on trial. Here is a challenge fit to overcome the doubts of our generation.[33]

This firm attachment to such liberal values as individual freedom and parliamentary rule went hand in hand with a Marxist stance, a heritage of Mosse's earlier antifascist militancy that accompanied him for a number of years. "In my youth in America," he stated in an interview, "I was very Marxist."[34] Such an attitude lies at the roots of his direct political involvement of the time, as Mosse actively participated as vice chairman of the Henry Wallace presidential campaign. Wallace, a native of Iowa, ran against Harry Truman and Thomas Dewey as the third party candidate in the presidential elections of 1948. He stood for civil rights against racial segregation and advocated a stronger social system directed by the state, sometimes coming very close to pro-Soviet positions. The campaign ended up in a complete failure, but Mosse's committed involvement bore witness to the depth of his beliefs, especially considering the risks a new citizen, as he was (Mosse became an American citizen in 1946), could incur by exposing himself to possible accusations of being a communist. Despite all this, Mosse also spoke against the Thomas Committee on Un-American Activities, arguing that it was against the liberty of conscience, and fiercely opposed McCarthyism.[35] Besides, he joined an informal seminar on Marxism at Harvard, jeopardizing his academic position when participants were denounced to the Un-American Activities Committee.[36] Years later Mosse explained this attitude, arguing that it "took time to shake a pro-Soviet stance that had begun with the antifascist movement and continued during the war": by the time he wrote his memoir, he could say that "today I know that Truman's policies were correct."[37]

The contrast between fascist totalitarianism and liberalism, as well as his opposition to radicalism and extremism, is fully reflected in Mosse's works of this period in the guise of a fight between the rising absolutist state and the defenders of individual rights in the early modern age. Introducing a course at the University of Iowa in 1946, he distinctly narrowed it down "to one central theme. The growth of the State and the individual's relation to the State."[38] Hence his focus on political power, which he took from Meinecke and which he defined the "chief unit in history,"[39] and which he stressed in all his early modern works analyzing it through the category of sovereignty. The whole of his historical output at this stage ought to be examined against the background of his political activity since the 1930s, and of his commitment to liberalism, whose fate was, as he stated, "one constant theme in my work, tying the earlier period of my interests to my preoccupation with modern history."[40]

Thomas Hobbes as the "Voice of the Future"

The fate of liberalism in Mosse's work on the early modern period can be depicted as an imaginary confrontation between two seventeenth-century thinkers: Sir Edward Coke and Thomas Hobbes. In the historian's mind, they come to represent two opposite poles, with the former embodying the struggle for the rule of law and individual rights, and the latter epitomizing the road leading from reason of state to totalitarianism. A vein of profound pessimism pervades Mosse's reflections as he viewed Coke as a "martyr for the liberal cause" who "in public life was above all a fighter, albeit in a lost cause," while Hobbes would be "the voice of the future": modern political persecution, Mosse once said, was "the new Leviathan."[41] In Mosse's scheme of things, a line had been drawn between the birth of the modern state and the Holocaust that would withstand all subsequent methodological and thematic turns, and which would inform all his writings and reflections thereafter.

The twentieth century and its tragedies had seen a growing skepticism among intellectuals toward the role and the power of the state, embodied in the concept of sovereignty.[42] The greatest influence in the early years of the historian's career was his doctoral advisor, Charles Howard McIlwain, whom Mosse declared "the greatest teacher that I've ever known."[43] Writing on Mosse's early modern scholarship, Johann Sommerville emphasized McIlwain's importance to his young student. On the one hand, the great scholar of Anglo-American constitutional history "came to believe that states are ultimately governed either by force or by law. The rights of individuals and minorities, he claimed, can only be safeguarded where law rules, for any person or group who is above the law can trample on everyone's freedoms and reduce people to the position of slaves. Freedom can be preserved only if government is subjected to constitutional laws that it cannot change." On the other hand, McIlwain drew a line between the "pernicious" concept of sovereignty as it had taken root in seventeenth-century England and its degeneration into fascism and National Socialism.[44] This dichotomy between law and force, as well as the deterioration of the concept of sovereignty, are integral parts of Mosse's historical output of this period. Though his tone was "calmer and more detached" than McIlwain's (as Sommerville put it),[45] Mosse often connected the rise of sovereignty to fascism, thus adding a very personal nuance to his analysis of early modern English history. In his doctoral thesis, he clearly stated that the leading theoreticians of sovereignty "were well on the road to a *Machtstaat*,"[46] a belief he expressed also in his first book when he argued that "in a world where the boundary lines between the rights of individuals and the power of the state are ever in dispute, the development of the idea of sovereignty takes on great significance," and that "the principle of individual rights as contrasted with privileges granted by authority is still at issue in our modern world."[47]

The Struggle for Sovereignty in England was published in 1950, four years after Mosse received his doctorate from Harvard University. The book deals with the "emergence of the modern idea of sovereignty," focusing on the role of law, which "must stand in the centre of any discussion of the historical evolution of the idea of sovereignty in England." In Mosse's view, this evolution implied the gradual passage from the law of nature (or common law) to the law of reason. It was a shift from the medieval ideal to a modern one, from the law of God to the law of man. The English common law was seen by Mosse as a guarantee of the rights of the individual, and therefore as a bulwark against the omnipotent authority of a sovereign body, be it the king or the parliament: "The law of reason as a succession to the law of nature took on the aspect of a higher law which, while still being above the sovereign power, yet was able to upset tradition, allowing new concepts to assert themselves with a hitherto undreamt of impunity." Civil law came then to be gradually identified with "the maxims of absolutism," and "the common law of England . . . could no longer function as a bar to absolute power."[48] From such premises, Mosse went on to tackle the problem he was mostly interested in, that of liberty and liberalism:

those who sought to stem the tide toward sovereignty tried to rally behind the common law as the best remaining shield to protect the liberty of the individual. In an age when both the King and the Parliament were engaged in a struggle for power, an age which tended to disregard the traditional view of the "body politic, knit together," common lawyers like Sir Edward Coke sought to protect liberty against both extremes. Perhaps here we can see the dawn of a modern liberalism which, like the common lawyers in an age of competition for sovereignty, tries to preserve a middle way which is supported as a guarantee of individual liberty against popular and extremist ideologies. Like many modern liberals, the common lawyers thought of "rights" in legal rather than in economic or social terms. A right was guaranteed by the common law against all powers and was to them vastly different from a privilege granted as a boon by a sovereign. The development which we are discussing will take us from a society of rights to a society of privileges. What emerges is omnicompetent power.[49]

This passage clearly reflects the concerns that animated the young refugee from totalitarianism: he clearly revealed his sympathies for those who tried to preserve a balance between contrasting forces in order to guarantee individual freedom against "popular and extremist ideologies," a phrase that unmistakably echoes the ordeal that Europe (and Mosse himself) had recently suffered.

Richard Schlatter, a reviewer of the book, was very much on point when he wrote that Coke "is the hero of his story";[50] indeed, Mosse regarded Coke as a defender of individual rights against absolute power, and strongly sympathized with his ideas. Mosse had spent much time studying the lawyer's works, and in the summer of 1949 had conducted research in Coke's private library. In an unpublished article on the subject, Mosse held that "Coke has come down to us in history as the opponent of the 'Divine Right of Kings,' as the lawyer who took his stand upon the Common Law of England against the encroachments of absolute power upon the liberties of the subject."[51] In a lecture, he praised "Coke's noble effort to stem the tide of absolutism in England";[52] Coke figures as the man guiding the defenders of the common law that, contrasting the emerging law of reason based upon human authority, act as a bulwark of the liberties of the individual.[53] Law seen as a check on arbitrary power, according to Coke, was the "perfection of reason," that reason being "legal reason," a thing for lawyers, in opposition to Hobbes's idea that reason comes from the sovereign.[54] According to the practitioners of common law, law has to do with practical experience and not abstract theory, and it cannot be put in the arbitrary hands of a sovereign. Mosse mentioned another common lawyer, Matthew Hale, who accused Hobbes of "basing his rejection of the Common Law on the necessity for emergency powers in stormy times."[55] "Fundamentally Coke," Mosse wrote, "was in the position of our modern liberals: constantly on the defensive, he had to maintain the middle road between the two new doctrines, both of which were challenging the liberties of Englishmen."[56] The conclusions drawn by the book were discomforting. Mosse quoted a passage from Harold Laski: "Legally we have no fundamental rights in Great Britain; we trust for their protection to the ordinary constitutional machinery of the state. And in quiet times, we need not doubt that such protection is ample for all necessary purposes. The problem lies in the fact that in periods of rapid social change the substance of what appears fundamental to one sort of opinion does not appear to be fundamental to another." He then commented that

> this was just what the common lawyers wanted to avoid. That is why they emphasized the "certainty" of the law. That is why Sir Mathew Hale preferred a certain law, however imperfect, to any kind of arbitrary government. Would they have relished a Parliament whose only external check was resistance by force? Would they have accepted the uncertain pressure of public opinion as a substitute for a certain law? And yet parliamentary sovereignty, without Bodin's *droit*, was the outcome of this competition for sovereignty.[57]

Mosse's pessimism toward the development of European history, which he regarded as a gradual erosion of individual liberty, was counterweighted by his enthusiastic introduction into his new American environment. *The Struggle for Sovereignty in England* was even perceived as a committed tribute to the American political system: for example, Schlatter wrote in his review that "the logical conclusion [of the book] would seem to be that England is governed despotically" in contrast to the United States.[58] As a matter of fact, if Mosse in the mid-1940s still thought of his new country as "they," he soon came to speak of "our" foreign policy and Constitution on public occasions.[59] This process of integration was also reflected in his published work. Mosse came to the conclusion that in New England the covenant theory and the tradition of the charter "pointed towards greater freedom and individualism"; in 1950 he wrote that "Sir Edward Coke's concept of legal reason, while failing to halt the struggle for sovereignty in England, was, through the concept of judicial review, to provide the citadel of American constitutionalism."[60] He believed that Coke's ideal had been applied in the New World rather than in England, thus making the

American constitution "in truth . . . a medieval document," and the United States the real heir of the English medieval past he so much admired.[61]

Mosse's exile condition, with all its fears and insecurities, was thus fully reflected in his first book, which, as another reviewer pointed out, displayed "the progressive destruction of the safeguards of the individual before the emergence of the supreme authority of the state."[62] The Nazi experience pervaded his very ideas about the goals and meaning of the historical profession: addressing a meeting in 1946, he wondered whether historical connections could be used "to cure present ills," concluding that historians had "failed to analyze or do anything to mitigate the conditions which brought about a Hitler."[63] Such concerns are evident throughout his writings and speeches of the Iowa period. In particular, there emerges the problem of the balance between individual freedom and national security in times of crisis.[64] If Coke was his "hero," Hobbes played the part of the villain as from his time onward, Mosse held; the "longing for peace and security would make people submit themselves voluntarily to such an absolute sovereign."[65] Mosse's historical analysis was haunted by that feeling of fear and insecurity that would make people "retreat behind the protective skirts of the State: a putting down of all opinion which might bring about any kind of change." Fascism and National Socialism, he said, fed on such feelings that endangered individual liberty and brought nations "closer to the police state."[66] Bourgeois conformity was the fatal outcome of this process: in the wave of the 1930s antifascist movement, very critical of "bourgeois" appeasement policies, Mosse came to admire Nietzsche's idea of the superman (or overman) as opposed to middle-class *Gemütlichkeit*: the superman, he wrote in a paper, is not a concrete possibility, it is rather a protest against mediocrity.[67] Hence his opposition to any kind of "putting down all opinion," to any attempt at dissolving one's individuality and submitting to a higher authority. The new nation-states, the process of centralization, the police state—all these, in Mosse's view, along with the Reformation and its liturgical uniformity, went into the direction of absolutism: "In Germany, the Hitlerian state Church seemed really to succeed in summing up four centuries of concessions to power in the name of the uniformity of a *Landesherrlicher Kirche*."[68]

In his "Chapel Talks," delivered in 1954 and strongly religious in tone, Mosse noted "how often have we come near to sacrificing some of our hard gained political freedom to the winds of an aroused public opinion or to the lure of political expediency. Let us beware of forced conformity: it is the road to the loss of our freedom before God. For to be a free man is to acknowledge differences: every man's conscience is equal in the sight of the Lord."[69] The talks' subject was persecution and liberty: Mosse told his audience (clearly referring to the fate of the European Jews) that modern persecution is the "new Leviathan," and advocated freedom of conscience against the all-engulfing state; one must "keep alight the flame of liberty." He then mentioned the example of Hermann Maas, the Protestant minister who helped many Jews flee from Nazi Germany and was eventually sent to a forced-labor camp, stating that we must make "no compromise at any price with those who would destroy man's conscience and man's liberty." Freedom of conscience in a religious sense will lead to freedom of humanity, but, Mosse continued, it will also lead to a great problem, that of the "relation of freedom of Conscience to the modern state": the struggle for freedom of conscience has become "a struggle for all our freedoms," and so he urges, "Let us rededicate ourselves to the preservation of our religious and civil Liberties: for one cannot stand without the other." With the example of Nazi Germany and of the people's democracies in the East before his eyes, Mosse stated: "where the Kings of a bygone era had left off, the modern state took over. Like a hungry dragon he sought to swallow up man entire: body and soul. . . . The modern state not only has lacked humility but has also tended to become a law in itself: to create a separate morality through which all arbitrary actions can be justified."[70]

The Serpent and the Dove: The Question of Political Morality

In the early 1950s Mosse's work acquired a new dimension: if the first phase was monopolized by the problem of the growth of the state in Hobbesian terms—that is, from a strictly political point of view—the new decade witnessed an enrichment of perspectives when the historian turned his attention to the problem of political morality through the study of Machiavelli's thought. Machiavelli, or rather his perception, as in "Machiavellism as Europe came to understand it,"[71] became the new historical villain in Mosse's scheme of things. These were the years when Mosse became fascinated with the study of reason of state in its Machiavellian formulation, particularly with regard to the term "policy." In 1952 he explained that reason of state

is essentially a systematization of the belief in the superiority of the state over all private rights and privileges. It was first widely used in the sixteenth and seventeenth centuries in order to rationalize the ruthless employment of political power. "Reason of State" furnished a principle of political action, a law of motion, to the state, based upon the rational faith that the state is the highest of all goods. . . . This belief in the overriding interests of the state finds a supplementary expression in the word "policy," which, according to Machiavellian usage, denotes an expedient but wicked action for the preservation of the state. . . ."Policy" might thus be said to be the concrete application of the idea of "reason of state."[72]

We find here one of the first formulations of Mosse's dialectical view of history, where ideas and reality (actions) interact. The word "wicked" associated with the word "action" entails a moral connotation inherent in his view of reason of state, which constitutes the basis for his reflections on that "separate morality" he referred to in his "Chapel Talks." A quote by the Florentine thinker served as inspiration: "A man who wants only to do good must perish among so many who do evil."[73]

The focus on the moral dimension of politics derived from Mosse's interest in religious issues on the one hand, and on the other it touched on the fascist experience. Reason of state acted as a common denominator, and the historian repeatedly reaffirmed the connection over the years. As early as in 1946 Mosse said that Machiavelli "was only leading to a new ethic."[74] In his doctoral thesis and in *The Struggle for Sovereignty in England* he discussed the nature of reason of state. Yet the problem seemed, at this stage, to lie at the margins of his preoccupation with constitutional history and the relationship between the individual and the state. The new phase began in the early 1950s. In an article on Puritanism and reason of state published in 1952 Mosse directly introduced the question of Machiavelli's double standard of morality, pointing to the "fateful divorce of ethics from politics" triggered by the Florentine's thought, which "supplied the inspiration for this double standard of morality," opposing public and private morals and endowing the state "with a moral personality of its own."[75] The totalitarian experience never left the historian's sight. Mosse defined the question of religion and political morality "the most modern of problems,"[76] and reason of state as a "constant and continuing historical problem."[77] When speaking of Christianity and politics, he referred to the ethical goals of the state under fascism, an idea he restated on another occasion saying that "the theme of relating Christianity to politics has today once more come to the public notice."[78]

The culmination of Mosse's efforts in dealing with such a delicate issue was the book *The Holy Pretence*, published in 1957. Inspired by Benedetto Croce's reflections on "the points of contact between the new Renaissance political thought and the apparently contradictory ideas of the Reformation," the book represents a too often neglected milestone in Mosse's work.[79] David Warren

Sabean referred to the book as a work "which George clearly saw as central to his intellectual biography": indeed, on sending him a copy, Mosse wrote on the jacket, "I (but hardly anyone else) consider it one of my most important books."[80] *The Holy Pretence* is a study in the history of ideas whose declared purpose was the examination of "the relationship between the Christian ethic and the idea of reason of state in the thought of important Divines."[81] However, the goal Mosse was seeking to achieve was more far-ranging, as he let emerge when he wrote that "perhaps the crux of the relationship between 'Machiavellian' ideas and the Reformation lies not in the thought of this or that reformer, or even in the direct influence upon them by Machiavelli himself, but rather in the general tension between religious presuppositions and political realities."[82] This tension entailed a dialectical dilemma that, as written above, Mosse considered ever recurring. Speaking on Cold War policies, he referred to Eisenhower's statement that human nature is dual, torn between good and evil, and that one should "keep [one's] head in the clouds and [one's] feet on the ground": the question the president was answering was about how reconciliation in Christian spirit with enemy countries could be achieved; Mosse found it extremely "significant" for the whole problem of Christianity and politics.[83]

It is small wonder that Mosse took Eisenhower's remarks as an example, since the idea of keeping one's head in the clouds and one's feet on the ground summarizes the attempt he was making to find and keep a balance between ideas and reality, between ethics and politics. Friedrich Meinecke had emphasized the need to "soar to the skies and yet keep a firm foot on earth,"[84] and Mosse built on Croce's and Meinecke's reflections on reason of state, believing that the dualism between ethics and politics had to be overcome, and that the two "systems of values" did not necessarily exclude each other. *The Holy Pretence*, from this perspective, is an attempt to establish a "positive relationship" between the two.[85] Mosse tackled the problem from the point of view of Christian casuistry, that is, "the adjustment of the general Christian framework of ethics to meet new situations and dangers": such an approach, he believed, could "furnish a fruitful approach to the problem of how far 'Machiavellian' ideas penetrated the thought of Western Christianity."[86]

Casuistry represented, in Mosse's eyes, the Christian response to the secularization process in Europe. It was also the means through which he tackled for the first time the problem of rationality in history: Mosse's work in the 1950s was also aimed at highlighting the contribution made by Christian theology to the development of a rationalistic attitude in Western culture that ran parallel to that offered by Renaissance political philosophy, the natural sciences, and the Enlightenment. "Such a point of view," Mosse held, "tends to ignore the greater realism toward nature and politics which developed within the Christian theological framework itself."[87] Religion itself, the historian insisted on another occasion, elaborated a rationality of its own when faced by the challenge posed by Machiavellian ideas, and the casuists eventually worked out a "rationalization of the use of reason of state" that implied its assimilation into the Christian framework of ethics.[88] Once again Mosse referred to the Nazi experience: the Church in Germany, he said, "was to learn the bitter lesson that faith itself had to come to grips with the reality of the State or to see its principles vanish from the land. The 'practical Divinity' of the Puritans had anticipated this realization."[89] The casuists, in his view, had realized the necessity of a balance between ideas and reality, something many Germans, including Mosse's family, had failed to do by clinging to an idealism devoid of realism, which entailed an underestimation of the Nazi threat.

Mosse's sympathy for these Divines was not, however, unbridled. Particularly in his earliest writings on the subject, he criticized their attempt to harness reason of state to Christian purposes, and he disapproved of their contribution to the development of the absolute state in the West (as in the case of John Winthrop, who claimed, as Mosse noted, that "the care of the public must oversway all private respects").[90] In the historian's opinion, many Puritans adopted a double standard of political morality, "thus giving added impetus to the fateful divorce of ethics from politics."[91] After all, casuistry had made Renaissance political thought respectable by preparing the soil for its theoretical acceptance in England, Mosse argued.[92] And yet his admiration for their efforts was greater than his criticism, perhaps in the light of his bitterness toward those Weimar intellectuals whom he blamed for their lack of realism when it was most needed to make an attempt to contest Hitler's rise to power.[93]

The message delivered by *The Holy Pretence*, and by all of Mosse's writings on ethics and politics, is a recommendation to live a moral life based on the balance between contesting forces. The sixteenth-century idea that "the stone must be joined to St. John's Gospel," where "the subtlety of the Serpent instructs the Innocence of the Dove, the Innocence of the Dove corrects the subtlety of the Serpent," was Mosse's credo for the modern age.[94] David Warren Sabean stressed the significance of *The Holy Pretence* as an expression of Mosse's enduring concerns. Among these, there was

a lifelong concern with finding a balance between contesting forces. George always thought that life's realities possessed powerful demands for people and that finding an ethical balance was crucial for living a moral life. He found unsatisfactory both the life of unexamined power and the life of the virgin moralist, unsullied by immersion in practical affairs. *The Holy Pretence* was an attempt to look at how a series of political thinkers and actors negotiated Christian morality and the practical exigencies of seventeenth-century state politics. . . . Mosse condemned a series of writers for failing to assimilate political thought within a Christian framework, and he admired the casuists who at least made the attempt. The people he most admired were those who did not skirt the issue and did not reject the concept of reason of state.[95]

The conclusion to *The Holy Pretence* sums up the more general goal of the study, stressing the fact that attempting to find the yearned-for balance between dangerous but necessary principles does not necessarily imply the hypocritical renunciation of one's principles. Rather, as Mosse firmly believed, it is the only way to survive in an evil world:

as long as tensions between religious presuppositions and the realities of life exist, such casuistic thought will always have great relevance in attempting to adjust the Christian tradition to various forms of worldly wisdom and secular necessities. The problem involved is to keep the balance between the Serpent and the Dove, so that neither obliterates the other: for the victory of the Dove can lead to unbridled idealism, and the ignoring of secular realities; while the victory of the Serpent means the total acceptance of what the sixteenth century called "Machiavellism." How well most of the Casuists in this study kept the balance is open to question. Prudence[96] as we saw did, in many cases, become "policy" under a different name. Reason of state was tied to God as the chief end, but here again the religious element seems at times to provide no more than a disguise for the secular concept. It must be stressed once again that the endeavor to combine the Serpent and the Dove does not imply hypocrisy. Rather these attempts raise the problem of what can be the Christian answer to the survival of a good man in an evil world.[97]

From Machiavellism to National Socialism

Mosse moved from Iowa City to Madison in 1955 "with the proviso that [he] specialize in the nineteenth and twentieth centuries."[98] This new opportunity offered him the chance to become a specialist in the history of National Socialism and fascism, an enterprise he was only too willing to undertake. The gap between life and work, which he had thus far filled by fusing his personal concerns with the history of a bygone age, could be finally closed in a more fulfilling way. The turn to the history of National Socialism provided him with the opportunity to follow the development of the state well into the twentieth century, when the principle of nationality found its highest, however bloody, gratification on a political and cultural level. In a lecture on the nineteenth century, Mosse summarized the path we have followed:

> The Nation State had risen in power and strength. The sixteenth and seventeenth centuries saw the acceptance of ideas of absolutism and of reason of state. Here Freedom was limited by the interests of the state. Here the Nation tended to become a good in itself above the unity of Western Civilization and ideas of liberty. To this the nineteenth century added "cultural Nationalism." The State now becomes not merely a political entity but a "way of life": a doctrine of superiority of one Nation over all others.[99]

This passage, which echoes Meinecke's thought, leads to nationalism, a phenomenon to which Mosse turned his attention in the second half of the 1950s, especially in its German version. His first writings on modern history were all concerned with the roots of National Socialism and anti-Semitism, which Mosse identified in the nationalist substratum underlying German history. It was nationalism that diminished the dignity of the individual, as Mosse made clear in the introduction to one of his major works on German nationalism and National Socialism, published in 1975. As he wrote,

> this book is the result of a longstanding preoccupation with the dignity of the individual and its challengers, so successful during long periods of our century in stripping man of control over his destiny. Many years ago I attempted to trace how a system of moral values, Christianity, was eroded through contact with political reality during the seventeenth century. The triumph of reason of state seemed to me then to lead into a realpolitik which answered Machiavelli's eternal question of how a good man could survive in an evil world. But while I still believe that the seventeenth century was an important turning point in the absorption of Christian theology by realpolitik, the nineteenth century with the development of mass movements and mass politics seemed to transform the political process itself into a drama which further diminished the individual whose conscious actions might change the course of his own destiny.[100]

Mosse was now ready to transpose his insights into a wholly new field, without losing sight of the guiding concerns that had animated his early efforts. This brought about not only a shift in the themes he was dealing with, but also a series of substantial methodological changes that saw him abandon the "respectable" way of writing history he had adopted so far. He had now firmly established his position in the academic world, and could finally expand his interests without concern.

2

Beyond the History
of Intellectuals

By what right do we introduce phenomena of collective psychology
into the study of history? They certainly are most difficult to grasp
with any degree of precision. We have immediate comprehension of
the meaning and life of an institution, the causes and effects of a military action or a political treaty. We even can reconstitute the variables
that have affected a human mind. But we are much less equipped to
enter the vast undefined realm of instincts, or of the beliefs and
undercurrents that move not individuals but crowds. Yet how can we
ignore this element when we are dealing, for example, with religious
faith, or with a revolutionary faith?

—HENRI FOCILLON

Before one could advance into the very heart of contemporary nationalism one would be forced to traverse the wide fields and devious
paths of anthropology.

—CARLTON HAYES

The "continuity of interests" in Mosse's work characterized his writings
over more than forty years. However, when he began his analysis of
modern European history in the mid-1950s, he had to face a new set of
historiographical problems. Mosse was now beginning to specialize in the history of National Socialism, a mass phenomenon typical of the modern age with
its diffusion of mass literacy, the growing involvement of the masses into politics, and the birth of mass movements. Such an attempt required new tools of
historical investigation into a phenomenon that sharpened more than ever the
problem of the loss of individual liberty in the midst of the crowd. This was true
particularly of totalitarian movements with their attempt to create a "new man"

through the participation of all citizens into the political machinery of consensus. While most historians at the time tried to interpret totalitarianism in strictly political, social, or economic terms, Mosse chose a completely different path. While his interpretation of German and Italian fascism will be dealt with in another part of this book, our concern here are two methodological turns that occurred in his work between the late 1950s and the late 1960s, and which constitute the theoretical backbone on which all his subsequent works would be based. The problem posed by the challenge to individuality will come to be dealt with by the historian in totally different terms on a methodological plane.

The two methodological turns divide three moments in Mosse's work: (1) the moment of the history of ideas, (2) the moment of the history of ideologies, and (3) the moment of the history of political liturgies and symbolism. The first phase, which we analyzed in the previous chapter, was concerned with the study of the ideas of first-rate thinkers in the early modern age. The second phase, inaugurated in the mid-1950s, saw the historian shift his focus to minor figures in history and in popular literature, and culminated in Mosse's first major book on National Socialism, *The Crisis of German Ideology*, published in 1964. The last phase was the outcome of a widening in the historian's perspectives that resulted in an anthropologically and aesthetically oriented kind of cultural history, theoretically supported by the article "History, Anthropology, and Mass Movements," published in 1969, and crowned by what is considered to be Mosse's most influential book in this period, *The Nationalization of the Masses* (1975).[1]

The Israeli historian Shulamit Volkov has argued that the first methodological turn was not a real watershed, but merely a widening of the scope of history of ideas and "not a complete turnabout."[2] If this was not a complete turnabout, it was surely an important step in the historiography of National Socialism when Mosse applied his new tools of historical investigation first to the study of the origins of German anti-Semitism, and then to those of National Socialist ideology.[3] *The Crisis of German Ideology*, the direct result of Mosse's new attitude, was without doubt a fundamental turnabout in the historiography on Nazism. The book offered a vast analysis of German *völkisch* culture from the age of the Napoleonic Wars to the eve of the Nazi seizure of power in 1933. Mosse also examined the culture through popular literature, paying attention to the thought of minor, often obscure thinkers and novelists. Mosse held that ideas are important only when they become institutionalized—that is, diffused among people through the educational system, through associations or political parties and organizations. He analyzed the prehistory of National Socialist ideology against the background of modernity and set the ideological factor at the center of his interpretation of National Socialism, which he eventually defined as an "anti-Jewish revolution."[4] Thus ideology, in this case anti-Semitic *völkisch* culture, came to play the main role in the study of Nazism and was set at its core: the analysis of popular culture was, in Mosse's mind, inseparable from the ideological factor when the impact of ideology on the majority of the population had to be assessed.

The Nationalization of the Masses was even more innovative. The book is an analysis of what Mosse labeled "the new politics," that is, a new political style born of the French Revolution, based on mass festivals and mass meetings where symbols are employed, and myths activated. Of paramount importance is also the setting where these festivals take place, and therefore the book is largely concerned with cultic spaces, national monuments, and architecture. Anthropology and aesthetics merge into this work: fascism has now, in his view, many characteristics of a religion. The consensus relies on a genuine belief in ideology, but this belief is kindled by a fully developed liturgy that integrates the masses into the nation through this new political style. *The Crisis of German Ideology*, based on written sources, stresses the ideological dimension of National Socialism. *The Nationalization of the Masses* focused on the aesthetic means of self-representation and paved the way for a wider interpretation of fascism that was not confined to the specific ideological content. Rather, it highlighted the differences among various fascisms and implied a unifying element, a common denominator among them, thus opening a door leading to the elaboration of a general theory of fascism that would occupy Mosse from the 1970s on.

This phase of Mosse's historiography was the result of numerous factors and influences that we will explore in the next two chapters. It needs to be pointed out from the outset that the two methodological turns carried a whole set of problems, issues that touched closely upon his own historiography as much as they had affected, if not haunted, the whole of the historical discipline over the last century. Though Mosse hardly ever systematized his theoretical beliefs, he acted as a catalyzer of many of the fundamental currents of thought of the age. He tackled, implicitly or explicitly, a number of crucial questions, such as the relationship between rationality and irrationality, the role played by ideas and ideologies in history, the religious nature of modern political phenomena, the correlated problem of the genuineness of myth in modern politics, and the very issue of what history should be about. His contribution was to prove enduring and has shaped our current views not only of nationalism and fascism, but also of racism and sexuality to a considerable extent. It is therefore important to try and elucidate the details of these methodological shifts, in order to shed light both on the development of Mosse's work and on the birth of the cultural history of modern mass movements, and of the myths that underlined them.

From Ideas to Ideologies: The Turn to Popular Culture

Over the course of the 1950s, Mosse consistently widened his perspectives on the role played by ideas in history, thus expanding his views to include ideologies among the causal mechanism that moves human events. In an article he authored in 1964, significantly titled "Puritanism Reconsidered," he blamed himself for having promoted, in his *The Struggle for Sovereignty in England* (1950), the English Revolution's prime cause "as a struggle over a new and modern definition of power and sovereignty," a struggle "for power within certain important vested interests . . . just a matter which concerned a few hundred members of Parliament."[5] The time had come for historians, he argued, to begin stressing the ideological connections between Puritanism and the English Revolution: Puritanism had to be studied as an ideology, as "a system of ideas which had to be taken seriously"; from this point of view, "a whole new historical perspective was illuminated," which would shed light on the fact that "a vigorous and systematic ideology stands at the beginning of American history."[6]

Though a precise line of demarcation cannot be drawn, the year 1957 could be taken symbolically as a watershed. In that year Mosse published a short article about the teaching of history to freshmen. If compared to a similar attempt he had made in 1949, some remarkable differences are present. By 1957, as Sommerville has written, "Mosse had come to attach greater importance to theories, metaphysics, and ideologies in the teaching of history to freshmen."[7] Indeed, in his 1949 article, Mosse's stress was almost entirely laid on the teaching of facts and chronology: reality must prevail over metaphysics; ideologies and philosophy come later.[8] To be sure, he emphasized the importance of freshmen reading extracts from philosophers in order to see "how men rationalize the changing features of our civilization . . . to understand the continuity and development of history"; and yet the goal he had in mind was pragmatic, at a time when his political involvement was particularly intensive in the wave of the Wallace campaign: education must serve the purpose of helping students "make intelligent political choices in our society"; they must be educated as "citizens" before they can become historians.[9]

The 1957 article has a far more historical flavor, and the perspective has changed remarkably. Mosse now laments that history as it is taught in the United States is only pragmatic, and "influenced by the contention that what moves history is the political and socio-economic surroundings in which the struggle for life has its setting. What this has meant is failure to deal with abstract thought and political rationalizations. Almost none of our texts show any realizations that ideas can be weapons . . . how men rationalize their actions often determines what actions they take."[10] The emphasis on ideas is linked with their rationalizations, which implies more than abstract ideas in themselves: they now serve as powerful motivating factors. It is not surprising that Mosse explicitly writes about nationalism in this article, comparing it to a "mood" rather than "something that can be analyzed through political or economic factors alone."[11] Moreover, he does not mention extracts from philosophers anymore: the key to understanding nationalism is popular literature: reading the works of Gustav Freytag, Mosse argues, makes nationalism clearer than a chronological or external account of its development. The focus has then shifted from ideas to their rationalizations, from ideas to ideologies (from "sovereignty" to "nationalism"), from philosophy to popular culture.

Mosse, in his usual fashion, did not feel the need to elaborate much on his methodological beliefs through organic and coherent theoretical essays. His interest in cultural history surely dates back to the very beginning of his career: introducing a course he held at the University of Iowa in 1946, he defined cultural history as "a rather new thing" that could be traced back to Jacob Burckhardt's *The Civilization of the Renaissance*, the "first book of 'cultural' history properly so-called." Cultural history, Mosse said, is a "generic term" that "includes all aspects of life," and yet he narrowed down his course to "one central theme. . . . The growth of the State and the individual's relation to the State." Though devoting much attention to the thought of important political thinkers, the course mainly focused on the social and chronological framework.[12] His published works between the late 1940s and the mid-1950s dealt exclusively with the analysis of ideas, and therefore they can be more properly categorized into what is known as intellectual rather than cultural history. This does not mean, however, that the backbone of Mosse's later interests was not present already. His belief in the totality of history (cultural history as including "all aspects of life," probably derived from his admiration for Hegel's philosophy and Croce's historicism) emerged occasionally, as when he argued, during another course held in the early 1950s, that the idea of cultural history had to be broadened to take in art and music, and that the sixteenth and seventeenth centuries could not be understood "without dealing with the Baroque style and all it implies."[13]

Mosse's real transition to cultural history was triggered by his inclusion of popular culture into his view of the discipline. A number of factors can help explain the origins of such a turn. Mosse's bent for Hegelianism rendered him receptive toward the stimuli offered by works like those of Burckhardt and Johann Huizinga (see below), which he profoundly admired. These other pioneers of cultural history shared an intense fascination for art and aesthetics, and a view of history that included human life in its totality. Their first contributions in the field of cultural history dealt with medieval or early modern history, and Mosse was familiar with them. When he moved on to the study of the modern age, he brought with him the heritage and the expertise of a scholar trained in Church history and theology, who nourished a particular interest in Baroque art, architecture, and liturgy. Mosse, who had studied the Baroque with passion, was impressed by *Roma triumphans'* "delight in grandiose religious ceremonies and in liturgical color and form," which stressed the "dramatic element in popular piety" in tune with that ceremonial impetus.[14] As he himself acknowledged, he had brought his knowledge "to bear upon the secularization of modern and contemporary politics"; he stated that "it was not such a big step from Christian belief systems, especially in the baroque period, to modern civic religions such as nationalism in its various forms—including fascism—which have occupied me for many decades."[15] While Mosse's view of the Baroque will be analyzed later,[16] it is important to stress here the connection he drew with popular piety, and with liturgy's aptitude to orchestrate vast numbers of people.

Johann Huizinga's *The Waning of the Middle Ages*, despite its focus on court life, stressed many themes that inspired Mosse in his interpretation of popular culture. Above all, the longing for a better world and the desire to turn such dreams and hopes into reality belonged to Huizinga's view of history, as they did to Mosse's. The Madison historian, however, pointed to the study of popular, millenarian, and prophetic ideas rather than to the art and writings of the court, as he himself made clear in an unpublished essay.[17] Ernst Bloch's *The Principle of Hope* served as another source of inspiration, with its emphasis on the influence of millenarianism and utopianism on men and women. Mosse firmly believed that the "need for hope," the "longing for a better world" and for the "release from daily misery" informed popular feelings and piety.[18] What the historian needed was a methodological key to grapple with the interpretation of such feelings, hopes, and aspirations.

The environment at the University of Iowa surely lent itself to such a purpose. Mosse said in his memoir that it was during the Iowa period that he turned to "what is sometimes called a history of mentalities, or, rather, . . . a kind of cultural history which I tried to make my own, dealing with perceptions, myths, and symbols and their popular appeal."[19] In this passage the historian fuses his two methodological turns and traces back their origins to the early 1950s, when his published works show no evidence of any interest in popular culture, not to mention myths and symbols. However, his lectures from the late 1940s reveal a precocious interest in the works of Burckhardt and Huizinga, an interest that was to develop and blossom over the following decade. It can be said that many of the elements that would later converge into his new methodology found their inspiration here. Indeed, Mosse's earliest contribution to the history of anti-Semitism and modern German culture acknowledged an important intellectual debt: the insights of his Iowa colleague William Aydelotte.[20] Aydelotte had been a leading figure in the development of social and intellectual history in the United States. He had also shown an interest in social psychology, particularly in explaining how human motivations manifest within the historical context. He had authored essays on the importance of the study of popular literature for historians, focusing in particular on detective stories: he believed that "a careful study of literature of this kind [might] reveal popular attitudes which shed a flood of light on the motivation behind political, social, and economic history."[21] The passage that caught Mosse's attention, and that he quoted, was taken from another article published in 1952, and regarded "the attitudes and preconceptions literature reveals—attitudes which, though they may be trivial in themselves, yet to the extent that they are widely shared, underlie and motivate basic historical changes."[22] Compared to Mosse's assertion that "if you find a whole body of literature, regardless of who wrote it, which has a certain point of view about peasants, which certainly changes the peasant images, then it is relevant," the citation reveals how important such ideas must have been, especially in the light of Mosse's deep concern with popular literature.[23]

Moreover, at Iowa City Mosse felt closer to colleagues from the departments of fine arts and literature than to historians, and he often actively attended cultural events and discussions that included participants from different disciplines. Among these he was engaged with were the Writer's Workshop and, above all, the Humanities Society, which he also presided over. The society "furthered a broadening of one's outlook," and surely played a substantial role in making Mosse more familiar with interdisciplinarity, favoring his bent toward literature.[24] Last but not least, he also mentioned the importance of Mary Ann Holmes's lectures in art history, real "cultural events": "When I heard about modern art," he wrote, "my eyes were opened to a new world, one I had not even considered before."[25] All this occurred against the background of a vivid interest in popular and mass culture, sparked by the critique of the Frankfurt School, the diffusion of pop art, and the works of many historians and social scientists who felt the need to analyze mass society.[26]

Despite the lack of outspoken theoretical elaborations, Mosse's conviction of the importance of popular literature to the historian was expressed through two unpublished writings, a lecture and an article, in which he enunciated some of his most important ideas. These papers, "Literature and History" and "The Cultural Historian and Popular Literature," were written respectively in the late 1950s and in 1967. In "Literature and History," Mosse invited historians to do for the modern period what Huizinga had achieved for the Middle Ages. The starting point, he argued, was the "extensive use of literature": not literature intended as source material on which psychological judgments must be passed, but literature "used as a source for 'attitudes' towards problems . . . not for historical events, but for the 'history of opinion.'" He referred to the need to deal not with the greatest authors, but with the "most popular," focusing on "the writer's sensitivity to his status in society."[27] The best approach, he said, is to

> get at some of the attitudes in popular culture . . . to take a mass of popular literature—novels which were, as far as we can tell—widely read, and to analyze these as the totality of material. Analyze it how? Here I think that the sociological concept of the stereotype or "image" can be most useful. Concretely the questions I would ask of such a body of material is what is the author's image of the "commercial classes," of the "working classes," of the "Jew." It is in reality taking the concepts of "types" and treating it as fluid. . . . In this way we can, I think, get at popular attitudes, and at popular culture. For it is the stereotype, the image (as Huizinga calls it in his chapter on religious thought crystallizing into images) which tends to dominate popular thought and popular feeling which becomes obvious in social and economic crisis, but which is ever present in that substrata of popular thinking at which the cultural historian tries to get. For cultural history tends to consist in a series of images and stereotypes which, in this way, find their reflection in literature. Not literature as the product of the individual artist, but literature as the product of many artists, considered as a whole. In this way we might yet get cultural history written.[28]

In 1967, in the middle of the second methodological turn, Mosse felt the need to reassert his convictions about the use of popular literature, now adding some of his newly acquired anthropological perspectives. He argued that historians should focus on the "history of readers rather than of authors": the very fact that a book attained mass circulation "must lead the historian to search for the common denominator of this literature and its enduring appeal." At this point, Mosse criticized Huizinga's focus on the culture of the elites and stressed the need to examine the lives of the masses with their millenarian and prophetic ideas, which are filled with "religious thought stimulating dynamic social myths." The goal is to penetrate "the turns and twists of the primitive mind which dominated among the peoples of Europe." This popular literature is, according to Mosse, imbued with a constant repetition of themes that reflect "utopian longings"; if it was so popular at a given time, this can be of help for the historian to fathom the "popular mind": "If we can find out why people liked an immensely popular work we may have opened a door to an understanding of their cast of mind." The crux of the matter is that all this, Mosse continues, "cannot but entail political and social consequences . . . the very repetitiveness of theme and content reveals a great deal about the popular cast of mind, and allows us to draw some concrete conclusions about the political importance which one can attach to such investigations." This approach, which Mosse had adopted in his earliest writings on National Socialism, could "answer the question of why so many people (and not only the Germans) accepted so easily the racial and rightist ideals which triumphed between the wars."[29]

The driving interest that led Mosse to concentrate on popular literature was, indeed, his personal urge to delve into the roots of Nazi consensus. He came to see the extensive use of literature as a key to the understanding of ideology. He believed that many people were convinced that ideology was only a façade: as he said, "here was a mistake typical of our time: underestimation of ideology. Most people in our age living pragmatically oriented lives find it difficult to believe in ideological commitment but they find it easy to believe that men want power. . . . It is an obsession with desirability of power for its own sake which blinded men to the real object of NS [National Socialism]. And which made possible what has been called with some justice this 'silent revolution.' We must not make this mistake again."[30] Again, in "Puritanism Reconsidered," he invited historians "to go down among the sects," referring to those radical and revolutionary sects he believed to stand at the core of Puritanism, and whose ideals of community reflected the same hopes and desires that could be found in popular piety.[31] Popular piety, in Mosse's definition, consisted in "folks beliefs and customs" that represented "the hopes and aspirations of the multitude whose religious awareness tends to be immediate and naive. The practices of popular piety functioned as dynamic social myths, reaffirming community and kinship ties, reconciling man to God and seeking to secure divine aid for the problems of human existence."[32]

When Mosse began to explore National Socialism, he did so analyzing its ideology, which he sought to grasp through popular literature in search of a key to comprehend the "hopes and aspirations" of the German people, to fathom the "social myths" they lived by, and to shed light on the popular basis on which the *Volksgemeinschaft* (community of the people) was built. His first writings on the subject, three essays published between 1957 and 1961, stressed the need to understand the content of the "popular imagination" through an analysis of literature in order to understand the intellectual foundations of German anti-Semitism.[33] He pointed out the fact that, despite decades of research, the intellectual origins of the Nazi movement were still unexplored territory, and that it was necessary to examine it as an ideology: "This is necessary because historians have ignored this stream of thought as too *outré* to be taken seriously. . . . Yet such ideas made a deep impression upon a whole nation. Historians who have dismissed these aspects of romanticism and mysticism have failed to grasp an essential and important ingredient of modern German history."[34] Thus the problem of ideology was brought to the fore in connection with popular literature and culture: ideology was important not only in the abstract, but also insofar as it permeated the "popular mind." Once applied to the study of National Socialism, this approach helped Mosse explain the origins of a phenomenon that had touched so closely upon his life, and whose legacy still preoccupied him.

Between Consensus, Nihilism, and Propaganda

In the early 1960s Mosse expressed his apprehension with the resurgence of Nazi sympathies in both Germany and the United States on several occasions. Following the desecration of the Cologne synagogue in 1959, he wrote an article with the significant title "A Ghost Come Alive," in which he lamented the fact that many former Nazis had been recycled to high levels in the German Federal Republic, and conveyed his anxieties on the influence still retained by anti-Semitism in the newly born German state.[35] Similarly, *The Crisis of German Ideology* was born out of a double concern with the past on the one hand, and the present on the other. In the introduction, Mosse pointed the finger at the persistence of *völkisch* ideas not only in Germany but also in the United

States, through those extremist groups that fused anti-Jewish and anti–African American sentiments, and did so drawing from German sources. Though such groups were little influential, Mosse believed they could still, in times of crisis, represent a potential danger, helping create a racist mood by slowly poisoning institutions from the inside.[36]

It should therefore come as no surprise that the years of his early interest in National Socialism were overshadowed by his concern with the "appeal of Nazi culture," a theme he dealt with on several occasions over the 1960s.[37] In the late 1950s, in reflections titled "National Socialism and Germany Today," he defined Nazism as "a regime with a mass following . . . a twentieth century totalitarianism which is based upon mass enthusiasm and mass support."[38] This definition bore the seeds of all coming reflections on the relationship between consensus and propaganda in Mosse's work, which were informed by the driving question that lay at the roots of the book on German ideology: "Why did millions of Germans respond to the Volkish call?" The answer lay in ideology, according to Mosse. He set himself to the task of dealing with the interpretation of fascism "from the ideological point of view," as he made clear at the seminar on fascism held at Stanford University in the fall of 1963.[39] To interpret fascism from the ideological point of view implied that ideas had to be taken seriously, on the assumption that they were instrumental in the success gained by fascist movements.

Such an attitude proved revolutionary, as up to the early 1960s it went against the grain of most, if not all, scholarship on fascism. As early as in 1952 Mosse had criticized American liberal historians for not understanding theology, and for not espousing the European interest in theory and ideas.[40] In 1957 he claimed that "it is surprising to what extent our Freshmen history texts have been influenced by the contention that what moves history is the political and socio-economic surroundings in which the struggle for life has its setting. What this has meant is failure to deal with abstract thought and political rationalizations. Almost none of our texts show any realizations that ideas can be weapons. . . . How men rationalize their actions often determines what actions they take." Unlike in Europe, where "the question of religion and political morality . . . is currently occupying some of the best minds," Americans, driven by their "fear of ideologies," tended to discard ideas, thus misunderstanding their own past and identity.[41] With regard to the interpretations of fascisms, the same could be held true at the time. Propaganda and will to power still represented the guidelines along which interpretations of totalitarianism revolved. The question of consensus was a taboo that still needed to be broken.[42]

Mosse himself, in the early 1960s, was torn between propaganda and consensus: in his view of fascism they cohabited, thus creating a contradictory tension that would be partially solved only through the second methodological turn and the consequent belief that fascisms were secular religions. This shift was, in turn, fueled by Mosse's interest in the roots of consensus. His writings clearly reveal the conviction that Italian Fascism and German National Socialism benefited from a vast popular support. The "mass enthusiasm and mass support" he referred to at the outset of his analysis were reaffirmed in many subsequent works. Popular literature in Germany had spread a stereotype of the Jew that was "widely shared" by the population,[43] and this image went "far to explain the surrender to National Socialism's anti-Semitism by even the more respectable elements of the population": *völkisch* ideas had "made a deep impression upon a whole nation."[44] As Mosse approached fascism and National Socialism directly for the first time, in his 1961 book on the culture of modern Europe, he expressed this belief with no hesitation, clearly stating that "there can be little doubt about the popularity of fascism, especially in the beginning": fascism had come to power legally in both Italy and Germany, Mosse observed, and was overthrown only because of a lost war.[45] He repeatedly wrote of fascism's attraction, pointing out how National Socialism had relied on a consolidated cultural atmosphere shared by many Germans and imbued with *völkisch* ideas.[46] *The Crisis of German Ideology* was the outcome of these concerns, its underlying idea being the conviction that "you cannot have any successful myth without historical preparation."[47] Mosse was pointing at the conservatism of popular culture, which required a tradition to stand at the basis of any successful political myth.[48] In 1966 he published an anthology titled *Nazi Culture*, a revolutionary concept in itself.[49]

An interpretation of fascism "from the ideological point of view" could seem at first incompatible with current views, mostly inspired by the widespread theory of totalitarianism, which mostly regarded mass support as a mere result of propaganda and manipulation. Indeed, Mosse himself believed at first that the latter were integral part of the fascist phenomenon: this belief relied on a view of ideology as a rationalized means of maneuvering the masses. The cohabitation of consensus and propaganda in *The Culture of Western Europe* (1961) is made explicit in a passage where the author stresses Mussolini's obsession with propaganda as a means to manipulate mass meetings side by side with a view of these meetings as "religious rites" in which "the devoted participated and renewed their fervor." Yet despite the popular devotion Mosse attributed to such meetings, they remained "manipulated," artificial, a form of "propaganda" that "sprang from a basically irrational view of human nature." Mass meetings, though "central to fascism," required a leader able to "manipulate the longings of the people." Mosse saw Mussolini and Hitler as "expert *creators* of powerful myths," in some contradiction with his belief in the necessity and genuineness of tradition.[50] The idea of myth that emerges here is that of a tool used by leaders to control and discipline the masses through rituals that added to the already existing attraction of the movement.[51] In fact, Mosse wrote that "fascism has been called government through propaganda and with some justice if by propaganda we mean the *objectification of ideology*," by which he meant mass meetings, whose religious content was both genuine and manipulated; in short, it was exploited "for a better understanding among the people." Fascist cultural accomplishments, Mosse clearly stated, were "restricted to the organization and manipulation of the masses of the population."[52] Two years later, at the Stanford seminar, he affirmed that propaganda was only a means to implement an idea, to organize the masses: here Hitler was in full accordance with Georges Sorel and Vilfredo Pareto. Hitler's propaganda was animated by what Mosse called "ideological pragmatism": his concept stems from a view that regards the Führer as a "cynic who became a master politician. Yet he always believed in the essential ideology. . . . His political maneuvering, even the German–Soviet alliance, was a tactical decision which, in the end, was meant not to hinder but to further the triumph of a fully worked-out ideology."[53] Yet this vision did apply exclusively to the leader, and not to the masses. This was Mosse's view in the early 1960s: the historian was torn between two concepts, that of propaganda and that of consensus, which could not be satisfactorily espoused. His cultural interpretation of fascism suffered from the contradiction inherent in the view of all fascism, of all totalitarian systems as resting on ideology "based upon a technique of terror."[54]

It was only in the mid-1960s that Mosse became fully aware of these contradictions, and slowly began to modify and clarify his approach to this apparently insoluble problem. Emilio Gentile has convincingly suggested that the turning point lies in Mosse's realization that ideology could not be associated plainly with conscious rationalizations aimed at the manipulation of the masses: the key is the passage from ideology to liturgy, where ideology is no longer identified with theoretical rationalism, and its irrational side is highlighted. This points to a view of ideology that no longer regards rites, symbols, and mass ceremonies as Machiavellian tools of power, but rather as animated by genuinely held beliefs in the ideology, which is now regarded as a secularized religion based on a fully developed liturgy. Gentile argues that Mosse solved the problem by separating irrationality from nihilism, and attributing to irrationality a rationality of its own. This rationality was "constituted by the logic inherent in the forms through which irrationality expressed and materialized itself as a political movement."[55] As Mosse wrote in *The Crisis of German Ideology*,

> Georges Sorel had said disparagingly that intellectuals never know what to do with the phenomenon of religion in history. They could not deny its historical importance, nor could they explain it. He held that men are motivated by irrational myths whose truth or falsehood is irrelevant to their appeal. It is hardly surprising to find that Sorel was a great source of inspiration for the fascists. But even the most irrational religion, to become effective, must express itself through outward forms. To move masses of men it must objectify itself. In the end the outward forms may become so important that they determine the content of the faith. That is what happened in Germany, both through the way in which the ideology was objectified and through the dominant role that the leader came to occupy. Moreover, the ideas of discipline and organization which Hitler stressed in place of "fanaticism" not only led to a more effective objectification of the ideology but also provided the basis for an awesome political effectiveness. The so-called eternal verities of nature, *Volk*, and race were channeled toward definite objects, consciously directed by the leadership.[56]

Ideology was thus objectified through liturgy, which implied discipline and organization over fanaticism: Mosse came to see the "taming" of irrationalism as a key element of the fascist revolution. The shift from ideology to liturgy entailed, as Gentile points out, two consequences: the first is the new balance in the relation between faith and pragmatism, as Mosse slowly abandoned the conviction that myths and symbols are solely a tool for manipulating the masses. The second factor is the definition of fascism as a religion: fascism, from a movement with analogies with religion, becomes itself a religious phenomenon. Mosse's divorcing nihilism from irrationality brought up a view of fascism as a religion, paving the ground for the turn to liturgy, which helped shed light on the problems of nihilism and ideology.

From Nihilism to Liturgy: The Religion of Fascism

The relationship between nihilism and ideology in Mosse's thought deserves to be analyzed in greater depth, in that it is crucial both to understanding the turn to liturgy and to elucidating the whole issue of fascist morality and values.

In 1961 Mosse, identifying ideology with myth and nihilism with activism and with the struggle for power for power's sake, stressed Mussolini's urge to "integrate activism and ideology," on the assumption that "no nation could be transformed on the basis of . . . nihilism": ideology was crucial in that it provided the goal, the necessary faith mirrored in a myth "which mystically fused the individual and the nation through the party," providing people with a "sense of commitment and belonging which destroyed that alienation from society which many men had felt so deeply. . . . [This] was no small part of fascism's attraction." Here Mosse argues that the essence of fascism could not be solely nihilism, that a powerful myth expressed in ideology was essential: though Italian fascism had in the beginning a "pragmatic base" as opposed to an "ideological vagueness," it slowly acquired a fully worked-out ideology that managed to combine nationalism and activism. However, Mosse continues, both in Italian fascism and in German National Socialism ideology came eventually to be brushed aside by a powerful nihilistic streak, embodied by the "struggle for the sake of struggling—action for action's sake." Both Italy and Germany ended up privileging "a certain kind of nihilism which became a naked urge for power" where activism "put a quest for power ahead of any dogmatism."[57] However, partly contradictorily, Mosse ended up setting nihilism itself within the scope of ideology when he wrote, referring to Hermann Rauschning's interpretation of National Socialism as a "revolution of nihilism," that the German historian

> was correct in using the term nihilism to describe that transformation of values which fascism accomplished. The ethical norms of society were no longer related to intrinsic standards or to eternal verities. Instead, duty to the fascist state and to its leader became the criterion of moral behavior. Where ethics had once been linked to Christian ideas, however vaguely defined, now they were linked to the fascist ideology of struggle and history.[58]

Mosse identified nihilism with activism (and therefore with struggle for power for its own sake): for him, ideology now comes to embody, in the last sentence, both nihilism and history, that is, the tradition upon which ideology had been built and which constituted the basis for consensus. We therefore face two contradictory views of nihilism: on the one hand, it represents activism and struggle for struggle's sake, and thus opposition to ideology (which provides "positive" values, that is, a goal, a myth); on the other hand, it becomes part and parcel of Mosse's interpretation—it describes the transformation of values brought about by fascism. But to speak of "transformation of values" means to claim that fascism possessed, in fact, "positive" values upon which criteria of moral behavior could be set. According to this scheme, if nihilism eventually won over ideology, it eventually espoused it to transform values and provide a goal, thus revealing a dual nature whose components, as Mosse came to realize, were irreconcilable.

The years between 1961 and 1968 marked Mosse's definitive abandonment of the concept of nihilism. At the Stanford seminar (1963), he expressed his refusal to interpret fascism as "merely a quest for power," and stressed its "ideological sincerity," though within the limits of "ideological pragmatism."[59] One year later, in *The Crisis of German Ideology*, he stated that National Socialism was "far from being purely nihilistic," in that it had a "positive ideology."[60] There is in this book no hint at the final triumph of nihilism over ideology that characterized *The Culture of Western Europe*, published only three years earlier: the eventual supremacy of the nihilistic streak had been considerably blunted. In 1966, both in the article "The Genesis of Fascism" and in the book *Nazi Culture* (1966), the word "nihilism" was replaced by a stress on the religious character of fascism and its liturgy, even though hints at "propaganda" and "manipulation" still occasionally emerged. Along with nihilism, these two other concepts will gradually abandon the stage.

The key question behind Mosse's discarding of nihilism had been posed in his first attempts to delve into National Socialism, and was clearly expressed at Stanford, where he introduced the topic of fascism by stressing the problem of consensus: why did so many people make National Socialism their intellectual commitment? Fascist ideology had a concrete appeal, Mosse argued, an appeal that could not be dismissed as a "hodgepodge."[61] At the time, he was fully immersed in the writing of the book on *völkisch* culture, and as he acknowledged years later in an interview, it was then that he had seriously begun in his work his investigation into the problem of propaganda.[62] In 1966, as we have said, the enthusiastic reception of Nazi ideals still cohabited with the concepts of manipulation and propaganda, and yet Mosse expressed his first doubts about the usefulness of the latter, arguing that "a much more sophisticated theory was involved."[63] By 1968 he could write that a "revolution of nihilism could not be expected to capture the true enthusiasms and dreams of men";[64] the next year, the article "History, Anthropology, and Mass Movements" would definitively embrace a different perspective that led to *The Nationalization of the Masses* (1975), the groundbreaking work on Nazi liturgy inspired by the conversations (which began in the late 1960s) with Albert Speer, the brain behind

Nazi festivals. It was Speer, as Mosse made clear, who once and for all convinced him of the inadequacy of the term "propaganda."[65] This was an idea Mosse had been cultivating for some time: in 1964 he had referred for the first time to liturgy, claiming that the *völkisch* worldview "was itself objectified in the form of a new religion with its own mysticism and its own liturgical rites"; in 1966 he wrote that mass meetings, with their appeal to the irrationality in human nature, were "liturgical rites."[66] Liturgy was taking up a central role in Mosse's view of fascism, thus orienting his interpretation toward the belief that "National Socialism was a religion; the depth of the ideology, the liturgy, the element of hope, all helped to give the movement the character of a new faith."[67]

Since his earliest writings on fascism, Mosse had displayed his penchant for the religious nature of modern political phenomena. His experience as an early modern historian provided him with the sensibility to read between the lines of propaganda and manipulation, perceiving a more genuine substratum of belief nurtured by the liturgy of mass movements. As early as in 1961 he had compared mass meetings to "religious rites" and written of the participants' "fervor" and devotion, defining them as "believers."[68] At Stanford he referred to Hitler's "religious fanaticism" and "intolerance," arguing that fascism was "essentially a religious movement" in its attempt to revolutionize the human soul.[69] In the conclusion to *The Crisis of German Ideology*, he states that National Socialism and the whole *völkisch* movement were "analogous to a religion."[70] However, these ideas remained scattered throughout Mosse's works until his focus shifted directly to liturgy, tackling the relation of nihilism to irrationality. As the two became separated in his mind, he came to see liturgy as the means through which "the irrational is made concrete through rational acts within the terms of its own ideological framework": *völkisch* ideology, however irrational it may have been, was formalized and tamed through "concrete, outward forms," since "even the most irrational religion, to become effective, must express itself through outward forms . . . to move masses of men it must objectify itself."[71] Nihilism could not therefore be associated to irrationality anymore, as irrationality now linked to an ideological basis that attributed to it a set of values that nihilism could not provide. Mosse's 1961 belief that nihilism described "that transformation of values" accomplished by fascism, where "the ethical norms of society were no longer related to intrinsic standards or eternal verities" (Christian ideals) but rather to "the fascist ideology of struggle and history," could no longer be held. Now the "cult element," as he wrote in 1966, focused its attention on the "eternal verities" of ideology upon which state ethics is built: they are "eternal," and this is stressed by the "liturgical element" with its "endless repetition of slogans, choruses, and symbols. These are the techniques which went into the taming of the revolution and which made fascism . . . a new religion with rites long familiar in traditional religious observance." If in Mosse's previous interpretation nihilism transformed values detaching the ethics of society from "eternal verities" linked to Christian ideas, now liturgy furthers the "eternal verities" of fascist ideology. Fascism is now a "new religion" whose liturgy found inspiration from traditional Christianity.[72]

The adoption of the concept of liturgy, and the view of ideology as religious truth, marked the end of nihilism intended as transformation of values. The year 1966 can be considered as a watershed if a line has to be drawn: in *Nazi Culture*, Mosse restated the idea, saying that "National Socialism was a religion."[73] Fascism is therefore no longer viewed as "essentially" religious or "analogous" to a religion: fascism *is* a religion. Through the analysis of popular culture, a new link was now established between the early modern and the modern part of Mosse's work as the historian of sixteenth- and seventeenth-century theology delved into the religious essence of modern mass movements. "Any phenomenon of our civilization," he said, "is in a sense a Christian phenomenon because Christianity is what people know. Any political theology grows quite naturally out of Christian theology."[74] Again, he also stressed his conviction that "the fascist revolutions built upon a deep bedrock of popular piety and, especially in Germany, a millenarianism which was apt to come to the fore in times of crisis. The myths and symbols of nationalism were superimposed upon those of Christianity—not only in the rhythms of public rites and ceremonies . . .—but also in the appeal to apocalyptic and millenarian thought."[75] Such an approach makes Mosse one of the fathers of late-twentieth-century political religions theory. In the late 1990s he lamented the fact that "in the past many failed to discuss fascism as a civic religion, and that, for example, it was only in the 1990s that Emilio Gentile gave us the first and masterful analysis of Italian fascism's sacralization of politics": Gentile's *Il culto del littorio* was indeed very much admired by Mosse, who saw in it the first "comprehensive analysis of fascism as a civic religion."[76]

If by 1966 Mosse was fully convinced of the religious essence of fascism, he found that the study of popular literature could no longer provide all the keys to the proper understanding of liturgy. The stress on written sources that had characterized *The Crisis of German Ideology* came to be replaced by a stress on the visual dimension of mass movements, necessary to grasp the substance of mass rituals, their dynamics, and their setting. The historian in search of a more satisfactory answer to the enigma of consensus needed a new set of historiographical tools. After all, Mosse's early modern interests ranged widely, from the written works of seventeenth-century Divines to the premise that art and ritual were pivotal to the comprehension of the Baroque age. Mosse was now ready to move on from Christian churches to the new pagan temples and statues erected in honor of the Nation, from Christian liturgy to the rituals performed in worship of new, secular entities. It was at this point that he received a timely request.

Beyond the History of Intellectuals

In February 1969 Professor R. K. Webb, managing editor of the *American Historical Review*, sent a letter to Mosse asking him to write a joint review of three recent books on the history of anthropology: "What I have in mind is a long, reflective review essay, approaching the subject not from an anthropological standpoint . . . but judged as contribution to the history of ideas."[77] Mosse took the opportunity to systematize the numerous reflections that had accompanied his transition from ideology to liturgy. The outcome was one of the historian's sporadic attempts to elaborate on theoretical issues, and it is significant that he decided to do so on this particular occasion: the article, as Roger Griffin put it, "crystallized Mosse's maturation from intellectual history and history of ideas to an anthropologically informed historiography."[78] The Madison historian turned the review article into a programmatic manifesto in which he fully embraced the adoption of anthropological, psychological, and aesthetic interpretive categories in order to analyze modern political liturgies.

The abstract Mosse sent to the *American Historical Review* summarizes the main themes he dealt with in this essay:

> The historian confronting problems raised by mass culture and mass politics needs new approaches in order to capture the structure of the popular mind. The anthropologists' use of myth and symbol can provide useful ways to penetrate the modern as well as the primitive mind. However, a purely techno-environmental approach ignores the importance of human consciousness and psychological factors in the formation of human attitudes. Claude Lévi-Strauss comes closest to posing the problem which confronts historians of mass phenomena through stressing the interplay between psychological attitudes and social functions. Though anthropologists assume the possibility of establishing orderly laws of behavior, historians in attempting to clarify irrational acts also impose a rationality upon the irrational.[79]

Mosse's need to find new interpretive tools to get to the core of mass society emerges here in connection with popular culture. The essence of the anthropological and visual turn is embodied by the formula of myths and symbols, which adds a visual dimension to the ideological and mythical structure. The historian set himself to the task of adopting the insights provided by anthropology and psychology: the goal was to find new ways of understanding the workings of the "popular mind" on the assumption that irrationality underlies both primitive and modern cultures. In the article, Mosse expressed once again the need to proceed beyond intellectual history as Arthur Lovejoy had conceived it (as the study of elitist groups) in favor of a "more thorough investigation of popular practices and sentiments. In an age of mass politics and mass culture," he continued, "the intellectual historian needs new approaches that take into account those popular notions that have played such a cardinal role in the evolution of man and society." As he made clear, he was not referring to the study of a "boring catalogue of curious notions," leisure time, or "pursuit of pleasure, excitement, and beauty": the subject "must attempt to fathom the minds of the majority of men at a given historical time in order to understand the nature and force of popular beliefs and predilections as expressed in politics and culture."[80]

Such considerations reaffirmed his first methodological turn and served as an introduction to the most innovative reflections that followed. The point of departure of Mosse's argument was the problem of irrationality in history. He lamented the fact that both Lovejoy and the sociology of knowledge had worked under the assumption that humans are rational beings; and yet he argued that in "the analysis of popular culture or mass politics the irrational seems to predominate," and therefore the historian needs new tools to capture the structure of what he called "the popular mind." These tools, he suggested, were offered by two disciplines that historians had mostly neglected: psychology and anthropology. Psychology had unmasked the importance of "men's unconscious drives and aspirations," while anthropology had focused not only on folkways and community customs but also on mythical and symbolic apparatuses. Hence, Mosse argued that mass politics and popular culture are fundamentally irrational, and therefore rational tools do not suffice to grasp the very essence of modern politics.[81]

This approach implied a view of human nature as universal in time and space, based on the assumption that the "primitive mind" and the modern are fundamentally the same, at least as far as certain mechanisms are concerned. Jacob Burckhardt, the father of modern cultural history, had stressed the need to focus on the constants in history: only these are really understandable at any time and in any place. According to the great Swiss historian, man with his hopes, yearnings, and sufferings must be the center of historical analysis: man as he has always been, and always will be. Hence, the "pathological" nature of Burckhardt's considerations.[82] Similarly, Mosse argued that

historians must also hesitate before they draw such close connections between primitive and modern man, but this connection does not have to consist in the similarity of the actual contents of myths and symbols. It may, rather, consist in the similarity of human wishes and aspirations, reactions and frustrations. The myths and symbols that modern mass movements use in order to manipulate their followers badly need historical investigation *as* myths and symbols. Throughout the centuries these myths and symbols have a sameness that cannot be ignored. Studies of popular literature have brought this to light. Totalitarian movements (and indeed most modern mass movements) "imposed" themselves upon their people by using familiar and basic myths and symbols. These found expression within the literature of the movement and in its liturgy as well, in festivals, mass meetings, and symbolic representations such as national monuments. Here indeed the great manifestations of society originate at the level of the unconscious, as Lévi-Strauss believes. Conscious and unconscious wishes, desires and frustrations are manipulated in order to produce adherence to the political movement. Historians have only arrived at the threshold of such investigations. They are important without denying the essential role played by the social and political situation. Without the right conditions, the appeal of the proper myths and symbols cannot be activated in a meaningful manner. But historical analyses of the myths and symbols used by such movements are essential, and neither the history of ideas nor the sociology of knowledge will suffice any longer for the intellectual historian. Anthropology can be helpful; at least one must be familiar with its methods.[83]

The emphasis Mosse was putting on irrationality was not aimed at the writing of an "idealistic" kind of history. It was, rather, intended to provide a twofold corrective: on the one hand, against merely political, social, and economic history, which he regarded as being too focused on the search for rational explanations to human behavior; on the other hand, as a means to "advance beyond the history of intellectuals" as it had been performed by Lovejoy but also by himself.[84] He was focusing on the interplay between myth and reality, between the unconscious and the conscious motivations that informed historical development.

"History, Anthropology, and Mass Movements" is a milestone in the development of Mosse's conception of history, as the most observant critics have pointed out. Emilio Gentile considers it the final point of the transition from ideology to liturgy and the opening of a new perspective centered on the rites and symbols of mass politics. Roger Griffin sees in it a "pretext for articulating his debt to such theorists as Ernst Cassirer and Claude Lévi-Strauss in coming to realize the value of anthropology to historians. . . . This review crystallized Mosse's maturation from intellectual history and history of ideas to an anthropologically informed historiography (or rather a historiography informed by a certain *idea* of anthropology and certainly not by a rigorous anthropological school of thought or theory)."[85] Indeed, Mosse's utilization of anthropological insights was, as Gentile put it, "very personal."[86] He certainly appreciated Lévi-Strauss's efforts directed at a rapprochement between anthropology and history, as well as his stress on "the interplay between psychological attitudes and social functions," his belief that the great manifestations of society originate at the level of the unconscious,[87] and his idea of the "cosmic rhythm," which, Mosse wrote, "possesses mankind from the earliest times onward" and which "we would define in a more pedestrian manner as the desire for permanence and fixed reference points in a changing world."[88] And yet, as Griffin points out, he never embraced any definite theory.

If the main stages of this methodological turn have been analyzed, it is still necessary to delve into its roots. Mosse elaborated a personal idea of myth that was based on various influences, as were his reflections on the role played by aesthetics. This process occurred through the turbulent 1960s, when the student movement reached its climax. Mosse's understanding of mass movements cannot be eradicated from the intellectual, social, and historical context that surrounded him in those years. The numerous influences that inspired the anthropological and visual turn mingled with a preexisting dialectical view of history that was only too fertile to absorb and integrate the new stimuli Mosse benefited from in the midst of his analysis of National Socialism.

3

The Roots of the Anthropological and Visual Turn

I think that a frankly speculative treatment has a place in historical method that has not always been sufficiently recognized. And this, like the whole notion of defining symbols, has an irremediable vagueness about it. Indeed, these are precisely the points where the whole element of art and literature enters into historical explanation—an element, as I have suggested, that history more particularly shares with cultural anthropology among the social sciences. At one point or another history necessarily passes over from science into art: the main thing is to be sure that this point of passage has been well chosen.

—H. STUART HUGHES

The similarities are startling: the national monument is, in a way, the totem pole of modern nationalism.

—GEORGE L. MOSSE

Mosse wrote in one of his earliest works that "rapid changes in history usually come about when the gulf between what is and what should be, between outward reality and the human condition, becomes painfully apparent": this belief lay beneath his later assertion that history consists of a dialectical interplay between myth and reality, where human perceptions of reality are "more than just the actual realities," and act as motivating factors.[1] Such a view of human events implied a kind of history that went far beyond what was generally written at the time when Mosse began his analysis of modern mass movements, and marked his own passage from intellectual history to a new approach within the realm of cultural history that embraced an interdisciplinary mingling of historiography, anthropology, and psychology.

His belief that perception informed by myth is a powerful motivating factor required the adoption of the anthropologist's as well as of the psychologist's tool kit in order to delve into the delicate issue of historical causation. Indeed, Mosse focused on the problem of the choices people make, and on the reasons they make them. These choices, he argued, are not necessarily rational: the world as it "should be"—that is, myth (in Mosse's view)—is more often than not linked with utopian longings, irrational hopes and aspirations, or unconscious needs. Once these forces are at play, human actions cannot be explained away through rational categories: the only way to grasp their meaning, he believed, is to understand them through empathy, to take the actor's point of view. In order to do this, anthropological and psychological categories are needed.

It can be said that, from the beginning, Mosse's anthropological turn, which came about in the late 1960s, was ingrained in his more general outlook. A similar concern can be found in his long-term fascination with aesthetics, which dates back to his emotive absorption in Baroque architecture as a young student in Salem, that was to blossom in the 1950s on an intellectual level. Such a foundation made fertile soil for the reception of the biographical and intellectual stimuli he received over the course of the 1960s, at a crucial stage of his exploration into the nature of National Socialism. Mosse's double outsiderdom, the problems raised by his research, and the cultural environment he found himself in intertwined, thus paving the way for a theoretical revision of his historical approach.[2] The article "History, Anthropology, and Mass Movements" and all of Mosse's subsequent works can be seen as an attempt on the part of the historian to integrate his personal experiences with his research interests against the background of the study of mid-twentieth-century cultural history, whose direction Mosse considerably helped determine.

Mosse's analysis of National Socialism stemmed from an eclectic mingling of the most diverse intellectual currents of his century. His work, as it has been pointed out, tackled a set of problems that had been haunting the historical profession since the turn of the twentieth century, notably the issue of relativism and the relation between rationality and irrationalism. In order to shed light on these problems, he had to draw from other disciplines, which he enthusiastically did. He regarded this not only as a way of delving into historical issues, but also as a means to express his deeper feelings in facing the challenge posed by racism and respectability to his double outsiderdom.

In 1895, in a surprisingly pioneering essay titled "The Relation of Anthropology to the Study of History," the American historian George E. Fellows lamented the fact that history as it was taught in his time was mainly textbooks and narratives, and admonished that "he who would teach history best cannot confine himself entirely to what is generally understood to be history. If he would get out of it its fullest meaning and lift it to its highest usefulness with students, he must run over into the borderland; he must study the origins of peoples and of customs, that is, he must invade the domain of anthropology." Fellows held that "man's mode of thought, habits of life and association, are essential to be known as being the sources of power which has produced and is producing history": history elucidated by anthropology assumed a new aspect, where causes and effects could be more easily explained.[3] Regarding history as "the whole of human life" and advocating the necessity to "understand" human acts, Fellows embraced a vision of history that set humanity at its center, and stressed the need to understand the distinctive character of each people through the anthropology-flavored analysis of modes of thought and habits of life, thus taking up a fully historicist stance.

This empathetic approach led Fellows to claim that, had civilized nations embraced the study of anthropology, their policies toward "savage" peoples would have been wise and tempered, and would not have ended up in a slaughter: such an enlightened policy, in his view, "could only be called into existence by an *understanding* of the distinctive character of the conquered savages, their capabilities and adaptabilities."[4] Such considerations were well espoused in Franz Boas's immensely influential anthropological historicism and his attempts to fathom the "mind of primitive man." In fact, anthropology and historicism shared many fundamental premises: understanding through empathy, the importance attributed to the point of view of the "other," the attempt to comprehend values and logic different from one's own, and last but not least, the implicit cultural relativism inevitably entailed by such an attitude. Anthropology came to play a role that was both critical and demystifying toward Western values and beliefs: it is therefore hardly surprising that in the mid-twentieth century, as it has been claimed, "nine out of ten anthropologists were, it seems, politically radical in one sense or the other."[5]

Mosse, in his own way, grew more and more radical in his critique of Western values, which he identified as bourgeois. He was also radical in attacking "traditional" historiography: cultural history, in Thomas Nipperdey's formula, was an *Oppositionswissenschaft* (opposition science).[6] Little wonder then that Mosse found in anthropological attitudes an ideal foundation on which to build his methodology, especially since he came from a historicist background and made full use of a tool for grasping "the way people think."[7] Moreover, as a double a double outsider, his life experiences were very close to those of many great anthropologists like Franz Boas, Bronisław Malinowski, or Claude Lévi-Strauss, all of them exiles, often for racial reasons. Many of these scholars came to the conclusion that all cultures must be analyzed without prejudice and believed that one must take the "point of view of people on the ground," developing a skepticism of decisions taken "from above."[8] Mosse, as an exiled Jew and as a homosexual, could easily feel in tune with the radicalism that derived from such experiences, and gradually came to expand his interests to include not only the fate of the persecuted, but also made full use of empathy to investigate the mind-set of the persecutors, whose ideas and actions seemed to escape the rationalist logic of most historians of National Socialism. The outcome of his disenchanted view of history was a vein of pessimism that he shared with other pioneers of cultural history like Johann Huizinga, whose preoccupied reflections on the fate of Western civilization mirrored a more widespread concern among European intellectuals.[9]

As a child of his century, Mosse fully participated in its intellectual and political life, and it is in this light that his innovative approach to history ought to be understood, especially in opposition to that "traditional" political history that had dominated the second half of the nineteenth century and—though under siege and in an obviously more elaborated form—was still influential in the twentieth. The purpose of this chapter is to elucidate the influences at play on the historian, be they direct (through an author he had read) or indirect (reflecting a widespread trend, or an attitude—and here to speak of "parallels" might be more appropriate). The mingling of history, anthropology, and psychology was by no means Mosse's original contribution to the discipline. The uniqueness of his approach lay rather in the eclectic way he combined them, without ever yielding to the temptation of writing a fully anthropological or fully psychological history. He benefited from all the insights these disciplines could offer without losing a strictly historical perspective on the problems he was dealing with. The outcome was a revolutionary approach to the history of nationalism, fascism, racism, and gender. However, while the momentous impact of such an approach has been dealt with extensively, few critics have focused on the roots of this methodological turn.[10] An analysis of these roots will shed some light on this thus far neglected aspect of Mosse's work, and on some equally neglected connections between German historicism and today's cultural history.

The Anthropological Turn: Myth

When Mosse came to view various manifestations of fascism as political religions, he also expanded his idea of myth, which now moved from the fringes
to the center of his work. Within his dialectical view of history, myth came to
play a pivotal role, one essential to the understanding of all those themes that
stem from this approach. The delicate balance between myth and reality constitutes, for Mosse, the source from which his history of perceptions springs,
along with the crucial insights regarding the relationship between history and
anthropology, history and psychology, and history and aesthetics. It is also the
necessary point of departure in analyzing fundamental issues in his work, such
as the relationship between rationalism and irrationality; the nature of mass
politics; the links between rationalizations, motivations, and perceptions; and
the whole issue of relativism, which lies at the core of historicism, anthropology, and cultural history.

It needs to be pointed out that Mosse's concept of myth always remained
elusive, even to himself. Writing to him in 1990, his friend and colleague
Emilio Gentile expressed his bewilderment about Mosse's idea of myth. The
Italian historian identified two divergent concepts of myth in his colleague's
work: on the one hand, there was myth as an "irruption of the sacred" originated by a sincere faith; on the other, myth appeared as an "artificial construction manipulated by a minority in order to achieve certain goals."[11] In his reply,
Mosse conveyed the difficulties with sincerity:

> I have never been able to get a satisfactory definition of myth, and as far back
> as 1960 Leonardo Olschki . . . told me that my use of myth was very problem-
> atical. I suppose it is, as you say, the idea of the artificiality which is at the root
> of the trouble. I look at myths too much from the nineteenth and twentieth
> century point of view. Myth is both artificial and a sincerely held belief. I don't
> think that they exclude each other, as I would say that all religions are con-
> structions. I think the word construction is better than the word artificiality,
> but it is not ideal either because a myth may be quite spontaneous. All that is
> certain is that the manipulators are themselves manipulated as you rightly
> say, that is to say, they come to believe quite sincerely in the myth which they
> have advocated.[12]

From this perspective, the concept of "ideological pragmatism" Mosse had used
in the early 1960s (though severely downplayed) appears to have lasted much

longer than his short-lived adoption of nihilism. Constructed or manipulated, myth retained its fundamental power in Mosse's view in that what eventually counted was perception: it is no accident that Mosse defined his own history as a "history of perceptions," since this concept allowed him to overcome the difficulties raised by the apparently insoluble problem of spontaneity and manipulation. Once myth comes to be believed, no matter if spontaneously or through manipulation, it affects one's perception, thus determining choices and actions.

Despite having written about myth for decades, Mosse, in his typical fashion, never made an attempt to give a proper definition.[13] And yet on several occasions he provided hints and suggestions on what he held myth to be, or on the influences that affected his views. It can be said that there emerge two ideas of myth in his work, one being of a more general nature, the other definitely more specific. In the draft for a lecture, he wrote that

> there is one thing more I want to answer: the confusion about the term "myth." Can be used: 1. In Sorel's sense as the activation of the subconscious for some action. This is the modern propaganda (fascist) use of it. 2. or as denoting an absence of reality: this is the us vs society of Youth Movement and of many who revolted against this society from the fin de siècle on.[14]

In this passage, Mosse outlines the two views that he merged. Myth as "absence of reality" is obviously the more generic one, the one that remained unchanged in his mind over the years. Here myth simply represents the dialectical counterpart of "objective reality": as he claimed in his 1976 interview with Michael Ledeen, "we realize after all, through the important schools of social history, that the dialectic is, in fact, between myth and social forces. I would say between myth and what Marx called objective reality, that is social, political, and economic forces."[15] In the same interview, he claimed that his idea of myth had been inspired by Huizinga, about which there is little doubt, especially as far as the idea of "dream" as a way of escaping reality is concerned.[16] Mosse also referred to myth as "metaphysics," and was deeply convinced that "there is a dialectic between myth and reality," and that "all of history must be viewed in a dynamic and dialectical fashion."[17] Yet this view of history as a grand dialectic between myth and reality is only one side of the coin: Mosse had drawn from many other influences, and his view of myth was far more complex.

In the early 1960s Mosse heavily relied on the fascist idea of myth to explain fascism itself. This view he had taken mainly from the thought of Georges Sorel and Carl Gustav Jung. The very expression of myth as "the activation of the subconscious for some action" seems to synthesize these influences. The book *The Culture of Western Europe* as it was first published in 1961 clearly elucidates Mosse's ideas about myth. Mussolini, according to Mosse, believed that "myth is a faith, it is a passion," and that it is necessary in order to transform reality, since activism alone is not enough. The task was to translate the fascist myth into reality. Myth appealed to the irrational in humanity, and it had to be created and manipulated in order to win the masses: "The intuition involved in the construction of an organic state was thought of as the ability to use and create 'myths' fusing government with the irrational mainsprings of human actions." According to Sorel, Mosse said, ideology has to be based upon one's irrational feelings, and that is what myth does: "Human beings acted upon illogical premises; therefore the creation of a 'myth' will stimulate their will for action."[18] A few years later, Mosse asserted that the conservatism of crowds preached by Georges Sorel and Gustave Le Bon, and taken up by fascism, implied that "the appeal must be made to this irrational conservatism and it must be combined with the 'magic' influence of mass suggestion through a leader. In this way mass man can be harnessed to a political mass movement, his tendency toward chaos can be curbed, and he can be redirected into positive action."[19]

The influence of Sorel and Jung on Mosse is clearly detectable. Sorel's view of history is profoundly dialectical, and the dialectic is between myth and "accomplished fact" (Mosse's "objective reality"): myths are the constructions derived from the pictures, or the images of coming action men make for themselves, which inform their acts; myths are therefore proper historical forces, "knowledge of which is so important for historians."[20] The French philosopher believed with Henri Bergson that myth and religion occupy the "profounder regions of our mental life."[21] Mosse, who came to regard ideology as a religious phenomenon, also believed that myths are adopted in order to make choices: these choices depend on social and economic circumstances, he stated at the Stanford seminar, but also on "ideological conditioning," which he saw as linked with psychological factors.[22]

In "History, Anthropology, and Mass Movements" Mosse wrote of the necessity of assimilating "twentieth-century discoveries concerning the importance of men's unconscious drives and aspirations," and stated that a century of psychological research cannot be ignored by historians.[23] The kind of psychology he turned to was not that of Freud, whom he blamed for having fused his extraordinary discoveries with the dominant morality of his time, thus ending up repressing the role played by irrationality. Mosse relied, rather, on Jung's work, despite his criticism of the Swiss psychiatrist's ideological affinity to National

Socialism and racialism, and of his having upset the balance between rationalism and irrationality in favor of the latter.[24] When discussing the personality of Adolf Hitler at the Stanford seminar, Professor Milorad Drachkovich, a historian of Marxism, told Mosse that, since he was entering fields that go beyond rational explanation, he should have relied on psychoanalysis; Mosse replied: "Yes, I think so. Obviously there is this whole problem of charisma. . . . I think perhaps Carl Gustav Jung came closest to it, but I hate to admit this in public, because of his involvement with National Socialism."[25] Mosse obviously distanced himself from Jung and plainly asserted that he was not a Jungian, but he believed that there is "a great deal of truth to Jung," and added:

> I think that more than anybody else Jung had a sense of what National Socialism was all about. I think for an intellectual historian Jung is fruitful to operate with, but within very definite limits. But the main idea is that you live in a world of images that you've made yourself, that have some tie with reality, but which can also escape it. And especially I think in a tight situation these images become aggravated into a kind of wish fulfillment, into a flight from reality, a flight into metaphysics.[26]

Like Sorel, Jung believed in myth as an image and opposed thinking in words to thinking in images, thus conferring on myth a deeply aesthetic nature, in line with Mosse's belief that the self-representation of the nation "has been more often visual and oral than solely through the written word."[27] Myth, in Jung's conception, is part of everyone's life, and he who thinks he can live without it is an exception; he is an "uprooted" person who "does not live inside a house like other men, does not eat and drink like other men, but lives a life of his own."[28] The idea of rootedness, the link the past, with tradition: all these are crucial elements in Mosse's work, in which one of the essential functions of myths and liturgies is to "provide a fully-furnished home" to live inside safely.[29] As Mosse was moving from the "history of the intellectuals" to the "history of the masses," Jung's belief in the masses' addiction to mythology, in the existence of the collective unconscious, and in the notion of collective representations must have been greatly influential.

Anthropology and Mass Movements

The American anthropologist Clark Wissler asserted that the concept of culture implies a sense of superiority when applied to an individual, while if applied to a group it simply expresses the "mode of life" of a people, devoid of any value judgment, as the culture of this group is merely "the aggregate thoughts and deeds of the tribe."[30] Anthropology, which is concerned with "men in groups," can only turn to the diversity of cultures, thus departing from ethnocentrism in the direction of relativity, as Alfred Louis Kroeber proposed.[31] The historian of religions Mircea Eliade believed that myth ought to be integrated "into the general history of thought, by regarding it as the most important form of collective thinking."[32] When Mosse turned his attention to the history of the masses he found anthropological and psychological categories necessary to interpret group consciousness and values. This brought about a widening of his concept of culture to include myths and symbols, with a focus on group mentalities and feelings rather than on individual ideas and systems of thought, thus moving from intellectual history to cultural history. The anthropological approach could not be confined either to the understanding of primitive cultures, nor to that of medieval or early modern history, as had hitherto been the case, with few exceptions. Adolf Bastian's idea of the "psychic unity of mankind" laid the foundations for many important attitudes in both anthropology and psychology, contributing to the cause of anthropocentrism as against ethnocentrism.

Mosse, who was already quite receptive toward the ideas of Le Bon, Sorel, and Jung, benefited also from another unexpected source: the student movement of the 1960s. Anson Rabinbach, writing of his first encounter with Mosse, recalled him

> arguing intensely with a group of students who were planning to sit in to block the Dow Chemical Company campus recruiter in the Fall (Dow was chosen because the company was manufacturing napalm). As it happens, they were discussing Lenin's theory of the vanguard, which according to the students, plainly justified a militant action opposed by the majority. "Lenin," George pronounced brusquely, "is *passé*. You should read Georges Sorel because you are all Sorelians."[33]

This is an important recollection in that it unmistakably reveals how Mosse was weaving into one single fabric his research interests and his actual life experiences. He himself admitted in an interview that it was precisely in the 1960s, when he was specializing in the history of National Socialism, that he "learned many things about crowds, about mass movements." He often engaged in conversations with his students, in the attempt to understand why they occupied public facilities, why they used sit-ins. The students, Mosse recalled, responded that they were looking for experiences of collective action in order to take part in a common experience: protest marches gave them an immense feeling of participation.[34] Emilio Gentile has rightly stressed the chronological liaison between the student revolt, the publication of the article "History, Anthropology, and Mass Movements," and Mosse's research on the new politics: all this occurred against the background of an antagonist political style that was based on "a long cultural and political American tradition of civic myths, rites and symbols."[35]

If Mosse learned from this experience, and often sympathized with the students, he was also very critical of the radicalization of the movement, as he seemed to recognize in it a "transition from thinking to mindless activity."[36] The turn to violence, culminated in the accidental killing of a university researcher in the bombing of Sterling Hall at the University of Wisconsin in the summer of 1970, definitively marked the end of his sympathy toward the movement. Besides, Mosse claimed years later, he never took the whole thing seriously in that he, as a historian of mass movements, knew that it was "only a game, in a way," and that it would eventually "blow over."[37] This was also due, he said, to the fact that deficiency in organization, excessive use of speeches instead of rituals and symbols, and a lack of "visual orientation" on the part of movement "intellectuals" made the creation of a successful mass movement impossible.[38] Such is the spirit in which he provocatively said to his students: "Oh boy, if I joined you, I could begin a movement . . . but what I would do would probably be more like a fascist movement."[39] Again in 1969 he asserted in a lecture that his attitudes toward the events of the year had been dominated by the consideration that tactics, leadership, and discipline were crucial to a successful mass movement. Emotions had to be kept at bay in favor of organization, political sense, reason, and sense of degree: in short, of objective reality.[40]

Mosse also blamed many left-wing Weimar intellectuals for the disregard for objective reality. He had been drawn to them in the 1960s by his students, who according to him "loved everything that came from Germany."[41] If the students felt attracted to ideals of democracy, individuality, and socialism espoused by Weimar intellectuals, and based their critique of society on these (as well as on the thought of the Frankfurt School), Mosse detected more implications in these ideals, which at the same time made him increasingly aware of his own German Jewish background. In his opinion, Stefan Zweig, Hermann Cohen, Martin Buber, Ernst Bloch, Aby Warburg, or Ernst Cassirer—all of them German Jews—failed in their opposition to National Socialism because they believed in absolutes, had no contact with objective reality, and fed on an unbridled idealism. Similarly, many intellectuals of the New Left got mired in a utopianism that had no contact with reality; this inability to propose concrete solutions could easily end up in indiscriminate violent revolt. Weimar intellectuals recognized the irrational forces in human history and fought against them; and yet they were linked to a rationalist and humanistic tradition of thought, which allowed them to brush irrationalism aside and therefore misunderstand National Socialism.[42]

Between Rationalism and Irrationality

If Mosse believed the Weimar Jewish intellectuals had been unable to understand and confront Hitler's rise to power, he greatly admired the ideas and the ideals they stood for, and he felt surely grateful to them for having provided him with the essential analytical tools for grasping the essence of National Socialism. Roger Griffin, emphasizing the role played by myth as a causal factor in Mosse's work and hinting at the Jewish background of such a conviction, wrote that "it is tempting to speculate that such an approach is second nature to those brought up to have a deep empathy and intimacy with the Jewish religious and mystic tradition yet who are excluded from full participation in it by a secular intellect steeped in Enlightenment rationalism."[43] Renato Moro has argued that Ernst Kantorowicz may have influenced Mosse with his interest in political mysticism, political theology, and the sacrality of power, and with his conviction of the existence of a continuity, based on Christian foundations, that linked the Middle Ages to the twentieth century: Kantorowicz, like Mosse, had turned his attention to the irrational character of modern "political religions."[44]

The American literary historian Paul Fussell saw in the First World War the moment when myth irrupted into the modern world, bringing about a rebirth of cult, mysticism, sacrifice, and sacrality; Carl Gustav Jung wrote that "where the masses are in movement, the archetypes begin"; Carlton Hayes described, as early as in the 1920s, the triumphant nationalisms as new religions.[45] Myth had, in the interwar years, forced its way to the attention of many intellectuals, even those initially reluctant to accept it as a historical factor, such as Benedetto Croce.[46] Ernst Cassirer, Walter Benjamin, Martin Buber, Ernst Bloch, Carl Gustav Jung, and many others realized the significance of myth in modern culture, as Sorel had done even before the Great War. Mosse was influenced by their ideas, which led him to a problem that he investigated for the rest of his career: the problem of the relationship between rationalism and irrationality in history. As a scholar of early modern Europe, his interest in Christianity and particularly Christian theology had paved the way and provided him with the necessary intellectual background for uncovering the Christian substratum of modern politics. *The Holy Pretence,* with its portrait of the delicate balance between faith and reason, appears in this light to be more than ever a crucial book in Mosse's intellectual biography. Renato Moro captured this aspect of Mosse's contribution when he defined him as a "historian of modern irrationalism."[47]

The problem of scholarship, Mosse said, is that

> it has to operate with the instruments of rationality into a so largely irrational world, it has to recapture the irrational rationally and thus it is in danger of getting it wrong. This was a problem for those Jewish scholars who in the Germany of the 1920s faced the ever longer shadow of National Socialism. Coming out of that tradition of emancipation which stressed rationality, they sought to exorcise the threat of the irrational. Thus they began to investigate myths and symbols, the visual which seemed to excite the irrational imagination. . . . If irrational symbols and myths could be understood then the rational mind could analyze them, and in this way exorcise the irrational.[48]

And yet he believed that such an attempt to "exorcise the irrational" had too often been held hostage by rationality, such as in Lévi-Strauss's turn to linguistics. Mosse saw too much of a "rational mental structure" in that for the French anthropologist human emotions can never become causes. A historian, Mosse continued, "may be disturbed by . . . presuppositions of human rationality that underlie . . . explanation of the meaning of myth and symbol, but since they must make sense out of the often irrational acts of men, they must form them into an explainable pattern and frequently assume a rationality even for the irrational."[49] Stanley Payne, in his major work on fascism, wrote that "any inquiry into fascism has to grapple with the fundamental problem which George L. Mosse once described as attempting to analyze the irrational through rational study. The goal is not to rationalize the irrational but to elucidate the historical problems and contradictions involved."[50] Mosse believed that any historical analysis needs a certain degree of rationalization, though one must be aware that life does not work in that way. As he once told his students in a lecture, "the historian's task is a terrible one: to make the irrational rational," to make the behavior of people and perceptions rational, but if he does so he necessarily falsifies, "because everything is really a totality"; and yet Mosse said that he could not transform the class into a church. But "unless we become a church ourselves, there is no way for a historian to start with the totality. We have to start quite differently than Blaise Pascal, we have to start and we order things logically for you . . . though we know very well that life doesn't quite work that way and that therefore we are in a certain way falsifying things"; what historians do is a "personal evaluation of individual perceptions in a historical framework, perceptions which do not work according to Voltaire, but more, I think, according to Pascal if the truth must be told, or more according to popular piety."[51] Though disagreeing with rationalistic views of human nature, Mosse realized that reason is the only tool that can be used to "order" history and explain it. After all, Mosse said, "I'm an Enlightenment man myself."[52]

Benedetto Croce had argued that Historicism had a deep rationalistic grounding, that it confronted experience as against the abstract thought of the Enlightenment, and could therefore accept and understand the importance of the irrational by discovering its rationality. To realize the importance of irrationality meant, according to Croce, to accept myth and utopia as historical factors.[53] Mosse, criticizing the approach of the intellectual historian Arthur Lovejoy, said:

> Arthur Lovejoy wrote . . . that ideas are derived from philosophic systems and he adds that logic is one of the most important operative factors in the history of thought. He warned of giving the non rational too much place in the new discipline. How strange and isolated even such intellectual Americans must have been in the 1930s! For most of the world was in the grip of irrational systems which had, to be sure, a logic of their own but not one opposed to irrationalism. This can surely not longer satisfy. Not only for the twentieth century but for the earlier centuries as well. How much irrationalism will face us here in the seventeenth and eighteenth centuries—perhaps the movement of mysticism, of social revolt for the sake of the millennium—these are in the long run as important as the supposedly rationalistic systems of the pre Enlightenment and the Enlightenment itself.[54]

As early as 1948 Mosse had shown an interest in irrational forces in history and traced it back into the period he was studying: in a speech on mysticism and the Renaissance given in 1948 he stressed (quoting Huizinga and Leonardo Olschki) the importance of mystical thought in the early modern age—despite the fact that the age is generally associated with the rise of secularism. Mosse drew a comparison with the modern world: "Within the cultural chaos of the modern world many have returned to the spiritual presupposition of the mystics of the thirteenth and fourteenth century."[55] Mosse saw European history as a gradual "erosion of rationality," and history "also confronts emotion with rational analysis through its criticism of ideology and 'myths'—which so often make up the essence of ideology."[56]

This character of history leads to the task of the historian:

> The chief problem facing any historian is to capture the irrational by an exercise of the rational mind. This becomes easier when the irrational is made concrete through rational acts within the terms of its own ideological frame-work. . . . The various expressions of radical nationalism which fill this book may seem irrational and even bizarre, but they are a logical consequence of the presuppositions and the functions of modern nationalism. An earlier generation of scholars working in the Weimar Republic, living in the shadow of National Socialism, believed that the irrational could be tamed into a frame-work of rational thought by an exercise of the rational mind. They examined the myths of the past in order to ensure a rational approach to the construction of present society. Men like Aby Warburg and Ernst Cassirer believed that a scholarly, historical, and philosophical investigation of myths and symbols would lead to the integration of what was nonrational in the rational critique of culture. We can no longer share the optimism of such men, based as it was upon the idea, as Cassirer formulated it, of humanity's progressive enlightenment until man realizes the rational basis of his existence.[57]

Commenting on this passage, Gentile has noted how Mosse "separated irra-tionality from nihilism, endowing it with a rationality of its own constituted by the logic inherent in the forms through which irrationality expressed itself and crystallized itself as a political movement."[58] The rationality of the irra-tional manifests itself in the systematization of an ideology, or in the organi-zation of a political movement through a fully developed liturgy. Mosse said that "Sorel's myth was the overt rationalization of the deepest feeling of the group."[59] Myth itself, the irrational side of the dialectic myth-reality, can be a rationalization. Nationalism as an ideology is also a rationalization that inte-grates and organizes the masses: it can be argued that the nationalization of the masses is, in a way, their rationalization.

History and Psychology:
Rationalizations, Motivations, Perceptions

Mosse's insights did not occur in a vacuum. Since the early decades of the twen-tieth century, many psychologists and social scientists had made attempts at interpreting historical events in the light of psychological discoveries. However, most professional historians seemed reticent and unwilling to take an inter-disciplinary approach. William L. Langer, in a well-known speech given at the annual dinner of the American Historical Association in December 1957, lamented that, unlike anthropologists and mythologists, historians had thus far been "reluctant to recognize and deal with unconscious motives and irra-tional forces." Langer continued, "If progress is to be made we must certainly have new ideas, new points of view, and new techniques. We must be ready, from time to time, to take flyers into the unknown, even though some of them may prove wide of the mark." The exploitation of the concepts and findings of modern depth psychology was the historians' "next assignment." According to Langer, historians would have to reckon with the concept of "collective men-talities" and to explore the individual and "his basic motivations, his attitudes, beliefs, hopes, fears, and aspirations."[60]

The idea that motivation, a concept derived from psychology, was central for historical explanation was supported by Goodwin Watson, who maintained that it had been too often biased by the "psychology of the Age of Reason," and that the irrational ought to be included in historical analysis. Public acts and statements, upon which the dominant political history was traditionally based, do not account for real motivations. In 1940 Watson wrote: "History that is not psychologically critical seems likely to lend itself to the perpetuation of fallacious respectability."[61] "Human motivation," argued Franz Alexander, is "the dynamic driving force behind the ever-shifting scenes of history"; his toriography then "should apply a correct knowledge of man's motivations." However, Alexander held, historians for centuries had seen only "surface moti-vations," that is, rationalizations, the way through which people deceive them-selves: since "people do not know the deepest and strongest motives of their behavior," they tend to select arbitrarily between motives in order to make things seem simpler and understandable, and thus, "rationalization makes it possible for a person to explain his actions in a self-complacent way, saves him from the necessity of admitting to himself his objectionable motives." This is the reason why historians at the time Alexander's essay appeared, in 1940, were "disillusioned by witnessing the power of the hidden, destructive forces."[62] Seen from an anthropological perspective, the problem of motivation took up collective connotations, as it referred to group behavior: the ethos of a group "supplies the secondary motivations and types of choice for biological actions and provides symbolic elaboration and rationalization for nonbiological actions and attitudes."[63]

H. Stuart Hughes claimed that the central question of historical interpre-tation in the German idealist tradition had been "the ascription of motives to the leading actors in the events of the past." Thanks to psychoanalytic theory, he continued, the investigation of these motives could move from an "intuitive" to a more scientific approach: "In this classic area of what the German idealists call inner 'understanding' (Verstehen) the application of Freudian and post-Freudian theory might well result in a wholesale revamping of conventional notions of historical motivation."[64] Mosse firmly believed that ideological conditioning and psychology went hand in hand with social and economic factors in determining human choices: "As historians," he argued, "we cannot be too interested in testing systems by abstract criteria. The problem is always: why did men take this kind of choice and not another? . . . Choices are our problem. Here human attitudes are what counts and these attitudes are formed by images men have of themselves."[65] History is made by people, and people have choices, Mosse told his students in another lecture: "the problem is why they make the choices they do?"[66] Here perceptions come into play in Mosse's scheme of things: perceptions provide a background against which choices can be made. They lead to practical action in a constant interplay between perception and reality. From this perspective, the intertwining of history, psychology, and anthropology acquires its full significance. As Wilcomb E. Washburn remarked, "greater research in the psychological aspects of perception will, I think, have to fill in the gaps for which neither the historical record nor the ethnological method can provide the answers."[67]

Anthropology and Historicism

William Langer attributed the excessive focus of historians on recorded fact and rational motivation to the prevalence of the methods and approaches of German historicism.[68] H. Stuart Hughes, on the contrary, focused on the widening of a historicist category (that of *Verstehen*) through the adoption of psychological tools, asserting that this opened new perspectives on human motivation.[69] Langer was, indeed, simply looking at the outer shell of historicism, while Hughes was fully aware of the potential insights of its approaches. The German historian Thomas Nipperdey, a solitary advocate of cultural history in a country largely hostile to such attitudes in the postwar period, saw the necessary precondition for a developed historical anthropology in the perfection of nineteenth-century historicism: he argued that the goal of knowledge in Hegel, Burckhardt, or Dilthey was always anthropological, in that its focus was on the transformation in humanity or in conscience. In Nipperdey's view, if historicism never did succeed in developing mature historical-anthropological researches, historians could now fulfill the premises posed by historicism through the study of attitudes—that is, through the adoption of anthropological and psychological perspectives (already inherent in historicism), and through their application not only to "simple" societies, but also to "complex" ones.[70]

The interpretive category of *Verstehen*, indeed, expressed a need for empathetic understanding. If human nature is regarded as immutable over time (as was the case from the anthropological point of view, which was habitually hostile to the idea of historical development, as was Jung's theory of the archetypes), then this approach could be valid for both primitive and modern societies. Whereas anthropology focused on primitive peoples, anthropologically oriented historians investigated the role played by culture in the Western world. The emphasis was initially on medieval or early modern history (from Burckhardt to Huizinga to the Annales School), and only toward the middle of the twentieth century did historians begin to realize that the numerous insights of psychologists and anthropologists could be applied to mass society, and then as a consequence to modern history.[71] Mosse was one of the pioneers in this field. The fact that his intellectual background had been forged by historicism, anthropology, and depth psychology should come as no surprise.

The mingling of historiography and anthropology that gave birth to the "new cultural history" of the second half of the twentieth century had deep roots in the historicist tradition. E. H. Gombrich, in a 1967 lecture titled "In Search of Cultural History," saw cultural history as an attempt to use Hegelianism without metaphysics, and praised the "Hegelian intuition that nothing in life is ever isolated, that any event and any creation of a period is connected by a thousand threads with the culture in which it is embedded": Hegel's idea of the "spirit of an age," of life as a totality, had informed many fathers of cultural history who approached their topic from different perspectives (he referred to Burckhardt, Lamprecht, Dilthey, and Huizinga). Dilthey's *Geistesgeschichte*, Gombrich argued, was "the school which has made it its programme to see art, literature, social structure and Weltanschauung under the same aspect."[72] Cultural anthropology, as Stuart Hughes put it, was an ideal partner of history in its attempt at fathoming the totality of a culture, the thoughts and emotions driving the individuals' choices within that society.[73]

As we noted above, the historicist and the anthropological approaches had many traits in common, "understanding through empathy" being the key factor in both. George W. Stocking Jr., looking at the issue from an anthropological perspective, wrote that the goal of the historian

is nothing more nor less than understanding—an understanding of context and of change in time, an understanding informed at every point by the traditional historicist belief that the individual historical phenomenon is in a certain sense ineffable. This sort of understanding is by no means specific to history as a discipline. On the contrary, it is an essential part of the dominant tradition in twentieth century American cultural anthropology—part of the required tool kit, as it were, of every field anthropologist. Though it is perhaps more difficult to apply it in looking at one's own disciplinary culture than in looking at the Sioux or the Tiwi, it is no less important.[74]

Anthropology and historiography, despite many mutual misunderstandings, eventually interacted. Claude Lévi-Strauss argued in retrospect that thanks to ethnologists, historians had become able to discover obscure and underground manifestations of social life, while historians helped ethnologists give a historical dimension to their work.[75] This exchange began in the interwar period, picked up steam in the postwar years, and blossomed after the 1960s. In order for this to occur, historians had to be shattered in their certainties, in their values, and in their optimism, and eventually many were to follow the steps of the historical pessimism that permeated the works of Burckhardt or Huizinga, moving on to a critique of Western society.

Roy Franklin Nichols, a noted American historian, effectively summarized this loss of certainty in a 1948 article. The starting point of his analysis was relativism and the slow adoption by historians of the philosophical implications of Einstein's and Heisenberg's revolutionary ideas after the catastrophe of the First World War:

> The historian found in some cases that he must modify his sense of certainty. He realized that his cherished objectivity and scientific accuracy were somewhat illusory and that he was bound to take into account the implications of relativism. It now appeared that the circumstances of the historian's existence established in him a frame of reference according to which he made his judgments; his findings were always influenced by this type of subjectivity. Such thinking in one sense was clarifying; it destroyed a specious optimism and sense of infallibility.[76]

Historians through the 1920s became more aware of the problems of studying human behavior, and came closer to the social sciences. The Second World War brought about new confusion and a renewed sense of uncertainty, thus making even more urgent the need for a new reorientation. Nichols emphasized society's need for "more knowledge of the basic behavior patterns which induce peril-producing phenomena," which would "make more possible an understanding of certain similarities between behavior patterns of peoples of various nationalities and thus take some of the emphasis away from rivalry and difference." In order to do this, he continued, the historian "must be able to relive, with understanding, human experience at varying epochal points in time . . . to reconstruct the conceptual framework of the period he is studying, to know the conditions dominating thought and action in that time, and then think in such terms rather than in those which his normal present-mindedness would dictate." Then new methods of historical inquiry were required, methods that would yield a picture of a community as a whole, which economic, social, or political history cannot do. The "understanding of the past comes from the use of the historian's best technique, that of understanding the past in terms of itself."[77]

It is at this stage that a thus far neglected part of the German historical tradition came to the aid of American scholars. At the turn of the twentieth century, the German historical school had entered American universities, and yet its impact had remained confined for the largest part to the adoption of scientific empiricism and the critical method—that is, of political history in Ranke's tradition.[78] Wilhelm Dilthey and his heirs had been totally disregarded in the United States, at least until the 1930s, according to Peter Novick, who has traced the influence of historicism and relativism in American history and the connection of historicist insights with those of anthropology and the new physics.[79] Yet this impact seems to have been, at first, far from momentous: as H. Stuart Hughes put it,

> the main job that needed to be done was simply to introduce the wisdom of Germany, Italy, and England to the New World. . . . [The] positivist-antipositivist controversy, which shook the universities of continental Europe from the 1890s to the 1920s, reached the United States in only muffled form. In America as in England, historians generally have adopted a highly pragmatic attitude toward their work and have been un-interested in epistemological or methodological polemics. Hence most practicing American historians have been neither positivists nor antipositivists in any explicit sense. By and large they have retained the concept of "causes," while rejecting the idea of "laws." Thus the dominant attitude in American historical writing has been a kind of residual or truncated positivism.[80]

The German idealist tradition, on the contrary, had been profoundly concerned with the motivations of historical actors: it is at this stage of the effort at "understanding" these that psychology, according to Hughes, is needed. Hughes went as far back as Gianbattista Vico, an intellectual father of historicism, to trace the importance "of learning from traditions, from linguistic usage, from architectural and technological remains."[81] The American historian, a few years earlier, in a book Mosse very much admired, had cited with approval the term "retrospective cultural anthropology" (referring to "popular ideas and practices . . . the whole of the vast realm of folklore and community sentiments"), though he focused his attention on "the history of the enunciation and development of the ideas that eventually will inspire such governing élites," which he regarded as the *"via regia* of intellectual history."[82]

Attempts in the direction of expanding the historical discipline had been under way in the United States since the beginning of the century. As early as 1912 James Harvey Robinson saw anthropology and psychology as the "new allies" of history: the "new history" he was advocating went in the direction of historical relativism, though it did not fully embrace it.[83] Arthur Lovejoy defined history as a "branch of anthropology" (even though his approach remained, in the end, that of a philosopher and an intellectual historian).[84] Franz Boas's historicism was very influential in the United States, bringing American historians to reconsider traditional concepts of culture, approaching it from a more German perspective, which implied an emphasis on "the totality of ideas in a society, popular as well as scholarly—in other words, low as well as high culture."[85] Caroline F. Ware's edited book, *The Cultural Approach to History* (1940), clearly advocated the adoption of new interpretive tools and the integration of other disciplines such as psychology and anthropology into historical study.[86] Ware focused on the urge to revise historical thinking in the light of the crisis of Western civilization, and pushed in the direction of a more "democratic" history that also considered the lives of the masses, stressing the "manner of living and the processes of change which affected the multitude."[87] Ware was concerned with interpreting societies as unique entities through their own cultural standards, their own point of view, and insisted that culture ought to be viewed in its wholeness, and societies as integral wholes. Such a concept of culture "forces recognition that human motivations are culturally conditioned and that, within the limits of universal human nature as revealed by biology and psychology, the historian must allow for the possibility of a pattern of motivation alien to that of his own culture."[88]

Perceptions and rationalizations constitute the basis for motivation, which leads to action. The problem of cultural causation, which lay at the heart of Dilthey's historicism in the distinction between *Naturwissenschaften* (natural sciences) and *Geisteswissenschaften* (literally, the sciences of the spirit, that is, the humanities), was one of methodology: different methods and tools were required in order to grasp logics as diverse as those of the natural sciences and those of the human spirit. This was in tune with anthropological perspectives. The anthropologist Alfred Louis Kroeber had stressed the difference between biological and cultural causation, which determined, respectively, biological and cultural events.[89] E. E. Evans-Pritchard regarded social anthropology "as being closer to certain kinds of history than to the natural sciences";[90] he, like Lévi-Strauss, believed in the affinities between the two disciplines and admired the work cultural historians, particularly those close to the Annales School (and preferably those who read anthropology like Marc Bloch), were doing. The humanities had a logic of its own, as Ernst Cassirer insisted, because a human is not an *animal rationale*, but an *animal symbolicum*, and therefore "Reason is a very inadequate term with which to comprehend the forms of man's cultural life in all their richness and variety."[91] Cassirer, who had been influenced by Dilthey, among others, drew much from anthropology in his attempt to account for human behavior. He was particularly interested in the mythical world and its own logic, which could not be grasped by ordinary reason: as against "explanation," he supported "interpretation" in order to account for the world of mythical perception and imagination. He implied that what seems to us irrational, prelogical, or mystical is different if seen "in the same light that primitive man does" instead of "from the point of view of our theoretical ideals of knowledge and truth." Cassirer saw no incoherence or lack of reason in myth and primitive religion: the coherence was simply based on feeling rather than on thought: he saw the primitive mind as having no "synthetic," "analytical" view of life, but rather a view of life as "an unbroken continuous whole." The historicist attitude evident in Cassirer's work, particularly the use of empathy, the relativistic stance, the distinction between explanation and interpretation (*Erklären* and *Verstehen*), allowed him to embrace anthropology (he defined his philosophy as "philosophical anthropology").[92]

Georg G. Iggers has noted how historicism, since Friedrich Meinecke's *Entstehung des Historismus* (1936), "has been identified less with the problems of historical relativism than with the discipline of history as it developed in the nineteenth century in Germany and with the professionalization of historical studies that became a model also outside of Germany."[93] Perhaps it is this association that has, more often than not, led many to associate the beginnings of cultural history in the United States mainly with the rapprochement to anthropology and psychology, thus disregarding the robust historicist theoretical foundation that had posed the premises for such achievements.[94] And yet the focus on the irrational side of human existence, and therefore of history, was a central element of an important part of German historicism.[95] This element was initially not integrated in American historiography, and came in, as it were, through the back door with the wave of German Jewish historians (including Mosse) who fled to America to escape National Socialism, and who brought with them an all-German awareness of irrationality.[96] Moreover, the intense interest the student movement took in German culture in the 1960s certainly allowed many students to become familiar with the thought of intellectuals who had investigated the depths of mythical thought, from Aby Warburg to Ernst Cassirer.[97]

Mosse abundantly drew from the thought of the Weimar German Jewish intellectuals. He argued that Cassirer, in his *The Myth of the State*, had come "tantalizingly close to an analysis of modern mass politics," and yet never explored the political implications of his concern with myths and symbols.[98] Ernst Bloch's *The Principle of Hope* was also often quoted by Mosse, who was particularly interested in the effects of utopian longings on the mass of humanity.[99] The "working definition" of myth had, in Mosse's view, really been given by the prominent Zionist Martin Buber, that is, myth as the "eternal function of the soul through which concrete events grasped by the senses were interpreted by the soul and the divine and the absolute."[100] Such ideas could only find fertile soil in the mind of a historian who was already imbued with German culture, and who considered himself, however debatably, "a Hegelian."[101]

Mosse's approach to myth was eclectic in that he drew from the most diverse sources and trends, picking and choosing the parts he found most congenial to his insights. Following his historicist attitude, he made an attempt at *comprehending* why people believe in myth; at the same time, loyal to his Enlightenment values, he tried to study it rationally, in order to *explain* why this happens. Fully aware of the power of irrationality, he tried to grasp it through rational study. He went right to the heart of the problem posed by historicism, the problem concerned with the two different attitudes of *Erklären* and *Verstehen*. He sought to combine both dialectically: on the one hand, he tried to comprehend; on the other, he tried to explain the results of sympathetic comprehension. His aim was to warn people against the dangers inherent in irrationalist approaches to life, though he was fully aware that they are an inextricable part of human nature (Buber's "eternal function of the soul"). Mosse acted, as it were, as a catalyzer, fusing different approaches and techniques into a forceful historical interpretation that managed to change interpretations of nationalism and fascism, and greatly influenced cultural history as an emegent discipline. He did so, however, not only through the influences and the parallels analyzed so far. His major methodological turn was, in fact, not only anthropological, but also profoundly aesthetic.

The Visual Turn: Aesthetics and Architecture

Beginning with the article "History, Anthropology, and Mass Movements," the term "myth" in Mosse's work came to be regularly accompanied by the term "symbol." Mosse's turn to anthropology and psychology went hand in hand with a visual turn, and it can be said that his historical production from the 1970s onward is a history of the political dimension of aesthetics. The focus on national monuments and the aesthetics of mass movements in *The National-ization of the Masses*, the moral and aesthetic dimension of racial stereotypes in *Toward the Final Solution*, the focus on the political masculine stereotype in *The Image of Man*, all these can also be viewed against the background of the "visual turn" that takes place in the 1960s, and which is deeply connected with the themes running below the surface of the anthropological turn. The way from Jung's and Sorel's idea of myth as an image, taken up by Mosse, to the close association of myth with symbol had been largely built on Mosse's interest in aesthetics.

William B. Hesseltine, Mosse's colleague at the University of Wisconsin–Madison, in a speech given in the late 1950s spoke of the "challenge of the arti-fact." Hesseltine reproached historians for disregarding artifacts as a "useful, viable source for the understanding of the human past." Historians were, he argued, too focused on written sources, but these were as much artifacts as any constructed object. Continuing, Hesseltine claimed that

> artifacts are historical facts, and as facts they should be as meaningful to the
> historian as the facts derived by the internal criticism of literary remains. It is
> in this meaningful relation that the facts of the historian differ from the facts
> of the antiquarian. The antiquarian collects facts much as the museum curator
> collects artifacts—for themselves. He displays them, much as the suburban
> housewife displays her antique furniture—for their patina, their lines, or their
> design. The historian, however, gathers facts for their meaning, for their utility
> in reconstructing a viable narrative of mankind's past. The facts which he gath-
> ers have relationships with one another; they present cause and effect, event
> and consequence, situation and response. They are not sterile items displayed

in showcases, but useful tools by which he can recapture some meaningful portion of human life on the earth. . . . It is the essence of anti-intellectualism to say that these walls cannot talk. Of course they can talk. It is only that we cannot talk to them, cannot ask them questions, and cannot understand the answers. But until artifacts can be subjected to internal criticism and made to bear their witness, the task of historical methodology is unfinished.[102]

In the first edition of *The Culture of Western Europe* (1961) Mosse did not particularly stress the aesthetic dimension of politics, and yet it was present. In 1961 Mosse conceived of mass meetings as "central to fascism," though they were mainly viewed as an instrument of manipulation of the masses.[103] As far as fascist architecture is concerned, he mentioned its classic themes, the desire for order it expressed, and the function that broad streets had for mass meetings. Moreover, this first edition of *The Culture of Western Europe* was enriched by numerous plates, some of which represented examples of Nazi mass meetings and fascist architecture. In addition, he referred to the Aryan ideal type and to the importance of its outward appearance through which an ideology can become "tangible."[104] In Mosse's notes for an address called "Nationalism and Patriotism," delivered in 1963, he referred to the symbolism of the mass meeting, remarking that one should "always show pictures when teaching it": such meetings could not be regarded as "American style publicity," which would "miss the whole point."[105] Indeed, the psychological and anthropological importance of aesthetics is not simply "publicity": it is an integral part of the "nationalization of the masses." The transition from *The Crisis of German Ideology* to *The Nationalization of the Masses* can be summarized in Mosse's remark on Lévi-Strauss's assertion that myth is language: this, he argued, must be broadened "to take in visual means of communication as well."[106] He was advocating an anthropological view of society, where human needs, as the anthropologist Geoffrey Gorer put it, "are given symbolic elaboration by means of ritual, mythology, and belief"—"symbolic elaboration" meaning "all the behavior, both non-verbal and verbal, which is commonly manifested by all members of a society on any given occasion."[107] In the 1988 edition of *The Culture of Western Europe*, aesthetics finds its place in the chapter on nationalism. The analysis of national monuments and mass festivals (*The Nationalization of the Masses*, 1975) and that of racism (*Toward the Final Solution*, 1978) had enriched the historian's perspective, as becomes evident in a new paragraph in which he adds that these ideas were representative of the nation's self-image, a symbol of eternity—a world of order and harmony. It was on this *concept of beauty* that the national "ideal type" was based all over Europe. . . . . Racial thought based many of its judgments upon a *concept of beauty* which had become part of the self-representation of the nation: in stone and mortar through national monuments or through the *outward appearance of the ideal citizen.* Nationalism presented itself through a world of myth *and symbol* in which the people could participate: singing, folk dancing, forming processions, or strengthening their body through gymnastics. Public festivals which accompanied the rise of nationalism used the symbols we have discussed and encouraged popular participation. All over Europe nationalism captured masses of people, the more so as the beginning of nationalism coincided with the beginning of mass politics. People longed for a *beautiful* and healthy world where order reigned and which exemplified the continuity of history among chaotic change of industrializing Europe. The myths and symbols of nationalism fulfilled this longing.[108]

There were many influences at play on Mosse's conception of aesthetics. He was surely much affected by his admiration for the work of Huizinga. The Dutch historian believed that, in times of crisis, people tend to escape from reality, and do so translating the forms of life into works of art, social forms, and play. Huizinga also believed that such a trend had been retained by the petty bourgeoisie well into the twentieth century. Aesthetics, as well as manners and morals, fulfill an all-important function on the path to the world of dreams: they make life beautiful, lifting humanity from reality to dream. He argued that the mere presence of a visible image made, in the eyes of the masses, the intellectual demonstration of some truth superfluous: politics acts on popular imagination through fixed and simple figures, images that he called books for the ignorant.[109] Mosse wrote that the "stress on the visual . . . made it easy for people to understand the thrust of the ideology," and often referred both to a passage from *The Waning of the Middle Ages* that "having attributed a real existence to an idea the mind wants to see it alive and can effect this only by personalizing it," and to Huizinga's idea that "the mere presence of a visible image of things holy sufficed to establish their truth."[110]

The whole process through which hopes, needs, and dreams were being objectified was one of "personalization." The term, which Mosse drew from Huizinga, ended up in his work through a synthesis of the workings of ideologies like nationalism or fascism, and of communities. "We can look at all of fascism as an attempt to personalize the abstract," he wrote, and regarded nationalism as an ideology where "dreams and longings were channeled toward national goals, led by a dictated leadership. This community was not abstract but personalized through camaraderie, through its liturgy and its symbols."[111] He believed that no movement survives in history that does not appeal to authority or certainty, and that does not personalize this certainty: you cannot be a Nietzschean man or woman, he told his students, adding: "I love certainties, I'm no different, I live by certainties. I personalize everything."[112]

The escape from reality in search for certainties was embodied, in Mosse's mind, by the liturgy of the Baroque. He had always been deeply fascinated with the Baroque style, which surrounded his youth at Salem and intrigued him in the 1950s, when he frequently traveled to Rome to study Baroque architecture.[113] Mosse's interest in the Baroque had already assumed a definite shape by the late 1950s. As Sterling Fishman colorfully recalled,

From the outset of his career George evinced a keen interest in the cultural symbols which mediate between abstract beliefs and popular piety. This has proved to be his most enduring historical concern. As a reformation scholar, he became quickly fascinated with the baroque period because of its dramatic symbolic elements—the canonization and cult of St. Theresa, the sculpture of Bernini, and especially the highly theatrical baroque church. I recall a trip to Mexico with George and Dick Soloway in 1956, when George was in search of expressions of the baroque. Struck by the inevitable intestinal plight of North American travelers, we took refuge in the small town of Zamora. Undaunted, George attended mass twice each day in the local baroque church. Our unscheduled stop permitted him to study religious rituals which several centuries had not altered. The local Indians must have marveled at the piety of this round-faced, bespectacled "gringo." A few years later, when George turned his full attention to the study of modern mass movements, his work was informed by his study of baroque religious rites. However broad the chronological spectrum of his interests, strong threads of continuity run through his works. He has demonstrated that, although the prevailing ideological systems may change, popular piety with all its rites and rituals persists. George has shown how the cultural symbols of popular beliefs blur the distinction between religious and secular beliefs.[114]

The Baroque represents one of the links between the early modern and the modern part of Mosse's work. As he himself explicitly stated, "my lasting interest in the Baroque as art and casuistry was directly related to my later understanding of fascism as a visually oriented ideology and way of life."[115] As early as in the 1950s, he stressed in his lectures that it was not possible to understand the history of the twentieth century without understanding the Baroque.[116]

The historian's attention toward mass movements cannot therefore be traced back exclusively to an anthropological interest in group behavior, but must be inserted into Mosse's long-lasting fascination with the Baroque. His private library in Madison, with its many volumes on the subject (mostly editions of the late 1950s), witnesses this deep interest. What emerges from an analysis of some of the passages he underlined is of interest. Mosse seemed to take a great interest in the building instructions of Jesuit churches, particularly as far as vast choirs, favorable acoustics, the cult of images, and good lightning are concerned. Commenting on Victor L. Tapié's *Baroque et Classicisme*, he marked a sentence where the author criticized Benedetto Croce's rationalistic attitude in interpreting the Baroque style, and emphasized passages explaining how the theatrical was put at the service of a religious idea in order to provide believers with a sense of infinity.[117] Sentences from other books are underlined, in particular with regard to the veneration of images as a "means of reducing anxiety," or with Baroque architecture's ability to deal with large numbers of people.[118]

In a lecture from the late 1950s Mosse spoke of the "delirious participation of the masses of the population in the visual arts," and focused on Baroque architecture and its churches, which were centered on the space for preaching; moreover, the classical idea of beauty was utilized to serve Christian purposes.[119] We will find such themes in *The Nationalization of the Masses*, where classical beauty was adopted in service to the cause of the nation in the secular religion of Nationalism. In another course, probably given in the 1950s, Mosse depicted the Baroque as the expression of an "effort at 'sensuous propaganda,'" of an "appeal to the senses rather than to the heart."[120] In a 1977 interview on Nazism he explicitly connected the Baroque with modern mass politics: "The baroque is full of myth, theater, and symbols which carry you away from the reality of this world. But the very success of the Jesuits was that while carrying you away from this world they really integrated you into their political system."[121] Writing of the "new politics," Mosse stated in 1975 that "here we are close to the theatrical and dramatic tradition of the Baroque as exemplified by the Baroque churches, though this tradition was rejected by nineteenth-century nationalists as frivolous. For the beauty which unified politics could not be playful; it had to symbolize order, hierarchy, and the restoration of a 'world made whole again.'"

Hitler's speeches, the focal point of Nazi meetings, "integrated themselves with the total setting and the liturgical rhythm much in the same way as famous preachers functioned in the churches of the Baroque."[122] In a 1994 interview Mosse, talking of the importance of Christian rituals for political practices, stated that he was one of the first to have studied National Socialism, racism, and nationalism as civic religions: "In fact, this overlapping of politics and religion has interested me for a long time, since my first works on the Baroque. Remember how Mussolini and Hitler grew up in Baroque surroundings . . ."[123] Asked what the Baroque concretely is, Mosse replied that it is "an experience of space, of its utilization. I have repeatedly studied how the Nazis, for example in Munich, lay as much importance on the buildings surrounding a central space as on the space itself. The same effort is to be found in Baroque architecture, which aims at controlling the crowds, at fostering certain emotions, at arousing certain fervors."[124]

The connection between architecture and nationalism was also inspired by the reading of what he defined as "the pioneer study of Thomas Nipperdey," an article published in 1968.[125] In *The Nationalization of the Masses*, Mosse wrote that "the historian Thomas Nipperdey has described national monuments as the self-representations of a democratically controlled nation, objectifying the ideals for which the nation is supposed to stand."[126] Nipperdey's article had a considerable influence on Mosse and might have been decisive in turning the historian's attention to the political implications of architecture. As we have seen, Mosse had hinted at an interest in fascist architecture as early as in 1961, but the theme remained marginal in his work. Reading Nipperdey's article, he may have found a confirmation of the aesthetic turn he was already conceiving and of the inclination for the visual he had always had. Nipperdey had participated in the "widening of historiography through his historical anthropology" through the analysis of culture, art, and religion.[127] In the article that inspired Mosse, Nipperdey lamented that only historians of antiquity had taken symbols into consideration, and the author set himself to the task of analyzing national monuments in order to fathom their connections with the German national movement and national idea in the nineteenth century. Nipperdey regarded national monuments as "objective expressions of ideas" that could make these ideas "visible."[128] These monuments were meant to "elevate mythically" the people or the events they represented.[129]

"Mythical qualities" were precisely what Albert Speer considered essential for a monument to be effective, as he stated in his diaries.[130] Speer, Hitler's favorite architect and later Minister of Armaments and War Production in the last years of the war, offered Mosse a unique chance to see National Socialism as it really saw itself. Speer was released from Spandau prison in 1966, and authored his first volume of memories in 1969.[131] That was the year in which Mosse's article on history, anthropology, and mass movements was published, at a time when he was fully receptive toward aesthetics. Speer laid great emphasis on the cultic aspects of his work for Hitler, and saw in architecture and its religious significance a central element in National Socialism. Moreover, he also stressed the influence of the Baroque on Hitler, and often depicted his architectural achievements as having an effect similar to that of Baroque art. Reviewing Speer's diaries, Mosse wrote that "Hitler, after all, had grown up in the Austria of the Baroque, and though he despised this art form as too frivolous, still, the future dictator must be analogous to the priest at the altar of a baroque church deriving his authority from the ritual and the theatrical *mise en scène* regardless of individual qualities."[132] Speer's view of National Socialism was crucial, according to Mosse, for the historian who wanted to understand the Third Reich: since "all modern mass movements are apt to be visually oriented," and liturgy fulfills the psychological needs of the people, "the historian has to recapture their enthusiasm as they felt it at the time and not to impose his own abstract categories upon it thirty years later"; ideas of class, social grouping, and conventional politics explain little, and "most historians have put the cart before the horse, and here Speer proved an invaluable corrective."[133]

When Speer was released after his twenty-year imprisonment, Mosse contacted him, as he did other former Nazis, out of the conviction that the best way to understand National Socialism was to see it as it saw itself. The encounter with Speer was to prove of great importance for Mosse's work; they exchanged letters for over six years and often met in the first half of the 1970s.[134] Their relationship was a sort of respectful mutual exploitation, where the historian was looking for precious insights, and Speer was trying to regain a respectable image in order to overcome his Nazi past.[135] Mosse found Speer a fascinating character who could offer the historian unique insights into the Third Reich. Moreover, he was the only survivor of Hitler's closest collaborators. When Martin Krygier, review editor for *Quadrant*, an Australian review, asked Mosse if he wanted to review the *Spandau Diaries*, Mosse replied: "How could I resist such an appeal?"[136] In a long interview at the United States Holocaust Memorial Museum, Mosse summarized his collaboration with Speer:

> I knew Speer quite well. I talked a lot with Speer. . . . When I first met Speer
> he was very suspicious of course. I said, look I'm not interested in your

morals. That's between you and God. I've come to ask you technical questions. I asked him why did you use this lighting at the Nuremburg Rally. For the effect, for the crowds. With that he saw these were questions he could answer, technical questions. Then we went from technical to other things and it worked I think very well. . . . I got everything out of him. He always picked me up in Munich. You noticed—this went over about five six years—he always picked me up in Munich in a car which had a Wankel motor—that was the alternative to our engine, our motor engine that he developed in the war. Off we went, and the embarrassing thing, the only embarrassing thing was whenever I ate with him in public people came up and wanted his autograph. Whenever, they must have thought I too was a Nazi. The other interesting thing about it was it's quite true, it gave me insights into other things. For example, whenever he talked about Hitler negatively, his eyes lit up. Hitler must have had a tremendous charisma because this man even, you know, denying everything, thinking everything was dreadful now, his eyes lit up when he talked about Hitler. Oh, I learned a lot from him. I never wrote about him. I wrote about him once in an Australian paper because I didn't want him to see it particularly. [Question: What did he teach you about Hitler, except for the army?] Everything that is in his excellent memoirs, but in a kind of different way. I mean Hitler's attitude towards women is remarkable. He never knew Speer was married and Speer was married with eight children or something like that. He's not only married, he's really married. Hitler never knew it. He never asked. He never knew it. You learn little tidbits like that.[137]

Speer respected and appreciated Mosse and his work, or so he claimed. One day, to his delight, Speer told him that he was the only historian who had ever understood what National Socialism really was.[138] Indeed, Speer held Mosse's work in great esteem and suggested that Mosse publish in Germany one single volume with *The Crisis of German Ideology*, *Nazi Culture*, and *The Nationalization of the Masses*.[139] As Mosse wrote *The Nationalization of the Masses* he discussed it constantly with Speer and indeed, in the introduction, he wrote that he "learned a great deal from Diplom Ing. Albert Speer, who on several occasions took the time to answer a myriad of questions and who read the manuscript of this book, keeping me from making several errors. . . . Albert Speer was an important link between the earlier history of the political liturgy in Germany and its use by National Socialism which he so largely directed."[140] Speer appreciated the book, saying that it was important to analyze the background of Hitler's period in order to understand National Socialism properly, and Mosse wished he could have met Speer when writing *The Crisis of German Ideology*, which he believed would have improved the book.[141] Mosse went so far as to state that, without Speer, *The Nationalization of the Masses* could have never been written: if he had been having doubts about the concept of propaganda in the mid-1960s, it was Speer who confirmed them, he revealed in an interview.[142]

Aesthetics thus played a crucial role in Mosse's rejection of the idea of propaganda. The power of images and symbols, which were the personalizations of myths, provided the cement holding a group together around a shared belief.[143] Art and architecture became integral parts of the historian's work, side by side with popular literature, adding a new dimension that fulfilled Mosse's conviction that history must be regarded as a totality. As Steven Aschheim put it, Mosse viewed history as a totality that becomes "a kind of updated Hegelian totality, a dialectic in which the political cannot be separated from the religious, the scientific from the aesthetic, the rational from the mythological."[144] In this perspective, Mosse's assertion that he considered himself a Hegelian falls into place, inextricably linking his historicist background with his adoption of anthropological and aesthetic interpretive categories.

Toward New Perspectives

The trends discussed in this chapter gave a decisive thrust to the full development of what we mean today by "cultural history." The inclusion of anthropology into the historical discipline opened up new interpretive scenarios for a better understanding of mass politics through the analysis of myths, rites, and symbols, while depth psychology provided new insights into human irrationality and its historical implications; a combination of both paved the way for the realization of the religious character of modern politics.[145] The rise of comparative religious studies helped develop new, more detached perspectives on Western history. Mircea Eliade was a firm supporter of these standpoints. He believed hermeneutics to be "Western man's response—the only intelligent response possible—to the solicitations of contemporary history, to the fact that the West is forced (one might almost say, condemned) to this encounter and confrontation with the cultural values of 'the others.'"[146] Renzo De Felice had praised Mosse's contributions, highlighting his attempt to make history even of phenomena that may appear to us preposterous and irrational, finally setting aside those apriorisms that derive from Western rationalistic culture.[147] Eliade had underlined how religious studies, ethnology, and depth psychology had helped understand "psychological attitudes which at first seem 'inferior,' 'strange' or 'disconcerting,'" and "ways of thinking that are so foreign to the

Western rationalist tradition," "even when those rites and myths reveal 'strange,' terrible or aberrant aspects."[148]

Eliade's stand for hermeneutics reflects a need for understanding that had been expressed both by historicism and anthropology, which shared this premise in pursuing their respective goals. Yet, if anthropology sought to fathom the mind of the "other" by looking outside of Europe, historicism attempted to apply empathetic "understanding" (*Verstehen*) to European history. What Mosse did was, as it were, to look at Western society with the eyes of an anthropologist intent on scrutinizing people from far-off lands. He belonged to those anthropologically oriented historians who, in the face of "conventional" wisdom, delved deeply into the irrational core of Western society, unafraid of disclosing its own "strange, terrible or aberrant aspects." The Holocaust viewed as an integral part of European society and the reconsideration of some of the basic values of Western society represent the two main tenets of Mosse's interpretation of the Jewish catastrophe, and are a direct consequence of the methodological turn examined in this chapter. A wholly new perspective was being adopted that was to overturn most common assumptions about European superiority in world history and politics.

The anthropological and visual turn had, by the end of the 1960s, come full circle, and Mosse's question about how millions of Germans had responded to the *völkisch* call had now a far more satisfying answer. And yet this long road took another turn, which opened new scenarios to the historian, paving the way for a "new season"[149] of his historiography. A new question replaced the previous one, as Mosse's focus shifted to the Holocaust: "How could this come to pass?"[150] Once again, life and work interacted in the 1970s and 1980s, orienting Mosse toward new themes and interests. The 1960s sexual revolution had made society more tolerant toward homosexuality, an attitude that was furthered during the following decade, when Mosse publicly acknowledged his sexual orientation. All this meant for him the opportunity to investigate subjects that had been so far considered taboo, and to slowly "come out of the closet." At the same time, the students in the 1960s had provided another contribution to Mosse's intellectual development, introducing him to the thought of the Frankfurt School: the influence of the school made itself felt on the historian. The outcome was a change of perspective in his view of the Enlightenment and of bourgeois society and values. Mosse began investigating racism and bourgeois respectability, an investigation that would lead him to the conclusion that the roots of the Holocaust lay deep within European culture, and that bourgeois values became part of nationalist and fascist ideology to the extent that he once asserted that the new man of National Socialism was the "ideal bourgeois." These were the years of Mosse's coming out as a double outsider: both a Jew and a homosexual, he criticized Western society and its values from within, attacking that "underside of the Enlightenment" that had called, in his interpretation, for racial classification and sexual repression.[151] Racism and sexuality are the themes Mosse dealt with in the late 1970s and early 1980s. Fully convinced of the power of aesthetics, and armed with his newly acquired anthropological arsenal, he made full use of them in order to delve into the dark side of Western culture.

4

The Dark Side of Modernity

Every society invents for itself a type, a model, an exemplar, of what
the perfect member of that society ought to be. These heroes and
heroines are much more than the products of existing social and
economic conditions: they are myths which repeat the legends of the
past and enhance the dreams of the future. In a materialistic age it is
salutary to remind ourselves of such fictions.

—HAROLD NICOLSON

The fate of outsiders is part of the essential working of our society.

—GEORGE L. MOSSE

The trenches were the concentration camps of the First World War.

—ROBERT KEE

The ethical purpose inherent in Mosse's works, embodied in the "from
Machiavellism to totalitarianism" formula, found a new and more challenging dimension when the historian turned more directly to the analysis of the cultural roots of the Holocaust in the 1970s. The idea that modern
persecution was the "new Leviathan," expressed by Mosse in his 1954 Chapel
Talks,[1] was now taken to its extreme consequence, completing the path leading
from Machiavellism (here expressed in Hobbesian terms) to the Holocaust.
The destruction of European Jewry thus came to stand, in his view, at the very
heart of modernity: on the one hand, at the heart of a "long" modernity where
the modern state was the presupposition for the implementation of mass murder;[2] on the other, in the context of a "short" modernity where a consistent part
of the cultural bases for the extermination of the European Jews had been laid
by the Enlightenment and by bourgeois manners and morals. The latter view
proved rather shocking in its radical and provocative essence. His assertion
that the new man of National Socialism was the "ideal bourgeois" must have

filled many a reader with wonder, if not with horror.[3] And yet this interpretation was part and parcel of Mosse's ethical thrust, as he made clear during a lecture by the unconventional title "The Holocaust and Modern Manners and
Morals":

> The Holocaust is often treated as unique, a static event, and yet we shall never
> realize its full dimensions unless we treat it as part of the historical process.
> If we do so it should make us reconsider some of the basic values of our soci-
> ety which we take as given but which are created through history. . . . Today
> I want to be concerned with a factor not usually considered, put in its most
> general sense: the Holocaust as integrating what society thought respectable,
> as building upon the ideas of normalcy and abnormalcy which informed
> norms of behavior, and which had become personalized through the stereo-
> types of respectability.[4]

The historicization of the Holocaust is therefore aimed at reconsidering "some
of the basic values of our society," an interpretation that, beyond opening new
perspectives on the cultural history of racism (but also, extensively, of fascism,
nationalism, and gender), was intended as an ethical warning against the dangers inherent in respectability. Respectability, by which Mosse meant "'decent
and correct' manners and morals, as well as the proper attitude toward sexuality,"[5] was envisioned by him as the "cement" of bourgeois society, as the
standard regulating the dynamics of inclusion and exclusion, in short, of the creation of social and racial stereotypes.[6] The Holocaust thus becomes not only a
phenomenon linked with the Third Reich, but the historical place where myth
showed all its power by becoming reality: to warn against the dangers inherent
in respectability, and as a consequence in conformity, was then the deeper goal
of Mosse's efforts, expressing the closest link between his life and his work.

The years from the 1970s onward represent, in Mosse's intellectual biography, the moment when his double outsiderdom was fully disclosed, leading to
a radical critique of bourgeois society and its values. These are the years when
Mosse could let his identity emerge forcefully: first, as a Jew engaged in retriev-
ing his roots; secondly, as a homosexual who could finally be visible without
running the risk of losing the integration it had taken him many years to attain.
This "coming out" coincided, not by accident, with his growing interest in the
Holocaust or, more precisely, in racism and the creation of the outsider's stereotype during the nineteenth and twentieth centuries. This new interest, which
had been only latent in his works since the late 1950s, finally took precedence,

adding new insights to his interpretation of National Socialism. The above quoted passage effectively summarizes the essence of Mosse's view of the Holocaust as well as the main tenets of his critique of bourgeois society. First, he stated the historicity of the Holocaust, integrating it into European history: an event that had too often been regarded as an aberration, or a deviation from the enlightened path of Western civilization, was placed by Mosse into a context where an attempt could be made to explain it historically. Secondly, he linked the attempted extermination of the European Jews to bourgeois respectability. From these premises, the foundations of a disruptive interpretation not only of the Holocaust, but also of the modern mass society, were laid.

In Mosse's work, the Holocaust occupies a central place. Driven by the question of how it could happen, all his writings point, in a rather teleological (and yet not deterministic) way to the Jewish catastrophe. Historiography and biography are indissolubly intertwined. As he wrote in his memoir,

> the Holocaust was never very far from my mind; I could easily have perished with my fellow Jews. I suppose that I am a member of the Holocaust generation and have constantly tried to understand an event too monstrous to contemplate. All my studies in the history of racism and volkish thought, and also those dealing with outsiderdom and stereotypes, though sometimes not directly related to the Holocaust, have tried to find the answer to how it could have happened; finding an explanation has been vital not only for the understanding of modern history, but also for my own peace of mind. This is a question my generation had to face, and eventually I felt that I had come closer to an understanding of the Holocaust as a historical phenomenon. We have to live with an undertone of horror in spite of the sort of advances that made it so much easier for me to accept my own nature.[7]

Mosse defined the Holocaust as a "constant presence for any Jew," and though he wrote only one book specifically dealing with its prehistory, he quite rightly referred to it as "a latent presence in many of my other writings."[8] And yet Mosse's Jewishness was only one side of his outsiderdom: homosexuality too was to play a crucial role. Here Mosse, breaking new ground in historiography with his analyses of the connections among nationalism, fascism, racism, and sexuality (in its political dimension), set himself to the task of exploring the process through which bourgeois society tackles the problem of normal and abnormal, of inclusion and exclusion, thus linking both racial and sexual outsiders. Mosse's reflections, which ran almost parallel to those of another

important thinker of the time, Michel Foucault, tackled the problem of "normalcy," analyzing the process through which society built, in the modern
age, types and antitypes based on the norms set by the dominant bourgeois
morality.[9]

Mosse developed his critique, like Foucault, from the point of view of an
outsider, and therefore in a very personal manner, writing that "while I have
addressed outsiderdom in general I have also been concerned with the specific minority groups of which I have been a member."[10] He dealt with the issue
of diversity in a sort of paradoxical way: on the one hand, he had spent decades
looking for integration into society through respectability; on the other, he
claimed, years later, to be happy to be an outsider, and to "have rarely en-
countered the temptation of normalcy."[11] He considered being an outsider an
important vantage point from which to look at the workings of society from
within, but with a different, more detached eye. Most of his colleagues and
friends refer to him as a "very respectable" person. Paul Breines, underlining
how Mosse's analysis of respectability has been "one of the central and most
challenging dimensions" of his work as a historian, has focused on his "manly
voice," connecting it to his historiographical evolution. "It was not only exile
as a Jew," Breines writes, "but also respectability and its stereotypes of hetero-
sexual masculinity, which incised themselves into George's vocal cords. . . .
George's is the voice of a man who has turned his wounds at respectability's
hands into a critical standpoint on modern western history, a standpoint that
redefines that history, making the history of modern Europe into a history of
respectability. For me, George's voice is that history's critical self-reflection." It
was during the 1960s, continues Breines, that Mosse's voice changed while he
shared with the students the experience of "unraveling" respectability: here
his voice "expanded . . . and it did so in connection with the emergence in this
country and elsewhere of two exemplary rebellions against respectability, the
movements on behalf of Jewish and homosexual self-affirmation. . . . My main
point, then, is that, in the 1960s, George embraced and integrated into his voice
two dimensions of his life—the Jewish and gay dimensions—that respectability had ensured would be difficult to embrace and integrate. This development
issued in his great works of the 1970s through the 1990s."[12]

The connection Mosse drew between respectability and the Holocaust was
intended to shatter common beliefs in the rationality of Western society. His
study of racism aimed to place it at the heart of European culture, to the point
that, he argued, the Holocaust is "built into our society and attitudes towards
life. Nothing in European history is a stranger to the Holocaust."[13] The story

of racism, he maintained, should not be told "as the history of an aberration of European thought or as scattered moments of madness, but as an integral part of the European experience."[14] His most shocking and provocative thesis was that racism sprang not only from romantic irrationalism, but also from the rationality of the Enlightenment, upon which European mainstream culture in the last two centuries has been built. If up to the early 1960s Mosse saw National Socialism as mainly a degeneration of romantic trends, in the 1970s he would claim that the ideal man of National Socialism was born of the degeneration of Enlightenment values. Mosse would underline what he called "the paradox of the Enlightenment," lying in the coexistence of toleration and conformity, and saw in modern anti-Semitism the "failure of the Enlightenment."[15] The 1960s were crucial to his personal and intellectual development: here the anthropological and visual turn took place, providing the historian with the historiographical tools necessary to study myths, symbols, and stereotypes; here, also, Mosse came close to the thought of the Frankfurt School, whose harsh critique of the Enlightenment would considerably inspire him. Finally, the changes brought to society by the 1960s, particularly the sexual revolution, made his "coming out" possible, and allowed him to deal with subjects such as the history of sexuality or of gender, which were not considered "respectable" before.

The road leading from a "positive" view of the Enlightenment to a more critical one is winding, since many of the themes he addressed since the 1970s were present before, if suppressed. Yet Mosse's critique of "enlightened" modernity eventually blossomed, and it strengthened with his preoccupation with the role played by the First World War in European history. He came to see the war as the event that triggered all the previous trends he had analyzed, and therefore as a key event. He was one of the pioneers of the cultural approach to the history of the conflict, and his dedication to this new field of investigation eventually had consequences for his views of the bourgeois side of the Nazi experience. This chapter will therefore deal with his interpretations of the Enlightenment, of racism, and of bourgeois respectability, and with Mosse's contributions to the history of the Great War. All these developments must be seen in a dual light. First, as part of the secularization process that Mosse began analyzing with his works on reason of state and Christian ethics, an analysis that continued through *The Nationalization of the Masses* (the cult of the nation and its liturgical aspects, that is, nationalism and fascism intended as secular religions) to *Fallen Soldiers*, where he saw in the Great War and the cult of the fallen the highest point of fusion between nationalism and Christianity.

His view of physicians taking over from the clergy as the guardians of public morality is paradigmatic in this respect. Secondly, the histories of racism and respectability are related to Mosse's growing concern, the connection between aesthetics and morality, an outcome of the visual turn. Morality, indeed, became a central issue in his work on several levels, as will be argued in the next chapter. The histories of racism, of respectability, and of the Great War, through *Toward the Final Solution* (1978), *Nationalism and Respectability* (1985), *Fallen Soldiers* (1990) and *The Image of Man* (1996), represent a continuum; they are different perspectives on the same topic: how could the Holocaust come to pass in the heart of "civilized" modernity?

The "Failure of the Enlightenment"

Mosse's controversial relationship with the Enlightenment unfolded over the decades in a rather paradoxical way. On the one hand, the cultural background of his family supplied him with a set of values he always clung to, such as cosmopolitanism, tolerance, individual freedom, rationality, and a critical attitude toward reality. On the other hand, his double outsider status motivated him to investigate the roots of conformity and discrimination, which he traced back to the Age of Reason. The two sides of the Enlightenment, the bright and the dark, coexisted in his view throughout his life. And yet he did not see this as a contradiction, he saw it as an inner dialectical relationship, and regarded his apparently ambiguous position as a privileged point of view, an advantage instead of a disadvantage, in that it offered him the opportunity to criticize bourgeois society from within. He summarized this twofold view in the interview on Nazism:

> About the Enlightenment I think there are two points of view possible, both of which are actually correct. There is the view of Peter Gay which looks at the Enlightenment from within. What the philosophers actually wanted was the predominance of the critical mind. From that point of view, they were in no way the ancestors of authoritarianism. But there is the other side, what I call the darker side of the Enlightenment (which in addition to Talmon, also the Germans of the so-called Frankfurt School, Horkheimer and Adorno pointed out)—namely the Enlightenment as depersonalization because of its abstract theories, its intellectualism. This depersonalization became in fact a forerunner of modern positivism, producing the first racial classification. That is another side of the Enlightenment. But this side called for Rousseau's

patriotic ceremony, a certain romanticism, and a certain attempt to personalize the depersonalized. We can look at all of fascism as an attempt to personalize the abstract. That is in my opinion the connection with the French
Revolution and the Enlightenment.[16]

This passage synthetically embodies Mosse's thought on the Enlightenment
in the mid-1970s, the decade that inaugurated his open "rebellion" against
bourgeois society. However, the path leading to such assumptions had been
rather rough, and it crossed with several events in the historian's life.

Mosse's mounting critique of the Enlightenment went hand in hand with
his critique of bourgeois society and its values. The young Mosse had engaged
in the antifascist movement in the 1930s with a critical attitude toward "bourgeois" appeasement, an attitude that was mirrored in his sympathies for the
Soviet Union, in his pseudo-Marxist political orientation, and in his contempt
for bourgeois mediocrity as expressed in the 1940 essay on Nietzsche.[17] Over
the course of the 1960s, he shared the student movement's hostility toward
middle-class respectability, which both were trying to unravel.[18] This was the
background against which his interpretation of the Enlightenment evolved. If
in the 1930s he had faced fascism "out of an enlightenment philosophy,"[19]
he eventually came to consider fascism as partly stemming from that philosophy, and to establish a connection between the Enlightenment and bourgeois
respectability and conformity, thus linking both to the Holocaust. The influence of the thought of the Frankfurt School on this process was considerable.

Mosse praised Adorno and Horkheimer for having brought to light the "long
overlooked . . . underside of the Enlightenment," particularly through their concept of "repressive equalitarianism," by which he meant the Enlightenment's
penchant for abstraction, typology, and depersonalization.[20] As he wrote in the
revised edition of *The Culture of Western Europe*, "perhaps these renewals of
Marxist theory were one of the chief Jewish contributions to modern times, and
the most original, for these theories influenced the 1960s' student revolts in the
United States and in all of Europe as well. They were an attempt to give Marxism a human face."[21] Mosse, who came to regard the Frankfurt School as "essential," eventually "applied the arguments of Horkheimer and Adorno's *Dialectic
of Enlightenment* to his cultural history."[22] *Dialectic of the Enlightenment* has much
in common with the new direction taken by Mosse's work since the 1970s.
In particular, Adorno and Horkheimer saw a connection between Enlightenment and racism (particularly anti-Semitism) that was based on an abstraction,

the concept of outsider, and that of anxiety. The "fully enlightened earth," Adorno and Horkheimer maintained, "radiates disaster triumphant": Auschwitz was an integral part of "enlightened," rationalist society, "its 'irrationalism' is deduced from the nature of the dominant *ratio* itself, and the world which corresponds to its image."[23] Enlightened society was viewed as a "system of order" that necessarily entailed persecution as part of defending that order against the idea of outsiderness: the fear and the anxiety evoked by social deviation from the accepted standard of conformity lay at the source of persecution. Enlightenment is "mythic fear turned radical. . . . Nothing at all may remain outside, because the mere idea of outsiderness is the very source of fear." The "tool of the Enlightenment," Adorno and Horkheimer argued, is "abstraction," the tendency to classify and dominate nature: abstraction allows one to define whoever does not abide by the norms of established society, whoever does not conform to such accepted standards, that is to say, the outsider, who thus becomes the enemy of modern civilization. Such devaluation of the individual, such an attempt to include all aspects of life into a definite standard of behavior lends enlightened society its totalitarian character, making the Enlightenment as "totalitarian as any system."[24] The exponents of the Frankfurt School thus set themselves "the task of defining the relationship between reason and brutality" where the Enlightenment failed to "effectively abandon the mythological": National Socialism represented its "corollary brutality."[25]

In his earliest works, Mosse rarely associated the Enlightenment and National Socialism. In the 1950s he drew a connection between Jacobin terror and the concept of "totalitarian democracy," establishing a link between fascism and the French Revolution, following Jacob Talmon's interpretation, but he merely regarded the excesses of the revolution as an "excessively perfectionist attitude" toward the idea of humans as rational animals who needed to be brought down to a common denominator into a "mass of rational individuals."[26] In 1958 he blamed the Enlightenment because, he claimed, it "had not fundamentally improved the popular image of the Jew; indeed, it had materially contributed to the creation of the stereotype."[27] Such ideas, seldom expressed over the late 1950s and the 1960s, remained fragmentary and never fully articulated. As a reviewer of *The Culture of Western Europe* pointed out in 1963, "the link between freedom and reason is the link [Mosse] is most anxious to sustain";[28] this was in line with Mosse's firm commitment to his family's Enlightenment ideals. When he came closer to his Jewish background during the 1960s, he surely felt in tune with the rationalistic values for which the interwar Jewish intellectuals he admired so much had stood, but at the same time he began distancing himself from the unconditional defense of Western liberalism he had, with few exceptions, championed until then. His antibourgeois élan finally blossomed, sparked by the ideas of the Frankfurt School and by the changing social context; by the early 1980s, his view of the Enlightenment was profoundly changed. Again, his new insights rested on prior intuitions.

Mosse's experience as a historian of religion in the early modern age was once again put to the service of his interpretation of the nineteenth and twentieth centuries. In 1961 he had highlighted the psychological function of faith when he pointed out that "the Enlightenment was not sufficiently aware of man's need of a faith, of a belief in a stable and eternal force impervious to ever-changing external realities, a force which would lead man toward a better and fuller life. Christianity had fulfilled this need and one could not simply pronounce it dead, as some of the *philosophes* did, without allowing for the need which it had filled."[29] His interest in religious architecture, as we noted in the previous chapter, led to the comparison between the function of liturgy in the Baroque age and in modern mass movements: liturgy, through the objectification and personalization of ideas and ideologies, provided fixed and apparently immutable points of reference that could give life meaning. The quest for security as against anxiety and uncertainty was a salient theme of the lectures on European cultural and intellectual history Mosse gave at the University of Wisconsin–Madison in the early 1980s:

> This is the truth of modern history: that we intend to sublimate the real uncertainties, the real catastrophes, in liturgy, in certainties like the nation, like nationalism, and religion; that we grasp for certainties in an uncertain world, and that determines what will be successful or unsuccessful in popular culture, and that determines what will be successful in politics, and unsuccessful in politics as well; and that determines of course the rise of the greatest political force of modern times, nationalism, and that determines the rise of the other greatest force of modern times, respectability, which comes out of the evangelical movement, the shame of your bodies, the shame of sexuality, and the classification of people into normal and abnormal. That is part of wanting security, and it only arises in the eighteenth century.[30]

During these lectures, Mosse made clear the main tenets of his interpretation: the great change brought about by the Enlightenment had been "impersonality."[31] In line with Adorno and Horkheimer's contention that "abstraction" is the "tool of the Enlightenment," Mosse viewed the age of mass politics and mass culture, of the nation and of the people, as an age of abstraction.[32] And yet he believed that since humans cannot live by abstractions, the abstract must be made concrete, which happens through the adoption of myths and symbols. The Enlightenment's unawareness of "man's need of a faith," its excess of intellectualism, was destined to fail on the popular level because the average person, Mosse held, needs security and a sense of totality, not abstract intellectualism. Despite the Enlightenment's search for authority in the classics and in natural law (science), which were supposed to provide certainty and immutability, these still remained impersonal. Popular culture and popular piety were more influenced by the religious revival through Pietism and Evangelicalism. Christianity therefore remained, on the popular level, a guiding force to resort to in order to make life meaningful: liturgy retained its importance because it had things cut down to a manageable size. In other words, the need remained for immediate symbols, for myths, for personalization.

And yet, according to his interpretation, the Enlightenment (which he personalized, as it were) eventually provided such personalizations in grasping for clear distinctions, for respectabilities and ideas of outward beauty, thus ending up with its own myths and symbols, which it substituted for those it had sought to destroy. Hence the "double-edged sword," as Mosse called it, wielded by the Enlightenment: on the one hand, there is the autonomy of man, symbolized by Lessing's Nathan the Wise and Rousseau's Emile; on the other, the "underside of the Enlightenment": the penchant for *classification*, which goes with mathematics and the new science of anthropology, and then the penchant for *conformity*; it is a "kind of dialectic": humanity is autonomous, but at the same time there is a trend toward conformity.[33] Conformity was to lead to "repressive equalitarianism," Mosse held, relying on Adorno and Horkheimer's concept when referring to Enlightenment abstraction, typology, and depersonalization.[34] Classification, on the other hand, was to symbolize personalization: Mosse saw no contradiction in this twofold legacy of the Enlightenment, since he believed that "there are no contradictions in history. Everything is in a dialectical relationship."[35] Thus, the Enlightenment could give birth to both liberalism and racism; it could be the age of tolerance (emancipation of the Jews) and at the same time of the reenslavement of blacks and Jews through the new sciences, above all anthropology with its racial classifications; it could be the climax of individual freedom that went hand in hand with a new authoritarianism imposed by respectability and the creation of racial, sexual, and national stereotypes that superimposed a new conformity upon society.

In the late 1970s, around the time Mosse published *Toward the Final Solution*, he wrote some notes for a lecture or a paper with the significant title "Modern

Anti-semitism: Failure of the Enlightenment?"[36] In this short essay, Mosse summed up his critique of Enlightenment by referring explicitly to Adorno and Horkheimer's theories, drawing a direct connection with anti-Semitism. The argument runs as follows: the Enlightenment, with its ideals of tolerance, individualism, and most of all de-Christianization, brought about the emancipation of the Jews, who would remain loyal to these ideals. And "yet this basis of the process of assimilation was flawed from the beginning. The Enlightenment emancipated the individual Jew and left the stereotype of Judaism intact." The "mania for the classification of nature and people" was a serious cause of weakness; here lies what Mosse called the "paradox" of the Enlightenment, its mingling of tolerance and conformity. The Enlightenment "facilitated the construction of a new type of 'outsider' who is at the heart of modern anti-Semitism and what Harold Nicolson called the 'onslaught of respectability' was to enter into this creation."[37] The Enlightenment, Mosse said, failed twice. First, inasmuch as it contributed to that radical nationalism that fed on racism and "which was eventually to exploit fully the underside of the Enlightenment"; here, aesthetic factors and classification are to be held responsible for having contributed to the creation of those stereotypes that stood at the center of modern anti-Semitism, "for in the mass society which was being born people looked and did not read—reached out for tangible symbols." Second, the "Enlightenment had another conformity inherent as well: manners and morals": though respectability was not born in the Enlightenment, it had been supported by it, Mosse argued, and classification had encouraged clear divisions through stereotypes.[38] Respectability and nationalism, as Mosse would more extensively maintain in a later book, would eventually contribute in a vital way to the Final Solution.[39] Nationalism used the conformities of the Enlightenment for its own ends, and became the "chief enemy of the Jews because it did not remain patriotism. . . . [The] Jew as outsider could now become the insider with the age of emancipation but at the same time outsiderdom was ever more clearly defined and took in the whole person."[40] Racism and respectability are the main themes Mosse dealt with during the 1970s and 1980s through the two major works of this period, *Toward the Final Solution* (1978) and *Nationalism and Sexuality* (1985). From the premises analyzed above, he would develop his harshest critique of Western society and its values.

Nationalism, Racism, and Respectability

Mosse's analysis of racism and respectability can be regarded as belonging to one major concern, that of the creation of types and anti-types in bourgeois society.

Type and anti-type correspond to the division between insider and outsider, and Mosse's double outsiderdom emerged forcefully inasmuch as he focused, when dealing with racism and respectability, respectively on anti-Semitism and sexuality. At this stage, the "visual turn" comes to play a prominent role for the definition of such stereotypes, in line with Mosse's view of the modern period as an intensely visual age. Between the first and the last edition of *The Culture of Western Europe* (1961 and 1988), there emerges all the innovations brought about by the anthropological and visual turn. In 1961 Mosse traced the origins of modern racism both to the romantic vision of history and to the nineteenth century's desire for scientific verification: the search for the mythical origins of the nation went hand in hand with the contributions of the rising sciences of anthropology, philology, and phrenology and their concern with the classification of data. Racism, Mosse held, reasoned in the abstract terms of "type," but romanticism provided the emotional basis: racism was, in Mosse's words, an "emotional presupposition" where "the scientific approach joined with the contemporary romantic ideology of the true inward spirit or 'sentiment.'" Racial thought, the historian argued, "was spread into the national consciousness of Europe . . . through the introduction into the popular mind of certain images which were spread through literature and, to a certain extent, by demagogues . . . What emerged from this imagery were certain stereotypes of peoples which determined the reaction of others toward them."[41] This early view of racism was not to change in Mosse's mind, but it would be largely enriched over the years. This is the definition of racism he gave in 1988:

a world view which relates all human behavior and character to the so-called race to which the individual or the group is said to belong. The importance of racism in modern times derives from the fact that it became a *secular religion* based upon science and history. . . . From the second half of the nineteenth century and the end of the *First World War* racism increased in intensity and assumed a more clearly defined direction. Between the world wars it became linked to European political *mass movements* like National Socialism and was able to put its theories into practice over much of the continent. Racism provides a total view of the world which besides science and history also encompasses *aesthetics and morality*.[42]

A number of new elements, derived from the anthropological and visual turn as well as from the critique of bourgeois society, appear in this definition: racism as a secular religion, the role of mass movements, aesthetics, and morality.

The First World War helped to mingle and intensify these elements. As Mosse specified, "the crucial new aspect of racism after the war was its growth as a mass movement. . . . National Socialism introduced a cycle of new national festivals to celebrate the mythical racial past, sun symbolism, and those martyrs who had died for the movement. As a mass movement racism annexed the traditional Christian liturgy for its own purposes." Besides, racism acquired a moral dimension through the worship of middle-class values such as "manliness, honesty, hard work, and family life";[43] if bourgeois morality was absent from Mosse's analysis of racism in 1961, by 1988 it had come to stand at the center of his interpretation in its connection with sexuality.

Toward the Final Solution, Mosse's book on racism in Europe, appeared in 1978. This work analyzed the development of those racial ideas that paved the way for the Holocaust, and was mainly concerned with tracing the roots of racism well into European culture, regarding it not as an aberration but rather as an integral part of European culture, stemming both from the Enlightenment and from the revival of Pietism and Evangelicalism in the eighteenth century. Racism is depicted as part of the reaction against the chaos represented by modernity and industrialism, and therefore as an attempt to find order and security in immutable principles, be they aesthetic or moral. The book was welcomed with both enthusiastic approval and harsh criticism, a clear sign that Mosse's critique of the basic rationalistic Enlightenment values upon which Western society had laid its foundations was bound to arouse lively debates.[44] As he pointed out,

to find the origins of racism in the eighteenth century has filled many readers of this book with both wonder and consternation. The Enlightenment, after all, was supposed to have torn down the old superstitions which had denied men and women control over their lives. . . . The Enlightenment marked a crucial stage in the history of liberty, but to the history of racism . . . it made a different sort of contribution. . . . The Enlightenment tended to fit all human beings into the same mold—not only by its fondness for classification and its idealization of classical beauty, but also through its assumption that all of humankind shared its goals and that its moral order was part of the natural order and thus set for all time and place. This was the "underside of the Enlightenment" that limited the "science of freedom." . . . The moral order was reflected in the aesthetic values which men had been taught to embrace. . . . The result of such an aesthetic definition of the moral order was a visual message, not theory hidden in weighty books which most people could not read, but ideas and ideals which could be readily apprehended, and were therefore attuned to the coming age of the masses. . . . Racism was a visual ideology based upon stereotypes. . . . But in addition racism, as an emotion-laden ideology, took advantage of the reaction that set in against Enlightenment. Many factors came together in the making of modern racism: the underside of the Enlightenment was a crucial one and so were those movements like romanticism and modern nationalism which had their proper beginning in the age of the French Revolution.[45]

The passage quoted above is taken from the 1985 prologue to the second edition of the book, where Mosse also mentioned that "the results of the alliance between racism and respectability are analyzed fully in the body of the book, but one aspect of this alliance—the association between racism and sexuality—deserves more extensive discussion than I was able to give it when the book was written."[46] Indeed, in 1985 his *Nationalism and Sexuality* had just been published: the two works (as well as the later *The Image of Man*, published in 1996) can be regarded as part of one single project in analyzing the connections between nationalism, racism, respectability, and sexuality in modern history.

Nationalism and Sexuality has certainly been a controversial, though generally appreciated book.[47] Arthur Mitzman praised "the connections Mosse makes between social, sexual and political matters" defining them as "unique and highly important for the understanding of the modern age."[48] Steven Aschheim, Renato Moro, and Emilio Gentile noted how Mosse innovatively emphasized the collective dimension and the political implications of sexuality, thus grasping the significance of the historian's effort on a historiographical level.[49] The book also had a great significance on a more personal level. Indeed, Jim Steakley called it Mosse's "coming-out book," and Mosse himself recognized that his "preoccupation with the history of respectability . . . was driven by a sense of discovery and of my own situation as a double outsider."[50] He regarded the history of sexuality and respectability as a "forgotten history": to write about that meant "overcoming some taboos deeply ingrained in our society."[51] These words summarize his intentions when he set himself the task of exploring this field: not only was he in search of a better understanding of the cultural roots of National Socialism, he also meant to go beyond those preconceptions that had shaped his life while at the same time he sought to "break taboos . . . to get people to think."[52] His work had a deeply provocative nature, aimed at a constructive critique of bourgeois society and values.

Speaking on anti-Semitism during a seminar held in Israel in 1978, Mosse told his students: "Don't take a haughty attitude: what I am talking about is alive, not just past but the present."[53] Yet while he believed racism to have lost part of its appeal after 1945, at least as a mass movement, he saw respectability as permeating the whole of Western society.[54] Respectability indicates, he argued, not only "decent and correct" manners and morals, but also the "proper attitude toward sexuality"; and sexuality, which stands at the center of the moral concern of respectability, is "basic to human behavior." If National Socialism "provided the climax to the alliance of nationalism and respectability," Mosse's reflections took in, more extensively, the whole of modern society.[55] His main concern was society's need for cohesion in a rapidly changing world since the time of the Industrial Revolution and of the French Revolution. In his interpretation, racism and respectability came to advocate a set of manners and morals "which were thought to symbolize the cohesion and define the status of bourgeois society . . . respectability provided security through fixed social norms."[56] And despite the fact that Mosse regarded manners and morals as "part of the historical process" and therefore relative values subject to historical development,[57] their appeal was to what he believed to be a universal human tendency to order and security. Hence the unifying element of bourgeois society before and after 1945: the need for a "cement" that can provide cohesion. This is the reason why, he wrote, "control over sexuality [is] vital to the concept of respectability, indeed, to the very existence of bourgeois society." The nineteenth-century struggle to control sex, Mosse maintained, "was part of a larger effort to cope with the ever more obvious results of industrialization and political upheaval"; it was the search for a "slice of eternity," for "stability amid change," for "control in a nervous age, to find firm structures for a bewildering world."[58]

From these premises, Mosse regarded nationalism as the ideology that embraced respectability and helped spread it to all classes of the population. Like racism, Mosse saw nationalism as a visually centered ideology: through ideas of beauty derived from the classicist revival during the age of the Enlightenment,[59] nationalism built a stereotype based on the ideal of manliness and on middle-class virtues, where manliness stood for "freedom from sexual passion, the sublimation of sensuality into leadership of society and the nation,"[60] and middle-class virtues consisted of cleanliness, honesty, hard work, and family life. Through physicians, educators, and the police, nationalism helped control sexuality and provided the means to tame changing sexual attitudes into respectability. Vice and virtue became, according to Mosse, a matter of health and sickness not only of the individual, but of the whole national community. The distinction between normal and abnormal, basic to modern respectability, assigned everyone a place in society: the breaking of these rules would provoke chaos and social disorder. Mosse came to focus on the role played by physicians in this process of exclusion: "To a large extent the physician took over from the clergy as the keeper of normalcy," he wrote.[61] With particular reference to sexuality, he argued that the medical analysis of homosexuality drew a clear boundary between normal and abnormal sexuality, and in doing so, medicine justified the criminalizing of homosexuality.[62]

As mentioned above, such a pessimistic and critical view of respectability did not imply, in Mosse's mind, a thorough and unilateral condemnation: he was well aware that respectability performs a "necessary function": "While I recognized its repressive aspect, using reason rather than emotion," he wrote in his memoir, "I also realized that respectability was essential for the cohesion and functioning of society itself. . . . I came to believe that the existence of outsiderdom was built into modern society as a prerequisite for its continued existence and the self-esteem of its insiders. The insider and the outsider are linked; one cannot exist without the other, just as there can be no ideal type without its antitype."[63]

Modernity and the Great War

Paul Fussell, in his groundbreaking *The Great War and Modern Memory*, highlighted how the First World War dramatically enhanced the polarization between enemy and friend.[64] Mosse's belief in the contraposition between outsider and insider, anti-type and type, was to be strengthened by his analysis of the war: the conflict intensified this division, paving the way to further exclusion, discrimination, and eventual extermination of so-called outsiders. Despite having already placed the war at the center of his interpretation of fascism, Mosse came to realize that he had not laid enough importance on the event: he considered this a serious weakness in his interpretation and meant to rectify the situation, as he stated in the mid-1980s.[65] At this stage, he had already been interested in the conflict for a few years, but the ripest fruit of his new research area was yet to blossom.[66] The new direction of his studies was to prove, once again, highly innovative and pioneering in the field. Moreover, the insights Mosse gained from his analysis of the war and its consequences had an impact on his view of the Nazi as the "ideal bourgeois" as well.

The cultural approach to the history of the First World War made its way into historiography in the late 1960s, mostly thanks to the pioneering work of Marc

Ferro. The French historian maintained that people's aspirations deserve "as much stress as the more strictly economic or political causes," and focused on the point of view of soldiers and their psychology, as well as on celebrations of victory, the cult of the dead, and masculine solidarity among the combatants, emphasizing how much National Socialism had originated in the trenches.[67] In a series of contributions published in the *Annales* in the second half of the 1960s, Ferro had repeatedly called for a widening of perspectives and for an interdisciplinary approach, insisting on the importance of feelings and mentalities in decision-making processes, and above all on the necessity to enhance the study of audiovisual documents that could provide, he argued, precious insights into the moods and mentalities of the people.[68] Alain Besançon, another Annales School historian, pointed to the role of the historian's *imagination* in reading *visual* documents.[69]

These "suggestions" caught Mosse's attention, though it is hard to tell whether they did so directly, or simply shared a parallel and independent orientation in historiography. As coeditor of the *Journal of Contemporary History*, Mosse was looking for new approaches to history in those years, when he was in the middle of the anthropological and visual turn. He tried in vain to edit a special issue on psychology and history, while his efforts at finding new satisfactory approaches to the study of the Great War met with greater success.[70] In 1966 the journal had already published a special number on the war, "1914," which focused mostly on foreign policy issues; soon after, however, the journal sought new perspectives on the impact of the war with a view to a more complex approach. Now the focus was being shifted to the "original expectations" rather than to "a narrative account of events," as Ernest Hearst, the assistant editor, explained to a potential contributor.[71] And Mosse himself depicted the journal's effort as an attempt to view the conflict as a point of transition from the nineteenth to the twentieth century, which could be accomplished by way of adopting new approaches, such as studying the impact of the war on writers.[72] It is significant that in the correspondence related to this special issue he mentioned again the intention to explore the connections between psychology and history, and even more significant, especially in view of the aesthetic turn he was conceiving, appears to be the inclusion of Marc Ferro's insights in the volume.[73]

In his essay "1917: History and Cinema," Ferro restated his beliefs in the importance of examining visual documents, especially referring to cinematographic evidence. He did not regard this approach as a substitute to more traditional ones, rather, he considered it as an enrichment that had been widely disregarded in the past, and wondered:

Can this be attributed to an excessive worship of the written document? Or to scorn for "audio-visual culture"? Or simply to negligence? We would suppose, rather, that historians have been so trained, in past centuries, to use certain research techniques that today they sometimes fail to see that they have at their disposal documents of a new type which register contemporary events in an entirely different manner. This is very surprising in view of the fact that these archives and the cinematographic language itself allow for an additional dimension to be given to our knowledge of the past.[74]

The compilation film, he continued, "enriches our vision of the past by presenting truths which could not be conveyed through the exclusive use of written archives": it "not only possesses value as illustration, but also adds a new dimension to historical knowledge: the mental dimension which is also that of collective psychology."[75] Other contributions to the journal issue put forward similar convictions. William L. Langer, whom we have already met in his heralding of the adoption of depth psychology by historians, invited readers to go beyond the analysis of merely political issues and to keep in mind the "revival of ruthlessness and violence," the "disillusionment about progress," the "profound spiritual deflation" brought about by the conflict; Patrick Renshaw stressed the importance of "popular attitudes" and people's fears; Pawel Jasienica pointed at the usefulness of photographs as historical documents, and stressed the influence of the "psychological situation and moral reflexes" as well as of "fear" on political events, which could be grasped also through an analysis of "literary works written under the spell of immediate impressions."[76]

These examples reflect the tone set by the special issue of the journal, and it is worth referring to them at some length because they also anticipated many trends that were yet to come in the historiography of the Great War, trends that Mosse would enthusiastically embrace when he turned to a deeper analysis of the conflict. The attention to mentalities and psychology, as well as anthropological approaches, belong to what has been termed the "de-materialization of historical study, a turn towards ideas and representations as independent of material conditions" in the interpretation of the First World War, which is an integral part of the cultural approach that came to the fore in the 1970s.[77] On the wave of a rising interest in the Great War incited by the *Fischer-Kontroverse* (a debate fueled by Fritz Fischer's book on German responsibility in causing the war) in the 1960s, which took on a social and cultural bend, a number of important works appeared in the 1970s that were to give a decisive thrust to the new interpretive developments. As Modris Eksteins has observed, cultural history was still a "minor byway," and little attention had been paid to the "psychological impact" of the war, or about the "experience of war."[78] In such a context, the novelty brought about by the works of Paul Fussell and John Keegan can be better understood.[79] Fussell, focusing primarily on the British experience and yet suggesting a more general interpretation, highlighted the psychological and cultural impact of the war as a major source of modern myth, where primitivism, superstition, mysticism, and sacrality came to the surface at the apex of modernity. Keegan paid attention to the point of view of the soldier, to his perceptions, to the real "face of battle" and its psychological impact: this reality of the war sharply contrasted with the picture offered by military and political histories, which were unable to explore the deeper consequences of the conflict. Mosse greatly admired Fussell's and Keegan's efforts. In 1978 he wrote that "a cultural history of the war does not really exist, especially as it relates to the European consciousness. Paul Fussell did write *The Great War and Modern Memory* which is a superb study of the effect of the war upon the consciousness of an English elite. But it is centered on literature and on England. The work for Europe therefore remains to be done, even on a comparative basis."[80] Mosse's *Fallen Soldiers*, his book on the cult of the fallen soldier and the myth of the war experience in the aftermath of the First World War, was indeed intended as a book on "how war was built into people's lives."[81] It is therefore hardly surprising that he also held in high esteem subsequent works such as Eric Leed's *No Man's Land* and Modris Eksteins's *Rites of Spring*, and actively participated in the creation of the research center of the Historial de la Grande Guerre de Péronne, inaugurated in 1989.[82]

Mosse's own contribution took, as usual, a highly original direction as he wove two different trends in historiography into one interpretive scheme. He eclectically combined an Anglo-Saxon cultural approach to the study of the First World War (Keegan, Fussell, and later Leed) with recent orientations of part of the French Annales historians that, though they did not focus on the war, provided him with great inspiration. The history of death, or of attitudes toward death, was a rather recent development in historiography, one particularly fostered by French historians, at the time when Mosse turned his attention to it.[83] As his research notes for *Fallen Soldiers* reveal, he had shown an interest in themes such as death and burial at least since the mid-1970s.[84] It may be no accident that his copy of Philippe Ariès's *Western Attitudes toward Death* is dated 1975, and that he underlined passages on the role of the state in the veneration of heroes' tombs and on the cult of the dead as "one of the forms or expressions of patriotism" that were greatly affected by the First World War.[85] The historian David Cannadine observed in 1981 that "the impact of the First World War on attitudes to death has been underrated by sociologists and historians."[86] Two years earlier, Mosse had opened his first contribution to the cult of the fallen with these words:

> the new interest in the history of attitudes to death has not yet considered the cult of the fallen soldier. This is a curious omission, not only because this cult is central to the development of nationalism, but also because it changed men's view of death itself. Indeed, its history is, on the one hand, part and parcel of the secularization of established religion, and on the other, one factor in the brutalization of consciousness which informed the violence between the two world wars.[87]

While Fussell and Keegan had focused on the changes brought by the conflict on European consciousness, including the deep brutalization and barbarization of life, French historians like Ariès (and also Michel Vovelle) had hinted at the process through which the nation-state took over the Church in the veneration of the dead.[88] Both these approaches flourished in the mid-1970s, when Mosse's reflections on the role played by the Great War were ripening: he combined these insights, finding them most congenial to his view of the secularization process and the religious nature of nationalism and fascism, and he eventually came to regard the First World War as the climax of the fusion between Christianity and nationalism.[89] A pioneering step in this direction had been taken more than twenty years earlier by Ernst Kantorowicz, who, in a 1951 essay known to Mosse, had outlined the secularization of the idea of the holy war and the appropriation by the state of religious attributes, highlighting how "death for the fatherland" came to be viewed in "a truly religious perspective."[90] The cult of the fallen thus became, in Mosse's perspective, a central aspect of the nationalization of death.

The First World War thus emerges, in Mosse's scheme of things, as a central event where all the trends he had analyzed intertwine, gaining new momentum. As he made clear in *Toward the Final Solution* and in *Nationalism and Respectability*, the war had helped radicalize racism, camaraderie, activism, the cult of youth, and the stereotype of manliness: in short, it had provided a cauldron where all the elements that paved the way for the Holocaust were assembled.

Nationalism came out of the conflict vigorously strengthened and ready to absorb to an even fuller extent cultural attitudes heightened and revitalized by the brutalizing events of 1914–18. The war thus comes to represent, in Mosse's view, the place where the dark side of modernity showed itself in all its terrifying power, the locus where the "apocalypse of modernity" (in Emilio Gentile's formulation) occurred.[91] Fussell, as we have seen, described the war as the archetypal model for all the violence to come, as the moment where the dividing line between friend and enemy was drastically dramatized, and human life lost good part of its value.[92] Keegan, quoting the British writer Robert Kee, wrote that "the trenches . . . were the concentration camps of the First World War," and added that

> though the analogy is what an academic reviewer would call unhistorical, there *is* something Treblinka-like about almost all accounts of July 1st, about those long docile lines of young men, shoddily uniformed, heavily burdened, numbered about their necks, plodding forward across a featureless landscape to their own extermination inside the barbed wire. Accounts of the Somme produce in readers and audiences much the same range of emotions as do descriptions of the running of Auschwitz.[93]

Mosse underlined this passage in his copy of Keegan's work: in his mind, the road to modernity leading from Machiavellism to the Holocaust took a decisive turn in the years 1914–18. The mechanization of death and the numbing before it, the brutalization of society, the strengthening of nationalism and racism— all these factors favored the radicalization of the type-creating process, rendering the singling-out, the persecution, and eventually the extermination of outsiders much easier, particularly in countries like Germany, where the consequences of war and defeat made themselves felt more harshly.

Yet what did brutality and murder have to do with bourgeois respectability in Mosse's 1977 assertion that the ideal man of National Socialism was the ideal bourgeois? If an answer to this contradictory argument can be found, the growing importance Mosse laid on the war can perhaps provide one. His interpretation of modernity as a secularizing process climaxing in the Holocaust heavily touches on the issue of morality in totalitarian regimes, that is, it involves the problem of ethics and politics on a new, extremely radicalized level. The link between the extermination of the European Jews at the hands of the Nazis and bourgeois respectability becomes, in this light, a central point in

Mosse's intellectual biography. If the "ideal bourgeois" assertion could seem to be the logical conclusion of his critique of bourgeois society, partly dictated, as he himself admitted, by his "anger over the fact that the strictures of respectability had made my own life so much more difficult,"[94] it must be pointed out that his interpretation was much more sophisticated, and it deserves further analysis.

5

From Machiavellism to
the Holocaust

As a matter of fact, the new man of National Socialism was the ideal
bourgeois.

—GEORGE L. MOSSE

The emphasis on action was supposed to distinguish the new man
from the bourgeois, associated in the fascist mind with passivity,
cynicism, and decadence.

—GEORGE L. MOSSE

The relationship between ethics and politics stands at the center of
Mosse's work, connecting his early modern writings with his major
works on nationalism and fascism. His interpretation of Machiavellism
lies behind both, strengthening the "continuity of interests" and attributing a
comprehensive quality to his ideas. His books before *The Culture of Western
Europe* stressed the link between Machiavellism and totalitarianism. His later
work points to the Holocaust, which appears as the triumph of Machiavellian
ethics over individuality. Corrupted bourgeois respectability, viewed by Mosse
as one major factor leading to the Final Solution, enters this scheme as part of
that ethical dimension of public morality that had its origins in the divorce of
Christian ethics from politics. Thus Machiavellism, intended as a component
of the secularization process leading to the creation of an ethics dictated by the
state, comes to play a crucial role on the road to the Holocaust.

In 1924 Friedrich Meinecke argued that Machiavellism had led to nationalism; in 1946, speaking of the modern age but referring in particular to National
Socialism, he wrote that "politics is no longer the affair of the few. . . . This widening of the circle of politically active people multiplies the keys to the chest of
poisons in which lie the essences of Machiavellism. From being an aristocratic

affair, Machiavellism became a bourgeois affair, and finally became mass Machiavellism."[1] Meinecke also referred to the amoral consequences of reason of state; Mosse wrote in 1961 that fascism had substituted nihilism for the "eternal verities" of Christian ethics. And yet he would soon substitute, in his scheme of things, bourgeois morality for nihilism, thus linking the former to fascism, and particularly to National Socialism, viewed as the most abhorrent outcome of reason of state. In 1976 he claimed that the new man of National Socialism was the "ideal bourgeois." Bourgeois respectability, once it became "everyone's morality," came to represent that cement of society that paved the way for the Holocaust: ethical principles shared by a mass society took the form of a secularized ethos that dictated the difference between good and evil, between normal and abnormal, leading to the persecution of the outsider: in Mosse's view, modern persecution was the "new Leviathan."

As early as in 1940, in a paper on Nietzsche in which a young Mosse passionately chastised bourgeois *Gemütlichkeit*, he wrote that "the relations between National Socialism and the doctrines of Machiavelli are very close."[2] At the Stanford seminar he defined totalitarianism as "the stretching of the old ideas of raison d'état."[3] Mosse regarded totalitarianism as one possibility inherent in the idea of reason of state: Machiavelli's ethics was the beginning of a new ethics linked with modern materialism, where the state substitutes for God and becomes a new source of virtue: this brings the need to "choose between the State as a thing of morality, or the good of the individual."[4] Thus, the problem of the relationship between ethics and reason of state, raised in the early modern context of the growth of absolutism, was apt to be transferred to the new field of studies Mosse was about to enter. Machiavellism lies at the core of modernity, he wrote in 1952, in that it leads to the "fateful divorce of ethics from politics": Machiavelli "supplied the inspiration for this double standard of morality," which confronted public and private morals and "endowed the state with a moral personality of its own."[5]

The concern with the liberty and dignity of the individual passed into Mosse's study of the modern age, which was in fact its point of origin. *The Culture of Western Europe*, Mosse's first contribution to the history of the nineteenth and twentieth centuries, was written as a warning against totalitarianism and as a passionate defense of the individual. The chapter on National Socialism is an outstanding example of Mosse's beliefs and ideas. "Individualism," he wrote, "was easily sacrificed for the sake of security and for the feeling . . . that life was worth living again." This climaxed in the National Socialist "destruction of individuality"; the concentration camp was the final tool for depersonalization. The

Final Solution is "the most frightening phenomenon of this century. Multitudes of men digging their own graves . . . without resistance. . . . [T]hey docilely went to their graves because they had been utterly robbed of their individuality, they had been systematically turned into obedient robots. Surely, here is the climax of that decline of liberty in our times which has been discussed so much in these pages. This is the ultimate price paid for viewing the individual as an integral part of larger, irrational cosmic forces."[6]

When Mosse began his analysis of modern mass society, he came to focus on the role played by public morality in crushing the individual. Once again, a larger force overshadowed the individual, endangering liberty and basic rights. In the case of National Socialism, a public ethos was embodied by *völkisch* ideology, which Mosse saw as imbued with bourgeois morality. The connection between bourgeois respectability and the Holocaust was then drawn, though not directly: the "double standard of morality" allowed for a private dimension where such morality was not murderous (even though it made it easier to identify and exclude outsiders), while on a "public" level this mass ethos could easily assume more violent, aggressive traits, and the "enemy," whose stereotype had been made familiar through the diffusion of racism and nationalism aided by such respectability, could be killed in the name of an "exceptional" situation, a matter of life and death of the nation.

Mosse's interpretation of bourgeois respectability has raised lively reactions and often harsh criticism. It has been said that he partly blamed it for the Holocaust, and yet it must be pointed out that his views on this subject were not so straightforward; he viewed this linkage as a *method* of perceiving the pervasive quality of respectability, and how difficult it was to judge its influences without a provocative analysis. His views also had changed considerably by the time he turned to the study of the cultural consequences of the Great War on European politics and consciousness. It also appears that his critique of bourgeois society is not only linked with his double outsiderdom and his coming out as a Jew and a homosexual: the link between morality and politics is an integral part of his work, and therefore the historical question of "morality" and the Holocaust cannot be separated from the rest of his writings. In the light of the connection between Machiavellism and the Holocaust, the problem of bourgeois respectability takes on a new, deeper significance.[7]

Steven Aschheim, referring to *Nationalism and Sexuality*, has noted that Mosse's view of bourgeois ethics had "been almost inverted" when compared to the basic interpretation in *The Crisis of German Ideology*.[8] And yet Aschheim was aware that Mosse's later thesis "also appears in previous works but . . . is now given systematic treatment and dominant emphasis."[9] Emilio Gentile also hinted at the presence of bourgeois morality as a component of fascism in Mosse's earlier writings.[10] Indeed, though all the factors examined in the previous chapter surely affected Mosse's views, the roots of the "ideal bourgeois" are deeper. In his memoir, he wrote:

> My omission of homosexuals from my early work on National Socialism had deep psychological rather than historical roots. I was by that time fully conscious of my sexuality, but homosexuality could not be mentioned, and certainly not admitted, without paying the steep price of being driven out of one's profession (especially as a teacher) and expelled from normative society. Any success, any attempts at assimilation, at overcoming exile and statelessness, would have been in vain.[11]

Mosse's initial interest in early modern history had been linked with his need for integration, an attitude that was to last well into the 1960s; and yet in these years, as Aschheim and Gentile observed, he already took the liberty to refer to sexuality in his writings. Mosse recalled that

> homosexuals were present indirectly, however, in *The Culture of Western Europe* when I wrote about the German poet Stefan George. . . . I would be more explicit in 1964 in *The Crisis of German Ideology*, where I was the first, as far as I know, to forge a link between male Eros, the German Youth Movement, and Volkish thought. . . . I did not discuss homosexuality for its own sake; at that time it was not considered to have a history of its own which deserved to become a part of the general history I was addressing. This attitude changed by the time I wrote *Nationalism and Sexuality*.[12]

There was, however, more than that in Mosse's works of the 1960s: he already connected the middle classes with that radicalization of nationalism that would eventually lead into National Socialism when he described them as those that set the "ideology of integration," which left no place for the foreigner and "put forward a view of the state which was to have fateful consequences for the future." This idea of "integration" is that society's need for cohesion he would vividly describe in the 1970s and 1980s. Moreover, he argued that Romanticism's antibourgeois élan was eventually tamed to preserve integration: indeed, "the movement was tamed into either a Christian or a national *respectability*." In *The Culture of Western Europe*, Mosse did not further elaborate on this concept

of "national respectability," and yet his assertion that respectability and genocide could coexist in a "split personality" sheds light on how much interest he
had at the time in the relationship between morality and murder, which he
extensively discussed not only in *The Culture of Western Europe* but also at the
Stanford seminar and in *The Crisis of German Ideology*.[13] In the latter he wrote
that "bourgeois respectability and traditionalism were successfully woven into
the ideological fabric of the Nazis, who, upon assuming power, took to championing the Volkish concepts of rootedness, puritan morality, and bourgeois
tastes, ethics, and values": the Nazi revolution was antibourgeois insofar as it
was directed against the Jews in order to protect the values of the middle
classes.[14] He insisted on this idea in 1966 when he maintained that "the Nazis
substituted racism for religion, but, once more, the morality was that shared
with the rest of the bourgeoisie."[15]

Mosse's "coming out" and his critique of the Enlightenment and of respectability must therefore be only partially associated with this interpretation, which
had clearly been lying beneath the surface for a long time, however repressed.
Rather, the major change consisted in the centrality these issues came to
occupy in his work, and in the progressive radicalization of his views. As noted
above, he was conscious of having overstressed in the 1970s and 1980s the
role played by respectability in the Final Solution, and he attributed this to
his "anger" over the strictures imposed by respectability upon his own life.
There is, however, another aspect of his personality that must be accounted for:
the deeply provocative nature of his works. His shocking assertion about the
"ideal bourgeois" must therefore be analyzed in the light of the complex relations among autobiography, intellectual development, and the role of agent
provocateur he liked to play. Provocation, in his mind, was intended as a warning against the dangers of conformity and ideology: from this point of view, his
work assumes a further ethical dimension that transcends the historiographical sphere and invades the domain of politics, since he regarded history as a
profoundly political effort, as a means to political education.

Thus the Holocaust becomes the place where all major trends in Mosse's
work merge: the Final Solution is the point of arrival of Machiavellism as
embodied by the concept of reason of state; it is also the outcome of the degeneration of bourgeois society's identity mechanisms, and of the process of depersonalization of humanity through ideology and conformity; finally, it is the
extreme consequence of the "faithful divorce of ethics from politics," and as a
consequence a constant warning against politics devoid of ethics. The two main
tenets of Mosse's earliest writings, the problem of the state and the question of

political morality, converge in his interpretation of the Holocaust with added meanings. The road leading from Machiavellism to the Holocaust is thus extended in its ethical dimension, and Mosse's 1954 statement that modern persecution is the "new Leviathan" appears now under a new light. To understand the development of Mosse's interpretation of respectability does not only involve the implications of the turn to liturgy and of his critique of bourgeois society: it goes to the heart of his view of modernity, and to grasp the ethical-political nature of his whole work.

Nihilism and the Holocaust

Most of the criticism of Mosse's view of the bourgeois side of National Socialism is based on two arguments: first, that bourgeois morality has nothing to do with violence and mass murder; and second, that Mosse ended up overemphasizing the bourgeois elements in his dialectical formulation of the antibourgeois revolution. And yet, though it cannot be denied that Mosse's own "anger" toward respectability affected his views (which Mosse himself had admitted), it must also be pointed out that his interpretation underwent significant changes over the decades, changes that were brought about by the development of his historiography and by the opening of new fields of research. In fact, apart from the assertion in the interview on Nazism about the new man of National Socialism as the ideal bourgeois, there is coherent evidence in all his other writings from the early 1960s through the late 1990s that points in a different direction. The antibourgeois nature of the bourgeois revolution ran along the divide between private and public morality, reflecting Mosse's ever-recurrent concerns about the dangers inherent in conformity, which he regarded as the obvious result of an ethics dictated by the state.

Mosse's early-1960s belief that Machiavellism entailed a "divorce of ethics from politics," supplying the "inspiration for a double standard of morality" and endowing the state "with a moral personality of its own," is profoundly connected with his view concerning the bourgeois aspect of National Socialism. The core of this connection lies in the previously quoted passage when Mosse argued that Rauschning's concept of the "revolution of nihilism" was valid as far as it referred to the "transformation of values which fascism accomplished. The ethical norms of society were no longer related to intrinsic standards or to eternal verities. Instead, duty to the fascist state and to its leader became the criterion of moral behavior. Where ethics had once been linked to Christian ideas, however vaguely defined, now they were linked to the fascist ideology of struggle and history."[16] This crucial passage touches upon the whole question of Nazi morality in Mosse's work, in its connections with Machiavellism: the Florentine's ideas paved the way for the State as the source of a new morality that was not linked to Christian values, but in large part to nihilistic ones such as will to power, action, and violence; the fascist state then was the expression of nihilistic values embodied in the nihilistic streak present in fascism.

Fascism was, in Mosse's interpretation, a movement of bourgeois youth oriented toward a critique of bourgeois values and society: it was not a revolution "in social or economic fact," but rather a "revolution in ideology" and thus an "ideal bourgeois revolution," in that it left class structure intact; fascism was "an anti-bourgeois revolution which the bourgeoisie could fully accept."[17] Fascists agitated "against bourgeois morality," Mosse wrote, and "yet this transformation of values did not penetrate the realm of personal morality. Here fascist movements tended to be prudish, to accentuate plain living as a part of the concept of the democratic leader. To this prudishness Hitler added a sexual Puritanism which was not found in Mussolini." Mosse then fully separated public from private morality in fascism: "Fascism retained a bourgeois morality in personal relationships but abandoned it in the dominant public ethic to which private ethic had, in the last resort, to be subordinate."[18] Public ethic was therefore a result of that "transformation of values" inherent in fascism's nihilism, while private ethic rested on "bourgeois morality." To understand this private–public dichotomy is basic to the understanding of Mosse's interpretation of National Socialism and the Holocaust.

Here the question of fascist dynamism and its taming needs to be addressed. Since fascism was, Mosse held, dialectically torn between activism (informed by nihilism) and bourgeois morality, during the struggle for political power this activism could be allowed free play. Yet once the fascist state was established, the activism needed to be tamed, and directed toward new targets. This is how Mosse explains, for example, the slaughter of the SA in 1934: a constraint had to be put on their social impetus, their restless activism, their doubtful morality. Thus, activism was tamed inside the state, or the nation, and unleashed on the outside: "Fascism was committed to an internal order based upon its complete dominance and an international disorder which would enable the dynamic to expand once the system had been established at home." Hence, the "paradoxical result" of the transformation of bourgeois values brought about by nihilism: family life and rootedness were retained; yet "bourgeois values as a whole were rejected in the struggle for domination." Nazism has a "split personality. . . . But this seemingly fantastic moral contradiction was really part of the movement's ideology. Bourgeois respectability and genocide could be fused into one, for neoromanticism was accompanied by the 'Revolution of Nihilism.'"[19] What emerges here is a view of fascism, and particularly of National Socialism, where the antibourgeois side is fully underlined, and the Final Solution is not linked to bourgeois morality; rather, it is part and parcel of the nihilistic streak of Nazism, where nihilism had separated the public ethic it pervaded from the private ethic, which remained informed by bourgeois values.

At the Stanford seminar, Mosse devoted a whole session to the "problem of National Socialist morality."[20] In this very significant contribution, he associated such values as honesty, probity, work, and family life with traditional bourgeois morality, and contrasted them with National Socialist morality: the concept of "struggle" was alien to bourgeois morality, Mosse said, and so was instinct, that racial instinct against the enemy that National Socialism had substituted for conscience (conscience being a bourgeois feature, he held). Violence, an antibourgeois value, could be applied against the enemy: "The race and its morality could only survive, and so could the nation, if towards the enemy this morality did not apply." Here Mosse drew a parallel with Christian ethics: the question of Nazi "split personality" is a "very ancient problem in our civilization, that of the permissible exception." Reason of state is such an example, Mosse said, implicitly hinting at Christian casuistry, but in National Socialism two new factors emerged. First, the contrast between mass murder and the Aryan bourgeois morality: for the Nazis, the contrast was mitigated by technology, which "depersonalized the act of murder, just as the murdered had already been depersonalized into stereotypes." Second, the disbelief typical of our civilization that such a thing could happen; Eichmann or Höss were labeled as "criminals," and National Socialism as "a movement of criminals taking off from the shaken morality of the Free Corps. The point is, of course, that their morality was not in daily life a criminal morality, but a common bourgeois morality, and that this raises the question of the relation of such a morality to exceptional situations. The Nazis built upon a western tradition and pushed it to the extent of a double morality: towards enemy and towards the friend."[21]

Mosse held that "all the *völkisch* ideology was intensely bourgeois on the moral level," and that only the ideology of race was that part of the morality that "allows for the 'exception.'" When confronted with the opinion that brutalization had nothing to do with bourgeois morality, that this was part of a "new morality," Mosse replied that "this means the widening of the exception, the struggle with the enemy, the execution of orders. I don't think they were brutalized in their private lives": perpetrators were "new men" when they kill; at home, they retained a traditional morality. There were, Mosse continued, two kinds of people involved in the Final Solution: those with a split personality, and the SS who has "sloughed off the bourgeois morality. These are the minority, these are just emerging"; Himmler belonged to the latter, but at the same time he shared the most traditional *völkisch* ideas. This led Mosse to assert that "before 1939, and I'm quite sure about that, it was emigration of Jews which was wanted by many Nazis, though perhaps never by Hitler himself." At the end of the session, Mosse significantly felt the need to specify that "I was not condemning bourgeois morality. . . . But I think the point is again how much exception was allowed. . . . I don't call this attitude bourgeois morality but the exception."[22]

At Stanford, Mosse hinted at the depersonalization through technology and stereotypes. Two years earlier, in *The Culture of Western Europe*, he had referred to the Aryan ideal type and to the importance of its outward appearance through which an ideology can become "tangible"; the "type," he said, was confronted with and opposed to the individual.[23] Therefore, "what the Commandant of Auschwitz was murdering were types that lacked all individuality to him. Murder, in these circumstances, was depersonalized and completely remote from that Aryan life whose ethics coincided with those of the bourgeoisie."[24] This passage clearly separates, once again, bourgeois morality from murder: the latter is absolutely nonbourgeois, it derives instead from the logic of the "permissible exception" and from that depersonalization furthered by racism through the creation of "types" and by technology. As a consequence, the creation of types with its process of depersonalization, technology, and the longing for authority paved the ground for the Holocaust. Mosse's stand for the dignity of the individual is fully reflected in this interpretation: National Socialism represented the "destruction of individuality," and the concentration camp was the final tool for depersonalization.[25]

The main themes in Mosse's work are now inseparably welded together: the concern with the liberty of the depersonalized individual and the conformity entailed by the ethics of the state appear here in their connection to the road leading from Machiavellism to the Holocaust. The anthropological and visual turn and the changing attitude toward the Enlightenment and bourgeois society were to widen these perspectives: the former brought Mosse to discard the concept of nihilism and to view fascisms as religions; the latter led him to emphasize the role played by bourgeois respectability in paving the road to the Holocaust. The Final Solution in Mosse's interpretation was, up to the mid-1960s, a by-product of the nihilistic streak of National Socialism that had its origins in the stretching of Machiavellian ethics. One question now arises: once Mosse discarded nihilism, how did he deal with the problem of the Holocaust? The double morality entailed by nihilism, which had perpetrators respond to bourgeois morality in private life and to a nihilistic state ethics in the struggle against the enemy, was to undergo a significant change when Mosse began to develop his critique of modern society.

Respectability and the Holocaust

In 1968, in the same article where Mosse definitively discarded the concept of nihilism, he also asserted that the fascist revolution "got mired in the very middle-class values which it was supposed to fight": no spiritual revolution was implemented, no new man was created.[26] Instead, the bourgeois values that Mosse had attributed to the *völkisch* ideology eventually had the upper hand. Mosse's harsh critique of respectability through the 1970s and 1980s appears to confirm that, in his scheme of things, bourgeois morality had taken over nihilism's role in paving the way for mass murder. Emilio Gentile has criticized Mosse's interpretation, arguing that "in his latest writings Mosse had gone so far as to assert a substantial identity between bourgeois respectability and fascism, an identity that historically, in my opinion, stood in sharp contrast to the very essence of fascism, with its culture, with its concept of man, of politics, of the national community, and of the totalitarian state." Following Mosse's definition of fascism as an "anti-bourgeois revolution of the bourgeoisie," continues Gentile, "one ends up ignoring the congeniality of anti-bourgeois polemic in fascism's fundamental attitudes that belonged to the essence of its origins and of its militaristic and collectivistic nature. . . . The identification of fascist respectability with bourgeois respectability underestimates the role the anti-bourgeois spirit played in fascism." There is instead, Gentile concludes, "a substantial difference between *respectability in civilian clothes* and *respectability in uniform,* and we must keep in mind that the latter, rather than the former, was the ideal of fascist morality. The new man of fascism was not the incarnation of traditional 'respectability in civilian clothes,' which was the ideal of the individualist and liberal bourgeoisie, but of the new 'respectability in uniform' of the collectively organized man who was raised according to the principles of a militarist and belligerent morality which was the antithesis of everything that was typical of the 'respectability in civilian clothes' of the bourgeoisie."[27]

Despite the considerable weight he laid on the bourgeois side of Nazi morality, Mosse did not identify bourgeois and fascist respectability as the same thing;
nor did he ignore the antibourgeois polemic in fascism's attitude. As early as
in 1961 Mosse had stressed the antibourgeois nature of fascism, especially (but
not exclusively) as far as it concerned attitudes toward the enemy. In 1963 he
contrasted bourgeois morality with National Socialist morality and mass murder when exceptional situations had to be faced, elaborating his views about the
"double morality." In 1977 he described the perpetrators as "victims or products of the *corrosion* and *corruption* of middle-class values through National
Socialism," thus attributing mass murder to the "corrosion and corruption" of
bourgeois respectability rather than to bourgeois respectability itself.[28] While at
the Stanford seminar he had stated that he was "not condemning bourgeois
morality,"[29] he surely did so after his "coming out" of the 1970s and 1980s, but
his critique was directed at the role played by respectability in the singling-out
of outsiders and the creation of types, and did not apply directly to the extermination process. His later works, especially those focused on the cultural consequences of the Great War and on the history of sexuality, show that he was fully
aware of the antibourgeois side of National Socialism, and of the deep differences between Nazism's "new man" and the "ideal bourgeois."

In *Nationalism and Sexuality*, Mosse emphasized how a "new challenge to
respectability" was posed by the Great War and by the antibourgeois attitude
of the generation of 1914; he stressed fascism's tendency to continue the war
in peacetime and remarked how this attitude "might easily leave respectability
a casualty on the battlefield." And yet, he argued, fascisms shared a "basic need
to maintain respectability" in order to "tame the putschist mentality" and
please the bourgeoisie: only when the struggle for power had ended could bourgeois morality become predominant. He maintained that there was a deep
ambiguity "based upon the Nazi wish to be dynamic and virile but also respectable, to attack the bourgeoisie for their formlessness and hypocrisy while nevertheless maintaining bourgeois values."[30] It was nationalism and racism, in
his scheme of things, that pushed respectability to the extreme, and "it would
be wrong to judge respectability simply by the use racism or fascism made of
it. One must not assess a system of thought and behavior solely by its abuses."[31]
His focus went then to the "abuses" of respectability, not to respectability itself,
echoing his previous assertion that perpetrators were products of the "corrosion and corruption" of bourgeois values.

The Image of Man (1996), Mosse's analysis of the political role of masculinity
in modern society, goes even further in separating bourgeois respectability

from fascist respectability.[32] Highlighting the influence of the Great War in exalting the "warrior elements of masculinity" that informed the "new fascist man," Mosse clearly said that "the emphasis on action was supposed to distinguish the new man from the bourgeois, associated in the fascist mind with passivity, cynicism, and decadence."[33] He linked this emphasis with the warlike features of the "new man":

> the new fascist or National Socialist man, then, was not so new after all. Most of his basic traits were shared with normative masculinity, but he extended them, giving them an aggressive and uncompromising cast as an essential tool in the struggle for dominance. There is, surely, a world of difference between the clean-cut Englishman, the all-American boy, and the ideal member of the SS. Yet all shared essentially the same masculine stereotype with its virtues, strength, and aesthetic appeal, whether it was restrained, nonviolent, and even compassionate, or uncompromising, ready to do battle by all means at hand. Fascism, and especially National Socialism, demonstrated the awesome possibilities inherent in modern masculinity when it was stripped down to its warlike functions.[34]

The new man of fascism and the traditional (liberal) ideal bourgeois share the same stereotype, but there is "a world of difference" between them—there is no confluence between the two in Mosse's mind. From this perspective, it is clear that Mosse was aware of the difference between *respectability in civilian clothes* and *respectability in uniform*, and that the latter was the ideal of fascist morality. Mosse ended up stressing the "warrior qualities of masculinity," and believed that it was racism that "brutalized them and transformed theory and rhetoric into reality."[35] In fact, his interests since the 1970s—racism and the Great War—consistently affected his views on the role played by respectability, adding new nuances and enriching his interpretation. While bourgeois respectability did not lead directly to mass murder, it surely helped to create the outsider stereotype, to draw a line between "normal" and "abnormal," it provided nationalism and fascism with a "cement" that gave society cohesion, but it was not identical with fascist respectability.

The background for the analysis of the "new man" is the Great War. In 1990 *Fallen Soldiers* was published. Examining the "myth of the war experience," the book is an analysis of the political impact of the mass death experienced during the war, which drastically changed attitudes toward death itself. This process led to the brutalization of nationalism and racism, opening a new phase in their histories where violence could become a means to any end. The myth of the war numbed its reality, it transcended and transfigured it; war and violence became associated with sacrifice in the name of a higher cause: the "cult of the fallen soldier" was now the central element of the civic religion of nationalism. The period of the French Revolution was once again crucial: it is here that a new kind of soldier, linked to the nation and ready to sacrifice for it, was born. After the First World War, a revolution aimed at the creation of a "new man" who was supposed to stand against bourgeois society seemed at hand. The brutalization of life and politics brought about by the war rendered violence against the enemy acceptable, numbing the reality of death and leading to the dehumanization of the enemy. It was the Great War, Mosse had argued as early as in 1975, that led to Holocaust morality.[36] Years later he stressed once again, and more organically, the link between the war and the Final Solution: the slaughter of 1914–18 had brought to many a numbness in the face of mass death, brutalization, an enhanced sense of camaraderie, and a heightening of the concept of masculinity, as well as a total lack of compassion at the service of one's cause.[37]

This picture of Mosse's thought is further enriched by his writings and his lectures on the new man, a theme that interested him in the 1980s and 1990s. Here the connection between the "new man" and Gentile's concept of "respectability in uniform" is strong, and the distance from the "ideal bourgeois" grows bigger. In Mosse's interpretation, the war had enhanced the ideal of manliness as well as its militarization: these were strongly antibourgeois values that entered into the idea of the fascist new man. The fascist ideal of manliness, Mosse held, was "built upon the Great War," and wartime camaraderie "was for all of fascism the paradigm of society and the state." Mussolini's new man "lived in a state of permanent war," which was exemplified by the "constant wearing of uniforms," the continuous marches, the emphasis put on physical exercise, on camaraderie, and on discipline: the "warrior elements of masculinity" were central to fascism.[38] The "new man" was a soldier whose idea was forged during the Napoleonic Wars, and the Great War had only hardened the stereotype. Ideas of force, violence, aggression, battle, decisiveness, and lack of compromise informed this man who was a "fighter and warrior."[39] He spoke a "soldierly language" and appeared preferably in military uniform and in action: the duce as warrior revealed the "true nature of the 'new Italian.'"[40]

Mosse emphasized the distinction between the ideal of a "new man" and the bourgeois on several occasions, stressing the constant tension between manliness and bourgeois respectability.[41] The "new man," be it the ideal of the right or of the left, or even the "new Jew" envisaged by Zionism, was supposed to set himself against the establishment, to oppose bourgeois complacency and self-satisfaction, to reject the lifestyle of settled society and the so-called weakness of bourgeois family life.[42] However, all this remained confined to the ideal and never became reality: the "new man" was never created, despite the efforts made by fascism, National Socialism, or communism to breed him. Indeed, Mosse spoke of the "development inherent in the idea of the 'new man' . . . but in reality the role of the 'new man' endowed with all the proper middle class virtues remained predominant—and even in fascism he did not follow the image of the nietzschean superman."[43] Mosse drew a distinction between the new man of the bourgeoisie and the revolutionary (fascist, nationalist, or communist) new man, basing it on the concept of manliness. The former corresponded to the liberal model, according to which manliness meant bodily health, good looks, hardness, and sexual purity. In England, Mosse said, rules like chivalry, fair play, or the protection of the weak counted: the nationalist new man broke them instead. In Germany, despite some exceptions, the new man had "sharper edges" than did his English counterpart.[44] The "revolutionary" new man aimed at the extremes, an attitude, Mosse said, that had no place in bourgeois society. Again, he focused on the distinction between private and public morality: in private life, the image of the true man did not "concentrate upon war or aggression."[45] Thus, the ideal remained unfulfilled, and this happened because bourgeois respectability tamed the new man's dynamism, which threatened to undermine bourgeois morals. The morality of the new man then became "nothing else but the bourgeois morality," and Mosse could speak of the "embourgeoisement of the 'new man.'" However, though respectability tamed the new man's warlike qualities, this "embourgeoisement" remained a "complex process": hard features of masculinity were indeed retained, but this happened only in public life, and when the enemy was involved.[46] Traditional, liberal bourgeois morality applied to the private sphere of life, while in the public domain this morality was easily corrupted in that process of self-definition of society Mosse had focused on in his works on the social dimension of sexuality and respectability. Indeed, he said, masculinity sharpened before the enemy, and yet these are "figments of the imagination, flights of fancy, while in reality the masculine image seemed to have lost some of its contours as it ceased to be representative of movements or nations and became part of daily life." Thus, the "hard side" of masculinity was retained only in the public sphere (movements or nations) and not in the private one (daily life).[47]

This picture of the "new man" is considerably different from the "ideal bourgeois" Mosse had depicted in the 1970s. Now the "new man" is profoundly antibourgeois, but since the fascist revolution "got mired in the very middle-class values which it was supposed to fight," this new man was never created, and bourgeois respectability had the upper hand. However, things change when a man is confronted with exceptional situations: here the dialectic inherent in the cohabitation of bourgeois and antibourgeois values in fascism fully emerges.[48] The Final Solution becomes the stage where the Nazi "split personality" plays its part. If in the 1960s Mosse contrasted the "bourgeois side" with the "nihilistic side" of this personality, now the dichotomy is between the bourgeois side and its corruption: society's need for cohesion, racism, fascism, and the Great War had stretched respectability to the extremes, disfiguring its original traits and eventually transforming it into something fairly close to Gentile's concept of *respectability in uniform*. Once again, the individual had been crushed by the needs of larger entities: from the necessities of the state to those of society. Mosse's work becomes again a warning against the strictures imposed by conformity, and respectability, be it "in uniform" or "in civilian clothes."

Reconsidering the "Ideal Bourgeois"

Mosse's analysis of bourgeois respectability has been at the same time illuminating and controversial. Criticisms of his approach have been raised by sympathetic observers such as Emilio Gentile, Steven Aschheim, or Saul Friedländer, and yet all of them recognized the great contribution offered by Mosse's insights into the historiography of fascism, nationalism, racism, and gender. The very nature of his approach, based on a very intuitive attitude and aimed at analyzing the "wider" mechanisms of ideologies in history rather than focusing on detailed accounts, surely led him to inaccuracies and paradoxes. The "ideal bourgeois" definitely belongs to this aspect of his historiography. Despite the fact that a distinction appears in Mosse's work between "respectability in civilian clothes" and "respectability in uniform," Gentile's observations show how he could emphasize one aspect or another of the problem according to his intellectual and personal context. The "ideal bourgeois" statement was pronounced in the 1970s, when his critique of "respectable society" was in full swing, and his "anger" toward respectability was being unleashed; it was only with the study of the brutalization process brought about by the Great War that Mosse toned down his critique. Friedländer noted how Mosse's "grand scheme" about

respectability did not take into consideration, when faced with the Final Solution, the different categories of "outsiders" (Jews, gypsies, homosexuals, the
mentally ill), and argued that Mosse remained "right in general terms," but
difficulties subsist when the analysis becomes more specific; he also hypothe-
sized a strong connection between Mosse's arguments and the anxieties of
an outsider who had perhaps been more shaken by his past than he himself
realized.[49]

Steven Aschheim has underscored how Mosse's connection between bourgeois respectability and genocide contains "suggestive insights," and yet it
calls for "more detailed discussion" since "bourgeois *Sittlichkeit*, after all, while
often illiberal, was seldom genocidal and it is surely in the processes of corruption and radicalization that such a transformation was engendered." Racism too, Aschheim held, is not necessarily murderous, and the German variant
ought to be examined more carefully. Nonetheless he stressed, like Mosse,
the corruption and radicalization of bourgeois values, and he wrote of the
"dual moment within Nazism itself: the combination of bourgeois and radical
anti-bourgeois elements," and he concluded by asserting that "precisely in the
combination of and tension between these elements, in the fusion of the conventional and the extraordinary, could Nazism transcend middle-class morality
at the same time that it embodied it. Whatever future research will bring, however, Mosse has performed a valuable service in alerting us to these important
middle-class dimensions of the Nazi experience. . . . [Mosse] has demonstrated
that such stifling discourses of normative conformity are also potentially murderous."[50] Aschheim's "dual moment" is nothing else than Mosse's concept of
"double morality," of the "Nazi split personality": it is a concept reminiscent of
that put forward by Robert Jay Lifton in his *The Nazi Doctors* under the term
"doubling," an unconscious psychological principle that he described as "the
formation of a second, relatively autonomous self, which enables one to participate in evil": it was a "mechanism by which a doctor, in his actions, moved
from the ordinary to the demonic."[51]

Aschheim's observations, however, also point to a fundamental aspect of
Mosse's analysis of respectability: the constructive debunking of myths through
deliberate provocation. Commenting on the reactions to *The Holy Pretence* in
1958, he wrote: "I have come to the conclusion that the only book worth reading
is one which puts forward new ideas, however controversial they might be. We
need much more of that sort of thing. . . . I may be wrong, but I wrote *The Holy
Pretence* and everything else I have done on the Puritans also to stimulate some
debate," a belief he certainly held on to in his later works.[52] As he wrote in his

memoir, "I like to provoke, to break taboos, but purely theoretically, as a myth destroyer, to get people to think—not in the practice of daily life."[53] Seen in this light, his 1976 assertion about the "ideal bourgeois" appears to be a provocation; and still it was a provocation dictated by the "anger" he felt at the strictures respectability put upon his life, which undoubtedly is the reason for his (sometimes overstressed) critique of respectability. This "anger" must have been particularly influential in the 1970s and 1980s, but then it must have, at least in part, faded away, leaving room for a more constructive critique of bourgeois respectability. In the revised version of "Toward a General Theory of Fascism," published twenty years after the original (1979), he took the trouble to modify the final part, highlighting how "settled, respectable society" rejected the idea of killing the "asocials," and how "the Nazis felt that the extermination process had to be kept a dark secret."[54]

This whole debate over Mosse's interpretation of respectability must not, however, divert attention from the great contributions his work has given to different fields of historiographical research. His reflections on the morality of the perpetrators have anticipated, and often inspired, themes and issues that have occupied historians since the 1980s: as Robert Nye has written, Mosse's "pioneering use of race and sexuality as categories that permitted the national community to define itself in the process of identifying racial and sexual 'others' has been widely taken up by historians and anthropologists of nationalism, sexuality, and gender and by students of both imperial and postcolonial societies."[55] And yet the study of nationalism, sexuality, and gender were, to Mosse, ways of approaching from a different angle the problem of totalitarianism in its fascist version, and of the Holocaust. Fascism has been a constant presence all through these pages, and it is now time to turn extensively to Mosse's interpretation of this phenomenon, which occupied him from the 1960s through the 1990s. Fascism is the necessary background against which his whole work must be analyzed: the anthropological and visual turn, the dark side of modernity, the whole road leading from Machiavellism to the Holocaust is marked by the historian's reflections on fascism, which stimulated the most important methodological turns, animated Mosse's ethical thrust, and represent the immovable hinge around which his whole historiographical project has been woven.

6

The Missing Link
The Nationalist Revolution

The frequent contention that fascist culture diverged from the
mainstream of European culture cannot be upheld. On the contrary,
it absorbed most of what had proved to have the greatest mass appeal
in the past.

—GEORGE L. MOSSE

The traditional nationalist myths and slogans, the use of the
nationalist liturgy, the constant and unremitting appeals to national
solidarity and greatness informed all of fascism, and should have
made nationalism's importance obvious—perhaps too obvious to
many historians of the movement who have not bothered to analyze
nationalism itself as a belief-system.

—GEORGE L. MOSSE

I believe we can speak without exaggeration of a "Mosse revolution" in
the historiography of fascism.

—EMILIO GENTILE

George Mosse's contribution to the historiography of fascism has been
widely praised as well as deeply influential. Emilio Gentile has written
of a "Mosse revolution in the historiography of fascism, a revolution
consisting first of all in the novelty of his method of analysis"; in the history of
nationalism and of mass politics, he wrote to his colleague and friend in a letter, "historiography can be articulated as 'before Mosse' and 'after Mosse.'"[1]
Stanley Payne has defined Mosse a "pathbreaker in fascist studies," and his
interpretation "one of the clearest, most forceful, and most cogent."[2] The noted
Italian historian of fascism Renzo De Felice, republishing in 1983 his book on

the interpretations of fascism, openly admitted his intellectual debt toward Mosse. In the new introduction to his book (the first edition was published in 1969), De Felice praised above all Mosse's belief that fascism ought to be understood "in the anthropological sense," thus viewing it as an "attitude toward life."[3] What De Felice considered one of Mosse's most essential contributions was the realization that ideological or rationalistic interpretations, be they Marxist or liberal democratic, did not suffice to explain the nature of fascism: a different approach was needed, based on the belief in human irrationality.

Without distancing itself from these convictions, Mosse's interpretation of fascism never remained static: it evolved over the years in tune with the methodological innovations in his historiography; moreover, as happened with other fields he investigated, autobiographical factors left a mark on his views, modifying his perspectives and bringing about new ideas and beliefs. Three main stages can be singled out in his interpretation: first, the analysis of fascism as a revolution in ideology; second, fascism interpreted from a cultural perspective through the study of nationalism, employing the interpretive category of the "new politics," a result of Mosse's anthropological and visual turn; third, fascism viewed as a nationalist revolution, a concept that embodied the previous two and related to Mosse's growing concern with nationalism as the dominant ideology of modernity beginning with the French Revolution. What he called the "missing link"—that is, fascism viewed as a nationalist movement—brought him back, figuratively, to Meinecke's original formula of the development leading "from Machiavellism to nationalism," thus adding a further nuance to the road "from Machiavellism to the Holocaust" as racism itself came to be regarded as a form of "heightened nationalism."

From the beginning, Mosse's approach was highly original: as he did so often in his work, he confronted "conventional wisdom" and insisted on the centrality of ideology in fascism. He stressed the revolutionary nature of a right-wing phenomenon at a time when most historians restricted the concept of revolution to left-wing movements. Moreover, he inserted fascism into the mainstream of European culture, and he put forward the idea that there had existed a "Nazi culture" worthy of serious historical consideration. The anthropological and visual turn broke new ground again as he came to view fascism as having many characteristics of a religion, and analyzed its liturgy, its myths, and its symbols: this approach paved the way for the elaboration of a general theory of fascism, which occupied him through the 1970s. Starting in the early 1980s, he did not specifically address his work to new theoretical interpretations of fascism,[4] but came to view fascism, as Emilio Gentile put it in his accurate analysis of the development of Mosse's interpretation, "only as part of wider phenomena such as nationalism, racism, the myth of the war experience, sexuality and respectability, and the construction of masculinity."[5] To be sure, nationalism became the center of his interests, eventually embodying all the above quoted phenomena: racism and fascism came to be viewed as extreme forms of nationalism, where bourgeois respectability and the cult of masculinity were absorbed into the worship of the nation, completing its fusion with Christianity through the cult of the fallen soldier and the myth of war experience.

Mosse's interpretation of fascism, perhaps his best-known historiographical contribution, has been exhaustively analyzed in recent years.[6] Fascism has been a constant presence in this study, and therefore it will suffice here to briefly summarize the main tenets and the development of his interpretation, laying a particular emphasis on one aspect that has not received the attention it deserves: the view of fascism as a nationalist revolution. To emphasize this aspect of his interpretation means to coherently weave together the numerous factors that interacted in its formation, including turns in methodology and growing political involvements. It also sheds additional light upon Mosse's rapprochement with nationalism and the new politics, which he came to regard with a more benevolent eye. Here the study of nationalism becomes indissolubly intertwined with Mosse's Jewish identity, something that certainly played a role in his ever more emphatic approach to modern mass politics.

The cultural interpretation Mosse put forward was based on empathy as a historical tool, on the belief that one must see the world "through the eyes of its faiths": this approach led him to formulate his definition of fascism in cultural terms. Despite the fact that he did not neglect the importance of economic, social, and political factors, he certainly felt the urge to stress those cultural factors that most historians had completely disregarded. This attitude raised criticisms toward an approach that focused almost entirely on the cultural dimension. However, most historians would argue that today's concept of fascism is largely based on his revolutionary interpretation, which has opened new vistas and greatly contributed to the study of political religions and of the connections between fascism and sexuality, as well as of the analysis of fascist political style, culture, and ideology.

The Fear of Ideology

During the Stanford seminar Mosse made clear from the outset that he meant to analyze fascism "from the ideological point of view." His approach met with harsh criticism. When he expressed his view that "I just don't think you can explain the policy without the ideology which such men came to accept," Paul Baran, a Marxist professor of economics, replied: "I say we can. You say we can't"; the dispute ended with Mosse's statement, "we're necessarily dead-locked." And yet he found all the criticism he received "fruitful," and ended saying: "I'm glad you have shot down—somebody asked me whether I felt like the Christians among the lions, and I don't know how they felt."[7] This episode is paradigmatic of the state of historical research on fascism in the early 1960s, and shows how Mosse's approach went against the grain of most scholarship.

Indeed, in the early 1960s historians had paid little or no attention to the ideological dimension of fascism. Two exceptions were Fritz Stern's *The Politics of Cultural Despair*, which dealt with the intellectual origins of Nazi ideology (yet without attempting an interpretation of fascism), and Ernst Nolte's *Three Faces of Fascism*, which examined fascism from a new perspective, considering it a "metapolitical phenomenon" with an ideology of its own that affected social and political realities.[8] When Mosse laid out the basis of his approach, he insisted on the inadequacy of liberal and Marxist political and economic theories: the former were, in his opinion, driven by a "fear of ideologies" that caused historians to dismiss ideas, and ideas, Mosse held, "can be weapons";[9] the latter lingered in a sterile economic approach. All through the 1960s he held to the belief that to grasp the essence of fascism meant to embrace a wider concept of politics, detached from rationalist attitudes and focused on the empathetic understanding of the irrational forces in history. Here he echoed the emphasis Benedetto Croce, Friedrich Meinecke, and Georg Lukàcs had placed on irrationality,[10] although he set such insights, especially after the anthropological and visual turn, within the scope of a general theory of fascism, and into a wider and more elaborated anthropological perspective. As he wrote in *The Nationalization of the Masses*, "whether a liturgy can be regarded as still more basic than social forces depends upon our view of human nature. A belief in man's inherent goodness and rationality, for instance, would view the new politics as mere propaganda and manipulation."[11] Referring to Franz Neumann's *Behemoth*, he argued that

> scholarship dealing with fascism has suffered through the application of a concept of political thought . . . modeled on the ancients' belief that true politics must be constructed in a reasonable manner: an emotional belief system does not constitute a legitimate political theory. That is why you will find in so many books fascism described as eclectic, lacking a system of ideas (Franz Neumann)—once again fascism seen from a liberal viewpoint, not from its

own . . . Such an approach can never understand how fascism could rule by consensus and enthuse so many respectable citizens.[12]

In the drafts for the introduction to *The Fascist Revolution*, Mosse repeated that approaches like Neumann's excluded the ideological factor because they saw fascism as "incompatible with any rational political philosophy": Neumann was a man of the Enlightenment and a rationalist and so failed to grasp the essence of fascism.[13] The misunderstanding of fascism, in Mosse's opinion, lay in such an "optimism about the good and rational nature of 'the people,'" a "heritage of the enlightenment which had long ago informed so-called pro-gressive political thought."[14]

Mosse regarded politics, as it has been noted, as being "more than the formal political process."[15] This conviction was at the heart of his approach to fascism since the early 1960s, when he criticized historians who tried to understand fascism "from traditional points of view taken from our own political organi-zation."[16] Indeed, in *The Crisis of German Ideology*, he insisted that ideas must be given "serious consideration," and that *völkisch* ideology was far from being "apolitical": "this type of thinking," he wrote, "is only apolitical if 'politics' is restricted to a description of traditional forms of activity and belief."[17] The pri-macy of ideology in fascism, he stated in 1966, implies a "fundamental redefi-nition of politics."[18] Fascism looked at from the liberal point of view—that is, from the perspective of parliamentary government—cannot be understood, because it regarded itself as a myth opposed to classical political theory, and this was the reason Anglo-Saxon historians "have such a difficult time discussing it. They're always looking for logical, consistent political theory."[19] Mosse thus viewed politics as a process that did not focus exclusively on the rational under-standing of the mechanisms of parliamentary government or of the decisions of leaders: instead, it included powerful irrational forces that motivated both the leaders and the masses.

From this perspective, to grasp a phenomenon like fascism—that is, a "flight into ideology, an irrational ideology"—required more than a merely rationalistic approach: this, however, did not preclude the possibility of rational analysis, because "if we penetrate into it, it will become apparent that even this emphasis on feeling has a dialectic, a logic, built into it which did make it a coherent world view. But we cannot measure it with a measuring rod taken from the eighteenth century or even our supposed American belief in rational-ism. Otherwise, like Shirer, we will call it a hodgepodge, and never understand its appeal."[20] Here empathy and the awareness of the irrational side of human nature become necessary for the understanding, for example, of *völkisch* ideology, whose premises "are presuppositions which you have to accept emotionally, intuitively, irrationally," he said at Stanford.[21] This was the reason why, as he wrote in one of his first contributions to the history of National Socialism, the intellectual origins of the movement were still unexplored territory, and it was therefore necessary to investigate it as an ideology, because "historians have ignored this stream of thought as too *outré* to be taken seriously. . . . Yet such ideas made a deep impression upon a whole nation. Historians who have dismissed these aspects of romanticism and mysticism have failed to grasp an essential and important ingredient of modern German history."[22]

The stress on the ideological dimension brought Mosse to develop a negative attitude toward the concept of totalitarianism. To be sure, this attitude was always ambivalent: he certainly used the concept, particularly in his earliest works, but on the whole, he rejected it.[23] In *The Culture of Western Europe* and in some previous writings and speeches, Mosse adopted the term "totalitarianism" in describing the erosion of the individual's dignity brought about by fascism and communism, connecting it not to the Enlightenment as Jacob Talmon would have it with his concept of "totalitarian democracy," but rather to the romantic and neoromantic aspiration to the totality of life. Indeed, in a lecture Mosse identified totalitarianism with opposition to parliamentary government driven by a "hunger for wholeness," by the longing for community.[24] Above all, Mosse rejected the political implications inherent in the concept (the liberal connotations it acquired in the Cold War context) and its lack of ideological differentiation between fascism and Marxism. As he said in the interview on Nazism, "I am opposed to the word totalitarianism because it seems to me an untrue generalization, or to put it better, it is a typical generalization from a liberal point of view. . . . This point of view uses totalitarianism as a general catch phrase for anything that is antiliberal." Totalitarianism, he continued, is "a typical Cold War phrase."[25] The anthropological and visual turn brought about an even harsher critique, since Mosse, despite establishing a connection between fascism and the French Revolution (thus coming close to certain aspects of Talmon's view), definitively rejected such words as "propaganda," "manipulation," and "terror": when he elaborated his concept of the new politics, he could not agree with previous approaches such as Hannah Arendt's. As he made clear in an essay,

the fear of mass politics has informed the use of the concept of totalitarianism ever since Hannah Arendt's *The Origins of Totalitarianism* (1951). Such a fear has blocked consideration of the new politics as more than just a means of manipulating the masses for the purposes of keeping the dictator in power. The contention of Montesquieu that tyranny depends upon the isolation of the tyrant from his subjects was accepted by Hannah Arendt and her successors. The very opposite prevails in modern times. The dictator must reflect the wishes and hopes of his people and must share their attitude towards life. The dictator and the people do not confront each other. Instead, the new political style mediates between them, taking the place parliament occupies in the liberal state. Through rites and festivals, myths and symbols, the people are drawn into active participation. To millions this was the true democracy and the use of the pejorative term 'totalitarianism' merely serves to obscure this fact.[26]

The anthropological and visual turn with the idea of new politics definitively dismissed the concept of propaganda, further convincing Mosse of the inadequacy of the category of totalitarianism, a path he had been treading since he sought to understand fascism from the point of view of ideology.

The Building Blocks of a General Theory:
Fascism as Revolution

In the late 1980s Mosse stated, "I do not believe in a long-time German *Sonderweg* [special path] which is more peculiar than the special characteristics of any nation."[27] This view appears to contradict the general structure of *The Crisis of German Ideology*, written in 1964: here Mosse emphasized the role of anti-Semitism in German culture, which attributed to National Socialism its unique character, turning it into an "anti-Jewish revolution." The revolt against positivism, stemming from romantic and mystical ideas, took in Germany a "special turn," and Germany differed from other European nations because of a "profound mood, a peculiar view of man and society which seems alien and even demonic to the Western intellect."[28] However, writing a new introduction to his great work thirty years later, Mosse argued that the book wasn't meant to provide an argument for a German *Sonderweg*, and certainly not to support the "from Luther to Hitler" thesis.[29] If there is little doubt that *The Crisis* never supported such a thesis, it seems reasonable to argue that it was inclined toward a "German uniqueness" interpretation, to use Jürgen Kocka's formulation.[30] However, the conclusion of the book added new light to the issue, in that Mosse combined the peculiarity of German history with the embryo of a general theory of fascism on a European scale. Indeed, he referred to "German fascism," to a "unique variety" of fascism that developed in that country and that differentiated it from other fascisms in Western Europe. This meant to imply that there was a European fascism, and to affirm the "uniqueness" of the German movement, Mosse wrote, "is not to deny that all fascisms had certain features in common."[31]

These statements were in line with Mosse's interpretation in the early years of his investigation. In *The Culture of Western Europe* he included fascism as part of European "culture," which was highly original in itself. He traced back the roots of fascism into European traditions (romanticism, the longing for wholeness and organicity as against atomization of parliamentarism, elitism, and the cult of leadership) and clearly argued that there were "diverse manifestations" of fascism that shared a "similar base in a common redefinition of freedom. Freedom meant not individual liberty but a mystical union with the whole."[32] Stressing the importance of ideology for fascism (on the basis of nationalism, activism, syndicalism, and corporatism), he discerned a common "positive" emphasis, thus chastising the view of fascism as an exclusively "anti" movement: indeed, fascism was "a revolution in ideology" based on different ideological bases, but still sharing common traits.[33] National Socialism and Italian Fascism shared indeed "a common world view" in their rejection of the bourgeois system of values and in the championing of an organic view of the state based on "contempt for representative government," an "urge for strong leadership" and authoritarianism, as well as an emphasis on the nihilism embodied in action and struggle.

At the Stanford seminar, he made a first attempt to elaborate a working definition of European fascism. First, he highlighted the revolutionary nature of the movement, comparing it to the other great revolution of the century, communism; second, he stressed again the ideological basis of fascism, defining it as a "serious movement of a revolutionary nature," an "ideological kind of revolution" with "ideological sincerity," in contrast to those who viewed it as a mere quest for power or as an anti-movement.[34] Fascism was a "flight into ideology, an irrational ideology" that defined humanity through aesthetic or spiritual criteria; it was also an "ideal bourgeois revolution, a revolution in ideology and not in social or economic fact."[35] From these premises, he formulated two definitions of fascism:

[Fascism was] a general European movement. It was a revolutionary movement which has its immediate origins in the rejection of the materialism of the *fin de siecle*. Because it centered its revolt against it, it turned toward the aesthetic, romantic, literary, the 'myth,' rather than towards the concrete and practical means of change. It became a displaced revolution, an anti-bourgeois revolution, which the bourgeoisie could fully accept. It came to objectify itself through the search for new forces of organization (I have mentioned the Bund) and ideals of beauty which became stereotypes. . . . It combined the Nitzschean ecstasy with its taming.

I would say that fascism, fully blown, is a mass movement, a mass movement which organized the proletariat . . . in a mass form, as an explicitly revolutionary movement. But a revolution which does not mean to and does not change the existing class or social structure.[36]

The bases laid at Stanford were not to change over the years. In *The Crisis of German Ideology* he insisted on the revolutionary nature of fascism, on the existence of "common elements" shared by "various fascisms," and on the stress on ideology rather than on social and economic realities.[37] In "The Genesis of Fascism" (1966) he emphasized the need to investigate the common traits of the various national movements, highlighting how they all "sprang out of a common set of problems and proposed a common solution to them."[38] The "primacy of ideology" in fascism made it a "revolution of the spirit" aimed at overcoming the unrootedness and alienation of the industrial age. Through activism, the cult of youth, and the identitarian nature of communities, fascism fostered an organic view of the world based on irrationality, which brought about a "fundamental redefinition of politics," now viewed as an "attitude toward life."[39]

Over the course of the 1970s, Mosse made the greatest efforts at posing the "building blocks" of a general theory of fascism. As a consequence of the anthropological and visual turn and of the critique of the Enlightenment and respectability, he associated middle-class values with the fascist "new man" and stressed the aesthetic nature of the movement, laying additional emphasis on its mass character and its religious traits. In 1979 Mosse wrote a long essay elaborating on a "general theory of fascism." Here he wove together all the ideas he had been working on for the previous two decades. He argued that "any general theory of fascism must be no more than a hypothesis which fits most of the facts": his was an attempt to bring together some of the principal "building blocks for such a general theory—there seem to be enough of them to construct at least a provisional dwelling." He emphasized the coherence of fascist ideology and its place in the heart of European culture, arguing that "the frequent contention that fascist culture diverged from the mainstream of

European culture cannot be upheld. On the contrary, it absorbed most of what had proved to have the greatest mass appeal in the past."[40] Singling out the main common traits shared by fascisms, he offered a view of fascism that was, in its basic traits, not too far from that given at Stanford sixteen years earlier:

> The building blocks for a general theory of fascism now seem to lie before us. Fascism was everywhere an "attitude towards life," based upon a national mystique which might vary from nation to nation. It was also a revolution attempting to find a "Third Way" between Marxism and capitalism, but still seeking to escape concrete economic and social change by a retreat into ideology: the "revolution of the spirit" of which Mussolini spoke; or Hitler's "German revolution." However, it encouraged activism, the fight against the existing order of things.[41]

The idea of fascism as a revolution is the most recurrent in Mosse's writings. The concept is expressed time and again, and it became the title of the collection of essays on fascism he assembled in the late 1990s, *The Fascist Revolution*. In his works, fascism appeared as a "revolution in ideology"; as an "ideal bourgeois revolution, a revolution in ideology and not in social or economic fact" (hence Mosse's concept of fascism as a "displaced revolution," a revolution that did not turn toward the concrete and practical means of change and was therefore an "anti-bourgeois revolution which the bourgeoisie could fully accept"); as a "revolution of the soul" aimed at the creation of a "new mind, a new man"; as an "anti-Jewish revolution"; as a "revolution of the spirit" that "thought of itself in cultural, not economic terms"; as a "revolution of the Right," or a "right-wing revolution."[42] Such views derived, Mosse argued, from an interpretation of fascism based on a cultural point of view: not only the left is revolutionary once revolution "is defined as the forceful reordering of society in the light of a projected utopia."[43] This projected utopia was soon to become, in his eyes, the nationalist myth, and fascism would come to be regarded as being part and parcel of the vaster ideology of nationalism.

The Missing Link:
Fascism as a Nationalist Revolution

The 1960s are not only the years of the anthropological and visual turn: they are also the setting in which Mosse became increasingly involved in exploring his Jewish identity. These two factors considerably affected his interpretation of nationalism, which was to become the main source of concern in his writings.

National Socialism, the "ghost come alive" of the 1960s, would retain, by the mid-1970s, only its "psychological base,"[44] and by 1993 Mosse could say that Germany was immune from it.[45] At the same time, he began expressing his worries about a nationalism that was "growing in strength" and was "still the principal integrative force among peoples and nations."[46] In the late 1990s, at the time of the Balkan wars, he worriedly stated that "a renewed interest in nationalism as collective self-understanding through a belief system has surfaced only recently, nearly half a century since the end of the Second World War, in the midst of clear signs that nationalism in Europe was alive and well— not merely a patriotism . . . but the integral nationalism which had found its climax in fascism."[47] He feared that a serious crisis of parliamentary government could reactivate the forces of nationalism: while *völkisch* thought (which he saw as "German nationalism at its most extreme") was "no immediate threat" in Germany, he wrote in 1997, "it is latent in all modern nationalism."[48] His worried reflections on the fate of the nationalist ideology in Europe were certainly inspired by his commitment to the Israeli reality of the 1970s and to Zionism. It is not a mere coincidence that his focus on nationalism went hand in hand with his growing awareness of his identity as a Jew, and he passionately studied the history of Zionism in an attempt to find a balance between extremist nationalism as it had manifested itself in Europe and a humane patriotism that he saw reflected in the thought of early Zionists. However, the realities of Palestine had pushed Israel, in Mosse's view, toward the adoption of an ever more aggressive nationalism that further drew his attention to the problem.[49]

Mosse had been concerned with the problem of nationalism from the outset. As early as in 1957 he viewed it as a "mood," as a "mode of thought" rather than as "something that can be analyzed through political or economic factors alone."[50] In the 1960s he focused on what he called "integral" or "radical" nationalism, that is, on the ideology that would eventually lead to National Socialism.[51] He saw it as a reaction against the industrial revolution, as a "flight from reality" in search of genuine roots in a rapidly changing world.[52] Romantic idealism, at least in Germany, would transform the nation into a "cultural fact," pushing it toward racism and leading it "directly into National Socialism."[53] Nationalism, in Mosse's interpretation, implied the "vision of a better life," "a means of self-identification and belonging": his was a "psychological analysis" that led to a cultural interpretation.[54] However, though he argued that "for all fascism, nationalism provided the basic appeal," he also claimed that, at least in Germany, the party's nationalism proved "phony" in the end, and "eventually the racial element completely swamped even the nationalist element."[55] This view was to undergo deep changes: in 1985, Mosse asserted that "racism was a heightened nationalism."[56] While still in 1966, in the article on the genesis of fascism, nationalism was hardly mentioned, the anthropological and visual turn brought about a radical change in his interpretation. In a speech broadcast in 1973 by the Australian Broadcasting Corporation, he said that there can be no fascism without nationalism;[57] interviewed on Nazism in 1976, he asserted that there could be no fascism in America, due to the absence of an integral nationalism; in the 1979 essay on the general theory of fascism, he held that fascism became ever more nationalist, and he spoke of the "fascist nationalist myth," concluding that "in the last resort, all fascisms were nationalisms."[58] Such a complete overturning was the consequence of the methodological turn and of one of its major outcomes, the concept of the new politics.

Mosse's interpretation of fascism as a civic religion passed through the analysis of nationalism. More specifically, the anthropological and visual turn led to a view of politics imbued with liturgical aspects: this was a "new politics," the new political style of the age of the masses, whose development Mosse saw epitomized in the history of nationalism as a mass movement. In the early 1970s the historian published and lectured extensively on nationalism, an effort that culminated in *The Nationalization of the Masses*, a study on how the ideology of nationalism was brought to the masses, involving them in the political process and paving the way for the National Socialist political style. It is therefore hardly surprising that, by the time he published again, and explicitly, on fascism in 1979, nationalism stood at the center of his interpretation.

The concept of new politics was also a tool Mosse used to further his cultural approach to the study of history. His critique of "traditional" analyses found in the new politics the much-needed category to fully formulate his views. As he repeatedly stated in his writings of the time, the "new style of politics was closely linked to a political theology" that people reared in the traditions of liberal or socialist thought could not grasp: their search for logics in the workings of modern politics led them to "forget that men have been captured more often by theology than by the canons of classical political thought. . . . [T]he liturgical drama . . . stood outside any sustained social, political or economic analysis."[59] Fascism and National Socialism, he held, "cannot be judged in terms of traditional political theory"; their political style "has little in common with rational, logically constructed systems."[60] And National Socialism (along with fascism) as the climax of the development of the new political style could therefore not be understood "apart from the long history of nationalism as a mass movement."[61] This meant that the fascist political style was built on a long tradition with which many people felt in tune. This explained the roots of consensus and put the role played by terror and propaganda in a different perspective.[62] Politics in the modern age ought not, Mosse argued, be seen merely as a process separating the rule of the masses from the rule of representatives: "in reality a secular religion mediated between people and leaders, providing at the same time the instrument of social control over the masses."[63] Public festivals and national monuments merged into a new political style "based upon a secularized theology and its liturgy," in which people could believe to be participating in the self-representation of the nation, thus objectifying their general will.[64] This style was not exclusively linked to nationalism, Mosse specified: it was "integral part of modern mass society . . . the political style of mass politics and mass democracy"; it was "one wellspring of modern politics."[65] This allowed Mosse to operate with a category not limited to the German context he dealt with: it offered a wider perspective on a European scale and it strengthened the basis for a general theory of fascism through an additional element shared by various fascisms. And yet his focus on the nationalist use of this political style heavily affected his interpretation of fascism: now he came to regard it as "an integral part of modern nationalism in the age of mass politics."[66] In an unpublished paper titled "Fascism as a Nationalist Movement: The Missing Link," written in all probability in the 1980s, Mosse closed the circle and drew his newly acquired insights to their extreme consequences. The study of nationalism provided the key for the understanding of fascism as a mass movement. In this essay, he described the political culture of fascism as "an expression of modern nationalism" and nationalism as "always the decisive factor," putting forward a "general definition of fascism as the child of European nationalism."[67] In the 1990s he built upon these convictions, claiming that fascism "must be seen as nationalism reaching its climax,"[68] "as an integral element of European nationalism," and as "a system of belief based upon heightened nationalism."[69] In the last resort, nationalism was the bedrock upon which all fascist movements were built: thus, Mosse merged his view of fascism as a revolution with his new belief, coming to the conclusion that "finally, fascism must be understood as a nationalist revolution."[70]

The World through the Eyes of Its Faiths

Mosse's interpretation of fascism as a revolution derived from the very manner in which fascism viewed itself as a movement: in order to grasp the appeal of fascism and its popular genuineness, he made full use of historical empathy. He often claimed that the historian has to "see the world through the eyes of its actors and its institutions": in fact, he argued that "the cultural interpretation of fascism opens up a means to penetrate fascist self-understanding, and such empathy is crucial in order to grasp how people saw the movement, something which cannot be ignored or evaluated merely in retrospect."[71] This led him to adopt a terminology directly derived from the fascist vocabulary. Giuseppe Bottai had defined politics as an "attitude toward life," as did Mosse; similarly, he noted that National Socialists called culture a "basic attitude toward life."[72] Mosse's concept of culture was not confined to ideas or popular culture: he defined culture as a "totality, as indeed the fascist movement sought to define itself."[73] And despite his concerns with individual liberty, he asserted that fascism was not anti-individualistic, because the "longing for a true community" it advocated was based on the idea that in this community "the individual could truly fulfill himself."[74] He defined fascism as a "revolution of the spirit," just like Hitler had done, and even the expression "nationalization of the masses" was taken from *Mein Kampf*. This appropriation of fascist terms and concepts is also reflected in Mosse's view of humanity and of human nature: indeed, the fascist view of humanity, he wrote, was "both irrational and conservative," and so was Mosse's.[75] In fact, his methodology absorbed without prejudice ideas stemming from intellectuals who had laid important bases for fascism, like Sorel and Le Bon, and even from those who had sympathized or been involved in it, like Jung or Eliade. Mosse was not afraid to adopt interpretive categories that he found useful, no matter where they came from, as long as they helped him to a better understanding of a historical phenomenon.

Mosse believed in liberal values, and yet this did not prevent him from criticizing liberal attitudes when they, in his opinion, represented an obstacle to historical understanding, or to an effective political strategy. His attitude toward the concept of "democracy" is an enlightening example in this regard. Mosse separated antiparliamentarism from being antidemocratic: fascism, in his view, had a deep democratic thrust, and it had fed on the neoromantic search for new forms of government that implied a direct participation in political life. Fascist views of the leader saw him as a "democratic leader, a primus inter pares": such ideas were part, Mosse argued, of a long-established tradition of popular democracy.[76] Moreover, the new politics added to the romantic idea of democracy a new impetus that stemmed from the idea of popular sovereignty. In fact, Mosse argued to understand that apparently antidemocratic movements like fascism were instead looking for a truer form of democracy meant to gain a "fresh view upon the anti-parliamentary alternatives," alternatives that, "longing for increased democracy," envisaged a "collectivist society which was anti-capitalist and anti-bourgeois, but was opposed to Marxism."[77] The concept of democracy, according to Mosse, could not be understood solely in its "representative" facet as embodied by parliamentary government: there is "another idea of democracy which has moved millions," which originated in the popular sovereignty of the Jacobins Talmon analyzed in his study on "totalitarian democracy" and, ultimately, in Rousseau's dream of "the people governing themselves," not mediated by representative governments, but by "games, festivals, ceremonials, communal mass action which we may call symbolic, but which were real enough to many people." In short, he maintained that Italian fascism and National Socialism were "not antidemocratic movements": they simply built upon "a different definition of democracy[;] . . . the monopolizing of the concept of democracy by one of its strands falsifies history and puts us in danger of repeating the same mistake apparently built into our liberal heritage. Here fascism and Bolshevism are not dead but can still serve to teach us a lesson."[78] Again Mosse criticized exclusively political or social approaches to the study of fascism such as those adopted by liberal historians, which prevented them from a deeper understanding of fascism. Equally important, this critique also touched on liberal politics in the West: on more than one occasion, Mosse advocated the need to adopt the new politics to involve the masses in the political process, since people need to participate in it, and the new politics, when correctly balanced with the use of reason and a critical mind, is essential to the harmonious workings of a modern state.[79]

Mosse's adverse reaction to monocausal explanations of fascism such as those from a liberal or Marxist perspective led him to explore the cultural self-representation of the fascist movements. This developed into a cultural interpretation that, however, did not mean to neglect social, economic, and political realities. All through his writings, Mosse stressed the importance of the rational and the organizational traits of fascism. At the Stanford seminar, he emphasized how the masses were organized according to the theories of Le Bon and Pareto;[80] in The Crisis of German Ideology, he showed how völkisch ideas were institutionalized, which allowed for their success;[81] in The Nationalization of the Masses, he rejected monocausal interpretations of fascism, and wrote that "liturgy is one crucial factor among others."[82] The rationality inherent in organization was expressed, in Mosse's view, by the objectification of ideology through discipline and organization, and through myths and symbols. "The irrational," he wrote in 1964, "is made concrete through rational acts within the terms of its own ideological framework."[83] Political pragmatism operates in this way, springing from irrational beliefs channeled into liturgy, and an ideology is systematized, as emerges from *The Nationalization of the Masses*. Sorel's myth, he explained on another occasion, "was the overt rationalization of the deepest feeling of the group": myth itself, the irrational side of the dialectic myth-reality, can be a rationalization.[84] Nationalism as an ideology is also a rationalization that integrates and organizes the masses: here the nationalization of the masses becomes their rationalization. This led Mosse to say that "liturgy and ritual would not have succeeded without organization at the base."[85]

Emilio Gentile, despite his great admiration for Mosse's work, has argued that his cultural approach runs the risk of becoming one of those single-key interpretations Mosse himself had harshly criticized. From the point of view of a cultural historian, Gentile states that

> in the elaboration of a general theory of fascism the primacy of ideology is to be preferred to the primacy of the economy or the social structure. . . . [T]he irrationality of fascist culture was politically effective not only because it fascinated the masses with myths, symbols and rites but because it was joined to the rationality of the organization and the institution. Without the rationality of the organization and the institution, without being a party and a regime, without becoming the ideology of a modern state, fascism would have probably remained an ideology at the margins of politics and history, confined to the fields of intellectual snobbery.[86]

Although, as shown above, Mosse surely was aware of the importance of rationality and organization in fascism, there is no doubt that, as Gentile remarked, he almost entirely focused his attention on the cultural aspects and on the irrational premises of modern mass movements, and his "building blocks" for a general theory rely exclusively on fascist self-representation. On the one hand, Mosse's goal was to shift the focus to the overly neglected cultural dimension; on the other, he became aware of the dangers inherent in this attitude and wrote in his memoir that "perhaps I have seen the world too much through the eyes of its faiths, but then the times in which I have lived have been dominated by belief systems, by an almost fanatical devotion to civic religions, and there are few credible signs that this will change."[87]

Gentile has also argued that Mosse "almost entirely left out" of his concept of fascism the "militarization of politics" and the "sacralisation of politics."[88] The militarization of politics has been discussed in chapter 5, and the sacralization of politics deserves further attention. In his memoir, Mosse described his book on the nationalization of the masses as a study of the "sacralization of

politics," borrowing the formulation from Gentile's *Il culto del littorio.*[89] It must
be said, however, that *The Nationalization of the Masses* is rather a study of the
aestheticization of politics.[90] And yet Mosse certainly was familiar with the idea
of the "sacred" in politics. Thomas Nipperdey's seminal article on national
monuments and German nationalism put forward the concept of *Sakralisie-
rung der Nation* (sacralization of the nation); Mircea Eliade referred to "sacred
spaces," be they the nation or the temple.[91] There is, moreover, a significant
number of references to the "sacred" in Mosse's works from the early 1970s on:
in "Mass Politics and the Political Liturgy of Nationalism" there are numerous
hints at the sacredness of symbols like the flame or the tree, and of the cultic
spaces used for national festivals; in *The Nationalization of the Masses* Mosse
argued that the "sacred" symbolized the "urge . . . to transform the political into
the religious," and that the Nazis tried to win the "monopoly of the sacred" as
against the Church; while in the first edition of *The Culture of Western Europe*
the word "sacred" did not appear, in the editions following the anthropological
and visual turn it is widely used in the reviewed paragraphs; finally, in his 1982
lectures on European intellectual and cultural history, he said that a modern
person, in order to cope with unpalatable things, develops a "tendency toward
sacredness," and sacralizes things.[92] Therefore, it can be said that Mosse was
aware of the "sacred" nature of modern politics, and though he never dealt with
it explicitly, it was a theme that touched on his reflections on secularization.
The view of fascism as a nationalist revolution, and of nationalism as a secular
religion, which stood at the center of Mosse's work since the 1970s, represents
a typical example of Mosse's ability to anticipate trends and themes without
elaborating much on them: from this perspective, with his analysis of the secularization process brought about by modernity, he can be considered with no
hesitation one of the pioneers in the study of political religions, which was to
thrive after the 1990s.[93]

As it has been stated above, his interest in nationalism derived also from his
growing involvement in Israeli politics and in Jewish culture. The emotions
raised in the masses by the cult of the nation with its liturgy, myths, and sacred
symbols constituted, in Mosse's interpretation, one of the principal reasons for
fascism's success. Thus, it would appear that nationalism was, in his eyes, the
archenemy, the ideology that dominated the modern age and, through its alliance with racism and bourgeois respectability, paved the ground for the Holocaust. And yet just like the new politics was eventually regarded by Mosse as a
vital tool in the life of modern democracies, so nationalism too could be a positive integrative force, capable of providing men and women with a strong sense

of identity and security, without necessarily taking on radical and intolerant traits. Nationalism in the form of patriotism, purged of its most aggressive features, could be an opportunity. Like the liberal patriotism of the early nineteenth century, Zionism in its early stages possessed (in Mosse's view) a positive potential that could be directed toward humanistic, even cosmopolitan goals. The unearthing of this potential became, to Mosse, part of the "true mission of Judaism."

7

The "True Mission of Judaism"

My journey to Jerusalem began in slow motion, picked up steam, and soon became one of the most meaningful involvements of my life. This does not mean that I approved of the Israeli government and its policies; I was a supporter of "peace now" from the very beginning. But when the state was in mortal danger I rallied to its defence.

—GEORGE L. MOSSE

If we do not succeed in giving nationalism a human face, a future historian might write what Edward Gibbon wrote about the fall of the Roman Empire: that at its height moderation prevailed and citizens had respect for each other's beliefs, but that it fell through intolerant zeal and military despotism.

—GEORGE L. MOSSE

In the course of this study one of the dominant and recurring elements has been Mosse's critical attitude: toward those mass movements whose irrationality diminished the individual, and toward those historians who clung to an excess of rationality and dismissed the irrational side of history. In opposition to what could seem the generalized critical attitude of an outsider fighting against social and academic strictures there is, however, a bright side in Mosse's work, which informed his writings and allowed for a certain optimism in the face of his deep historical pessimism. On a methodological level, the study of ideology and the anthropological and visual turn offered a positive contribution to historiography through the recognition of the importance of irrational factors in the dynamics of history. With regard to the themes Mosse dealt with, and particularly the new politics and the history of nationalism, a less pessimistic view gradually surfaced, which eventually led him to consider both as useful means to improve the workings of parliamentary democracies. This bright side as opposed to the dark side (as Mosse himself defined them) emerged once a stronger relationship with Israel was established, affecting his beliefs about mass politics and nationalism: his involvement in Israeli cultural and political life brought the historian face to face with the more emotional side of his personality, exposing his own sensitivity toward the appeal of identitarian and communitarian mechanisms, and reorienting his criticisms in a more constructive and less fatalistic direction.

Giving a speech at a Jewish organization, Mosse once said that he felt "perversely a kind of gratitude" for his Jewishness: if he hadn't been a Jew in Germany at the time of Hitler, his life would have taken a totally different turn, and he would have just remained, to use his own words, a "spoiled brat."[1] There is, however, much more about his relation to Judaism: his being a Jew not only affected his personal life, leading him into exile and away from his life as the scion of a rich and influential family. Indeed, his experience in Jerusalem represented, as he put it, a "milestone in my personal and intellectual growth."[2] On the one hand, the anthropological and visual turn originated, at least in part, from the Jewish intellectual tradition that was brought to his attention by his restless students in the 1960s; on the other, the consequent view of fascism as a form of heightened nationalism was abundantly fuelled by the growing awareness of his identity, by his involvement with the Hebrew University in Jerusalem, and by the emotional impact Jewish nationalism had on him.

Mosse's first works regarding the Jews came about as early as the late 1950s, but they were all studies in German history and did not deal with the history of Judaism in its own terms; even his definition of National Socialism as an "anti-Jewish revolution" had little to do with Judaism itself. Only in the late 1960s did Mosse begin a more comprehensive, personal, and committed investigation into his own past. His family had been part of a traditionally liberal-oriented German Jewish elite that pursued political, cultural, and artistic goals though their newspapers: "The last voice of liberalism, tolerance, and pluralism in Germany," Mosse wrote, "is to be found in Jewish newspapers and writings in the Third Reich."[3] And yet these liberals failed, in Mosse's opinion, to grasp the essence of mass politics and irrationality: their idealism was too detached from political realities, and their attachment to culture and *Bildung* blinded them to the reality of political necessities. They were chasing, as he put it, a "noble illusion."[4] His father, Mosse recalled, did not take Hitler seriously, believing that he belonged to the humoristic supplement of the newspaper: he was imprisoned in his "Enlightenment worldview," and tried to fight irrationality logically, an attitude shared by "many, perhaps most Jews of his standing."[5]

These considerations were taken by Mosse as a warning, and just as he made the attempt to balance rationality and irrationality in the writing of history, so he sought to combine them in practical, political terms, in accordance with his belief in history as a political endeavor. Hence his conviction that idealistic values need to go hand in hand with the necessities of reason of state, in line with Meinecke's assertion that one needs to "soar to the skies and yet keep a firm foot on earth."[6] Here Mosse drew generously from his early modern works on casuistry, reasserting the centrality of The Holy Pretence in his intellectual biography when he came to advocate a "new Casuistry" capable of assimilating nationalism and the new politics in order to fulfill the human need for a fully furnished house, a house that Mosse the "eternal emigrant" had never had, and perhaps found, at least intellectually, in his Jewish roots. Just as the Divines of his 1957 work had done, men and women in the contemporary world should seek a balance between ideal and reality, coopting the identitarian, positive energy of the new politics and of nationalism, and turning it toward humanistic goals. The experience in Jerusalem forced Mosse to confront feelings similar to those he had critically analyzed in his studies on fascism: as he admitted, "when I saw the new Israeli Army or attended the swearing-in of the paratroopers on Masada, my heart beat faster."[7] His goal became the finding of a balance between reason and irrationality, and he came to believe that this was possible as long as emotion remained "tempered by reason."[8] In this way, nationalism could be humanized and cleansed of its chauvinistic, aggressive component. Mosse believed he had found these ideas embodied in the thought of early Zionists and in the tradition of the Bildung. And yet Israel itself, confronted with the realities of war and survival since its foundation, appeared to him to be losing its way and plunging into the currents of radical nationalism. To unearth the original roots of Zionist ideology and to build a Jewish identity based on cosmopolitan and humanistic values was the method, he believed, to confront resurgent nationalistic radicalisms. This was not only, in his eyes, for the education of the Jewish people: rather, it represented a universal message for all humanity, and was what he termed "the true mission of Judaism."[9]

George Mosse, Zionism, and the Reality of Israel

One day, when the Mosse family still lived in Berlin, the young Gerhard expressed the wish to become a rabbi. His father had the chauffeur take him to that part of Berlin where the nonassimilated Jews from Eastern Europe lived and then asked him if he wanted to become like them. Gerhard, rather impressed, replied that he did not, "of course."[10] This example is telling of the mentality shared by a large part of the German Jewish liberal bourgeoisie at the time of the Weimar Republic: Mosse's father, who lived by liberal Enlightenment ideals and values, considered anything irrational, including religion, a "humbug," "without substance, nothing but smoke and mirrors," and to him orthodox Jews wearing prayer shawls had something of the Middle Ages about them.[11] Such an environment could have hardly been affected by Zionist ideals: the members of the German Jewish bourgeoisie conceived of themselves, as Mosse has put it, as both German Jews and Jews in Germany, without seeing any contradiction in that.[12] "I did not even know about the existence of Zionism until I had left Germany," Mosse wrote in his memoir, and such a "lack of interest was typical for the vast majority of German Jews; indeed, my family remained hostile toward Zionism all of their lives. . . . I myself never doubted that I was German." And even though, as 1933 approached, Mosse slowly became more aware of his Jewishness, this "did not mean that I felt myself any less German."[13]

During the Second World War, when Mosse was already in the United States, he gave and attended anti-Zionist speeches, motivated by the belief that England had to be helped win the war, while the Jews in Palestine were becoming increasingly hostile toward the British, who were, at the time, trying to contain Jewish immigration in the area. "I was no Zionist, in any case, but instead thought that planting a Jewish colony in Palestine was asking for trouble," Mosse recalled.[14] However, he admitted, he felt "happy that such a refuge existed," which was a "sign of refugee mentality," though he had even supported settlement in Ethiopia.[15] In 1947, when an agreement was reached under the aegis of the newly born United Nations about the division of Palestine into two states (one Jewish and one Arab), Mosse fiercely opposed this solution. In his opinion, the split would only have the effect of balkanizing the area: the two states would not remain "static," Arabs and Jews would "want to expand into each other," and would call for help from America and Russia, thus creating a situation very much similar to that in the Balkans at the time. The only way out, Mosse said, would be a unified Arab–Jewish state under the trusteeship of the United Nations.[16] Mosse had by then accepted the idea of a Jewish settlement in Palestine and now leaned toward a two-state solution of the problem. Though he was no Zionist in 1948, he supported the Jewish State out of an emotional involvement affected by the shadow of the Holocaust and by the fact that seeing Jews fighting was an exhilarating "experience" to him.[17]

In 1951 Mosse made his first trip to Israel and was deeply impressed. From then on, his attitude would change. Despite the fact that he traced his deep involvement with Israel back to the 1960s and 1970s, he had already stated in the early 1950s that the newly born state of Israel represented a new model of individualistic socialism that could be compared to the Yugoslavian example in its difference from and opposition to the soviet system. Both countries embodied a new, enthusiastic form of nationalism that represented the hope for a different society. The kibbutz experience was a symbol for this, and Mosse contrasted it with Israel's party politics that sought to suffocate this more traditional view of politics in the name of reason of state. "Israel is here to stay, another new man has arrived to take his place in our civilization," he emphatically stated.[18]

In the early 1960s Mosse began his series of ever more frequent trips to Israel, first meeting members of German Jewish circles in order to gain new insights about the German Right and German nationalism (he was working on the Crisis book), and then establishing his first links with the Hebrew University. He became acquainted with such Jewish intellectuals as Gershom Scholem and Jacob Talmon, and was later introduced to a group of South African Habonim (the members of a Zionist youth movement) who introduced him to a Zionism "whose idealism—still strong and untainted—I found most attractive."[19] From the 1970s onward, he began teaching the history of anti-Semitism and racism at the Institute of Contemporary Jewry as visiting professor, and in 1979 he was appointed to the Koebner Chair in German History at the Hebrew University. Over the 1970s he lectured at "several of the educational institutions which trained young Zionist leaders."[20] This meant a deepening of his commitment to Zionism: his lectures were not propagandistic (these institutions were already Zionist), they were intended, as he put it, "to give some historical depth to this commitment." However, his relationship to the Jewish state remained always "ambivalent."[21] In a 1972 interview he stated that

I still don't know whether I'm a Zionist or not—the word really has no meaning for me . . . I became involved in Israel under the influence of my own studies and scholarly work. I came to the conclusion that it was vital for the Jews to have a homeland, largely because of past history, it is for that reason that I got involved. But I got involved much later than in 1948 after my study and work on Jewish history had led me to that conclusion.[22]

In the early 1990s he still claimed to be a Zionist "mit vielen Fragezeichen" ("with many question marks"), since Zionism was torn between a humanistic patriotism with its intellectual origins in the thought of Western European Jews, and a chauvinistic nationalism that came from Eastern European Jews and whose outstanding incarnation had been, in Mosse's eyes, Menachem Begin.[23]

Mosse's relationship to Israel was not based on religion or on a mystical love for the land, but, as he recalled in his memoir, "rather, a secular awareness of the Jewish fate in our century determined my basic attitude toward Israel, but beyond that also a love for the 'new Jew' and what he had accomplished. This love was stimulated by my awareness of the undesirable Jewish stereotype which has accompanied the Jews in modern times, and which most Jews in the Diaspora (including myself) had internalized. This stereotype the Zionists had set out to abolish." Mosse felt joy when seeing "sturdy," "self-confident" Jews, and was aware that such a feeling came out of a Jewish stereotype he had internalized: "I knew full well that this 'new Jew' represented a normalization, an assimilation to general middle-class ideals and stereotypes which otherwise I professed to dislike. But I could not help myself; faced with this Zionist ideal my reason and historical knowledge were overcome."[24]

To be sure, despite all the attraction Mosse felt toward Israel, he was also critical of Israeli policies. In 1972 he stated in an interview, referring to the peace process:

> I think that it has to be a peace without much annexation. I believe that in the twentieth century it is not feasible for one nation to annex populated areas of another nation. Nor do I approve of one nation putting colonies of itself into populated areas of another. I believe also, quite strongly, that such a peace has to take the security of Israel into consideration. But I believe, as many people in Israel believe, that this security can be assured without any annexation.[25]

Long-term occupation, he continued, corrupts also the occupier in the long run, leading to a moral corrosion that is bound to endanger the Jewish State. Mosse did not express himself on the legitimacy of Israel: it now exists, this is a matter of fact and nothing can be done, he said, and he asserted the necessity of a critical stance before Israel: American support for Israel is "institutionalized," "almost an article of faith," he lamented. "Critical support" is needed, since uncritical support is not helpful, and American Jews should understand this and back that part of the Israeli left that stands for peace as against the

"status quo" party, the Likud.[26] A blind support for Israel's military and economic positions would only harm the country, he insisted in 1974 and in
another long interview with the *Capital Times* in 1979: "Criticizing a country
constructively is the higher form of patriotism," Mosse concluded.[27] Here,
Mosse held fast to his belief in a federal solution, claiming that in the Palestin-
ian case the principle of self-determination would be impossible and a Pales-
tinian state would only make things worse and endanger Israel. And yet he
drew a distinction between Israel's government and its people, lamenting the
fact that the lively critical debate in the country was neglected by the foreign
media, and claiming that the American Jewish community should have pressed
for a Jewish–Arab dialogue instead of taking an uncritical stance that entailed
a tacit support for Menachem Begin's policies, which Mosse opposed along
with those of Golda Meir. He believed Meir should have solved the problem of
the West Bank by giving it back to Palestinians in some way: this had been,
Mosse said, a "missed opportunity."[28] However, his lasting opposition was to the
Likud Party: "I oppose the Begin government," he stated in 1980, and in 1996
he expressed his preoccupation with Benjamin Netanyahu's electoral victory.[29]
Mosse's commitment to the federal solution of the conflict would last into the
1990s, along with his conviction that power as well as the occupied land had to
be given back to the Palestinians. Not to do this, he said in 1980, would destroy
Israel ethically, morally, and politically.[30] He remained, after all, "all for Peres'
scenario of a federation between Palestine, Israel and Jordan."[31]

A Heritage Rediscovered: Redemption by Judaism

Mosse's relationship to Zionism and, by extension, to Jewish culture has a
long history and does not lend itself to a monocausal interpretive key. Shulamit
Volkov has written that Mosse had a "great deal of circumspection" approaching the study of Jewish history: though Jews were "clearly on his mind" already
in the 1960s, "he still kept his distance": indeed, Mosse's first writings that
touched upon the Jews were "still within the boundaries of German history,"
and only gradually he started to deal with Jewish life itself, fundamentally since
the 1970s.[32] Yet what were the reasons that led Mosse to the study of Jewish
history? These reasons are the key to the understanding of Mosse's relationship with Jewish culture, and shed light on his political views as well. After
all, his interest in Judaism was, by his own admission, animated by "political
concerns."[33] Such concerns are reflected on two levels: on the one hand, on the
American political and social scene in the 1960s; on the other, on Israeli politics and nationalism.

Mosse noted that it was young Americans who brought him closer to his roots: his family tradition had been linked to what Mosse considered the "mission of Judaism," that is, it promoted the idea of *Bildung* as self-cultivation as well as cosmopolitanism and rational attitudes toward life. This ideal of *Bildung* belonged to the German tradition, and when Mosse left Germany for England and, later, the United States, he immersed himself in another environment where he did not need to take an interest in this cultural heritage: in America, Mosse said, *Bildung* was an instrument of isolation rather than of integration as had been the case in Germany during the age of Jewish emancipation (from the late eighteenth through the nineteenth centuries), and at that point of his life he was in desperate need for integration. The American New Left in the 1960s, attacking the dominant system of thought, awakened Mosse's "own consciousness to the lasting importance of the German-Jewish intellectual tradition": these students in search for meaning in life became interested in that German Jewish legacy that had expressed itself in the thought of left-wing Weimar intellectuals and had continued its impetus through the teachings of the Frankfurt School. Intellectuals as Georg Lukàcs, Herbert Marcuse, Theodor Adorno, and Max Horkheimer turned to Marxism, and they did so not toward its orthodox version as embodied by Soviet ideology, but rather in search for a less rigid left-wing identity that was the climax of the German Jewish tradition of the Weimar years. This tradition emphasized the "ideal of a common humanity based upon *Bildung* and the Enlightenment as essential for the autonomy of the individual."[34]

In 1985 Mosse published a book by the title *German Jews beyond Judaism*, a book that he defined, in his autobiography, "my most personal book, almost a confession of faith." If his studies on fascism and nationalism represent what he termed the "dark side of my writings," he could claim that "I have nevertheless been interested in what I consider the points of redemption of the human spirit, even if I did not discuss them in as many articles and books."[35] Mosse explained in his memoir his attempt to "recall above all the liberal and Enlightenment spirit which had given German Jewry a positive role within the constantly narrowing nationalistic universe"; moreover, he also turned his attention to Marxism, not in its Bolshevik version, but in its connections with humanism, according to Mosse's

dream of marrying socialism to liberalism; Marxist humanism substituted the power of reason for the violence of the class struggle, and put the autonomy of man into the center of socialism—man who was the end and must

never become a means. Marxist humanism based itself on the Enlightenment. . . . Interest in this type of humanism revived in the 1960s as a result
of books by Erich Fromm and the rediscovery of the thought of unconventional Socialists like Gustav Landauer. This was a humanistic instead of a
Bolshevik Marx, one that was based on Kant rather than on Hegel.[36]

In *German Jews beyond Judaism*, however, Mosse not only dealt with left-wing
intellectuals like Karl Marx, Ferdinand Lassalle, Kurt Eisner, or Lukàcs, Adorno,
Horkheimer, Benjamin, and Marcuse. Their attempt to give Marxism a human
face, to make use of the critical mind in order to preserve the dignity of the individual belonged, according to Mosse, to a vaster, though unconscious, attempt
to preserve a heritage that "contained much of what was best and most noble
in German culture. . . . [I]t was the German-Jewish *Bildungsbürgertum* which,
more than any other single group, preserved Germany's better self across dictatorship war, holocaust, and defeat."[37] Here socialists were not alone: Mosse's
book dealt, as Jost Hermand has written, with four groups of German Jewish
intellectuals. Apart from these socialists, there were such popular writers as
Stefan Zweig, Emil Ludwig, and Berthold Auerbach; scholars Sigmund Freud,
Hermann Cohen, Aby Warburg, and Ernst Cassirer; and Zionists Martin Buber,
Robert Weltsch, Hans Kohn, and Hugo Bergmann.[38] All these German Jewish
intellectuals believed in the individual as opposed to the mass, in the "critical
use of reason," in cosmopolitan views based upon humanistic values derived
from Enlightenment ideas: extending a phrase Mosse used with regard to
socialist humanists, they shared a "categorical imperative centered upon man's
dignity and his ability to control his own destiny."[39] The underlying principle,
common to all of them, was the belief in *Bildung*, the German ideal of self-
cultivation to which Mosse devoted numerous articles, lectures, as well as his
"confession of faith."[40] As Anson Rabinbach observed, Mosse himself "embodied
the Bildung—cultivation—that was second nature to those thinkers and scholars who had been forced to flee Germany"; Jost Hermand, writing that "most
German Jews had . . . sworn allegiance to reason and self-cultivation, i.e., had
seen themselves as adherents of the German Enlightenment," defined the four
categories of intellectuals cited above and argued that "nothing is easier than to
apply this thesis to George Mosse himself. He too is a popular writer in the best
sense of the world, a German-Jewish scholar and *Bildungsbürger*, a cosmopolitan-
minded left intellectual, as well as a Zionist committed to a humanistic, i.e., non-
religious universalism . . . he has incorporated himself into this so lovingly
portrayed tradition of German humanism."[41]

This tradition, however, had been tainted in Germany, and Mosse had experienced this directly: "The concept of *Bildung* had meant to me simply the usual humanist education which in Germany conferred social status. But as I studied the origins of this concept I found it was far removed from the rote learning and strict obedience to rules laid down by teachers as I had experienced them during my brief time at a humanist Mommsen Gymnasium in Berlin"; indeed, according to him, Germans had eventually coopted *Bildung* to belief systems, "thus precluding an emphasis on individualism and open-endedness."[42] Instead, in Mosse's view, it was German Jews who preserved this tradition that had characterized their emancipation at the turn of the nineteenth century: at the end of that century, while they were clinging fast to that ideal, nationalism in Germany was pushing toward a nationalization of *Bildung* that tended to exclude non-Germans. The same thing happened with those middle-class ideals based on respectability that Jews in Germany embraced in search for integration, and which were to be turned against them.[43] Most German Jews had turned to liberal ideals that had their bases in *Bildung* and the Enlightenment. Even socialists such as Kurt Eisner, Georg Lukàcs, or those of the Frankfurt School, though they rejected capitalist society, embraced ideals that lay at the basis of liberalism, and Mosse expressed his admiration for intellectuals such as Carlo Rosselli, who, showing a great realism, had claimed that the spirit of capitalism could be upheld only in a socialist society.[44]

Such ideas and ideals had fascinated American students in the 1960s. Herbert Marcuse had been crucial in transmitting them, Mosse held, asserting that Marcuse's *One-Dimensional Man* laid the bases for a humanist foundation of socialism with its critique of alienating modern mass culture, which coopts the critical mind through an established system of cultural domination. Only the "outsider" (students or members of the intelligentsia), from his or her vantage point outside the system, can rescue the individual through critical reason, which, according to Mosse, is based on *Bildung*.[45] Indeed, Mosse continued, Marcuse and the other philosophers of the Frankfurt School, though attacking liberalism (and the Enlightenment) and embracing a form of socialism, shared the ideological roots of the former in adopting the intellectual concepts of the German Jewish tradition of *Bildung* and Enlightenment values and simply bringing this tradition to the service of socialism.[46] In Mosse's view, these intellectuals were part of that German Jewish tradition that had flourished in Weimar culture, a great object of interest for the students in the 1960s. However, Mosse said, these students generally did not realize the link with such heritage, and neither did they catch the connections with liberalism rather than those with

Marxism; nevertheless they "made me think about the implications of this tradition, but political concerns led me to undertake this task," the task being the
writing of *German Jews beyond Judaism*.[47] What were these political concerns?
The answer lies in Mosse's ever growing involvement in Israeli cultural life and
politics. In Jerusalem he had engaged in much debate about nationalism with
a human face, which had played with the idea of a binational solution for the
Jewish question in Palestine, and expressed itself in the peace movement. This
led Mosse to think that "perhaps there was a certain German-Jewish tradition
at work, which, if it could be rediscovered and articulated, might yet help to
rehumanize modern nationalism."[48] This was to become one of Mosse's main
concerns over the decades to come, gaining momentum and increasingly
absorbing the historian in what he considered the "true mission" not only of
Judaism" but, extensively, of all humanity: the German Jewish symbiosis as
reflected in humanistic nationalism, that is, in patriotism, laid the bases of a
"Jewishness beyond Judaism."[49]

Between Nationalism and Patriotism

It may appear paradoxical, in light of Mosse's harsh critique of nationalism,
that he claimed to think of Israel "in terms of nationalism."[50] In a 1979 interview he stated: "I think that all nationalism is bad. All my books are written
against nationalism"; and yet in the same interview he also claimed that "criticizing a country constructively is the higher form of patriotism."[51] The great
prosecutor of nationalism and irrationalism, when faced with his own emotions
toward Israel, found himself at a crossroads: How was he supposed to consider Israel's own nationalism? Did he have to condemn it as he had done
with all other forms of this ideology? The answer can be found in the words he
chose in that interview: he condemned nationalism, but he favorably considered patriotism. In the difference between the two concepts lies the importance
the Israeli experience had in his historiography. As we have seen when we have
analyzed the changing focus on nationalism in his interpretation of fascism,
his concern with nationalism grew exponentially since the 1970s: this was also
the result of his emotional and intellectual commitment to the state of Israel.

Addressing a meeting called "The Teaching of Patriotism" in 1963, Mosse
had spoken only about the dangers inherent in nationalism, that is, only about
its dark side.[52] Less than two decades later, he defined nationalism as both "a
problem and an opportunity"; a more optimistic élan seemed to motivate Mosse,
who in the same years asserted that "nationalism will not vanish; it fulfills legit-
imate hopes for community, for a richer life. Rather than calling for its abolition

we should recall its potential, the hopes it once held in the midst of ever latent ideas of domination and assertions of superiority."[53] In November 1995 Mosse delivered a lecture in Tel Aviv that, as he himself said, "expressed my own credo, a guarded optimism about nationalism": the lecture was significantly titled "Can Nationalism be Saved? About Zionism, Rightful and Unjust Nationalism." Reminding the audience of the ever-present power of nationalism's appeal, Mosse turned to the analysis of early Zionism and its humanistic attempt to combine love for one's country with individualism and cosmopolitanism: the lecture, he stated, addressed the "promise of nationalism and not its negative implications."[54] Referring not only to the intellectuals he mentioned in *German Jews beyond Judaism*, but also to those who joined the Brit Shalom (Covenant of Peace), a Jewish organization founded in 1925 and committed to the creation of a dual Jewish–Arab state in Palestine, he emphasized their attempt to draw a line between a rightful and an unjust nationalism: they sought to distinguish between nationalism based on *Bildung* and nationalism based on borders. Thus national identity came to be "an integral part of individual self-knowledge and self-development open to outside influences": these intellectuals drew mostly from German Enlightenment culture, and "the symbiosis between the classical German liberal spirit and Jewish memory was among the most fruitful."[55]

Mosse saw such nationalism, however commendable, as excessively utopian, and here lay the reasons of its failure. The cultural nature of the movement clashed against the political reality of an already occupied land, and "their humanist nationalism proved impractical in the midst of a continuing war for survival and independence." Lack of realism and detachment from reality proved fatal in the last resort, and yet Mosse praised their efforts because "men must dream before they act."[56] These dreams were soon to collapse before the radicalization of Israeli nationalism since the foundation of the Jewish State. In 1996 Mosse expressed his "growing disillusionment with Zionist reality," a concern that had accompanied his writings from the beginning but that was destined to grow more acute over the decades.

In 1967 he had written an essay called "The Influence of the Volkish Idea on German Jewry" that showed how a small though significant part of the latter had been affected by ideals of community, *Bund*, of the "new man."[57] He had also investigated with particular attention the thought of the noted nineteenth-century Zionist leader Max Nordau, writing an introduction to the 1968 edition of his *Degeneration* and later an article.[58] Nordau, in Mosse's view, had internalized the middle-class stereotype of the Jew and had elaborated an ideal of a "new Jew" based on manliness, discipline, beauty, and respectability, a "muscle

Jew" at the service of the Zionist cause. All this remained, however, bound to a liberal and humanistic background, Mosse argued; and yet this stereotype, devoid of its liberal façade, was adopted by the Zionist Revisionist Movement, which provided the background of Menachem Begin's Irgun and of the Likud Party. Here, military values were glorified, and the struggle for survival meant everything.[59] In a lecture titled "Zionist Nationalism," Mosse argued that in the 1920s the Zionist hero could still be a mixture of ethical socialism and the practical need for defense, but after the founding of the state "the triumph of the tough Jews was a logical consequence of statehood under the circumstances, of the longing for normalization," it was a "matter of physical security" much less, if at all, concerned with humane values that ever fewer people in Israel still thought worth fighting for.[60] Even though the tradition of humanistic nationalism remained alive in Israel, the perpetual struggle in which the country found itself inevitably led to a corrosion of that heritage. A rupture was created, Mosse maintained on another occasion, between Israelis and the Jews of the Diaspora: this led to "two conflicting Jewish traditions: the liberal and indeed even socialist heritage of Jews in the Diaspora, and the ever more rightward course of the Israel government, policies of occupation, deportation etc which seem difficult to face coming out of the Diaspora traditions, to realize that Israel is not just Kibbutz, or bravery, or a state with a special ethical dimension."[61]

Mosse described Zionism in Palestine as a civic religion: Theodor Herzl and Martin Buber, he wrote, envisaged a national liturgy imbued with symbols and rituals such as flags, monuments, and songs. Their nationalism remained, however, centered on an "inner revival" and an "educational process" rather than on militarism; this was not the case, he argued, with Vladimir Jabotinsky, the founder of the Zionist revisionist movement (1923), who infused his ideology with a paramilitary spirit; and yet these attitudes remained exceptions to the general Zionist scenario before 1948.[62] After the creation of Israel, humanistic Zionism became, in Mosse's interpretation, constantly besieged: however, he pointed out that it was "remarkable that it held through three wars" without totally degenerating into an aggressive, exclusive ideology.[63] Mosse never abandoned the hope that nationalism could be tempered by humanistic ideals: to revive its humane side was "a worthy mission for all people."[64] The fact that Israel, despite repeated conflicts, was still witness to a debate between chauvinism and patriotism was a sign of hope for Mosse; and yet this hope remained fraught with doubts: "Returning Zionism to the realm of humane nationalism would certainly bridge the growing gap with American Jews," he said in 1988, "but does it constitute a recipe for survival?"[65]

The "True Mission of Judaism"

If humanistic nationalism was under siege in an Israel that was faced with political realities, it could still remain strong in the United States.[66] Here the German Jewish symbiosis, brushed away by the Holocaust, survived through the large number of refugee intellectuals to which Mosse belonged. To be sure, when he first arrived in America, he found himself in a rather hostile environment. Anti-Semitic prejudices were widespread in the United States, and many universities had Jewish quotas—Mosse's application to graduate school at Columbia University was rejected "quite overtly because the Jewish quota was full," he recalled.[67] Despite this, he managed to become one of the first Jews to teach history in important state universities. Then the civil rights movements, which Mosse obviously fully supported, initiated a change that was, eventually, to lead to more complete integration. This change, he said in 1992 during a lecture at Hadassah, the Women's Zionist Organization of America, was a "change which I call the triumph of assimilation in the United States."[68] And yet, once assimilation was established, what could be the future of Zionism, what should become its role? Could it not be in danger of extinction? With such questions in mind, Mosse set to the task of preserving the German Jewish legacy, enriching it with new goals and meanings.[69] The "ideas of liberalism, of ethical socialism are among the noblest our civilization has to offer," they represent "a tradition of which we can be proud," he said in the opening speech for the inauguration of the Kaplan Center for Jewish Studies and Research in Cape Town.[70] The Jews who transmit these ideas are the "custodians of a German tradition," a tradition that, according to Mosse, "contained much of what was best and most noble in German culture."[71]

This salvage operation, he believed, could be successful only through the aid of Jewish studies at universities and in high schools.[72] Indeed, he left a very large contribution to the University of Wisconsin in his will, most of which was intended to further Jewish studies and the Mosse Exchange Program in History, which called for the exchange of students and faculty between Madison and Jerusalem. He had also encouraged and furthered the creation of the Center for Jewish Studies in Madison, which eventually became reality in 1991: through this program "students can explore their heritage and their present situation in society," he said.[73] As early as in 1971 he gave a pioneering course in modern Jewish history, in the attempt to explain and divulge Jewish culture and the ideals it stood for: as he argued in a speech, Jewish history must be taught not only in its negative (persecution, anti-Semitism, the Holocaust) but also in its positive aspects, so that the history of Zionism can teach solidarity among future generations.[74] To base Jewish identity only on the Holocaust, he lamented in 1982, was wrong: therefore he opposed the creation of more museums of the Holocaust;[75] he preferred institutions devoted to educational efforts to combat racism and sectarianism. He also lamented what he called the "embourgeoisement of the Holocaust," that is, its trivialization through the endless repetition of photos. This caused, in his opinion, a numbing effect similar to the one the Great War had on attitudes toward mass death: thus, the "reality of death" is "not faced but transcended," he argued.[76] The history of Zionism, he believed, must be taught "in the affirmative," revealing its values and ideals in order to teach solidarity among future generations.[77] The further-ing of Jewish studies, in this light, becomes a duty that all Jews should accom-plish: as Mosse passionately stated in a speech at a Jewish organization, "the persecution of learning and the persecution of the Jews went hand in hand. . . . A Jew who rejects scholarship therefore puts himself on the side of those who have persecuted his people as well as the freedom of thought and inquiry."[78]

In his classes, Mosse tried to present this heritage for his Jewish students, stressing the humanistic potential of Jewish identity and the Enlightenment tra-dition. This approach might have been a little old fashioned, Mosse admitted, but "perhaps that gave the students the glimpse of a kind of Jewish commitment beyond religion and present-day nationalism," he said. It was a secular and cos-mopolitan Judaism that Mosse pursued, an outlook on the world "which is not static but a constant process," he specified in a speech at the Hillel Foundation, where he also emphasized the need for "a crusade for modern Jewish history."[79] In 1981 Mosse spoke at the memorial service for Manfred Swarsensky, a Ger-man rabbi from the Jewish reform community of Berlin who survived the con-centration camps and moved to Madison after the Second World War, becoming a leading figure in the ecumenical movement of the 1960s. Of Swarsensky, Mosse stressed the appeal to tolerance and the "desperate task to humanize our only too inhuman society": the ethical imperative in our society, as embodied by his teachings, was derived from Judaism and its love for the dignity of the individual, the acceptance of diversity, and the love of humanity. The end was the building of "a more human world where all men could realize their potential."[80] Mosse's speech at the Kaplan Center for Jewish Studies in Cape Town, given on the occasion of its inauguration in 1980, epitomizes his beliefs. He said:

> I have suggested that the tradition of Diaspora, a tradition of which we can
> be proud, be joined to a nationalism which sought to create a living people
> devoted to their own personal and national growth with the aim to serve the

unity of all mankind. I have suggested that this may not be as vague as it sounds, but exemplified by Israel's own history of restraint which I hope and pray will not have ended. . . . [T]here must be emotional involvement with the community, but if it is not tempered by reason, by an intellectual commitment and the awareness of humanity as a whole, it will not really last. Euphoria must be overcome or tempered by the intellect. And that must in some sort of manner be based upon historical knowledge. . . . [W]ithout learning modern Jewish history one will be lost, for Jews are children of assimilation. I would go further: that our own history is illuminating for any ethnic minority.[81]

The pursuit of a humanistic nationalism at the service of all mankind, the necessity of emotional involvement as long as it is "tempered by reason" and filtered through a critical mind, history as the means to promulgate values, and Jewish history in particular as an example from which all minorities should learn: Mosse hoped the Kaplan Center would become an example of scholarship to further what he called "the true mission of Judaism."[82] The German Jewish tradition, he held on another occasion, could still play a role in modern society: as an attitude toward life, it could and should be a "prism through which to view and humanize society."[83]

Despite the awareness of the impracticality of these ideals, Mosse never ceased to remark that "men must dream before they can act": his speeches and writings repeatedly stress the need to hope and to dream, inspired by Ernst Bloch's conviction that "without utopia no progress is possible."[84] In order to solve this dilemma about the balance of utopia and reason of state, the solution Mosse came up with can be seen as an updated casuistry. It was Mosse's "journey to Jerusalem" that gave the decisive thrust to his efforts, begun in the early 1950s and inspired by Croce and Meinecke, at balancing ethics and politics. Only when confronted with his own emotions toward Zionism, which echoed so strongly those anthropological mechanisms of nationalism he had so vividly chastised in his major works, Mosse must have fully realized that reason of state, nationalism, and the new politics are indeed necessary components of a working society, thus overcoming his hostility and providing him with a way of finding the long-yearned balance between ideals and reality.

Mosse's memoir contains a very telling passage:

my view that European nationalism had been and was the greatest enemy of the Jews never changed, and yet when I saw the new Israeli Army or attended the swearing-in of the paratroopers on Masada, my heart beat faster. I knew the danger of being captured by images and liturgy and had written often enough about their use in manipulating people, but I myself was far from immune to the irrational forces which as a historian I deplored—especially when it came to that group which I regarded as my own.[85]

It appears that the experience in Jerusalem drove Mosse to reconsider some of his basic idiosyncrasies, and to look with conviction for a "positive" use of liturgy. What he elaborated was, as Emilio Gentile effectively defined it, a "Machiavellism of democracy."[86] Indeed, Mosse eventually urged democracies to adopt the new politics to provide the masses with a sense of belonging and participation.[87] Lecturing in Tel Aviv, he blamed liberals and socialists for being unable, unlike nationalists, to use myths and symbols: rationality alone cannot be enough, he argued; it had to go hand in hand with emotions. Nationalism with its character of a secular religion is necessary, he held, and political liturgies fulfill the needs of any national community and should be encouraged.[88] If in 1975 the "nationalization of the masses" was seen as threatening the dignity of the individual, now festivals, myths, and symbols were deemed necessary. If it was not possible to eradicate nationalism, this must become patriotism, not as an abstract ideal but, rather, in combination with a practical and necessary political liturgy that, in turn, must always be "tempered by reason."

And yet Mosse never ceased, in his classes, to debunk myths, which led Gershom Scholem to accuse him of not loving the Jewish people enough. Mosse replied that he could love only individuals, thus reaffirming that, in spite of his "new casuistry," he remained a man of the Enlightenment. Also, he always refused to learn Hebrew: this was surely a handicap, he conceded, but also "one way to keep from being swallowed up by my new environment, to keep a distance between myself and Zionism—to preserve the rational against the strong pull of emotion."[89] Whether or not Mosse achieved this form of detachment, as he himself partly conceded, remains debatable. His enthusiasm when faced with the power of a long-lost identity surely affected his views, and his attempt to maintain his emotional balance partly failed. The "true mission of Judaism" he so passionately advocated was nothing less than an attempt to find a solution to the "eternal problem" of the relationship between ethics and politics, which seems to contradict a belief he had often expressed, and which informed many of his writings over the decades: that the historian can be a diagnostician more than a prophet, and can only "show you the problems which impeded Utopia rather than the way to Utopia."[90]

The reception of his works in Jewish historiography mirrors these difficulties, yet without diminishing the great contributions and innovative insights these writings offered. According to Steven Aschheim, the fact that Mosse did not "ghettoize" Jewish history but, rather, included it within wider perspectives shocked Israeli conservative historians and their "prevailing ethnocentric bias that Jewish history by definition followed its own unique narrative and immanent laws." Mosse's idea that the German Jewish heritage is that of *Bildung*, that Jewishness is synonymous with German culture was, to traditionalists, "profoundly shocking, even subversive," and yet, Aschheim says, "it was a sentiment that was remarkably prevalent within large circles of liberal German Jewry." Mosse had been accused of writing from the perspective of the wealthy, assimilated German Jewish elite, and though this is partly true, Mosse dissented and radically departed "from the constricting 'normalcy' and 'respectability' of his background." Whatever the criticisms he received, the fact remains that Mosse's approach was highly innovative, it helped make new connections, it offered "productive insights within the field of Jewish history," and "it crucially shifted and deepened our perspectives on German and European developments by uncovering the often crucial (positive as well as negative) roles that Jews— either in fact or in stereotypical fantasy—played within post-emancipation and post-Enlightenment society." Referring to Mosse's works on the relationship between German Jews and middle-class values, on how Jews in Europe had internalized Christian symbols (such as the cross in war cemeteries), on how they were affected by *völkisch* ideas, Aschheim states that Mosse "defined the connections in mischievously unorthodox, yet illuminating ways."[91]

However, Mosse's deep personal involvement had its downsides as well. Shulamit Volkov stressed the

undisguised note of apologetics in Mosse's writing about the Jews. Despite the tale of his youth as a rebel, despite his distance from his immediate family, despite his sharp, critical mind, Mosse was attached to the world he had lost. He never ceased to seek the Jews' dignified and admirable sides. He never ceased to try to exonerate them of explicit and often implicit reproach. Jewish right-wing tendencies, according to Mosse, never went as far as those of their German counterparts.[92]

Mosse's writings on Jewish nationalism, Volkov continued, are "the most striking example" of this attitude: in the 1990s Mosse was "even willing to transpose this claim onto the Israeli scene. Unlike some former supporters and later critics of Zionism, Mosse's strong ties to Israel made him uphold even *its* human, enlightened face—a most unusual stance in this day and age, indeed." According to this criticism, Mosse was torn about Jewish nationalism, and ended up making every Zionist into a liberal, and every liberal into a Zionist.[93] Aschheim, for his part, criticized Mosse's oversimplification of Jewish culture in Germany: in fact, many Jews, even in Weimar, were attracted to less rational and morally elevated aspects of German culture. Scholem, Benjamin, and Ernst Bloch had questioned the *Bildung* tradition just like Jünger, Spengler, or Heidegger had done.[94] Nevertheless, Aschheim's critique of Mosse was admittedly based on the "vital Mossean premise" that Jewish self-definition is "embedded within the wider cultures of which they are a part," thus recognizing Mosse's contribution.[95] Recalling conversations he had with Mosse, Aschheim provided an insightful picture of his insistence upon the difference between Zionism and integral nationalism:

> I sometimes would playfully nudge him to go beyond these assertions and examine in his scholarship—as apart from private conversation or journalistic comment—some of the darker faces of Jewish nationalism but this (perhaps given his status as a refugee and his first-hand experience of Nazism) he was always loathe to do. With all of George's delight in outraging his listeners and readers, here, I think, was a threshold he would not cross.[96]

Yet Mosse's Zionist affirmation, Aschheim continued, may "have had as one of its sources a (largely unstated) appreciation of the need for force and collective self-defense in a very imperfect, uncultured world," a kind of "corrective" to the utopianism of the *Bildung* intellectuals.[97]

As the last resort, Jerusalem did not mean for Mosse mere research interest or search for identity: it combined and embodied both in an inextricable manner, fusing his life with his work perhaps even more than it had been the case with the study of National Socialism. The rediscovery of his Jewish identity gave his work, and his life, a new purpose and reinvigorated his faith in the goal of the historian. Here the balance between ideal and utopia and the task and use of history seen as a "mission" took on a special significance that further added to the deep commitment he had poured into the study of totalitarianisms. A slightly more optimistic view of history emerged from this, casting some light upon the dark pessimism that generally shrouded his historiography. "I know full well that men and women do not as a rule learn from history, but it seems to me that at least the historian can do so," he said in 1985.[98] And yet he regarded history as his "faith," and in the face of his pessimism, he always sought to charge it with an ethical goal and bring its teachings to his students and readers: this was the meaning of history; this was the task of the historian.

8

The Granitic Foundation
of a Faith

Culture in our case must not be narrowly defined as a history of ideas,
or as confined to popular culture, but instead understood as dealing
with life seen as a whole—a totality, as indeed the fascist movement
sought to define itself. Cultural history centers above all upon the
perceptions of men and women, and how these are shaped and
enlisted in politics at a particular place and time.

—GEORGE L. MOSSE

What was [Mosse's] method? It concerns . . . how he deals with
culture, with culture as a systematic way of perception and a set of
powerful symbols. Culture, to get back to another central concern, was
always linked to the political, and his interest lay in describing "habits
of mind" that establish ways of living that in turn inform political
reality.

—DAVID WARREN SABEAN

The past is, in a sense, "present politics."

—GEORGE L. MOSSE

In the course of this study we have seen how Mosse's work underwent two
grand methodological turns and two thematic shifts. Yet despite these significant changes, there remained marked elements of continuity that characterized a dialectical view of history that never really changed significantly.
Thus we can speak of a "granitic foundation" of his historiography where a
"continuity of interests" merges with a "continuity of intents," reflecting both
his concerns with the liberty and dignity of the individual, and the profoundly
pedagogical nature of his work. Mosse hardly expressed himself directly about

theory in his books: as David W. Sabean pointed out, "I have always perceived a strong theoretical substructure to Mosse's historical practice, although it was one that he did not usually make explicit. There was no particular concept that he underlined so as to call attention to an innovation, nor was there any extended theoretical apparatus. . . . There was no overarching 'theory' here but rather a myriad of theoretical points and analytical critiques pushing their way into and opening up spaces in the plot he was constructing."[1] However, if Mosse's books are scarcely filled with explicit historiographical theory, his unpublished lectures and speeches are rich in theoretical elaboration. They shed light on what history meant for him, its meaning, its nature, its function, and its goals. The same assertions he made in the 1950s remained valid into the 1990s as far as his view of history is concerned. Here lies the continuity of interests and beliefs in his work, which was laid no later than the 1950s, and rests on a European frame of mind stemming from the influence of historicism. The thought of Croce and Hegel lies at the base of his conception of history in terms of dialectics and of its totality and contemporaneity. Reason stands at the center in its ever-recurring conflict with irrationalism. Steven Aschheim has defined Mosse as *"the* historian of modern irrationalism," thus highlighting the complexity entailed by his attempt to study the irrational through rational means.[2] Mosse, despite having immersed himself in the irrational psychology of his persecutors, did so with a rational attitude, loyal to his liberal heritage. Despite his harsh criticism of the Enlightenment and liberal bourgeois society, he held fast to the belief that they represent the best chance of survival of freedom and individualism. The defense of reason represents one more element of the continuity of interests: Mosse remained, after all, an "Enlightenment man." In the interview on Nazism, Mosse clearly stated:

I've always believed one should be interested in problems and not chronology, and so the problems I have worked on—the problem of the relationship between reason and irrationalism, the problem of Reason of State—which occupied most of my work in the earlier centuries, aren't so far removed from the problems I worked on later.[3]

Indeed, he repeatedly stressed the connections between his early modern and modern works. "The tension between Christianity and Reason of State," he argued in 1955, "was to be a constant and continuing historical problem; and the relationship between these ideas which was constructed at the beginning of the Nation state may well have lasted into modern times"; more than forty years later, in his memoir, he stated these continuities again, stressing the connections between the Baroque and modern mass movements, and saying that "this is how I see my work, how it falls into place in my own mind."[4] Emphasizing the same connections, he said in the 1970s that he saw no major break in his work, but rather "a continuity of interests."[5] His concern with the dignity and liberty of the individual obviously went hand in hand with the problem of the relation of ethics to politics, and was just as recurrent and constant. "The fate of liberalism is one constant theme in my work, tying the earlier period of my interests to my preoccupation with modern history," he wrote in his autobiography.[6] And just as *The Struggle for Sovereignty in England* displayed "the progressive destruction of the safeguards of the individual before the emergence of the supreme authority of the state,"[7] *The Culture of Western Europe* culminated in the "depersonalization of man" brought by National Socialism.[8] Similarly, *The Nationalization of the Masses* was "the result of a longstanding preoccupation with the dignity of the individual and its challengers"; it focused on how "the nineteenth century with the development of mass movements and mass politics seemed to transform the political process itself into a drama which further diminished the individual whose conscious actions might change the course of his own destiny."[9] Mosse evinced a "lifelong concern with finding an ethical balance between contesting forces," a balance necessary in order to safeguard the dignity of the individual and based upon a "commitment to humanistic—or perhaps better, humane—values."[10] As he made clear when introducing a beginning history course, "How come that modern history in Europe, instead of leading, as the Enlightenment of the eighteenth century had hoped, to the dignity and freedom of the individual man, led by 1939 to an acceptance of Man's depersonalization? These are some of the problems which will go through my head as I interpret this history for you."[11]

The problem of depersonalization and personalization has an apparent paradoxical nature: Mosse saw in totalitarianism the climax of the deprivation of personality or individuality, and yet he read the new politics, which lay at the base of totalitarianism, as a "personalizing" agent. The turn to myth, symbol, and liturgy was an understandable reaction to the excess of abstraction brought about by the Enlightenment with its penchant for conformity, with Voltaire's "clockmaker" God.[12] And Mosse believed that no movement in history survives that does not appeal to authority or certainty, and that does not personalize these certainties through myth and symbol. Indeed, one problem posed by his approach to history is the danger of suffering from what Marina Cattaruzza has defined "Hegelian sickness":

In my opinion, historical research on "political religions" in some cases still suffers from a kind of "Hegelian" sickness. Religious manifestations in the sphere of politics are analyzed and depicted as something barely "occurring." A stronger analytical effort might perhaps cast some more light on how the sacralisation of politics develops, on historical subjects in the context of creating rituals, cults and sacred writings, and on intentions and reciprocal relations between "officials" and the "liturgical mass." In this context, it is worth stressing that Mosse declared himself a "Hegelian." Emilio Gentile confronts this issue in his differentiated conclusions to the *Sacralisation of Politics*, where he underlines the intentional character of Fascist lay religion: "Once in power, Fascism instituted a lay religion by sacralising the state and spreading a political cult of the masses that aimed at creating a virile and virtuous citizenry, dedicated body and soul to the nation." But he also honestly admits that the problem of the sincerity of faith, of manipulation "from above," of the dialectic between rulers and masses, is still far from having been solved.[13]

Mosse was far from immune from this "sickness": he very often ended up personalizing the abstract himself, using "fascism," "nationalism," and "racism" as the subject of sentences. Isabel Hull raised the problem while reviewing his 1982 article on nationalism and respectability:

The major question, it seems to me, that Mosse's essay leaves open is: what were the actual, historical agents which forged nationalism and respectability together? Which institutions began to mix the discourses of two such different value-systems? Once we ask this question, we get nearer to the motives behind the process, whether they were conscious or not, the product of transient historical conjunction or of a longer, structural pattern, or whether they grew out of some dynamic internal to the institution(s), unrelated either to nationalism or respectability.[14]

Eric Leed pointed in the same direction, commenting on *Nationalism and Sexuality* in a 1988 letter to Mosse that "the terms are interesting, the notion of respectability seems to be one that is worthy of respect even though one isn't getting it and is a kind of magical self-evolution, a gest toward an unseen eye, a compensatory complex which creates itself. It is this boot-strapping feature of respectability which interests me, respectability creates itself and contains, inherently, the aspect of self-generation."[15]

As had been the case with respectability and nationalism (in the form of patriotism), personalization is also necessary when not stretched to its extremes. Mosse's philosophy, it can be argued, was a "philosophy of the balance," both in historiographical matters and in actual, concrete attitudes toward life. Dialectics seen as the maintaining of the balance lies at the core of Mosse's view of life and history as an open process that can never reach a conclusion. "I was never to close the gap between ideal and reality," he once said, "and I learned myself what I used to tell my students: true maturity is reached only when one realizes that there exist insoluble problems."[16] And, however insoluble, these problems need to be addressed in an analytical manner. Mosse contrasted analytical history with narrative history:

> There is a difference between history considered as the explanation of causes of human events and history considered as narrative only of events—as you have it in most of the kind of books of history the layman reads. I do not deny the fascination of stories of bygone days, when Kings, Emperors and Popes moved about in regal procession, when men seemed to be men and women very much the unfortunate creatures of their sex. But history has a deeper meaning than this. It is a manner of explanation of the condition of life itself. Analysis is thus as important as narrative[;] . . . everything on this world had an explainable cause, a cause explainable usually chiefly by its history. Even if some of you may not want to go so far as to say "what man is only history tells." It is analysis based upon data which makes up history. . . . The "Why" is all important and you must keep it constantly in mind. The narrative of history is an essential framework, a tool, but by itself it explains nothing.[17]

In order to understand the Why? Mosse made full use of empathy, which he deemed necessary to grasp people's attitudes toward life, the core of his cultural history. As he stated in the 1990s, and as has been argued above, "the cultural interpretation of fascism opens up a means to penetrate fascist self-understanding, and such empathy is crucial in order to grasp how people saw the movement, something which cannot be ignored or evaluated merely in retrospect."[18] In 1958, referring to the Puritans, he similarly claimed to have sought to "analyze their thought as I think these men themselves understood it."[19] Empathy then represents one major tenet of his methodology, in line with Wilhelm Dilthey's historicist precepts and with attitudes drawn from psychology. In his memoir Mosse said that "empathy means putting contemporary prejudice aside while looking at the past without fear or favor"; he then added that "it is my firm belief that a historian in order to understand the past has to empathize with it, to get under its skin, as it were, to see the world through the eyes of its actors and its institutions," and as a consequence "empathy is for me still at the core of the historical enterprise, but understanding does not mean withholding judgment. I have myself mainly dealt with people and movements whom I judged harshly, but understanding must precede an informed and effective judgment."[20] The historian, said Mosse in a lecture, "must be able to understand attitudes which are to him, personally, distasteful. . . . Understanding means empathy—to look at the world, at least for a moment, through the world view of others, however distasteful. This all important fact . . . is vital. It comes easier the more one knows, the more one is learned. But it is most difficult, I think, for that person who himself is committed to an absolute as a truth which stands outside history."[21]

The Meaning of History

The methodological side of Mosse's "granitic foundation" was laid no later than the 1950s and rests on a European frame of mind stemming from the influence of historicism. The thought of Hegel, Croce, and Meinecke is present in his work from the outset, soon to be joined by that of Dilthey, Cassirer, or Nipperdey. Mosse eclectically mingled such diverse influences, giving birth to an original view of history that embodied the most variegated insights into one coherent historical attitude. He envisioned history as a totality following Croce's Hegelian approach, while at the same time relying on Dilthey's psychological bent that clearly separated the humanities from the natural sciences, thus touching on the problem of rationality and irrationality and the related reflections put forward by Meinecke about the need to find a balance between the two, a problem Mosse made his own.

Steven Aschheim has defined Mosse's history as "a kind of updated Hegelian totality" based on the dialectical interplay of politics and religion, science and aesthetics, rationality and myth.[22] Mosse himself claimed to consider himself a Hegelian.[23] Giuseppe Galasso held that the greatest and most enduring influence on Mosse was that of Hegel. According to the Italian historian, Mosse's historicism derives far more from Hegel than from Croce, though in a very personal and sometimes diffident manner. Galasso highlighted the considerable role played by reason both in Hegel's and in Mosse's work, along with the common concern with dialectics as the dynamic element of history and with the idea of "culture" as manifestation of the "popular spirit": he praised Mosse's efforts at distinguishing the liberal and rationalistic aspects of young

Hegel's thought from current views focusing exclusively on his later idealism.[24] Indeed, Mosse had turned to Hegel's early thought and its liberal potential: as he argued in a review of George Friedman's book on the philosophy of the Frankfurt School, "the Hegel discussed here for the most part is the old Hegel preoccupied with the end of history and not the young Hegel with his open-ended dialectic and his emphasis on the mediation of reality."[25] The concept of "mediation," as will be shown below, was another important feature Mosse derived from the thought of the German philosopher. It remains debatable whether, as Galasso held, Hegel's was the most enduring influence on Mosse: Benedetto Croce's ideas played, in my opinion, an equally crucial role.

Recalling his historical training, Mosse wrote:

> like all of my generation, I was taught his [Ranke's] canon of writing history: to abstract myself as much as possible from my historical writing. It took me many years to realize that writing about historical problems which have affected one's own life was no barrier which stood in the way of understanding historical reality; indeed, I was helped to this realization by a colleague at the University of Iowa who once observed that I was so interesting while my books were so dull. I now think that the reason I never wrote about problems which in reality were always present in my thoughts during those early years, was not merely the quest for academic respectability or desire for integration . . . but also my graduate training: the ideal of historical scholarship without the personal involvement of the historian. After some forty years of training graduate students . . . it is my opinion that the best results are achieved if the student has some personal or at least internal relationship to his historical work. I suppose that for my generation which has seen so many wars and oppressive regimes . . . history must needs be present politics.[26]

It is not true that Mosse's early books were written in a detached fashion. There is little doubt that when he started writing on National Socialism and racism his personal involvement became stronger, but it has been shown that from the beginning his concern with individual liberty and with the question of political morality deeply affected his work. The historian's personal involvement in his work was a belief Mosse inherited from the thought of Benedetto Croce, who also inspired him in another crucial aspect of his historiography: the centrality of the mind of the historian, the connection between the historian's life and his interest in the past, the belief there is no reality outside history, and perhaps also the religious nature of ideologies and the function of myth.

In a speech titled "Culture and Civilization: The Function of the Historian," Mosse mentioned Croce and embraced his belief that "as all analysis of history passes through the mind of the historian, it follows that in as much as he himself lives in the present 'only an interest in the life of the present can move one to investigate the life of the past.'"[27] The centrality of the mind of the historian is connected with the problem of objectivity. Mosse said:

> this task of organizing and interpreting also becomes more than ever bound up with the historian's personal experiences. . . . It is basic to understand that no history is ever "objective" for it always passes through the mind of the historian. Its central focus is analysis and organization: facts do not, after all, speak for themselves—nor do the dead. You must recognize the evidence (data) . . . and then you must come to a conclusion about them. This must be as near to historical reality as you can make it but it will still be a personal thing if it [is] worth anything at all . . . Analysis passes through the mind laden as it is with some prejudices, some preconceptions and your own place in history—that, above all.[28]

Croce believed that, since history is necessarily filtrated through the historian's mind, "each real history is contemporary history" in that it originates from a present concern: "the past—he argued—is the eternal and living present."[29] The contemporaneity of all history entails, in Croce's view, a link with practical necessity, in that it springs from the "vital problems" the historian faces in his own time, however remote the facts he is analyzing are.[30]

Croce also emphasized the deep rationalistic structure underlying historicism, which allowed for a confrontation with the irrational: he believed that the rational mind must accept and understand the importance played by irrational factors in history, unveiling their rationality and defining their peculiar forms. This attitude must lead, he maintained, to the acceptance of myth and utopia as motivating factors: myth and utopia, he wrote, translate human desires into images, often leading men and women to perilously turn them into reality.[31] Croce and Mosse, as did many contemporary intellectuals, shared a similar pessimism toward the masses and their need for myth rather than for reality: as Mosse stated, people do not generally learn from history, but at least intellectuals should, so Croce distinguished between "political truth" and "popular myth," attributing a similar role to intellectuals.[32] Both historians believed in the social function of myth as giving society cohesion, in a dialectics between myth and reality, in the religious nature of ideologies.[33] As Steven Aschheim has remarked,

George Mosse is a historian who analyses phenomena that go against his grain—a humanist pushed into the study of the inhumane. But, like Benedetto Croce . . . he accepts the notion that this is an unavoidable task, for outside history there is no reality. The only way, therefore, of confronting the reality is by coming to grips with history from the inside and in a committed, rather than a positivistic and descriptive manner. History for him, must be a passion, certainly not "a profession like any other." Like Croce, Mosse insists that the mind of the historian is central to historical analysis; as a result, only history relevant to one's present situation is worthy of its name. Like Croce's work, too, Mosse's writings are animated by a commitment to individual liberty in a world threatened by the forces of mass irrationality and mass politics.[34]

And Mosse openly admitted his intellectual debt to the Italian historian, emphasizing ideas such as the totality of history, the fact that outside history there can be no reality, that all history must necessarily be contemporary history.[35]

Such a view of history as committed involvement on the part of the historian was well attuned to Croce's ethical political spirit. As James Wald has put it, "Mosse never ceased to remind us that the writing of history is a political endeavor. By this, of course, he did not mean that it should be crudely partisan, but rather, that it should derive from our convictions, that it should help us to understand the world in which we live."[36] And history according to Mosse was, indeed, deeply political. "Scholarship must never be sterile," he said during a speech; "it must entail an intellectual and social commitment and must ask itself constantly about its contribution to the outer world. . . . What you will do with your scholarship is indeed relevant for our common future, its failure, or as we hope, its eventual success."[37] Moving from the conviction that each man and woman is a "political animal," early in his teaching career he urged his students to think historically in order to grasp how the world works: here history comes to the fore dressed as the theory that lies behind a well-informed political action, revealing a practical side to the discipline that went beyond its purely theoretical applications.[38] To be informed is a duty, and no one can pretend to live outside history, since it pervades our whole lives. Like Croce, who insisted on a view of historiography as the source of practical action, he furthered a history that necessarily had to be ethical-political.[39] Culture and education must make men and women aware of their historical environment on the one hand, and prepare them for action on the other. As he told his audience during a lecture, "I hope that you also realize a little bit the importance of knowing about things which are neither immediately practical in the sense of offering a monetary return—or contemporary in the sense of dealing only with the here and now. Such knowledge as we have been able to give you is the very minimum necessary so that you can partake in forming the future, to help by intelligent political action to solve problems which, unless they are solved, will transform our Civilization into a civilization in which most of us would not care to live."[40]

This was the reason he argued that scholarship can achieve the best results "if the student has some personal or at least internal relationship to his historical work."[41] Such relationships express themselves in the political arena in that "the past is, in a sense, 'present politics.'"[42] Indeed, the goal of history is, he believed, that of attempting to cure present ills through an analysis of the "essential analytical relationships between past and present."[43] Thus the writing of history becomes a "political endeavor," and politics is, like the promoters of a symposium in his honor argued,

> more than the formal political process. It is even more of behavior of men in institutions related to the state, in cultural, economic, and military organizations. In everyday life, all human interaction is thoroughly permeated with political implication. Methodologically, this view makes Mosse skeptical of analyses of political action that content themselves with the in-and-out trays of a foreign ministry or statistical studies of parliamentary and election votes. Morally, just as Christianity views sin as composed of acts of omission as well as of commission, so it is impossible to be unpolitical. Each person is answerable for the political effects of his/her actions, whether participating directly in the formal polity or attempting to ignore or flee such involvement. Mosse dismisses as self-delusion the ideological cocoon which many a *Bildungsbürger* constructed to wait out the future, while avoiding contact with the perpetual dirty, compromising, often humiliating business of politics. His powerful pedagogical talent barely conceals a fundamental moral indignation against the aspiration to the apolitical.[44]

For these reasons, he believed that "no one has a right to be ignorant about his social, moral and intellectual origins": the meaning of history is precisely that of learning about these origins in order to become well-informed citizens able to live in society and understand its workings. The "use of history" becomes then the understanding of our society, and the "task of history" is "to confront your [emotional] commitment with the world in its historical dimension.

Confront: for it does introduce a sense of limitation, of possibilities rather than absolutes: this is not pessimism but a guideline to success. All change must be built upon realities, and not a blind Utopianism."[45]

With the totalitarian experience before his eyes, Mosse warned against the danger of an emotional drift toward demagoguery and thinking in slogans.[46] Knowledge, then, was the tool to resist such temptations. Individuals should keep a rational attitude, and the task of the historian is to provide them with the necessary intellectual weapons. The preservation of freedom, both intellectual and political, was Mosse's main concern. Freedom was, in his eyes, the goal of education, which in turn was crucial for preserving freedom, for not falling "prey of popular hysterias."[47] This knowledge is our price for freedom: "Freedom for what? Freedom to be well informed individuals who will not be swayed by passion but be guided by secure knowledge, who will not abdicate their rights and judgments to any almighty state," he said.[48] History, being part of education, is therefore connected to the necessity of preserving one's individual rights, one's freedom: history according to Mosse is crucial for living one's own life in the present. In the late 1960s Mosse told his students: "I think that we can all agree that in the late 1960s the battle is, once again, focused against the destruction of individual freedom from the aroused Right. . . . I believe with Romain Rolland that it is the primary duty of the intellectual to keep the torch of freedom alive in an age of iron. The task is not to let that age arrive, and here I think I have illustrated some of the relevance of the course: even if in quite personal terms."[49]

This deeply personal involvement pervaded Mosse's historiography with a "sense of mission," as he wrote in his memoir. He considered history "as a faith," as history for him "took the place of religion."[50] This attitude was in line with cultural history envisaged as a "political endeavor" in contrast with the Rankean parameters for a "detached" history without the personal commitment of the historian. And yet, as James Wald pointed out, Mosse's historiography was not meant to be partisan; instead, it sought to be as objective as possible, always based on the facts without prejudices and yet springing out of the historian's deepest convictions. As Ze'ev Mankovitz elegantly put it, Mosse "has taught us the art of passionate detachment."[51] Mosse pursued his pedagogical enterprise through an imaginative historiography and a way of teaching that transformed his classes into popular events. His tools were intuition and provocation: he made full use of both to break new ground in historiography and to champion his "faith."

The Devil's Advocate

Sterling Fishman, describing Mosse's approach to history, stated that "George's historical genius does not rest on his commitment to theoretical models. He is an artist with a vision rather than an architect with a carefully drawn plan"; similarly, Emilio Gentile defined Mosse's sensitivity as that of an "artist of history."[52] Such descriptions fit into Mosse's way of doing history, into his emphasis on an intuitive approach rather than on complex theoretical elaborations. To be sure, he was deeply immersed in the historical literature and in the archives, and he formulated some principles of his methodology in unpublished papers such as "Literature and History" and "The Cultural Historian and Popular Literature," or in "History, Anthropology, and Mass Movements," but the changes in his methodology generally reflected necessities posed by his research and teaching, and not the opposite: he never built a systematic theoretical structure on which to base his research, and thus he remained open to new ideas and inspirations he drew from the materials he was dealing with. During the Stanford seminar, when faced by pressing criticism about his supposed lack of a theoretical apparatus or failure to use precise definitions, Mosse commented: "I'm still troubled by these academic abstractions, power structures, social structures and so on. What I was interested in is to see why people went along, actually and in fact."[53] Indeed, he had always showed little patience with rigorous and disciplined scholarship, which did not suit his "adventurous bent of mind," as he defined it: he openly declared he had patience only for those matters that fascinated him, and he gratefully recalled how his intellectual curiosity had been first awakened by his English teacher at Bootham School who, on occasion, allowed the class great freedom without imposing that strict discipline that had caused Mosse so many troubles at the Mommsen Gymnasium in Berlin.[54] Indeed, he had hardly been a particularly brilliant student, as he himself pointed out: once he had become a professor at Iowa, he recalled, "I could teach and I could write books, skills for which no one who had met me in Germany or England would have given me credit. As my former headmistress put it when I visited her in Germany after the war, 'How come you are a professor when you were such a dreadful student?'"[55]

Such anecdotes shed much light on his approach to history: his work was always based on extensive research and comprehensive reading of primary and secondary sources; and yet, although he often admired the results of their work and used them in his research, he was never keen on historians who limited themselves to a disciplined scholarship. He preferred to see the "bigger picture,"[56] to find the hidden connections, placing much importance on intuition and a feel for history that surely accounts for the innovative and original books he wrote, but also for the numerous imprecisions they may contain. He often expressed disdain for historians who viewed their role as akin to that of the antiquarian who seemed never to come to any conclusions on the results of the collections of facts and figures.[57] As Walter Laqueur has written, "he was neither a saint nor a perfectionist. His spelling was uncertain in all languages . . . and he had the disdain of a grand seigneur vis-à-vis dates in history. In a memoir about his parents he had written that his father had invited Edith Piaf to perform in Berlin in 1919. I pointed out that this seemed unlikely since Piaf was five years old at the time. Did he mean perhaps Yvette Guilbert or Mistinguett? Yes, of course, he said, but did it really matter?"[58]

James Wald, speaking of the "general nature" of Mosse's work, has vividly described his peculiar approach to history, in which lay, according to him, the "secret of his success":

His innovation lies in having a broad vision, in putting seemingly disparate topics together, in getting the big picture. He transcends the specificity of his researches to arrive at a synthetic analysis. One senses that he is not the type that prefers detailed studies. He has too many ideas to allow himself to stay put for long, he feels the constant need to move on. To be sure, he has carefully reconnoitered the historical landscape that he has chosen to write about; but his is not the nature given to producing elaborate topographical maps. A scout rather than a settler or surveyor, his aim is not to stake out an exclusive claim to a homestead, but rather to blaze a trail, sketching the salient features so as to enable others to join or follow his search.[59]

David W. Sabean, underlining the importance of analogy and comparison for the generation of theoretical questions in Mosse's work, wrote:

On the one hand, narrative provided for him the dimension of practice, while on the other hand, theory was useful for generating questions, rigorously linked to context. He uses narrative to structure what he has to say. Theory for him is not directly linked to the narrative but involves a series of meaningful questions that are often only loosely linked to the matter at hand or to the overarching story he is telling. The questions often seem unprompted by the material itself: they come at right angles, so to speak, to the text he is developing. They can arise from his extensive reading, from his experience, or from something suggested by his imagination—a leap, an analogy, a comparison—

and any of these things can seem at once compelling for the reader and wildly out of place. He could be writing on some late-nineteenth-century text at the same time he was reading Philippe Ariès's *Centuries of Childhood*, the latter providing an insightful question, which he would sometimes make explicit and sometimes leave for the reader to guess where the flash of insight came from. There was no overarching "theory" but rather a myriad of theoretical points and analytical critiques pushing their way into and opening up spaces in the plot he was constructing. The plot itself usually involved an expository reading of text after text, each one chosen for its thematic usefulness. He treated the texts of Western (German) thought much as a biblical expositor might treat Scripture, moving back and forth, explaining here and there, bringing the texts from quite different places into juxtaposition. He takes a theme, builds a central focus, and explores variations.[60]

Such descriptions offer an effective and insightful overview of Mosse's historiography, highlighting the crucial role intuition played in it, and stressing its asystematic nature. Mosse himself had already exposed the foundations of his conception of history in the 1950s; these were not to change over the years. In a speech given at a graduate club, he gave a comprehensive overview of his ideas and beliefs. He argued that historians, in order to teach effectively, should not exclusively rely on textbooks, but rather embrace a definite thesis:

> Any Academic course to have a sense must have a thesis—a clearly defined viewpoint, if it is to be more than "a textbook wired for sound." Here the very limitations of the Historian's day are a help rather than a hindrance. If my knowledge of the religious struggles of the sixteenth century leads me to develop a thesis about politics which I believe also has value for subsequent centuries then my courses will make sense. Facts can be gotten from the textbooks. This I think plays into what constitutes good lecturing. You will only lecture well, I think, if you have the sense of giving the students something new: some theses which you have arrived at, on the bases of your researches—that is, if these researches have a value above the mere digging process. In my own case the work I did for my Ph. D. on the concept of sovereignty, and the work I have done subsequently on the relationship of Christianity to political thought, has given me a perspective over all of modern history. There is, I think, a great deal to be said for Ph. D. topics which are analytical in nature and deal with segments of constant problems in modern history. It must be plain that all this means that I regard the difference

between research and teaching as non existent. Only on the basis of continuing research can you be any kind of inspiring teacher who has developed his own scholarly point of view. Otherwise you will indeed be just a text book wired for sound.[61]

This meaningful passage refers to a belief that was to inform all of his work. It stressed the conviction that facts alone, that is, history "as it actually happened," cannot provide any key to historical understanding; it emphasized the view of history as a totality also in the diachronic sense, where problems posed in one epoch can provide answers for another time, thus reflecting the belief that all history is contemporary history; it expressed his belief in the need to put forward new theses, new ideas, in order to catch the students' attention and to attribute a concrete meaning to teaching beyond the simple exposition of facts; it advocated a fusion of research and teaching in contrast to the tendency of many historians, he continued, to consider research a "luxury," thus creating "operators," "wheels" in the system whose focus was exclusively on academic success in order to become a "successful businessmen." Concluding the speech, Mosse again contrasted "ideas," "imagination" and "research" to "fleeting antiquarianism."[62]

This championing of an imaginative approach to history, furthered by the stress on the importance of putting forward new ideas, went hand in hand with the deeply provocative nature of both his work and his scholarship. Mosse, convinced that the task of the historian was that of unmasking the myths people live by, often sought to accomplish this task by adopting provocation as a tool. Many who have written on his work have highlighted this important aspect. It has been pointed out that Mosse could make "apparently outrageous assertions," thereby inviting the criticism of colleagues and students, or how he loved to make "irreverent judgments . . . both playful and serious."[63] Jeffrey Herf called him a "provocateur," stating that he "offered one provocation after another to the conventions of the discipline," and observing how his history was never "politically correct."[64] George Mosse the historian always retained the personality of the mischievous young Gerhard, who, upon meeting the Soviet foreign minister Georgy Chicherin at a formal reception in the very respectable, luxurious Berlin house of his parents, noticed that he was wearing a tuxedo and asked him in his "usual loud voice how a Communist could possibly wear such a bourgeois garment."[65] Interviewed in the late 1970s Robert Nye colorfully recalled how "if an audience [had] a certain point of view . . . [Mosse] adjust[ed] his lecture to antagonize their feelings," thus inspiring students to search for the correct answer in an attempt to support their original conclusions, arousing "in people their interests in a subject by challenging certain set assumptions." Mosse was, according to Nye, an "intellectual devil's advocate."[66]

Provocation, innovation, deep personal commitment: all this was channeled in Mosse's works, written "to stimulate some debate."[67] And such fervor was also vital part of his lectures, as his former students tell us. Sterling Fishman effectively described his style of teaching:

> he brought with him a booming voice with dramatic modulation, clear, slightly accented diction, memorable descriptions, powerful phrasing, and the ability to make transcendent ideas comprehensible and personal. If George had chosen to be an evangelist and used his oratorical gifts for converting the faithless, he could have conducted a successful cross-country crusade—although it is hard to picture him in that role. George did not practice demagoguery with his students, but he has always been able to reach his most passive hearers. Without employing oversimplifications he has been able to make the ideas of even Calvin or Hegel exciting and personally meaningful.[68]

Paul Breines is equally vivid:

> George's lecturing style was not merely dramatic; it was intensely engaged with the students present. Characteristic gestures included gripping the lectern with both hands, arms extended, posture erect, as if to channel the intellectual and moral passion inside him; leaving the lectern to pace slowly back and forth as he spoke, then returning to it, leaning forward over it as he peered out intently at his listeners. At such a moment, he might have been saying something of the following sort: *yes, you should realize, you student-radicals especially, that you can learn a great deal from John Calvin. For he understood what you so often forget—that real social change doesn't come from what you love to call militancy and certainly not from theory, to which some of you are addicted, but from the two things you lack* (and here he would apparently become stern): *organization*, he would say, then pause, shifting to a provocatively satisfied grin, *and a sense of the symbolic in politics*. Astonishing combinations of erudition and political-moral challenges, George's lectures, as countless students have said, were events.[69]

This teaching style, born to a "tragic" and ironic vision of history, always bore a "didactic element" and a "pedagogical intent," as Sabean has pointed out.[70]

Mosse, never daunted by his pessimism, held to the hope that education, contributing to the formation of a critical mind, could warn people against the power of myth and conformity. The "sense of mission" that pervaded his "faith" was present in all his writings and represents a "continuity of intents" that runs parallel to the "continuity of interests" he saw in his work.

The "History of Perceptions"

The anthropological and psychological nature of Mosse's cultural history as elaborated in the late 1960s had deeper foundations in an attitude toward human nature that had been ingrained in his thought since his first works in early modern history. Even his assertion that it was Georg Lichtheim who introduced him to Hegel's dialectics in the late 1950s needs to be deemphasized to a considerable extent.[71] Indeed, in 1953 Mosse wrote that "rapid changes in history usually come about when the gulf between what is and what should be, between outward reality and the human condition, becomes painfully apparent": this unmistakably implies a profoundly dialectical vision of history where myth and reality interact.[72] He saw a "continuing unity" in the "basic myths and reality rhythm of history"; "all of history," he argued, "must be viewed in a dynamic and dialectical fashion," where the dialectics is "between myth and social forces. I would say between myth and what Marx called objective reality, that is social, political, and economic forces."[73] This illuminates his belief that exclusively social, political, and economic history cannot suffice to come close to historical reality, since it does not consider the importance of one whole half of the equation, that is, the power of myth.

The fact that Mosse focused almost exclusively on the mythical side of history must not draw attention away from the crucial importance he attributed to the "concrete side." The "rhythm of history," he explained in a lecture, is represented by "utopia and its obstacles": "reality sets the framework and cannot be ignored," reality "always stands in the way."[74] This framework is provided by historical narratives, because "theory cut loose from its concrete context becomes a mere game, an amusement of no particular relevance": problems need to be addressed within this essential framework.[75] As he told his students, "all these mediations, longings, angsts, take place within history—chronology. That is why you must not only know the problems but also the chronology, when what happened," for social and political events are important "as limitations within which man moves."[76] Mosse firmly believed that "every cultural movement, however much it thinks of itself as separated from the troubled world, *affects it and is affected by it*"; indeed, in his works, cultural movements are never analyzed in a void, their rhythm is always marked by what he referred to as the "crucial social, economic and political events."[77] He saw the French and the industrial revolutions at the wellspring of his cultural interpretation of modern European history, the German wars through the nineteenth century as determinant elements in the history of the new politics, and the First World War as a turning point in the history of fascism, racism, masculinity, and the "new man." As he wrote in 1961, "Romanticism would be unimaginable without the thought of the eighteenth century and the political events of the age of the French Revolution; Marxism could not be envisaged apart from the Industrial Revolution, and existentialism aside from the First World War and the crisis of European thought which followed it. Though all of this may seem obvious, it needs restatement; cultural history has so often been discussed outside of a proper historical framework."[78] He stated that ideology "is never isolated from the problems faced by an age; it is rather a response to them"; and he asserted that conscious and unconscious wishes, desires, and frustrations of the people "are important without denying the essential role played by the social and political situation. Without the right conditions, the appeal of the proper myths and symbols cannot be activated in a meaningful manner."[79] Referring to nationalism, he clearly said that "certain social, economic and political conditions were necessary in order to activate this cult and to make it effective,"[80] and with regard to the new politics in Germany, he felt the need to specify that "again, we are not claiming that the Third Reich could have succeeded without tangible results in ending unemployment and in foreign policy. The liturgy is *one* crucial factor among others."[81]

The emphasis Mosse placed on myth represented the basis of his cultural history. If his earliest approach to the history of fascism was from the point of view of ideology, "culture" was a concept he had already in mind and lay at the basis of *The Culture of Western Europe*. Here he provided an anthropologically oriented view of culture, which he defined as "a state or habit of mind which is apt to become a way of life intimately linked to the challenges and dilemmas of contemporary society."[82] In the 1950s there emerged, in his work, the embryo of his later approach: in 1953 he wrote of "cultural attitudes, indeed attitudes towards life itself," and twenty years later, in the interview on Nazism, he saw fascism, intended as a cultural phenomenon, as an "attitude of mind, an attitude towards life."[83] Mosse's 1961 definition of culture was an expression of what he held to be history's dialectical nature. A "habit of mind" becomes a "way of life": idea and reality are "intimately linked" in a dialectical interplay. Indeed, Mosse believed that "cultural development does involve an interaction of ideas between intellectuals conscious of what they were about and the general mood of their times": this "general mood," as he explained in the third edition of the book, "consists of reactions to the complexities of daily life as well as of images of a better future. Such hopes and reactions can be expressed by political or social action."[84] Following Johann Huizinga's and Ernst Bloch's insights, he heavily stressed the importance of popular dreams, hopes, and aspirations for historical developments. He saw a common mechanism at work in both early modern popular piety and modern ideologies,[85] where the irrational manifests itself in the human need to strive for a better world, a better future, a "fully furnished house." Just as popular piety had provided the popular support for the Reformation, so *völkisch* ideology paved the way for National Socialism.

Ideology, in Mosse's view, is "the formation of basic attitudes," as he put it at Stanford. Here he admitted that he used the concept "in a whole gamut of ways," and yet he stated that "by and large I come back always to the role of ideology in forming attitudes, because the attitudes of people depend on the image they have of themselves and their place in the world, and they always have several choices."[86] Ideology thus becomes a lens that allows the "believer" to look at the world according to certain criteria, which eventually determine the actions one takes. From this perspective, a link can be established between Mosse's concept of "ideology" and that of "culture." As he stated in 1961,

the system of thought, the ideology, is primary, for it produces attitudes toward life and thus toward all that life means to people. Let us also remember that ideology is never isolated from the problems faced by an age; it is rather a response to them. What is of importance in cultural history is not people's mode of life but their attitudes toward that life and the possibilities it holds. . . . Perhaps we should broaden the definition of culture upon which this book is built. Culture is a state or habit of mind which becomes an attitude toward life, intimately linked to the challenges and dilemmas of contemporary society; indeed, through the formulation of ideologies culture becomes an allegiance to a way of life itself.[87]

Culture formulates ideologies that, in turn, produce attitudes toward life; through ideology, then, culture becomes itself an attitude toward life. Attitudes toward life are the background against which actions are taken, and yet these attitudes are "linked to the challenges and dilemmas of contemporary society": ideologies are responses to the problems faced by an age and at the same time they produce those attitudes that are linked to reality. This is what Mosse later called the "interplay between perception and reality" that drives history: years later, commenting on his book on European culture, he gave a "clear definition of culture—not the history of ideas, but habits of mind which become ways of receiving reality. Underlying: that what drives history is how reality is perceived, rather than what it is, or better, the interplay between perception and reality."[88] In this scheme of things, a perception is a "way of receiving reality," a sophistication of the "attitudes towards life." Ideologies, formulated by culture, produce attitudes toward life (and, by extension, perceptions), but at the same time they are influenced by them in a dialectical connection, since culture itself has become a perception.

By 1988 the concept of "culture" in Mosse had almost completely supplanted that of "ideology," marking the passage from intellectual history to cultural history that took place in the late 1960s. Culture, being a habit of mind, has a character of immediacy, unlike ideology, which is a "system of thought" that needs intellectual formulation. Intellectuals can be a "barometer of ideas, voicing them clearly and formulating a mood," while the "mood of the population . . . interacts with the ideas built up by intellectuals" provided that the latter elaborate an accurate "analysis of the mood, hopes and needs of the times." These considerations, which Mosse expressed in revising *The Culture of Western Europe*, are but another example of how his historiography moved away from the thought of intellectuals toward a history of the masses.[89] And yet, as is often the case in Mosse, his early works already bore the seeds of future developments, although he did not deal, at least directly, with certain issues: concluding his book on the Reformation, Mosse expressed his conviction that the theological disputes between Catholics and Protestants were not confined to theology, that they encompassed the whole culture of the epoch: "The difference between Protestantism and Catholicism did not remain confined to theology alone, they came to encompass divergent attitudes to the whole texture of religious experience and, through this, toward life itself. . . . Two different views on the nature and capabilities of man confronted each other[;] . . . the style of life of the inhabitants was deeply affected"; there were "deep differences between Catholic and Protestant attitudes toward life. Thus, the Reformation had consequences that far exceed any theological quarrels; it led to a division which was one of cultural attitudes, indeed attitudes toward life itself."[90] And the history of the whole sixteenth century could be interpreted as follows, in Mosse's words: "The sixteenth century is a crucial age in the development of European supremacy: not because it managed to conquer the world by force, but because it laid the foundations for an attitude towards life which, in the end, proved favorable to those political, economic and social changes essential to the evolution of Europe into the modern age."[91]

The juxtaposition of attitudes toward life with political, economic, and social factors is nothing else but the dialectics between myth and reality, and to be aware of this interplay was, according to Mosse, the key to proper historical understanding. Myth's relation to reality was, in his view, embodied by the concept of "perception." As he said in a lecture, "we must say at the very beginning: what we are concerned with is the interplay between myth and reality, people's perception which leads to their action and the reality with which they interact. Thus we must avoid single causes. . . . Only in this way can we come close to historical reality."[92] Thus, perceptions become the essence of history. As he said in an interview,

[the] kind of history I do might really be called a history of perceptions, that's what I would think 'cause I believe people act on their perceptions, and their perceptions sometimes have very little to do with reality. I used to say to my students . . . you also live by perceptions, 'cause if you saw yourself as you really are, you would commit suicide. Thank God we don't see each other as we really are. . . . Your perceptions are, however, also reformed by reality. I mean, that depends on the person. If they are formed by reality, you know what happened, you try to move away from it, obviously, yes. But the whole world is now perceptions: What do we know about the people who rule over us? What do we know about anything? We don't, it's all mediated, yeah. It all plays on our perceptions or tries to manipulate them.[93]

Stemming from the belief that "what man is, only history tells," there emerges a view of history that is not only anthropological, but also anthropocentric, and the human mind stands at the center: "Man's mind," he said, "is central to perception and perception determines the view of himself and the world." The view of the world is nothing less than a worldview, a *Weltanschauung*, which is what an ideology provides. Ideology and myth can coincide in Mosse, or, perhaps better, "myth becomes a faith—a beleaguered faith in the view of the ideology."[94]

These considerations led him to believe that history is driven by "how reality is perceived, rather than what it is, or better, [by] the interplay between perception and reality."[95] Men's and women's perceptions as products of their minds thus provide them with the background against which they make their choices, driving them to practical action: in this process, men and women manifest their individuality through their freedom of choice.[96] Such a view, Mosse explained, rejects any historical determinism, and he criticized those historians who focused exclusively on one side of the dialectics, thus reducing history to a deterministic account of how social, political, and economic forces shaped human existence. Men and women, instead, make choices that are informed by their perceptions, by the myths and symbols through which they perceive objective reality.[97] Reality, in turn, is crucial in that it determines the limits, the framework of human perceptions, but "human perceptions are more than just the actual realities," for men internalize reality; they infuse it with their wishes and hopes, their wish for security, for eternity.[98] "Reality sets the framework and cannot be ignored": in contrast to the human "need for utopia, need for fairy tales . . . reality always stands in the way"; this is, according to Mosse, the "rhythm of history: utopia and its obstacles."[99] In the last resort, perceptions constitute, in Mosse's view, the backbone of cultural history: "Cultural history centers above all upon the perceptions of men and women, how these are shaped and enlisted in politics. . . . [T]hese perceptions may at times correspond to what historians or sociologists with hindsight conceive as their true situation in society, and yet, people act upon their perceptions true or false as they might be, rather than upon what historical or sociological analysis tells us as to their actual place in the scheme of things."[100] Defending himself from accusations of "over-valuing ideas," Mosse replied that "once the need for myth, for mediation, is understood there is no over-valuation, but a clarification of the link between ideas and reality. Thus ideas, a world view, have consequences in action: not just by ideologues and revolutionaries, but by everyone. Reality is never received, understood, unmediated. Here social myths [are] elaborated."[101]

The concept of "mediation" is of paramount importance here, in that it adds depth to Mosse's "history of perceptions," thus transforming it into a "history of mediated perceptions." "What do we know about anything?" he mused in an interview. "We don't. It's all mediated."[102] As a consequence, "mediation is what our history is all about: how people perceived themselves and their world, the myths they lived by and the symbols they sought."[103] The concept of mediation was derived from Hegel and Cassirer. Discussing Cassirer's approach, Mosse praised "his conception of how men mediate between their own minds and reality," which "is useful at all levels of historical analysis. Myths and symbols can be analyzed historically because the human mind works within definable categories of cognition. Cassirer shared with anthropologists the presupposition that all freedom of action is checked by the recognition of certain objective, inner limitations upon the reaches of the human mind. This assumption becomes all important when one uses myth and symbol for an understanding of the human mind and the society within which it has to work."[104] Myths and symbols viewed as images act as concrete political forces when they mediate between people and reality; they are the filters through which reality is perceived.[105] In the introduction to *Masses and Man: Nationalist and Fascist Perceptions of Reality*, Mosse clearly defined nationalism as a "mediating force" between intuition and reality, and he described the whole book (a collection of essays) as an investigation into the history of human intuitions, of those mediating forces that connect the individual to the world and determine one's personal and political choices.[106] The strength of Hegel's influence in this regard is revealed by a telling passage taken from his lectures: "Man's mind mediates reality through its comprehension, its consciousness. . . . [I]t is no surprise therefore that Hegel sees man defined through his actions which are a result of his consciousness."[107] As Seymour Drescher, David Sabean, and Allan Sharlin have effectively maintained, "Mosse argues that symbols are the meaning in themselves, that they order perceived reality, have multiple dimensions, and mediate between subjects and between subject and object. Historical actors perceive their own interests in distorted form. The very processes actors set in motion for their purposes rarely function exactly as intended and do so under conditions that often mask sources of tension from them. The only way to handle the problem is for the historian to incorporate the dialectic into historical practice."[108] To understand that history is dialectical means to be able to grasp its irrational, apparently inexplicable side. Without such an approach, said Mosse, a phenomenon like National Socialism cannot be explained:

A unicausal explanation of this phenomenon will not do. . . . [Y]ou have to bring in people and the desires and myths of people which are not always directly determined by their so-called objective class position. Usually people have false rather than true consciousness in this regard. As history is still made by people and based on people, certainly this has to be part of the historical dialectic. It seems to me very sterile to mouth slogans of class, capitalism, or reactionary without defining them in terms of their situation and without connecting them to the kind of world people want. In other words, these categories, useful though they are and investigated though they must be in detail, should be connected to the myths by which people live, to their attitudes of life. And these attitudes are never so crudely determined by the political and economic environment as some historians seem to believe. We must finally discard unmediated and positivist analyses for the examination of a mediated dialectic.[109]

Bending Marx's concept of "false consciousness" as ideological conditioning to his own purposes, Mosse implies in the above passage that most people are inclined to yield to the power of myth and therefore submit to an explanation and justification of a certain existing condition, thus subjugating their freedom to the existing order of society.[110] Consciousness, on the other hand, represents humanity's awareness of politics and of its position in history. The centrality of the historian's mind, and of the human mind in general, then touches on this problem: false consciousness means false perception of the interplay between myth and reality that takes place in the mind. To disregard this meant, in Mosse's view, to lose the much-needed balance between myth and reality both in personal life and in historiography: these, in his view, fully coincided.

Conclusion

George L. Mosse's Legacy

I was never to close the gap between ideal and reality, and I learned
myself what I used to tell my students: true maturity is reached only
when one realizes that there exist insoluble problems.

—GEORGE L. MOSSE

Our enemies have been and will always be those who lack tolerance
toward individual rights and freedoms, who seek security in a rigid
conformity and in emotion not tempered by reason.

—GEORGE L. MOSSE

George Mosse must certainly be considered one of the founding fathers
of cultural history as we know it at the turn of the twenty-first century.
If his ideas, as James Wald remarked, "strike us as insightful, but not
quite new it is precisely because Mosse was a pioneer in cultural history";
similarly, Jay Winter argued that he "developed a kind of cultural history which
was not fashionable in his time, but which seems amazingly familiar today."[1]
It has been written that Mosse was "years ahead of his times," that he had an
"extraordinary gift for anticipating what would become the important historical questions for the future, what taboos had to be transgressed, what myths
shattered."[2] Stanley Payne maintained that "it is no exaggeration to say that
Mosse pioneered what have become some of the main trends of research at the
beginning of the twenty-first century."[3] As noted above, Emilio Gentile wrote
of a "before Mosse" and an "after Mosse" in the historiography of fascism.[4]
Mosse, as Steven Aschheim put it, was "instrumental in transforming the very
idea of what we understand to be 'cultural history.'"[5] His work has been widely
praised in many countries, he was awarded numerous prizes and honorary

degrees, and a number of *Festschriften* have been published to honor and assess his contributions and his personality.[6]

It therefore appears surprising that influential accounts of the development of cultural history, and even of the historiography of fascism and National Socialism, completely ignore Mosse's contributions. With regard to National Socialism, classic summaries of historical interpretations of fascism such as Ian Kershaw's *The Nazi Dictatorship* and Klaus Hildebrandt's *Das Dritte Reich* hardly mention Mosse, let alone his cultural approach to the study of German fascism.[7] As far as the historiography of nationalism is concerned, many accounts either consign Mosse to the footnotes, or just plainly ignore him. At any rate, his contribution rarely receives thorough treatment.[8] In the field of cultural studies, it is astonishing that such leading historians as Peter Burke or Geoff Eley never mention Mosse or the influence of his work in their classic analyses of the birth and development of cultural history, not even when they refer to anthropological approaches to history.[9] What are the reasons for this neglect? The main motive certainly lies in Mosse's intuitive approach to historiography; as Jeffrey Herf put it, he worked "without a specific theoretical program,"[10] which caused many of his intuitions to go almost unnoticed, if only to be rescued later, and often without mentioning him. In Anson Rabinbach's words, Mosse was "a pioneer, but he never stayed long enough in any one of those territories to post fences and mark disciplinary boundaries."[11] Rudy Koshar argued that Mosse's idiosyncratic attitude toward theoretical elaboration led him to ignore relevant debates on modernization and social movements, which could have enriched his works; moreover, he did not participate in current debates on historical theory, and as a result, he did not leave a distinctive, easily traceable mark on various disciplines.[12] Indeed, as mentioned earlier, Mosse confined his theoretical beliefs mostly to his lectures or to unpublished writings. His precocious and unfashionable intuitions often broke new ground, and brushed against the grain of established scholarship: only later would his insights be incorporated into historiography, with or without his direct influence on other historians.

Mosse's contribution had been innovative from the outset. In his early modern works he focused on original themes and posed connections that had not received much attention: among these, the resistance to the process of state-building on the basis of the common law, the centrality of Jesuit casuistry in the theological discourse of the seventeenth century (as well as the parallel drawn between Catholic and Protestant casuistry), and the emphasis on the significance of popular piety as opposed to established religions.[13] Many of his books on early modern Europe went through several reprints, and some are still in print and valuable contributions to the subject.[14] However, there is little doubt that his greatest and most enduring work is on the history of the nineteenth and twentieth centuries. Books like *The Crisis of German Ideology*, *The Nationalization of the Masses*, *Toward the Final Solution*, and *Fallen Soldiers* are by now classics in the field, and in the case of the first two, published respectively in 1964 and 1975, they still are (more than thirty years since their publication) must-reads for anyone who approaches the history of National Socialism and of fascism.

Mosse's innovative approach is self-evident from the titles of his works, not to mention their historiographical significance. *The Crisis of German Ideology* broke new ground in two respects. First, in its opposition to dominant liberal and Marxist interpretations; second, because this work gave "'sub-intellectual' ideas a place in the writing of the intellectual and cultural history of fascism and Nazism," showing the importance of such ideas: here Mosse "blurred the boundaries between political, intellectual/cultural, and social history," thus attempting a synthesis, a reconciliation between these diverse disciplines.[15] Moreover, Mosse's work contended that the historian must examine the penetration of ideas into the broader public and institutions: it is when they are institutionalized that they become effective. As long as they remain abstract entities detached from political realities (which had been the standard set, for example, by Arthur Lovejoy's work on the history of ideas) they remain ineffective. Also, the book linked the rise of National Socialist anti-Semitism to the more general pattern of the crisis of modernity, thus viewing it in a historical perspective and not as something above history.[16] *Nazi Culture* was another outstanding example of Mosse's going against the grain. A book on Nazi "culture" at a time when Nazi ideology was regarded as subintellectual and therefore unworthy of serious consideration was "shocking," and the title's association itself between National Socialism and culture seemed an "oxymoron."[17]

The anthropological and visual turn brought about even more drastic innovations, inaugurating what Emilio Gentile has rightly defined as the most original and fruitful phase of his historiography.[18] The role he attributed to myths, stereotypes, and symbols "opened up new approaches on the study of mass politics, fascism, racism, Jewish history, sexuality, and personal identity."[19] *The Nationalization of the Masses*, as argued above, was a milestone both for the historiography of fascism and for cultural history at large. Moreover, by connecting fascism with the mainstream of European history and culture, it defied those interpretations that regarded it as an aberration, a "parenthesis," a drift from the liberal-oriented course of European development. These views, already inherent in *The Culture of Western Europe*, were furthered by Mosse's later works, as he focused on the "dark side of modernity."

Steven Aschheim saw in *Toward the Final Solution* the first attempt to write a major interpretation of the Jewish genocide based on the European tendency toward aesthetics and the visual. The book's originality, Aschheim argued, lay in the "emphasis on the centrality of visual stereotypes" and in the crucial role attributed to aesthetics.[20] The book, with its analysis of the Enlightenment's contribution to the Holocaust, paved the way for more studies on the connections between bourgeois values and mass murder. *Nationalism and Sexuality* highlighted the collective dimension of sexuality and respectability in their political implications. Aschheim defined this work as a landmark that posed a "strikingly new perspective" not only for the history of anti-Semitism, but also for that of all groups of people (homosexuals, Gypsies, the mentally ill) who were depicted as "outsiders"; the book addressed, just as *Toward the Final Solution* had done, the whole of European society, pointing the finger at the process through which so-called "respectable society" had excluded a portion of its members, thus paving the way for their further isolation and eventual extermination under the Nazis.[21] Mosse's concern with sexuality continued with *The Image of Man*, "one of the first histories of stereotypes and images of 'masculinity,'" but also one of the first comprehensive analyses of the "new man" of fascism.[22] *Fallen Soldiers* was instrumental in inaugurating the "memory boom" of the 1990s, as Rabinbach pointed out, referring to the myriad of studies on the Great War that appeared after Mosse's book.[23] Last but not least, the emphasis Mosse placed on liturgy left a lasting imprint on the development of political religions theory as it developed in the 1990s, beginning with Emilio Gentile's *The Sacralization of Politics in Fascist Italy* (1993) through his *Politics as Religion* (2001).[24] The historical analysis of nationalism and fascism as religious phenomena, put forward by the American historian Carlton Hayes as early as in the 1920s and then theorized by Eric Voegelin, was continued (although not always explicitly relying on their works) by émigré historians as Hans Kohn and Mosse;[25] Mosse's work in particular profoundly inspired Gentile, as the Italian historian wrote in a 1982 letter to his colleague.[26]

Mosse's Work between Recognition and Neglect

The reception of Mosse's work has varied from country to country, in tune with cultural and historiographical backgrounds. Any attempt to offer a comprehensive analysis of the impact of Mosse's historiography on different national scenes would require a book in itself, and therefore must necessarily remain outside the scope of this study, which is primarily focused on the inner development of his thought. In the light of some important contributions to the subject matter in recent years, however, a tentative analysis can be offered here; this analysis, based on general considerations, can shed additional light on certain aspects of Mosse's work, highlighting the historiographical setting of his contributions as well as the intellectual background against which his innovative approach was furthered. If certain cross-national aspects have been already dealt with, such as Mosse's impact on the historiography of fascism or of the Great War, or wider considerations on the development of cultural history or, still, his contribution to Jewish studies and to gender studies, a provisional balance can be drawn with regard to his reception in some major countries.

The impact of Mosse's work has been perhaps greatest in Italy. To this day, only two comprehensive studies on Mosse have been published, both by Italian historians: in 2007 Emilio Gentile's *Il fascino del persecutore* ("The fascination with the persecutor") appeared, a detailed analytical account of Mosse's historiography and a vivid description of him as a person; in 2010 Donatello Aramini published *George L. Mosse: L'Italia e gli storici* ("George L. Mosse: Italy and historians"), a comprehensive analysis of Mosse's reception by Italian historiography.[27] Also in 2010 an important conference was organized in Rome to take stock of Mosse's influence on historiography eleven years after his passing.[28] In addition, a great number of essays on Mosse have been published by Italian historians over the decades, and his influence is still very present on different generations of scholars, as Aramini has clearly shown.[29]

Mosse himself, on receiving a prestigious award in Italy, attributed his favorable reception also to the Italian "widespread disposition to think visually": the fact that his best received book in the country was *The Nationalization of the Masses* seems to confirm this thought.[30] Mosse's work entered the Italian historiographical debate through Renzo De Felice and Emilio Gentile. De Felice, who already had an interest in the incidence of the religious on modern politics, highly appreciated Mosse's efforts at writing his book on the new politics: the two had first met in 1967, in the middle of Mosse's anthropological and visual turn, which also focused on the search for the roots of fascist consensus, a theme that lay at the heart of De Felice's historiographical preoccupations.[31] De Felice was instrumental in promoting his colleague's work in Italy: his wife translated *The Nationalization of the Masses*, which was published at the same time as the original, and Mosse won the prestigious Premio Acqui-Storia in 1975 (De Felice was on the jury).[32] Emilio Gentile too pinpointed the originality

of Mosse's work, which diverged from the mainstream of Italian traditional historiography, still dominated by a view of fascism based on propaganda rather
than on consensus.[33] The historians grouped around De Felice and the journal
Storia contemporanea grasped the importance of Mosse's contributions: Gentile
defined him as "one of the greatest contemporary historians," Niccolò Zapponi
saw in his work a real "historiographical turn," and De Felice wrote an important introduction to the Italian edition of *The Nationalization of the Masses*
praising Mosse's achievements.[34] The work of the German American historian
opened new vistas that influenced an important trend in Italian historiography,
thus paving the way for an approach that directly affected the work of De Felice
and Gentile.[35] Apart from the favorable reception of these historians, Mosse's
work remained substantially ignored or misunderstood by other scholars of fascism until the mid-1980s, when the tide turned.[36] Aramini attributes this turn
to the crisis of the "fascist interpretive paradigm" and to the new interest in the
irrational, which was no longer interpreted as merely manipulative and propagandistic, and which had been furthered by the translations of important works
on the Great War (Paul Fussell and Eric Leed), and by the influence of the works
of the last generation of the Annales historians.[37] At the turn of the 1990s,
Mosse's works reached the height of success, affecting the reflections on the aesthetics of politics on the one hand, and those on the nation-building process on
the other. However, though Mosse was no longer attacked and criticized directly,
and his contributions were widely praised, many historians stuck to their views
based on the concept of propaganda, thus overturning the very essence of
Mosse's concept of "nationalization of the masses."[38] Since the 1990s Emilio
Gentile has built on Mosse's premises with considerable success and influence,
though following his own path, which investigated the "sacralization of politics"
rather than its aesthetic dimension, which had been Mosse's concern.[39] Moreover, since the mid-1990s the first analytical essays on Mosse appeared: in 1995
Mosse was awarded a *laurea honoris causa* by the University of Camerino, and on
the occasion Renato Moro wrote the first important overview of Mosse's whole
work; five years later, Giuseppe Galasso published another comprehensive
essay on his historiography; Emilio Gentile analyzed the development of his
interpretation of fascism in an important 2004 article, and then wrote the first
book entirely devoted to Mosse's work (2007).[40] Striking a balance, Aramini
wonders if Mosse's readers in Italy really grasped the actual content of his theses, since many were accepted but developed in a different direction. At any
rate, he concludes, *The Nationalization of the Masses* above all other works by
Mosse deeply changed the perception of fascism in Italian historiography.[41]

The reception of Mosse's work in his native land, Germany, is very different from what he enjoyed in Italy. Moshe Zimmermann examined this question in 1985, and noted that it took almost fifteen years before *The Crisis of German Ideology* was translated into German, and that the book was ignored by the Historikerzunft, the German Historical Association. According to Zimmermann, the reasons for this neglect lay in the fact that German historiography in the 1960s and 1970s was dominated by social history on the one hand, and engaged in the *Fischerkontroverse* on the other. This left little room for discussion of Mosse's work. Social historians had no interest in intellectual and cultural history, and were reluctant to accept anthropological approaches such as those Mosse had adopted. Moreover, German historiography at the time tended to regard National Socialism as an "accident" in German history, whose roots were to be found in the 1920s and 1930s. This plainly contrasted with Mosse's view of National Socialism, whose origins lay deep in German history from the time of the wars of liberation against Napoleon. Zimmermann wrote of a "typical German uneasiness" at establishing a direct line between German nationalism and Nazism, which was exactly what Mosse was aiming at. Indeed, German historians were making the "attempt to rescue Germany from Nazism in retrospect," and claimed that *völkisch* thought had played no concrete role in politics, thus betraying the "paranoia plaguing German historical understanding."[42] Mosse himself, speaking on the *Historikerstreit*, had lamented the fact that nationalism was "a word that will hardly be found in any discussion about the Historikerstreit," and this was due to "the dominance of social history" and to the fact that nationalism had been discredited after 1945, especially among those Germans who had overdone it before the war; but, Mosse continued, "without confronting the problem of nationalism not only can the whole period not be properly understood but even what the Historikerstreit is really all about." Nationalism, according to Mosse, is the key to understanding German history, and if it was not addressed in the *Historikerstreit*, that was because the problem went "to the heart of a crisis of national identity tied to this past."[43] To be sure, Mosse's poor reception in Germany improved beginning in the late 1970s, when the taboo was broken and his works on the nationalization of the masses and on racism were immediately translated. Zimmermann held that, while Mosse's work on National Socialism had been initially disregarded, he was considered from the beginning an authority on Jewish history, which seems to confirm, in Zimmermann's opinion, Germany's general uneasiness in coming to terms with its Nazi past.[44] However, as Aschheim observed, since the late 1980s Mosse's historiography was recognized in Germany, and he was the recipient of various academic honors, including the Goethe-Medaille from the Goethe-Institut in Munich in 1988 and an honorary doctorate from the Universität-Gesamthochschule in Siegen, in 1998.[45] Since 1997 the Institute for German Literature at the Humboldt University in Berlin has organized the Mosse-Lecture Series, a sign of how the attitude toward Mosse's work in German historiography is rapidly changing.

Mosse's work has also had an impact on French historiography, although rather belated. As of the late 1990s, few of his books had been translated into French.[46] Stéphane Audoin-Rouzeau, in his essay on Mosse's reception in France, looked for an explanation for this neglect. On the one hand, he attributed this to the fact that Mosse's works hardly dealt with France, if not to connect the French Revolution with fascist political style, or to stress the strength of French anti-Semitism before 1914.[47] Audoin-Rouzeau wrote of Mosse's poor knowledge of the country's history, which accounted, in turn, for France's poor knowledge of his work. On the other hand, he criticized the exclusive nationalism of French historiography, inviting French historians to retrieve the wasted time and pay the due attention to this "great historian."[48] To be sure, if Mosse's work has generally been ignored, his contributions to the history of the Great War were very influential in France, where they represented one of the rare points of encounter between Mosse and French historians.[49] His work on fascism had a less fortunate reception, especially insofar as he directly connected fascism with the thought of Rousseau and with the French Revolution. His essay "Fascism and the French Revolution" fueled a lively debate with the French historian François Furet, who rejected Mosse's connections, calling them anachronistic, and lamenting the little emphasis laid by him on the contrast between revolutionary ideals and fascist values.[50] If Mosse was not very familiar with French history, the same cannot be said for French historiography: he fully appreciated the tradition of the Annales as represented by the works of Marc Ferro and Philippe Ariès, as it has been shown above, and his own interpretation of the Great War heavily relied on their insights.

Mosse as Émigré Historian

On the American scene, Mosse's contribution to the understanding of German and Jewish history was deep and long lasting.[51] He was awarded the American Historical Association's Award for Scholarly Distinction and the Leo Baeck Medal, and important symposia in his honor were held in the country (before and after his death), which often resulted in *Festschriften* that attempted to draw a balance between his work and influence.[52] As Anson Rabinbach recalled, in the course of his career Mosse "trained a generation of historians who now teach at distinguished universities around the world."[53] Mosse helped lay a bridge between German and American historiography, and in this respect he certainly belonged to those German Jewish refugee historians who, as Kenneth D. Barkin put it, "transformed the way Americans studied the German past," who "taught Americans how be historians of modern Germany."[54] German history, widely neglected since the "anti-German hysteria" that followed the First World War, became "critical part of the curriculum of every major [American] university" after the second conflict, and this happened, Barkin argues, also thanks to the contributions of German Jewish émigré historians in the face of the widespread anti-Semitism that informed the American academe.[55] The émigrés "were able to ensure that German history would become an accepted part of the American university curriculum. . . . Their own commitment to a liberal-democratic interpretation of German history meshed well with the democratic values of young, educated Americans of the postwar era." They were primarily concerned with the question of why radical fascism came to power in Germany, the fruit of the almost obvious heritage they brought with them from their native country.[56] Barkin notes how the Nazi period was mainly ignored by historians at the time, and Neumann's *Behemoth* and Shirer's *Rise and Fall of the Third Reich* were the most read books on the subject. The refugee historians focused on the roots of National Socialism instead, and did so stressing the importance of ideas and "the conviction that intellectual history provid[ed] a vehicle for understanding the failure of democracy to take root in Germany," thus emphasizing the country's divergence from the liberal-democratic tradition other European nations had made their own.[57]

Mosse belonged to the so-called "second generation" of German Jewish refugee historians, that is, to those historians who left Germany after having experienced the rise of Nazism, but before completing their studies.[58] Steven Aschheim argued that these historians (along with Mosse, he refers to Peter Gay, Walter Laqueur, and Fritz Stern) "virtually reinvented German cultural and intellectual history and recast our understanding of it. They did so in the 1960s, long before the 'linguistic turn,' and on the basis of epistemological assumptions and contextual emphases quite different from the 'constructivist' and textual insistencies of the later 'new cultural history.'"[59] Aschheim drew an interesting comparison between these cultural historians and the German social historians (Hans-Ulrich Wehler, Jürgen Kocka, Hans and Wolfgang Mommsen, Martin Broszat, Wolfgang Schieder, and others), a comparison that sheds much light on the émigrés' original contribution as well as on the reasons

Mosse's approach, and cultural history in general, have found such a poor reception in Germany. Aschheim also highlights the importance "ethnonational
identities, generations, and geographical locations" have for the historical profession. This helps to further stress and clarify the link between life and work
in Mosse. These two groups of historians, active since the 1960s, had much in
common: all of them were Liberals or Social Democrats; all of them sought
to read German history against the traditional, conservative trend of German
historiography; and all of them searched for a distanced and critical evaluation
of the German past. They tried to link National Socialism to "immanent elements within German society itself," and leaned toward a *Sonderweg* view of
German history.[60] Aschheim maintained that, despite these similarities, these
two trends "emerged from significantly different, emotionally fraught textures
of feeling, experience, and perception and resulted in rather differently nuanced
representations of that traumatizing past." Despite the shared focus on the
same period, and the attempt to delve into the historical roots of National
Socialism, German social historians centered around 1933 as symbolic date,
while the émigrés focused on 1941–42: "For the social historians . . . the *Sonderweg* was the collapse of liberal democracy; for the cultural historians it was
anti-Semitism, genocide, and related Nazi atrocities."[61] The émigré historians
"instinctively turned to 'culture' (in its broader sense) as an explanatory key, to
ideology, issues of self-identity under crisis. . . . The turn to 'culture' was . . .
deeply connected to an awareness of the enormous power of ideological and
symbolic forces within German history and National Socialism. These émigrés
had, after all, experienced the weight of these forces directly on their own per-
sons. . . . The kind of history they composed was an expression of this inherited
sensibility."[62] German social historians, Aschheim argued, fully ignored their
work, perhaps also because they did not grasp the deeply innovative character
of their cultural history, since they stuck to a view of it that was traditional and
conservative (that of *Kulturgeschichte*), thus overlooking the radical transformations they brought about. These German Jewish scholars focused on the role
of irrationalism, if only to confront it with their own humanist, Enlightenment
ideals. Moreover, Aschheim interestingly maintained that, "perhaps," German
Jews, "when it came to issues related to National Socialism . . . both because
they were above suspicion and beyond the border, could openly address these
ideological issues, the putative magnetism of right-wing radicalism and Nazi
politics, in a way that would have been taboo for Germans in Germany."[63]
Thus, German Jewish historians could offer a great contribution to modern
German history, in a way complementing the works on the sociopolitical

process of social historians, but also shedding light on a phenomenon that most Western observers had, in the 1950s and 1960s, almost totally neglected: the Holocaust.[64]

Enzo Traverso has investigated the reasons that brought these refugees "to see and think about something that was almost invisible to their contemporaries," how they were able "to act as pathfinders for our later historical consciousness."[65] They had "a common feature: they were exiles, marginal people and outsiders," and "one should not consider this characteristic—exile—anecdotal or accidental; on the contrary, it was probably an essential precondition for their clear-sightedness and analytical sharpness. In other words, they illustrated the *epistemological privilege* of exile."[66] Traverso regards this privilege as "a kind of intellectual compensation, doubtless at a very high price, for the privations and uprooted life of exile."[67] This search led to a significant result, since these émigrés, in the midst of the triumph of Western democracies against fascism and their belief in a return to "a new era of Enlightenment," "like unwelcome Cassandras theorized a terrible and irreversible civilisational break. . . . [W]hile Western culture seemed to return to an idea of Progress eclipsed in the cataclysms of the modern Thirty Years' War, exiles played the role of killjoys identifying progress with catastrophe."[68] Mosse's provocative critique of bourgeois society and values must be seen also in this light. Traverso sets the point of view of the outsiders at the center of their innovative perspectives on history: "As strangers, extraterritorial and 'free-floating,' refugees were free of many of the social, cultural, political and also psychological constraints of the context they lived in. Indeed, they looked at war and Nazism with different eyes than did American or even Europeans. . . . Objectively forced to see the world with critical eyes, refugees adopted the position of the outsider, the heretic, the destroyer of orthodoxy and accepted norms." The refugee historians shared a "lack of prejudice," a "great sensitivity to injustice"; they "escaped from national stereotypes"; they perceived the death camps "not only as a Jewish tragedy but also, more deeply and universally, as a wound changing our image of humanity and our interpretation of history."[69] Many refugees embraced Marxism, not as "a state's theory" or "a revolutionary strategy" but rather as "a critique of domination," an inclination Mosse shared in some way in his attempt to fuse socialism with liberalism, thus giving it "a human face." Traverso concludes his reflections by pointing at the legacy of these emigrants who "created something new in American culture," and at the same time saw their intellectual background based on *Bildung* be affected by "'Atlantic' ideas of freedom, law and norms." The path was, he writes, summed up by Mosse's "brilliant

dictum: 'from *Bildung* to the Bill of Rights,'" which perfectly fuses Mosse's combination of German Enlightenment values and his preoccupation with individual rights and freedoms as represented by American society.[70] As Renato Moro
observed, Mosse, along with Hannah Arendt, Ernst Cassirer, Jacob Talmon,
Léon Poliakov, Raymond Aaron, Eric Fromm, and Zeev Sternhell, contributed
to that "rethinking of fascism from a Jewish perspective" that has been so
important for modern historiography; Jeffrey Herf wrote that Mosse, Stuart
Hughes, Peter Gay, and Fritz Stern vitally contributed to the "salvage operation" for humanism and liberalism, an operation, they would have perhaps
added, that sought to preserve an important part of German culture that had
been so severely damaged under the Third Reich.[71]

The centrality of the Jewish experience, and particularly of the Holocaust,
in Mosse's work raises the question of whether his history can be regarded as
"teleological." Rudy Koshar, commenting of *The Crisis of German Ideology*, stated
that the rise of National Socialism is set into a teleological interpretive frame,
where the final outcome seems inevitable.[72] In his memoir Mosse conceded
that such accusations were "not without reason," and yet he specified that "fascism did provide the climax of many of the trends which have interested me,
and if I have shown how what was latent or inherent in nationalism or in the
discrimination of the outsider became overt through these movements, then I
have filled in a neglected piece of history, one which is also relevant to the present."[73] Moreover, although Mosse certainly viewed German and European history as overshadowed by the Holocaust, this does not necessarily mean that he
believed it to be the inevitable outcome of German history. In the introduction to *The Crisis of German Ideology* he clearly stated that his object was by no
means any historical determinism, and that concrete causes had determined
the eventual triumph of a *völkisch* ideology, which "grew out of a historical
development."[74] As James Wald put it, in Mosse's interpretation "the triumph
of Nazism was . . . not the 'inevitable' outcome of German history . . . but
rather, *one* logical outcome, contingent on a particular constellation of social and
intellectual circumstances."[75] Mosse himself, in the preface to the 1997 edition
of the *Crisis*, discussed the contingent nature of the National Socialist victory.[76]
Moreover, his growing concern with the First World War since the late 1970s
had the effect of stressing the deep caesura that this event has meant for German history. The crucial role of the war in Mosse's work has been rightly
pointed out by Aschheim and Herf, who have highlighted it as a fundamental
"element of contingency," thus wiping out any determinism.[77] This is valid for
Mosse's entire historiographical production: his history was teleological only

insofar as this is understood as an interest in trends which culminated in a determinate event, and not as an attempt to read history "backwards."

The Message of a Life

When confronted by his own sensitivity before irrationality, Mosse must have felt to some extent like the Divines he had written about in *The Holy Pretence*, torn between his ideals and the necessities of reason of state. Thus he came to recognize society's need for cohesion, even for respectability, and Paul Breines pointed out how Mosse himself was very "respectable."[78] He eventually advocated the importance of the new politics and of nationalism in the form of patriotism, with its emphasis on communities: as Anson Rabinbach wrote, Mosse "made it clear that there was a community of his former students, a camaraderie that still exists to this day," and that he "was a relentless critic of the search for 'authenticity,' yet he himself was uniquely authentic. The consummate historian of communitarian doctrines created communities everywhere he went."[79] Fully aware of the power of myth, Mosse developed a "philosophy of the balance" that he came to regard as the "true mission of Judaism." This was the "bright side" of his work: when faced with powerful ideologies, Steven Aschheim observed, Mosse never reacted through a "mindless opposition," since he believed that these forces "answer deep needs for human community and meaning," that they address "real human desires." Therefore, he did not stand for their abolition but, rather, for their humanization. He proposed no solution, and "his personal response is rather a meliorating one, based always on the compassionate mode. The task is to reassert the positive potentials of these forms of community and to stress solidarity and humanization over domination and superiority."[80]

The real danger, Mosse never ceased to repeat, is the trend toward conformity, toward the putting down of all opinion. The antidote he proposed was the adoption of a critical mind through education. As he put it down before his students in the 1960s, the university is a teacher of scholarship, and scholarship

means knowledge defined as respect of facts, as an open mind for rational argument, a primary belief in freedom of inquiry, which means freedom of opinion arrived at through using rational qualities of mind upon a body of fact. It is the aim of understanding to come as near to "realities" as possible. This does not exclude hypothesis, of course, or the commitments to the search of truth. It does, however, mean a check upon sheer emotionalism—something into which moral indignation unchecked by understanding through scholarship can easily escape. This means, in the end, a denial of freedom, a denial of rationality. For there is no doubt that an emotion, however praiseworthy, unless controlled by the attitudes which the University seeks to instil, becomes a real danger to all of humanity. . . . [The university must] teach the knowledge, the scholarship, the attitudes which control the emotions, which bend them, if possible, towards respect for facts and reason. To ignore this imperils the causes in which the new student generation and to a certain extent I myself, very much believe.[81]

He deemed rational attitudes essential: reason must always stand against the "longing for Utopia," he said on another occasion in 1968, adding his belief that rational learning must always precede action: radical change needs a strong theoretical foundation if is it to succeed, while mindless activism brings about only violence.[82] And yet he believed that history is no logical process that can be understood exclusively through reason: Mosse defined himself an "Enlightenment man," and indeed he was a "rational man, a humanist, pushed into the study of the irrational and the inhumane," whose enterprise was "to bend the irrational into the rational; to tame it into a framework of rational thought."[83] This did not mean, however, that a strong idealistic basis ought not be retained: after all, "men must dream before they act," he argued passionately, as long as emotions remained "tempered by reason." Hence, he advocated the necessity of keeping the balance, which, at any rate, did not mean to hypocritically bend the ideal in front of reality. As he put it in *The Holy Pretence*, "it must be stressed once again that the endeavour to combine the Serpent and the Dove does not imply hypocrisy. Rather these attempts raise the problem of what can be the Christian answer to the survival of a good man in an evil world."[84] Mosse believed he might have found a possible answer in the humanization of the great villains of his books: respectability and the new politics. Hence the "two vital tasks" that, in Paul Breines's formulation, faced Mosse's humanistic socialism: "intensive study of the history of popular culture as the soil from which modern mass movements have sprung; and investigation of the symbols, images, and fantasies adequate to a movement for change that is at once massive and humane."[85]

Mosse did not believe in instant utopia: the lack of patience to build a cohesive society without destroying human rights would only lead, in his opinion, to fanaticism and dogmatism. The survival of parliamentary government and of human rights, he said, relies on the balance between individual freedom and social cohesion.[86] He held this to be true well into our age, which he believed to be, as he argued in the late 1990s, still a visual age to which the "new politics" of fascism were so attuned. The method used to appeal to the masses (or public opinion as it is called today), if not the form or content, is in our time, for example, reflected in the public relations industry and refined through the use of television as an instrument of politics. Symbols and myth are still used today though no longer in order to project a single and official attitude, but instead a wide variety of attitudes towards life. The danger of successful appeals to authoritarianism is always present, however changed from earlier forms or from its present worldwide manifestations.[87]

Echoing Ernst Bloch while reflecting on political indoctrination in the second half of the twentieth century, Mosse said that indoctrination means "carrying the myth to the people":

This is still the age of mass politics and the same longings which were operative until 1945 are still with us surely—the political process is still a drama transmitted to us by the media. We participate indirectly through emotions aroused, a mood induced. Politics is still symbolic action—governmental actions create a common perception and beliefs, myths and symbols are still used to mobilize support . . . the old traditions seem to have broken down, but now we have them again under a different form, mediating between us and the world, between us and our hopes in escaping from the crisis of our time which is the crisis of mass politics and mass democracy. Indoctrination is in reality this mediation and it would not work if it did not represent a principle of hope. Rather than condemn it we must understand its function: then perhaps we can begin to escape its all pervasive present.[88]

Mosse once wrote that "rapid changes in history usually come about when the gulf between what is and what should be, between outward reality and the human condition, becomes painfully apparent."[89] He had always shown a profound concern with times of crisis, when humanity easily turns to utopia as against the hardships of reality. National Socialism had been, in his interpretation, the most brutal example of such tendency to escape reality. The keeping of the balance depends on not allowing this "gulf" to expand. This despite the fact that he realized the difficulties inherent in this attempt: he himself had sought respectability and had directly experienced the fascination of nationalism; as he admitted, "I was never to close the gap between ideal and reality, and I learned myself what I used to tell my students: true maturity is reached only when one realizes that there exist insoluble problems."[90] Mosse claimed that the task of the historian is to unmask myths and symbols in order to understand the past, and consequently the present. In turn, the teaching of history is to provide people with the necessary intellectual weapons to resist any temptation to plunge into utopia (what should be) on the one hand, and to fall prey of conformism (what is) on the other. There is always, he said, "the tempter who will ask you to adjust unquestioningly to 'what is,' to admire power and prestige for its own sake, to ignore facts which may hurt. To him you must give a clear 'no'—he is the Mephistopheles of modern society."[91] Mosse undertook this task armed with a solid realism and with a personal urgency to deliver his message, and although he believed that people do not usually learn from history, he devoted his life to passionate writing and teaching, infusing both with his "sense of mission"; it may well apply to him what he once said about Rabbi Manfred Swarsensky: "The greatest message one can preach is one's life."[92]

NOTES

Introduction

1. George L. Mosse, *Nazism: A Historical and Comparative Analysis of National Socialism* (Oxford: Blackwell, 1978), 28.

2. George L. Mosse, "Response by George Mosse," in *George Mosse: On the Occasion of His Retirement, 17.6.85* (Jerusalem: Hebrew University of Jerusalem, 1986), xxix.

3. Seymour Drescher, David Sabean, and Allan Sharlin, "George Mosse and Political Symbolism," in *Political Symbolism in Modern Europe: Essays in Honor of George L. Mosse*, ed. Seymour Drescher, David Sabean, and Allan Sharlin (New Brunswick, NJ: Transaction Books, 1982), 3.

4. Anson Rabinbach said that Mosse wrote everything with a "political impulse." See Rabinbach, "George L. Mosse 1919–1999: An Appreciation," *Central European History* 32, no. 3 (1999): 335.

5. Mosse, "Response by George Mosse," xxx.

6. George L. Mosse, "Europe and the Modern World—Final Lecture, 1969," 1969, AR 25137, box 19, folder 33, George L. Mosse Collection, Leo Baeck Institute, New York.

7. George L. Mosse, draft for a letter to Merle Curti, October 16, 1967, box 3, folder 2, George L. Mosse Archive, Memorial Library, University of Wisconsin–Madison.

8. Peter Novick, *That Noble Dream: The "Objectivity Question" and the American Historical Profession* (New York: Cambridge University Press, 1988).

9. Charles A. Beard, "Written History as an Act of Faith," *American Historical Review* 39, no. 2 (January 1934): 219–31.

10. There are many publications on Rudolf Mosse, the Mosse family, and their newspapers. The most comprehensive work is Elisabeth Kraus, *Die Familie Mosse: Deutsch-jüdisches Bürgertum im 19. und 20. Jahrhundert* (Munich: Beck, 1999). Other publications include Fritz Härtsch, *Rudolf Mosse: Ein Verleger revolutioniert das Werbegeschäft* (Zürich: Mosse Adress AG, 1996); Werner E. Mosse, "Rudolf Mosse and the House of Mosse

1867–1920," *Leo Baeck Institute Year Book* 4 (1959): 237–59; and Andreas Halen and Uwe Greve, *Vom Mosse-Verlag zum Mosse-Zentrum* (Berlin: dbm Media-Verlag, 1995).

11. On Theodor Wolff, see Gotthart Schwarz, *Theodor Wolff und das "Berliner Tageblatt": Eine liberale Stimme in der deutschen Politik 1906–1933* (Tübingen: Mohr, 1968). For an overall view of the role played by the Jewish community in Wilhelmine and Weimar Germany, see the three volumes edited by Werner E. Mosse: *Entscheidungsjahr 1932: Zur Judenfrage in der Endphase der Weimarer Republik* (Tübingen: Mohr, 1965); *Deutsches Judentum in Krieg und Revolution 1916–1923* (Tübingen: Mohr, 1971); *Juden im Wilhelminischen Deutschland 1890–1914* (Tübingen: Mohr, 1976). As to the role played by the Jewish press, and particularly by the *Berliner Tageblatt* in the first decades of the twentieth century, see Werner Becker's essay, "Die Rolle der liberalen Presse," in *Deutsches Judentum in Krieg und Revolution,* 67–136. For a general survey of the democratic press in Germany (with a large section devoted to the Mosse publishing house), see Modris Eksteins, *The Limits of Reason: The German Democratic Press and the Collapse of Weimar Democracy* (London: Oxford University Press, 1975).

12. To be sure, he felt close to his brother and particularly to his sister, especially once in exile. He felt also very close to his stepmother, whom his father married during their exile after divorcing his first wife.

13. As he left Germany, he also changed his last name from Lachmann (his father's) to the more pronounceable Mosse (his mother's), thus becoming George Mosse or, better, George L. Mosse. George L. Mosse, *Confronting History: A Memoir* (Madison: University of Wisconsin Press, 2000), 97.

14. Mosse, *Confronting History,* 81. Leslie Gilbert was a renowned history teacher who had had among his pupils A. J. P. Taylor and Geoffrey Barraclough, historians who achieved (like Mosse) academic distinction.

15. Mosse, *Confronting History,* 94.

16. Ibid., 114.

17. Ibid., 115.

18. George L. Mosse, "The Idea of Sovereignty in England, from Sir Thomas Smith to Sir Edward Coke" (PhD diss., Harvard University, 1946). The dissertation was published (in a widely revised form) four years later as *The Struggle for Sovereignty in England: From the Reign of Queen Elizabeth to the Petition of Right* (East Lansing: Michigan State College Press, 1950).

19. The Army Specialized Training Program was a military training program aimed at training soldiers for occupation duties in Europe.

20. Mosse's most important works from this period are *Struggle for Sovereignty; The Reformation* (New York: Holt, Rinehart and Winston, 1953); *The Holy Pretence: A Study in Christianity and the Reason of State from William Perkins to John Winthrop* (Oxford: Blackwell, 1957), as well as a number of articles on early modern history.

21. Mosse, *Confronting History,* 6. See also the interview with I. Runge and U. Stelbrink, *George Mosse: "Ich bleibe Emigrant": Gespräche mit George L. Mosse* (Berlin: Dietz Verlag, 1991).

22. Mosse, *Confronting History*, 142. Mosse concludes the passage by remarking that in the course on Western civilization held at Iowa he had "already began to emphasize the fascist experience."

23. Stanley Payne, "The Mosse Legacy," *Wisconsin Academy Review* 43, no. 3 (Summer 2000): 9.

24. Mosse, *Confronting History*, 4. John Tortorice, Mosse's life partner, said that he "used history almost to understand himself." Interview with John Tortorice, *Wisconsin Academy Review* 46, no. 3 (Summer 2000): 12.

25. Jay Winter, "De l'histoire intellectuelle à l'histoire culturelle: La contribution de George L. Mosse," *Annales* 1, no. 56 (2001): 181; unless otherwise noted, all translations are mine.

26. Emilio Gentile, *Il fascino del persecutore: George L. Mosse e la catastrofe dell'uomo moderno* (Rome: Carocci, 2007), 42.

27. Ryszard Kapuściński, *The Other* (London: Verso, 2009).

28. Mosse, *Holy Pretence*, 154.

29. See, for example, Steven Aschheim, "George Mosse: The Man and the Work," in *George Mosse: On the Occasion of His Retirement, 17.6.85*, xi–xviii; Steven Aschheim, "George Mosse at 80: A Critical Laudatio," *Journal of Contemporary History* 34, no. 2 (1999): 295–312; Drescher, Sabean, and Sharlin, "George Mosse and Political Symbolism"; Giuseppe Galasso, "Il Novecento di George L. Mosse e le sue origini," *Nuova Storia Contemporanea* 1 (2000): 43–76; Roger Griffin, "Withstanding the Rush of Time: The Prescience of Mosse's Anthropological View of Fascism," in *What History Tells: George L. Mosse and the Culture of Western Europe*, ed. Stanley Payne, David Sorkin, and John Tortorice (Madison: University of Wisconsin Press, 2004), 110–33; Jeffrey Herf, "Mosse's Recasting of European Intellectual and Cultural History," *German Politics and Society* 18, no. 4 (Winter 2000): 18–29; Jeffrey Herf, "The Historian as Provocateur: George Mosse's Accomplishment and Legacy," *Yad Vashem Studies* 29 (2001): 1–18, http://www.yadvash em.org/odot_pdf/Microsoft%20Word%20-%202027.pdf; Rudy Koshar, "George Mosse and 'Destination Culture,'" in Payne, Sorkin, and Tortorice, *What History Tells*, 164–82; Renato Moro, "George L. Mosse, storico dell'irrazionalismo moderno," in *La grande guerra e il fronte interno: Studi in onore di George Mosse*, ed. Alessandra Staderini, Luciano Zani, and Francesca Magni (Camerino: Università di Camerino, 1998), 21–36; Payne, "The Mosse Legacy"; Anson Rabinbach, "George L. Mosse 1919–1999"; James Wald, "Cultural History and Symbols," *New German Critique* 37 (Winter 1986): 169–84; Winter, "De l'histoire intellectuelle," 177–81.

30. Gentile, *Il fascino del persecutore*, 13.

31. Two exceptions in this regard are Paul Breines and Emilio Gentile. See Paul Breines, "Finding Oneself in History and Vice Versa: Remarks on 'George's Voice,'" *German Politics and Society* 18, no. 4 (Winter 2000): 3–17; Paul Breines, "With George Mosse in the 1960s," in Drescher, Sabean, and Sharlin, *Political Symbolism in Modern Europe*, 285–99; Gentile, *Il fascino del persecutore*.

32. Herf, "The Historian as Provocateur," 8.

33. See essays in Caroline F. Ware, ed., *The Cultural Approach to History* (New York: Columbia University Press, 1940).

34. George L. Mosse, "Is Fascism Alive?—Australian Broadcasting Corporation," 1973, AR 25137, box 17, folder 47, George L. Mosse Collection, Leo Baeck Institute, New York.

35. For the persistence of respectability in the late twentieth century, see Mosse's observations in George L. Mosse, "Il declino della morale," *Prometeo* 14, no. 53 (1996): 6–13.

36. Mosse's historiographical approach could be, in my opinion, very useful for an analysis of today's politics. This approach could address the shattered balance, in parliamentary democracies, between individual rights and issues of national security in times of crisis, as is the case after September 11, 2001. It could also offer a key to the understanding of society's continuous creation of enemy stereotypes and of its need for conformity. An examination of popular cultural artifacts in this regard could provide the historian of this age with useful insights into the making of public opinion and its consequent political relevance. See, for example, the extremely popular TV series *24*, which, following the fictitious adventures of an American counterterrorist unit, implicitly renders extreme, violent measures such as torture "acceptable" and "reasonable" if implemented in the name of national security. Another interesting example is the recent, equally controversial Zack Snyder film *300* (2007), a fictionalized retelling of the battle of the Thermopylae in which masculine, honorable, and heroic Greek soldiers confront effeminate and lascivious Persians.

37. Friedrich Nietzsche, *Beyond Good and Evil: Prelude to a Philosophy of the Future* (Cambridge, New York: Cambridge University Press, 2002), 6.

38. Mosse, *Confronting History*, 83.

39. Aschheim, "George Mosse at 80," 304; Moro, "George L. Mosse," 36; Emilio Gentile, "A Provisional Dwelling: Origin and Development of the Concept of Fascism in Mosse's Historiography," in Payne, Sorkin, and Tortorice, *What History Tells*, 44–47. The "fascination of the persecutor" is also the title of Gentile's recent book on Mosse, *Il fascino del persecutore*.

40. Runge and Stelbrink, *George Mosse*, 77.

41. Mosse, *Confronting History*, 70. Mosse never tired of repeating that the landscape of Salem always remained his ideal landscape.

42. Ibid., 197.

43. Ibid., 180. Unlike with sexual repression, Mosse did not seem to feel (according to most accounts) any kind of resentment toward his country of origin, Germany, which sets him apart from other emigré German Jewish historians. The difference in attitude between Mosse and, for example, Peter Gay is telling. See Peter Gay's memoir, *My German Question: Growing Up in Nazi Berlin* (New Haven, CT: Yale University Press, 1998). A different story, as reported by John Tortorice, is told by Jay Winter, who recounted how, in a meeting in Germany, he heard Mosse refuse to speak the language of a country that had exiled him and his family. This is an interesting and rather isolated anecdote

that brushes against the grain of all other accounts I have been able to find (conversation with John Tortorice, April 2013).

44. George L. Mosse, "Hillel Talk," speech given at Hillel, Iowa State University's Jewish Student Organization, n.d., AR 25137, box 17, folder 31, George L. Mosse Collection, Leo Baeck Institute, New York.

45. Mosse, *Confronting History*, 181.

46. Mosse, *Holy Pretence*. The importance of this work has been strongly emphasized by one critic, David Warren Sabean, in his "George Mosse and *The Holy Pretence*," in Payne, Sorkin, and Tortorice, *What History Tells*, 15–24.

47. George L. Mosse, Early Modern History Course, 1969. I thank John Tortorice for having supplied me with the transcripts of these lectures.

48. George L. Mosse, "Warburg College Lecture," 1965, AR 25137, box 19, folder 20, George L. Mosse Collection, Leo Baeck Institute, New York.

49. Wald, "Cultural History and Symbols," 181–82.

50. George L. Mosse, letter to Christopher Browning, September 29, 1979, AR 25137, box 33, folder 57, George L. Mosse Collection, Leo Baeck Institute, New York.

51. Gerhard L. Weinberg, review of *The Crisis of German Ideology: Intellectual Origins of the Third Reich*, by George L. Mosse, *Political Science Quarterly* 81, no. 1 (March 1966): 109.

52. These reviews of *The Crisis of German Ideology* are by Peter Pulzer, "How Nazism Grew," *Jewish Chronicle*, October 21, 1966, 20; and A. J. Nicholls, *English Historical Review* 82, no. 325 (October 1967): 860–61.

53. Walter Laqueur, "The Roots of Nazism," review of *The Crisis of German Ideology*, by George L. Mosse, *New York Review of Books*, January 14, 1965, 15.

54. Stephen M. Poppel, "Understanding Germany," review of *The Crisis of German Ideology*, by George L. Mosse, *Midstream*, January 1970, 67.

55. Ken Minogue, "Nazi Rituals," review of *The Nationalization of the Masses: Political Symbolism and Mass Movements in Germany from the Napoleonic Wars through the Third Reich*, by George L. Mosse, *Quadrant*, September 1976, 79.

56. See Peter N. Stearns, review of *Nationalism and Sexuality: Respectability and Abnormal Sexuality in Modern Europe*, by George L. Mosse, *Journal of Modern History* 58, no. 1 (March 1986): 257.

57. Walter Laqueur, foreword to *Confronting History* by George L. Mosse, xi; George L. Mosse, "Fascism Once More," in *The Intellectual Foundations of National Socialism*, seminar held at Stanford University in 1963. The transcript of the seminar, completed in 1964, has never been published.

58. I thank Steven Aschheim and Jay Winter for this significant anecdote.

Chapter 1. From Machiavellism to Totalitarianism

1. Books like *The Reformation* and *Europe in the Sixteenth Century*, written with Helmut Koenigsberger (London: Longman, 1968), met with more success as textbooks and received the most positive reviews.

2. Mosse, *Confronting History,* 142.

3. Mosse, "Response by George Mosse," xxviii–xxix.

4. George L. Mosse, "Notes on the Marginalia of Sir Edward Coke at Holkham," unpublished article, 1950, George L. Mosse Archive, box 6, folder 68, Memorial Library, University of Wisconsin–Madison.

5. Mosse, *Nazism,* 28.

6. George L. Mosse, "The Pragmatism of the Freshman History Course," *Social Studies for Teachers and Administrators* 48, no. 8 (December 1957): 290; George L. Mosse, "They Worked for Hitler: the Problem of the German non-Nazi Collaborationists," speech, n.d. (between 1946 and 1952), AR 25137, box 17, folder 44, George L. Mosse Collection, Leo Baeck Institute, New York.

7. George L. Mosse, "The Problem of National Socialist Morality," in *Intellectual Foundations of National Socialism* seminar.

8. For a discussion of Mosse's controversial usage of the term "totalitarianism," see chap. 6.

9. Friedrich Meinecke, *Machiavellism: The Doctrine of Raison d'État and Its Place in Modern History* (London: Routledge and Kegan Paul, 1957). The original German edition, published in 1924, was *Die Idee der Staatsräson in der neueren Geschichte.*

10. Friedrich Meinecke, *Die deutsche Katastrophe, Betrachtungen und Erinnerungen* (Wiesbaden: E. Brockhaus, 1946). Here I have relied on the English translation: *The German Catastrophe: Reflections and Recollections* (Boston: Beacon Press, 1963).

11. Meinecke, *The German Catastrophe,* 34.

12. Ibid., 51, 34.

13. Ibid., 52.

14. George L. Mosse, "The Christian Statesman," *History of the Ideas News Letter* 1, no. 2 (March 1955): 4.

15. George L. Mosse, "Does History Have Any Meaning?" speech given at the Newman Club, 1946, AR 25137, box 17, folder 44, George L. Mosse Collection, Leo Baeck Institute, New York.

16. Drescher, Sabean, and Sharlin, "George Mosse and Political Symbolism," 3.

17. Ze'ev Mankovitz, "George Mosse and Jewish History," in *George Mosse: On the Occasion of His Retirement, 17.6.85,* xxiv.

18. Mosse, *Confronting History,* 100.

19. Ibid., 101.

20. Ibid., 105. Mosse defined himself as a left-liberal. See ibid., 197.

21. With regard to Mosse's sympathies for Marxism, see ibid., 147, and the interview with Laura Smail, 1982, University of Wisconsin–Madison Archives, Oral History Project, Interview #227. Mosse's was, however, an antifascism that sought to coexist with liberalism and did not coincide with the official antifascism of the Comintern. See Anson Rabinbach, "George Mosse and the Culture of Antifascism," *German Politics and Society* 18, no. 4 (Winter 2000): 36.

22. Mosse, *Confronting History*, 107. Anson Rabinbach wrote: "Although he himself remained dedicated to liberalism, George became something of a socialist and an admirer of the British intellectual Harold Laski" (Rabinbach, "George Mosse and the Culture of Antifascism," 31).

23. George L. Mosse, "The Significance of Nietzsche's Proposed Ethic of Masters," paper, 1940, George L. Mosse Archive, Memorial Library, University of Wisconsin–Madison, box 5, folder 6.

24. Mosse, "Hillel Talk." See also George L. Mosse, "What Price Freedom?" speech given at high school commencements, n.d. (between 1946 and 1952), AR 25137, box 17, folder 44, George L. Mosse Collection, Leo Baeck Institute, New York.

25. Mosse, "What Price Freedom?"

26. Ibid.

27. See George L. Mosse, "Thomas Hobbes: Jurisprudence at the Cross-Roads," *University of Toronto Quarterly* 15, no. 4 (July 1946): 350–51.

28. Mosse, *Confronting History*, 111.

29. Ibid., 146. Mosse's speeches shed additional light on his thought and beliefs. His unpublished speaking engagements are very important in that they complete what he expressed in his historical works; moreover, they allowed him to speak, as it were, more freely, outside the scope of academia, and to express his personal opinions directly.

30. Reported by *Daily Iowan*, May 10, 1945, March 4, 1952, and March 1, 1955; also, some years later, by *Wisconsin State Journal*, March 14, 1959.

31. See *Marshalltown Times*, March 30, 1950; *Press Citizen of Iowa City*, February 6 and 12, March 6, 1952; and *Des Moines Sunday Register*, September 26, 1954.

32. Reported by *Daily Iowan*, March 31, 1955; *Des Moines Tribune*, March 30, 1955. See also *Daily Iowan*, February 25, 1948.

33. Mosse, "What Price Freedom?"

34. Mosse, interview with Laura Smail.

35. Reported by *Daily Iowan*, November 24, 1947. In 1952 Mosse even spoke for the Republican party, since he was impressed by Senator Robert Taft (Ohio) and his stance for civil liberties against the hysteria of McCarthyism. See Mosse, *Confronting History*, 147; and Runge and Stelbrink, *George Mosse*, 42.

36. Mosse, *Confronting History*, 121. The seminar was given by the mathematics professor Dirk J. Struik, a noted Marxist of Dutch origin. Mosse said to have lived "anxious months" as he was, at the time, not a citizen of the United States, and his position at the University of Iowa was "far from secure." While other participants lost their academic jobs, Mosse benefited from Iowa's more liberal and less populist political orientation, which sheltered him. In Cambridge, Massachusetts, Mosse also became active for a brief period in the Oratory of St. Mary and St. Michael, which combined Catholic theology with Marxism. It was the only time, he recalled, that he "departed even slightly from [his] usual and accustomed agnosticism" (Mosse, *Confronting History*, 121–22). John Tortorice suggests that this may have been an attempt, facilitated by his Quaker education, to attain further integration, perhaps also driven by the search for that faith, for that sense

of identity, he lacked (conversation with John Tortorice, July 2010). Stanley Payne notes how at Harvard Mosse seriously considered converting to Anglicanism; he eventually translated a religious background into a strong sense of professional "calling" (perhaps also with certain Anglican and Lutheran roots), though secularized (conversation with Stanley Payne, July 2011).

37. Mosse, *Confronting History*, 147. Despite his sympathies for Marxism and liberalism, Mosse never dealt with them directly on a historiographical level, with the exception of the paragraphs in *The Culture of Western Europe*. Any attempt at explaining such an attitude is necessarily tentative, and probably related to psychological reasons. First, his exile condition and the fate of Judaism were more directly related with National Socialism; second, his closeness to Marxism in his early years may have prevented him from developing a full critique of that political system; third, he was surely more fascinated by irrationalist ideologies such as fascism: as he once told Seymour Drescher, who as a young scholar decided to take on the study of Tocqueville, "Seymour, why are you interested in studying such a sane man?" (conversation with Seymour Drescher, August 2011).

38. George L. Mosse, lecture notes for the Cultural History Course, 1946–47, George L. Mosse Archive, Memorial Library, University of Wisconsin–Madison, box 5, folder 8.

39. George L. Mosse, "Historismus," notes, n.d., George L. Mosse Archive, Memorial Library, University of Wisconsin–Madison, box 6, folder 38.

40. Mosse, *Confronting History*, 175.

41. George L. Mosse, speech given at the Des Moines Conference on Individual Freedom, 1955, AR 25137, box 17, folder 44, George L. Mosse Collection, Leo Baeck Institute, New York; Mosse, *Struggle for Sovereignty*, 172; Mosse, "A Re-Examination of the Liberties of Englishmen," lecture, n.d., AR 25137, box 18, folder 45, George L. Mosse Collection, Leo Baeck Institute, New York; Mosse, "Chapel Talks," 1954, AR 25137, box 16, folder 19, George L. Mosse Collection, Leo Baeck Institute, New York.

42. An excellent overview of early twentieth-century critical theories of the state is the anthology edited by Waldo R. Browne, *Leviathan in Crisis: An International Symposium on the State, Its Past, Its Present, and Future, by Fifty-four Twentieth Century Writers* (New York: Viking, 1946). The book also contains writings by thinkers who influenced Mosse, such as Harold Laski and Johan Huizinga.

43. In the introduction to *The Struggle for Sovereignty in England*, Mosse wrote: "This work was originally undertaken at the suggestion of Professor Charles H. McIlwain of Harvard University. Those who are familiar with the writings and teachings of this great scholar will recognize how greatly I have relied upon the contributions which he has made to the understanding of English political theory" (Mosse, *Struggle for Sovereignty*, v); in an earlier article, he had written that "C. H. McIlwain's discussion of Parliamentary Supremacy and his mention of Bodin's influence in this regard . . . has served as the inspiration for this paper" (George L. Mosse, "The Influence of Jean Bodin's République on English Political Thought," *Medievalia et Humanistica* 5 [1948]: 73).

44. Johann Sommerville, "George Mosse's Early Modern Scholarship," in Payne, Sorkin, and Tortorice, *What History Tells*, 28, 29.

45. Ibid., 29.
46. Mosse, "Idea of Sovereignty," 27.
47. Mosse, *Struggle for Sovereignty*, 1, 7.
48. Ibid., 2, 4, 5.
49. Ibid., 5–6.
50. Richard Schlatter, review of *Struggle for Sovereignty*, by George L. Mosse, *Archiv für Reformationsgeschichte* 42, no. 1 (1951): 2.
51. Mosse, "Notes on the Marginalia."
52. George L. Mosse, "A Re-Examination of the Liberties of Englishmen," Humanities Society Lecture, n.d., AR 25137, box 18, folder 45, George L. Mosse Collection, Leo Baeck Institute, New York.
53. This view was also held by McIlwain. See George L. Mosse, "Change and Continuity in the Tudor Constitution," *Speculum* 22, no. 1 (1947): 18–28.
54. Mosse, "Idea of Sovereignty," 188–89; Mosse, "Thomas Hobbes."
55. Mosse, "Thomas Hobbes," 351.
56. Mosse, *Struggle for Sovereignty*, 172.
57. The quote from Laski is taken from his *Parliamentary Government in England*, New York 1938. The passage is first cited by Mosse in "The Idea of Sovereignty," 237–38, and it is kept in its entirety in *Struggle for Sovereignty*, 178–79.
58. Schlatter, review of Mosse, *Struggle for Sovereignty*.
59. Recalling his gradual Americanization, Mosse wrote in his memoir, referring to the mid-1940s: "I was not yet fully American and, as a matter of fact, still often thought of the United States as 'they,' however much I continued to admire some American characteristics. What was refreshing at the time was precisely the absence of the stifling nationalism which I had found in Europe" (Mosse, *Confronting History*, 125). The passages referring to his enhanced sense of belonging to his new environment are in Mosse, "What Price Freedom?"
60. George L. Mosse, "Puritanism and Reason of State in Old and New England," *William and Mary Quarterly* 9, no. 1 (1952): 78; Mosse, *Struggle for Sovereignty*, 179.
61. Mosse, "A Re-Examination."
62. J. Hurstfield, review of *Struggle for Sovereignty in England*, by George L. Mosse, *History*, n.s., 39, nos. 135 & 136 (1954): 150.
63. Mosse, "Does History Have Any Meaning?"
64. See Mosse, speech at the Des Moines Conference on Individual Freedom.
65. Ibid.
66. Mosse, "What Price Freedom?"
67. Mosse, "The Significance of Nietzsche's Proposed Ethic of Masters."
68. George L. Mosse, in collaboration with David Hecht, "Liturgical Uniformity and Absolutism in the Sixteenth Century," *Anglican Theological Review* 29, no. 3 (1947): 165.
69. Mosse, "Chapel Talks." The tone of the talks was so deeply felt that one listener even thought that Mosse was a reverend, and a "wonderful preacher" (Mosse, "Chapel Talks," letter to Mosse).

70. Mosse, "Chapel Talks."

71. Mosse, *Holy Pretence*, 15.

72. Mosse, "Puritanism and Reason of State," 68.

73. George L. Mosse, "Christianity and Politics," speech, n.d. (undoubtedly dating back to the early 1950s), AR 25137, box 16, folder 20, George L. Mosse Collection, Leo Baeck Institute, New York.

74. Mosse, lecture notes for the Cultural History Course, 1946–47.

75. Mosse, "Puritanism and Reason of State," 71, 68.

76. Mosse, "Pragmatism of the Freshman History Course," 290. Commenting on *The Holy Pretence*, Robert Weltsch wrote to Mosse: "I am not an expert on Puritan theology, so your book interested me more from a general point of view as I think the problem is a perpetual one and very topical today" (Robert Weltsch, letter to Mosse, April 18, 1958, AR 25137, box 14, folder 29, George L. Mosse Collection, Leo Baeck Institute, New York).

77. Mosse, "Christian Statesman," 4.

78. George L. Mosse, "Christianity and Reason of State," n.d., AR 25137, box 16, folder 21, George L. Mosse Collection, Leo Baeck Institute, New York; Mosse, "Christianity and Politics."

79. Mosse, *Holy Pretence*, 5. Mosse refers to Croce's *Grundlagen der Politik* (*Elementi di politica* [Laterza: Bari, 1925]). In an article on Machiavelli's assimilation in English thought, Mosse wrote that Croce "thought that the assimilation of Machiavelli's ideas in the West might contain valuable clues as to how such contact had been accomplished" (George L. Mosse, "The Assimilation of Machiavelli in English Thought: The Casuistry of William Perkins and William Ames," *Huntington Library Quarterly* 17 [August 1954]: 315).

80. Sabean, "George Mosse and *The Holy Pretence*," 15.

81. Mosse, *Holy Pretence*, 9. The most important Divines whose thought Mosse analyzes are William Perkins, William Ames, and John Winthrop.

82. Ibid., 5.

83. Mosse, "Christianity and Politics."

84. Meinecke, *The German Catastrophe*, 10.

85. Mosse, *Holy Pretence*, 9.

86. Mosse, "Assimilation of Machiavelli," 315.

87. George L. Mosse, "The Importance of Jacques Saurin in the History of Casuistry and the Enlightenment," *Church History* 25, no. 3 (1956): 195.

88. Mosse, "Christianity and Reason of State."

89. George L. Mosse, "Puritan Political Thought and the 'Cases of Conscience,'" *Church History* 23, no. 2 (1954): 117.

90. Mosse, "Puritanism and Reason of State," 76 (see also 69–70).

91. Ibid., 71.

92. Mosse, "Assimilation of Machiavelli," 326.

93. See Moro, "George L. Mosse," 29; see also Drescher, Sabean, and Sharlin, "George Mosse and Political Symbolism," 1.

94. Mosse, "Christianity and Politics."

95. Sabean, "George Mosse and *The Holy Pretence*," 19–20.

96. "Prudence" being the Christian word for "policy," that is, policy oriented toward a Christian goal.

97. Mosse, *Holy Pretence*, 154.

98. Mosse, *Nazism*, 27.

99. Mosse, "Europe and the Modern World," lectures.

100. George L. Mosse, *The Nationalization of the Masses* (Ithaca, NY: Cornell University Press, 1975), vii.

Chapter 2. Beyond the History of Intellectuals

1. Through his anthropologically oriented cultural history Mosse intended to widen the scope of his own research and to elaborate on a critique of the works of other émigré historians like Fritz Stern and Peter Gay, who at the time developed a "traditional" kind of intellectual history.

2. Shulamit Volkov, "German Jewish History: Back To Bildung and Culture?," in Payne, Sorkin, and Tortorice, *What History Tells*, 225.

3. Mosse's earliest works on the modern age were "The Image of the Jew in German Popular Culture: Felix Dahn and Gustav Freytag," *Leo Baeck Institute Year Book* 2 (1957): 218–27; "Culture, Civilization and German Antisemitism," *Judaism* 7, no. 3 (Summer 1958): 256–67; "The Mystical Origins of National Socialism," *Journal of the History of Ideas* 22, no. 1 (January–March 1961): 81–96.

4. George L. Mosse, *The Crisis of German Ideology: Intellectual Origins of the Third Reich* (New York: Howard Fertig, 1964).

5. George L. Mosse, "Puritanism Reconsidered," *Archiv für Reformationsgeschichte* 55, no. 1 (1964): 44.

6. Ibid., 37, 38, 41.

7. Sommerville, "George Mosse's Early Modern Scholarship," 27.

8. George L. Mosse, "Freshman History: Reality or Metaphysics?" *The Social Studies for Teachers and Administrators* 40, no. 3 (March 1949): 99–103.

9. Ibid., 101.

10. Mosse, "Pragmatism of the Freshman History Course," 289.

11. Ibid., 290.

12. Mosse, lecture notes for the Cultural History Course, 1946–47.

13. George L. Mosse, "Old Lectures, 1950–1956," AR 25137, box 18, folder 33, George L. Mosse Collection, Leo Baeck Institute, New York.

14. George L. Mosse, "Changes in Religious Thought," in *The New Cambridge Modern History*, vol. 4, *The Decline of Spain and the Thirty Years War, 1609–48/59*, ed. J. P. Cooper (Cambridge: Cambridge University Press, 1970), 183.

15. Mosse, *Confronting History*, 178.

16. For a more detailed analysis of Mosse's view of the Baroque and its connections with modern mass movements, see chap. 3.

17. George L. Mosse, "The Cultural Historian and Popular Literature," 1967, AR 25137, box 7, folder 6 and 7, George L. Mosse Collection, Leo Baeck Institute, New York.

18. Mosse, "Changes in Religious Thought," 173, 195. Though published in 1970, Mosse's contribution had been completed in 1959, according to Sommerville in "George Mosse's Early Modern Scholarship," 26. In this essay, Mosse refers to the seventeenth century, but the idea can be held true for all of his work.

19. Mosse, *Confronting History*, 136.

20. Mosse, "Image of the Jew."

21. William Aydelotte, "The Detective Story as a Historical Source," *Yale Review* 39 (1949): 91. Quoted in Allan G. Bogue and Gilbert White, *William Osgood Aydelotte 1910– 1996: A Biographical Memoir* (Washington, DC: National Academy Press, 1997), 12.

22. William O. Aydelotte, "The England of Marx and Mills as Reflected in Fiction," in *The Making of English History*, ed. Robert Livingston Schuyler and Herman Ausubel (New York: Dryden, 1952), 512. The passage is quoted in Mosse, "Image of the Jew," 218–19.

23. George L. Mosse, "The Peasant and the Ideology," in *Intellectual Foundations of National Socialism* seminar.

24. Mosse, *Confronting History*, 132. In his memoir, Mosse also stresses his great passion for literature, which dated back at least to his York years at the Bootham School.

25. Ibid., 130.

26. See for example the volume *Mass Culture: The Popular Arts in America*, ed. Bernard Rosenberg and David Manning White (Glencoe, Ill.: Free Press, 1957). Mosse was also familiar with the work of José Ortega y Gasset (*The Revolt of the Masses* [New York: W. W. Norton, 1932]) and Elias Canetti (*Crowds and Power* [New York: Viking, 1962]), two authors he surely relied upon in his reflections on mass behavior and the fate of the individual in relation with the mass. With regard to the necessity of investigating fascism as a mass movement, he praised Hannah Arendt's *The Origins of Totalitarianism*: "I do not have priority in that," he said. Mosse, *Nazism*, 78.

27. George L. Mosse, "Literature and History," n.d., AR 25137, box 17, folder 44, George L. Mosse Collection, Leo Baeck Institute, New York.

28. Ibid.

29. "The Cultural Historian and Popular Literature" was never published. A draft of it, along with the correspondence with Howard Fertig, whom Mosse wanted as editor of the article, is in the Leo Baeck Archive: AR 25137, box 7, folder 6 and 7, George L. Mosse Collection, Leo Baeck Institute, New York.

30. Mosse, "Hillel Talk."

31. Mosse, "Puritanism Reconsidered," 44–47.

32. Mosse and Koenigsberger, *Sixteenth Century*, 135, 130.

33. Mosse, "Image of the Jew"; Mosse, "Culture, Civilization and German Antisemitism"; Mosse, "The Mystical Origins of National Socialism."

34. Mosse, "The Mystical Origins of National Socialism," 81. Mosse had emphasized the same ideas in a 1959 speech, "History as the Teacher of Life?," 1959, George L. Mosse Archive, Memorial Library, University of Wisconsin–Madison, box 6, folder 7.

35. George L. Mosse, "A Ghost Come Alive," article, 1960, AR 25137, box 17, folder 26, George L. Mosse Collection, Leo Baeck Institute, New York. Mosse referred to Hans Globke and Theodor Oberländer, and to the Gesamtdeutscher Block/Bund der Heimatvertriebenen und Entrechteten (All-German Bloc/League of Expellees and Disenfranchised). The league, originally founded in 1950, was represented in the Bundestag only for a few years during the 1950s and was part of Konrad Adenauer's coalition government; it was the party of those expelled from former German territories in the East, and espoused anticommunism and Pan-Germanism. Mosse also warned against revisionism, in reference to Ernst von Salomon's *Fragebogen*, published in 1951, which harshly criticized American denazification policies in Germany after 1945 by ironically replying to the questions posed in the questionnaire (*Fragebogen*) the Allies issued to investigate the activities of former or suspected Nazis under the Hitler regime.

36. Mosse, *Crisis of German Ideology*, 9–10.

37. Mosse gave at least three speeches by that title between 1966 and 1970 (reported by the *Bucknellian*, April 14, 1966, and by the *South Bend Tribune*, December 1, 1967). The speech was then also given at the Initiation Banquet of the Phi Alpha Theta at Marquette University on December 3, 1970 (the text presented on this last occasion is "The Appeal of Nazi Culture," 1970, AR 25137, box 16, folder 6, George L. Mosse Collection, Leo Baeck Institute, New York).

38. George L. Mosse, "National Socialism and Germany Today," n.d., AR 25137, box 18, folder 20, George L. Mosse Collection, Leo Baeck Institute, New York. The paper, though undated, can be chronologically located in the years following 1955, in that Mosse refers to the "silent reception, at this very moment, of the play about the *Diary of Anne Frank*," which had been first performed in Broadway precisely in 1955.

39. George L. Mosse, "What Is Fascism?," in *Intellectual Foundations of National Socialism* seminar.

40. George L. Mosse, "Die Amerikanische Geschichtsschreibung—Ein Überblick," *Die Welt als Geschichte* 12 (1952): 264–73.

41. Mosse, "Pragmatism of the Freshman History Course," 289–90. Indeed, Mosse said that it was significant that the only historian who really appreciated *The Holy Pretence* had been Giorgio Spini, an Italian. Mosse, *Nazism*, 28. In this regard, see Giorgio Spini, "Il periodo coloniale della storia Americana nella recente storiografia," *Rivista storica italiana* 73, no. 2 (1961): 321–34.

42. For Mosse's contribution to the interpretations of fascism, see chap. 6.

43. Mosse, "Image of the Jew," 218.

44. Mosse, "Culture, Civilization and German Antisemitism," 34; Mosse, "The Mystical Origins of National Socialism," 81.

45. George L. Mosse, *The Culture of Western Europe: The Nineteenth and Twentieth Centuries; An Introduction* (Chicago: Rand McNally, 1961), 343.

46. Ibid., 347–71.

47. Mosse, *Nazism*, 32.

48. See Mosse, *Nazism*, 36; Mosse, *Nationalization of the Masses*, 72 (where Mosse wrote that "traditionalism is built into every popular faith"; see also Mosse, "Europe and the Modern World," lectures).

49. George L. Mosse, *Nazi Culture: Intellectual, Cultural and Social Life in the Third Reich* (New York: Grosset & Dunlap, 1966).

50. Mosse, *Culture of Western Europe* (1961), 348–49, 350 (my italics).

51. Ibid., 368.

52. Ibid., 350, 363, 365 (my italics).

53. George L. Mosse, "Adolf Hitler," in *Intellectual Foundations of National Socialism* seminar; Mosse, *Culture of Western Europe* (1961), 366.

54. Mosse, *Culture of Western Europe* (1961), 371.

55. Gentile, *Il fascino del persecutore*, 83–84.

56. Mosse, *Crisis of German Ideology*, 316–17. The passage is also quoted in Gentile, *Il fascino del persecutore*, 85.

57. Mosse, *Culture of Western Europe* (1961), 346–47, 344, 351–52 365–66.

58. Ibid., 352. Rauschning's book is *The Revolution of Nihilism, Warning to the West* (New York: Alliance Book Corporation, 1939).

59. Mosse, "What Is Fascism?"; Mosse, "Adolf Hitler."

60. Mosse, *Crisis of German Ideology*, 312–13.

61. Mosse, "What Is Fascism?"

62. Interview with George Mosse, "Du Baroque au Nazisme: Une histoire religieuse de la politique," *European Review of History—Revue européenne d'Histoire* 1, no. 2 (1994): 250. The interviewers were Bruno Cabanes (Ecole Normale Supérieure, Paris), Christopher M. Clark (St. Catharine's College, Cambridge), and D. L. L. Parry (Hertford College, Oxford).

63. Mosse, *Nazi Culture*, xxiii.

64. George L. Mosse, "Fascism and the Intellectuals," in *The Nature of Fascism*, ed. S. J. Woolf (London: Weidenfeld and Nicholson, 1968), 205.

65. Mosse interview, "Du Baroque au Nazisme," 250. Speer's influence on Mosse is dealt with in chap. 3.

66. Mosse, *Crisis of German Ideology*, 312; Mosse, *Nazi Culture*, xxv.

67. Mosse, *Nazi Culture*, xxxi.

68. Mosse, *Culture of Western Europe* (1961), 348, 368.

69. Mosse, "National Socialist Morality"; Mosse, "What Is Fascism?"

70. Mosse, *Crisis of German Ideology*, 316.

71. Ibid., 316–17.

72. George L. Mosse, "The Genesis of Fascism," *Journal of Contemporary History* 1 (1966): 16–17.

73. Mosse, *Nazi Culture*, xxxi.

74. Mosse, *Nazism*, 36.

75. George L. Mosse, "Introduction: Towards a General Theory of Fascism," in *International Fascism: New Thoughts and New Approaches*, ed. George L. Mosse (London: Sage Publications, 1979), 9.

76. George L. Mosse, *The Fascist Revolution: Toward a General Theory of Fascism* (New York: Howard Fertig, 1999), xiii; Mosse, "Fascinating Fascism," lecture, n.d., AR 25137, box 17, folder 7, George L. Mosse Collection, Leo Baeck Institute, New York. The lecture was given soon after the publication of Emilio Gentile's *Il culto del littorio: La sacralizzazione della politica nell'Italia fascista* (Rome: Laterza, 1993).

77. R. K. Webb, letter to Mosse, February 7, 1969, AR 25137, box 8, folder 2, George L. Mosse Collection, Leo Baeck Institute, New York. The three books, all of them published in 1968, are George Stocking, *Race, Culture and Evolution: Essays on the History of Anthropology*; Marvin Harris, *The Rise of Anthropological Theory: A History of Theories of Culture*; and Wilhelm E. Mühlmann, *Geschichte der Anthropologie*.

78. Griffin, "Withstanding the Rush of Time," 116.

79. George L. Mosse, letter to the AHR, 1969, AR 25137, box 8, folder 2, George L. Mosse Collection, Leo Baeck Institute, New York.

80. George L. Mosse, "History, Anthropology, and Mass Movements," *American Historical Review* 75 (December 1969): 447.

81. Ibid., 448.

82. Jakob Burckhardt, *Reflections on History* (London: G. Allen & Unwin, 1943).

83. Mosse, "History, Anthropology, and Mass Movements," 451–52. It must be noted that the concept of manipulation still appears, though in a radically different context. Though he discarded the concept of propaganda, Mosse never denied that myths and symbols might also be used to manipulate, despite the huge emphasis he came to put on the sincerity of consensus.

84. Ibid., 452.

85. Gentile, *Il fascino del persecutore*, 91; Griffin, "Withstanding the Rush of Time," 116.

86. Gentile, *Il fascino del persecutore*, 89.

87. Mosse wrote that Lévi-Strauss had posited "an interplay between psychological attitudes and social functions. The great manifestations of society originate at the level of unconscious existence. Many historians will recognize the truth of his assertion that there is bound to be a discrepancy between the working of the human mind and empirical reality . . . Empirical data are necessary for Lévi-Strauss, but by themselves they cannot provide an explanation of causes. The human mind imposes form upon content, and therefore it is the structure of the human mind that must concern us" ("History, Anthropology, and Mass Movements," 451).

88. Mosse, *Nationalization of the Masses*, 451–52.

Chapter 3. The Roots of the Anthropological and Visual Turn

1. Mosse, *Reformation*, 1; George L. Mosse, "European Cultural and Intellectual History, 1660–1870," lectures given for the University of the Air, fall 1982, University of Wisconsin–Madison, lecture 01.

2. Emilio Gentile has written of a "circular connection" between research, methodology and theoretical elaboration in Mosse's work. See Gentile, *Il fascino del persecutore*, 69.

3. George E. Fellows, "The Relation of Anthropology to the Study of History," *American Journal of Sociology* 1, no. 1 (July 1895): 46.

4. Ibid., 47 (my italics).

5. Thomas Hylland Eriksen and Finn Sivert Nielsen, *A History of Anthropology* (London: Virginia Pluto Press, 2001), 55.

6. Thomas Nipperdey, "Kulturgeschichte, Sozialgeschichte, historische Anthropologie," *Vierteljahrschrift für Sozial und Wirtschaftsgeschichte* 55 (1968): 145. Peter Novick has written that conservative historians in the interwar period attacked relativism on the grounds that it was seen as a "nihilistic campaign against fundamental axioms of a stable and comprehensible world, against the quest for certain and absolute truth, against the very notion of rationality": the rebellion led by those historians who believed in relativism was "anti-intellectual" and "irrationalist." See Novick, *That Noble Dream*, 164.

7. George L. Mosse, "The Way People Think," Contemporary Trends, lecture, 1958–1959, AR 25137, box 16, folder 26, George L. Mosse Collection, Leo Baeck Institute, New York. Mosse himself stated that his main influences had been Hegel, Croce, Meinecke, and Huizinga: see Mosse, *Nazism*.

8. Among these "founding fathers" of anthropology as an academic discipline, apart from the exiles there were also many women and scholars coming from Europe's colonies overseas. See Eriksen and Nielsen, *A History of Anthropology*, 55.

9. See, for example, Johann Huizinga, *In the Shadow of Tomorrow: A Diagnosis of the Spiritual Distemper of Our Time* (London: W. Heinemann, 1936).

10. Two exceptions are Griffin, "Withstanding the Rush of Time," and Gentile, *Il fascino del persecutore*.

11. Emilio Gentile, letter to George L. Mosse, September 12, 1990, AR 25137, box 35, folder 9, George L. Mosse Collection, Leo Baeck Institute, New York.

12. George L. Mosse, letter to Emilio Gentile, October 15, 1990, AR 25137, box 35, folder 9, George L. Mosse Collection, Leo Baeck Institute, New York.

13. James Wald has written of the "general nature" of Mosse's work, referring to the fact that he always looked for the broad vision without trying to be systematic or to provide the reader with precise definitions (Mosse's definition of "culture" in *The Culture of Western Europe* is a rare exception to this rule). See Wald, "Cultural History and Symbols," 181.

14. George L. Mosse, "European Culture since 1870—Old Lectures—Not Used," n.d., AR 25137, box 20, folder 14, George L. Mosse Collection, Leo Baeck Institute, New York.

15. Mosse, *Nazism*, 29–30.

16. Johan Huizinga, *The Waning of the Middle Ages: A Study of the Forms of Life, Thought, and Art in France and the Netherlands in the XIVth and XVth Centuries* (New York: St. Martin's Press, 1924). Carl Gustav Jung had asserted that myths are "dreamlike structures" (Carl G. Jung, *Symbols of Transformation: An Analysis of the Prelude to a Case of Schizophrenia* [1912; Princeton, NJ: Princeton University Press, 1967], 24), while Mircea Eliade had drawn a line between myth and dream, on the grounds that he saw

the former as being a collective, universal phenomenon and the latter as a strictly individual one, a distinction in line with Mosse's own "history of the masses" (Mircea Eliade, *Myths, Dreams and Mysteries: The Encounter between Contemporary Faiths and Archaic Realities* [New York: Harper & Row, 1960], 16 [original French edition, 1957]).

17. George L. Mosse, "Conservatism," in *Intellectual Foundations of National Socialism* seminar; Mosse, *Nazism*, 29–30.

18. Mosse, *Culture of Western Europe* (1961), 344, 346.

19. Mosse, "The Genesis of Fascism," 16.

20. Georges Sorel, *Reflections on Violence* (1908; repr. New York: Collier Books, 1961), 41–42. Mosse wrote that myth is "an image which can inspire men" (*Nazi Culture*, 93).

21. Sorel, *Reflections on Violence*, 52.

22. Mosse, "Fascism once More."

23. Mosse, "History, Anthropology, and Mass Movements," 448–50.

24. See "Freud and Psychoanalysis," in Mosse, *Culture of Western Europe* (1961), 263–76.

25. Mosse, "Adolf Hitler."

26. Mosse, "Conservatism."

27. George L. Mosse, *Confronting the Nation: Jewish and Western Nationalism* (Hanover, NH: Brandeis University Press, 1993), 2.

28. Jung, *Symbols of Transformation*, xxiv.

29. George L. Mosse, "Mass Politics and the Political Liturgy of Nationalism," in *Nationalism: The Nature and Evolution of an Idea*, ed. Eugene Kamenka (Canberra: Australian National University Press, 1973), 51.

30. Clark Wissler, *Man and Culture* (New York: Thomas Y. Crowell Company, 1923), 1, 49.

31. Alfred Louis Kroeber, *Anthropology: Race, Language, Culture, Philosophy, Prehistory* (1923; repr. New York: Harcourt Brace and Company, 1948), 1, 12.

32. Eliade, *Myths, Dreams and Mysteries*, 24.

33. Rabinbach, "George L. Mosse 1919–1999," 331.

34. Mosse interview, "Du Baroque au Nazisme," 248–49. The emotive impact of student protests on Mosse can be detected also in a passage of a letter he wrote to Professor R. K. Webb in February 1969, while he was writing "History, Anthropology, and Mass Movements": "I am not sure if you could read my scribble on the postcard I sent yesterday. You must excuse this—the presence of National Guard and protestors does produce a certain disorientation" (George L. Mosse, letter to R. K. Webb, February 15, 1969, AR 25137, box 8, folder 2, George L. Mosse Collection, Leo Baeck Institute, New York). To be sure, Mosse had already experienced directly the seductive power of participating in a "movement" during his antifascist struggle in the 1930s: as he wrote in his memoir, "The Spanish war was the first modern war in which propaganda was used on a massive scale. I myself and my friends entered wholeheartedly into what our opponents (and later historians) called propaganda but for us was like any liturgy; it was an emotional and creative expression of truth, and the songs cemented our community. Here I received

one more insight which I later elaborated in my own work on National Socialism and nationalism: the word 'propaganda' is usually a hostile term which obscures what those involved felt about the self-expression such movements provide through their mass meetings, posters, dances, songs" (Mosse, *Confronting History*, 102).

35. Gentile, *Il fascino del persecutore*, 96.

36. George L. Mosse, "New Left Intellectuals/New Left Politics," in *History and the New Left: Madison, Wisconsin, 1950–1970*, ed. Paul Buhle (Philadelphia: Temple University Press, 1990), 235.

37. Mosse, Interview with Laura Smail.

38. Mosse, "New Left Intellectuals," 237–38.

39. Mosse, Early Modern History Course, 1969.

40. George L. Mosse, "Final Lecture," 1969, AR 25137, box 19, folder 33, George L. Mosse Collection, Leo Baeck Institute, New York.

41. Mosse interview, "Du Baroque au Nazisme," 248. See also George L. Mosse, "The End Is Not Yet: A Personal Memoir of the German-Jewish Legacy in America," *American Jewish Archives* 40, no. 2 (1988): 197–201.

42. See in particular George L. Mosse, *Germans and Jews: The Right, the Left, and the Search for a 'Third Force' in Pre-Nazi Germany* (London: Orbach & Chambers, 1971). Mosse had also surely in mind his own family, whose rationalistic attitude, in his view, prevented them from realizing the seriousness of the Nazi threat.

43. Griffin, "Withstanding the Rush of Time," 114.

44. Moro, "George L. Mosse," 34–35. In fact, Kantorowicz was related to Mosse, and Mosse was familiar with his work. Kantorowicz also wrote a pioneering article that anticipated Mosse's arguments by over twenty years and inspired Mosse's reflections on the cult of the fallen soldiers; see Ernst Kantorowicz, "Pro Patria Mori in Medieval Political Thought," *American Historical Review* 56, no. 3 (April 1951): 472–92. For an extensive discussion of Mosse's analysis of the cult of the fallen soldiers, see chap. 4.

45. Paul Fussell, *The Great War and Modern Memory* (Oxford: Oxford University Press, 1975). The Jung passage is taken from his *Wotan*, as quoted by Mosse himself in Mosse, "What Is Fascism?" Carlton J. H. Hayes, "Nationalism as a Religion," in Carlton J. H. Hayes, *Essays on Nationalism* (New York: The Mac Millan Company, 1926); see also Hayes's *Nationalism: A Religion* (New York: The Mac Millan Company, 1960).

46. See in particular Benedetto Croce, *La storia come pensiero e come azione* (Rome: Laterza, 1943), and his "La concezione liberale come concezione della vita," in Benedetto Croce, *La mia filosofia* (Milano: Adelphi, 1993).

47. Moro, "George L. Mosse."

48. George L. Mosse, "Nationhood and Diaspora," speech, 1980, AR 25137, box 18, folder 27, George L. Mosse Collection, Leo Baeck Institute, New York.

49. Mosse, "History, Anthropology, and Mass Movements," 451.

50. Stanley Payne, *A History of Fascism: 1914–45* (London: UCL Press, 1995), xiii.

51. Mosse, "European Cultural and Intellectual History, 1660–1870," lecture 02.

52. Ibid., lecture 05. Jung wrote that "although we, with our rationalism, think we can block this source of fear by pointing to its unreality, it nevertheless remains one of those psychic realities whose irrational nature cannot be exorcized by rational argument" (*Symbols of Transformation*, 156).

53. Croce, *La storia come pensiero e come azione*, 53, 254.

54. George L. Mosse, "European Culture 1600 to 1800," lectures, n.d. (probably late 1950s), AR 25137, box 19, folder 41, George L. Mosse Collection, Leo Baeck Institute, New York.

55. George L. Mosse, speech on mysticism and the Renaissance, 1948, AR 25137, box 17, folder 44, George L. Mosse Collection, Leo Baeck Institute, New York.

56. George L. Mosse, "Culture and Civilization: The Function of the Historian," speech, n.d., AR 25137, box 16, folder 31, George L. Mosse Collection, Leo Baeck Institute, New York; Mosse, "Europe and the Modern World—Final Lecture."

57. George L. Mosse, *Masses and Men: Nationalist and Fascist Perceptions of Reality* (New York: Howard Fertig, 1980), 15–16. Earlier, Mosse said that "the irrational is made concrete through rational acts within the terms of its own ideological framework. If this were not so, no political movement based upon irrational premises could exist or succeed. But this also means that in cultural terms it is, at times, possible to detach the rational from the irrational and to ignore the latter, especially if there exists a predisposition to accept the goals of such a movement. This was certainly the case in the relationship of many Germans towards National Socialism" ("The Appeal of Nazi Culture").

58. Gentile, *Il fascino del persecutore*, 84.

59. Mosse, "The Genesis of Fascism," 15.

60. William L. Langer, "The Next Assignment," *American Historical Review* 63, no. 2 (January 1958): 284, 286, 290.

61. Goodwin Watson, "Clio and Psyche: Some Interrelations of Psychology and History," in Ware, *The Cultural Approach to History*, 36–37.

62. Franz Alexander, "Psychology and the Interpretation of Historical Events," in Ware, *The Cultural Approach to History*, 42, 50, 55–57.

63. Geoffrey Gorer, "Society as Viewed by the Anthropologist," in Ware, *The Cultural Approach to History*, 25.

64. H. Stuart Hughes, "The Historian and the Social Scientist," *American Historical Review* 66, no. 1 (October, 1960): 31.

65. Mosse, "European Culture 1600 to 1800."

66. Mosse, "Europe and the Modern World," lectures. "The task of the historian is to explain the variety of choices made by the actors on the stage of the past": George L. Mosse, "The 'Non-Political' Youth Movement," draft for a review, 1960–1969, AR 25137, box 11, folder 17, George L. Mosse Collection, Leo Baeck Institute, New York.

67. Wilcomb E. Washburn, "Ethnohistory: History 'In the Round,'" *Ethnohistory* 8, no. 1 (Winter 1961): 39.

68. Langer, "The Next Assignment," 286.

69. Hughes, "The Historian and the Social Scientist," 31.

70. Nipperdey, "Kulturgeschichte, Sozialgeschichte"; see also his essays "Die anthro-
pologische Dimension der Geschichtswissenschaft" and "Historismus und Historis-
muskritik heute," in Thomas Nipperdey, *Gesellschaft, Kultur, Theorie: Gesammelte Aufsätze
zur neueren Geschichte* (Göttingen: Vandenhoek & Ruprecht, 1976), 33–58, 59–73.

71. Lévi-Strauss argued in 1949 that ethnology and history were essential to each
other, and stressed the importance of their cohabitation in studying contemporary societies. See Claude Lévi-Strauss, "Histoire et Ethnologie," *Revue de Métaphysique et de
Morale* 54 (1949): 391.

72. E. H. Gombrich, *In Search of Cultural History*, the Philip Maurice Deneke Lecture,
vol. 1967 (Oxford: Clarendon Press, 1969), 27, 30.

73. Hughes, "The Historian and the Social Scientist."

74. George W. Stocking Jr., "Cultural Darwinism" and "Philosophical Idealism," in
"A Special Plea for Historicism in the History of Anthropology," ed. E. B. Tylor, special
issue, *Southwestern Journal of Anthropology* 21, no. 2 (Summer 1965): 143–44.

75. Claude Lévi-Strauss, "Histoire et ethnologie," *Annales: Histoire, Sciences Sociales*
38, no. 6 (November–December 1983): 1217–18. See also Lévi-Strauss, "Histoire et Ethnologie" (1949); and Margaret Mead, "Anthropologist and Historian: Their Common
Problems," *American Quarterly* 3, no. 1 (Spring 1951): 3–13.

76. Roy F. Nichols, "Postwar Reorientation of Historical Thinking," *American Historical Review* 54, no. 1 (October 1948): 79.

77. Ibid., 83, 84, 85, 88.

78. Jurgen Herbst, *The German Historical School in American Scholarship: A Study in
the Transfer of Culture* (Ithaca, NY: Cornell University Press, 1965).

79. Novick, *That Noble Dream*.

80. Hughes, "The Historian and the Social Scientist," 24.

81. Ibid., 42.

82. H. Stuart Hughes, *Consciousness and Society: The Reorientation of European Social
Thought, 1890–1930* (New York 1958), 9, 10. (Mosse reviewed the book in 1959: George L.
Mosse, "Retreat from Reality," *The Progressive*, July 1959, 27). Hughes referred to
three ways of approaching intellectual history. The first deals with "popular ideas and
practices—with the whole of the vast realm of folklore and community sentiments,"
where historians "proceed in much the same fashion in which anthropologists approach
the study of 'primitive' culture"; such efforts have been labeled "retrospective cultural
anthropology." The second is "the kind of history that Croce called ethical-political—the
study of the activities of ruling minorities and of the rival minorities striving to supplant
them." The third is "the history of the enunciation and development of the ideas that
eventually will inspire such governing élites." By his own admission, Hughes's study fell
into the third category, which he regarded as the *"via regia* of intellectual history." See
Hughes, *Consciousness and Society*, 9–10.

83. James Harvey Robinson, *The New History: Essays Illustrating the Modern Historical
Outlook* (New York: The MacMillan Company, 1912). Along with Charles Beard, Robinson was instrumental in fueling the debate on relativism in the United States. See Beard,

"Written History as an Act of Faith"; Charles A. Beard and Alfred Vagts, "Currents of Thought in Historiography," *American Historical Review* 42, no. 3 (April 1937): 460–83. On Beard, see Lloyd R. Sorenson, "Charles A. Beard and German Historiographical Thought," *Mississippi Valley Historical Review* 42, no. 2 (September 1955): 274–87; David W. Marcell, "Charles Beard: Civilization and the Revolt against Empiricism," *American Quarterly* 21, no. 1 (Spring 1969): 65–86; see also Peter Novick, *That Noble Dream.*

84. Arthur O. Lovejoy, "Present Standpoints and Past History," *Journal of Philosophy* 36, no. 18 (August 31, 1939): 484.

85. Robert Beckhofer, "Clio and the Culture Concept in Historiography," in *The Idea of Culture in the Social Sciences*, ed. Louis Schneider and Charles M. Bonjean (Cambridge: Cambridge University Press, 1973), 82. The passage is quoted in *The Cultural Turn in U.S. History: Past, Present, and Future*, ed. James W. Cook, Lawrence B. Glickman, and Michael O'Malley (Chicago: University of Chicago Press, 2008), 6. On Boas's influence on American culture, see Richard Handler, "Boasian Anthropology and the Critique of American Culture," *American Quarterly* 42, no. 2 (June 1990): 252–73.

86. Ware, *The Cultural Approach to History.* On Caroline Ware and her intellectual background, to a certain extent affected by German culture, see Ellen Fitzpatrick, "Caroline F. Ware and the Cultural Approach to History," *American Quarterly* 43, no. 2 (June 1991): 185–89.

87. Ware, *The Cultural Approach to History*, 8.

88. Ibid., 12.

89. Kroeber, *Anthropology*, 186–87.

90. E. E. Evans-Pritchard, *Anthropology and History*, lecture delivered in the University of Manchester with the support of the Simon Fund for the Social Sciences (Manchester: Manchester University Press, 1961).

91. Ernst Cassirer, *Essay on Man: An Introduction to the Philosophy of Human Culture* (1944; repr. New Haven, CT: Yale University Press, 1962), 26. See also Ernst Cassirer, *The Logic of the Humanities* (New Haven, CT: Yale University Press, 1961).

92. Cassirer, *Essay on Man*, 79–81.

93. Georg G. Iggers, "Historicism: The History and Meaning of the Term," *Journal of the History of Ideas* 56, no. 1 (January 1995): 142.

94. A recent example is Cook, Glickman, and O'Malley, eds., *The Cultural Turn in U.S. History.*

95. Friedrich Meinecke, for example, interpreted the modern age against the background of the irrational/rational dualism between *Homo sapiens* and *Homo faber.* Similarly, Ernst Cassirer, inspired by Dilthey's distinction between *Geisteswissenschaften* and *Naturwissenschaften*, drew a distinction between *Homo magus* and *Homo faber.* See Meinecke, *The German Catastrophe*, 38; Ernst Cassirer, *The Myth of the State* (New Haven, CT: Yale University Press, 1946), 281. Mircea Eliade argued that "the man of traditional societies is admittedly a *homo religious*, but his behaviour forms part of the general behaviour of mankind" (*The Sacred and the Profane: The Nature of Religion* [New York: Harvest Book, 1959], 15).

96. See Steven Aschheim, *Beyond the Border: The German-Jewish Legacy Abroad* (Princeton, NJ: Princeton University Press, 2007).

97. Mosse, *Germans and Jews*. By the 1950s and 1960s the concern with myth and anthropology was rapidly gaining ground in the United States. The field of American studies, with its focus on myth and symbol, fully flourished thanks to the works of Henry Nash Smith and Leo Marx. The journal *Ethnohistory*, whose first issue appeared in 1954, sought a rapprochement of history and ethnology in the study of American native peoples. On American studies, see Henry Nash Smith, *Virgin Land: The American West as Symbol and Myth* (Cambridge, MA: Harvard University Press, 1950); Leo Marx, *The Machine in the Garden: Technology and the Pastoral Ideal in America* (New York: Oxford University Press, 1964); see also John Higham, "American Intellectual History: A Critical Appraisal," *American Quarterly* 13, no. 2, suppl. (Summer 1961): 219–33; Richard E. Sykes, "American Studies and the Concept of Culture: A Theory and Method," *American Quarterly* 15, no. 2, suppl. (Summer 1963): 253–70; Leo Marx, "American Studies: A Defense of an Unscientific Method," *New Literary History* 1, no. 1, New and Old History (October 1969): 75–90 (in which Marx draws a distinction between the method of the sciences and that of the humanities, stressing the necessity to describe and understand "the state of mind of a group of people at some moment in the past," as well as the need to consider culture as a whole. Marx draws the terms "image" and "symbol" from literary criticism, focusing on popular literature); Bruce Kuklick, "Myth and Symbol in American Studies," *American Quarterly* 24, no. 4 (October 1972): 435–50; a recent synthesis is *Locating American Studies: The Evolution of a Discipline*, ed. Lucy Maddox (Baltimore: Johns Hopkins University Press, 1998). As to *Ethnohistory*, its goals and approaches, see Erminie W. Voegelin, "A Note from the Chairman," *Ethnohistory* 1, no. 1 (April 1954): 1–3; Erminie W. Voegelin, "An Ethnohistorian's Viewpoint," *Ethnohistory* 1, no. 2 (November 1954): 166–71; James C. Olson, "Some Reflections on Historical Method and Indian History," *Ethnohistory* 5, no. 1 (Winter 1958): 48–59; Gene Weltfish, "The Question of Ethnic Identity, an Ethnohistorical Approach," *Ethnohistory* 6, no. 4 (Autumn, 1959): 321–46; Richard M. Dorson, "Ethnohistory and Ethnic Folklore," *Ethnohistory* 8, no. 1 (Winter 1961): 12–30; Wilcomb E. Washburn, "Ethnohistory: History 'In the Round,'" *Ethnohistory* 8, no. 1 (Winter 1961): 31–48; William C. Sturtevant, "Anthropology, History and Ethnohistory," *Ethnohistory* 13, nos. 1–2 (Winter–Spring 1966): 1–51; Charles Hudson, "Folk History and Ethnohistory," *Ethnohistory* 13, nos. 1–2 (Winter–Spring, 1966): 52–70; James Axtell, "Ethnohistory: An Historian's Viewpoint," *Ethnohistory* 26, no. 1 (Winter 1979): 1–13.

98. George L. Mosse, *German Jews Beyond Judaism* (Cincinnati: Hebrew Union College Press, 1985), 54.

99. Mosse, "The Cultural Historian."

100. George L. Mosse, "European Fascism—Lectures—Not Used," n.d., AR 25137, box 16, folder 41, George L. Mosse Collection, Leo Baeck Institute, New York.

101. Mosse, *Nazism*, 30.

102. William B. Hesseltine, "The Challenge of the Artifact," *Wisconsin Magazine of History* 66, no. 2 (Winter 1982–83): 123, 126, 127; the essay was originally published in *The Present World of History; A Conference on Certain Problems in Historical Agency Work in the United States*, ed. James H. Rodabaugh, (Madison: State Historical Society of Wisconsin, 1959), 64–70.

103. Mosse, *Culture of Western Europe* (1961), 348.

104. Ibid., 360.

105. George L. Mosse, "Nationalism and Patriotism," address to the meeting "The Teaching of Patriotism," Institute for Social Studies Teachers at Wisconsin State College, April 18, 1963, AR 25137, box 18, folder 23, George L. Mosse Collection, Leo Baeck Institute, New York.

106. Mosse, "History, Anthropology, and Mass Movements," 451. The importance of the "visual" as contrasted with the "written document" had also been emphasized by the French historian Marc Ferro in an article published in 1968 in the *Journal of Contemporary History*, coedited by Mosse: Marc Ferro, "1917: History and Cinema," in "1918–19: From War to Peace," ed. George Mosse and Walter Laqueur, special issue, *Journal of Contemporary History*, 3, no. 4 (October 1968): 45–61. In this regard, see chap. 4, section "Modernity and the Great War." See also Marc Ferro, "Vers le renouvellement de l'histoire des relations internationales," *Annales: Histoire, Sciences Sociales* 20, no. 1 (January–February 1965): 175–78; Annie Kriegel, Marc Ferro, and Alain Besançon, "L'expérience de 'La Grande Guerre,'" *Annales: Histoire, Sciences Sociales* 20, no. 2 (March–April 1965): 327–36; Marc Ferro, "Société du XXe siècle et histoire cinématographique," *Annales: Histoire, Sciences Sociales* 23, no. 3 (May–June 1968): 581–85.

107. Gorer, "Society as Viewed by the Anthropologist," 21–22.

108. Mosse, *Culture of Western Europe* (1988), 66–67 (my italics).

109. Huizinga, *Waning of the Middle Ages*.

110. The quote can be found in George L. Mosse, "The Poet and the Exercise of Political Power: Gabriele d'Annunzio," *Yearbook of Comparative and General Literature* 22 (1973): 33; and in George L. Mosse, *Toward the Final Solution: A History of European Racism* (New York: Howard Fertig, 1978), 233, but also in Mosse's lectures: see, for example, Mosse, "European Fascism—Lectures."

111. Mosse, *Nazism*, 95; George L. Mosse, "The Community in the Thought of Nationalism, Fascism, and the Radical Right," in Mosse, *Confronting the Nation*, 42.

112. Mosse, "European Cultural and Intellectual History, 1660–1870," lecture 03. This is reminiscent of that quote of Huizinga's Mosse often cited: "Having once attributed a real existence to an idea, the mind wants to see it alive and can effect this only by personalizing it." The "visible," the "tangible," noted Mosse in the drafts for a lecture, is "holy." See George L. Mosse, "European Culture 1815–1970—Enlightenment and Pietism," lecture notes, n.d., AR 25137, box 20, folder 3, George L. Mosse Collection, Leo Baeck Institute, New York.

113. Mosse wrote in his memoir that "the buildings of Salem, mostly constructed during the seventeenth and eighteenth centuries, were decorated in the style of the

South German baroque. . . . There were many churches and houses nearby constructed and decorated in the South German baroque style, and it is from these surroundings that I had acquired a lifelong love of that style; indeed, in the 1950s I often led friends on a tour of the South German baroque, specifically in its Lake Constance setting" (*Confronting History*, 54). In the later years of his life, he returned ever more frequently to his Salem experience (conversation with John Tortorice, March 2007).

114. Sterling Fishman, "GLM: An Appreciation," in Drescher, Sabean, and Sharlin, eds., *Political Symbolism in Modern Europe*, 278–79.

115. Mosse, *Nazism*, 36–37.

116. Conversation with Seymour Drescher, November 2010.

117. Victor L. Tapié, *Baroque et Classicisme* (Paris: Plon, 1957).

118. Wylie Sypher, *Four Stages of Renaissance Style: Transformations in Art and Literature 1400–1700* (New York: Anchor Books Original, 1955), 187; Giulio Carlo Argan, *L'architettura barocca in Italia* (Milan: Garzanti, 1957).

119. George L. Mosse, "Renaissance and Reformation," lectures, n.d., AR 25137, box 18, folder 46, George L. Mosse Collection, Leo Baeck Institute, New York. The lecture from which I have quoted dates back to the late 1950s, in that Mosse mentions his "just published" book *The Holy Pretence*, which was printed in 1957.

120. George L. Mosse, "Renaissance and Reformation," lectures, n.d., AR 25137, box 18, folder 47, George L. Mosse Collection, Leo Baeck Institute, New York. These lectures were surely given after 1953, and in all probability in the 1950s.

121. Mosse, *Nazism*, 31.

122. Mosse, *Nationalization of the Masses*, 9, 200.

123. Mosse interview, "Du Baroque au Nazisme," 250.

124. Ibid.

125. Mosse, "History, Anthropology, and Mass Movements," 452. The reference is to Thomas Nipperdey, "Nationalidee und Nationaldenkmal in Deutschland im 19. Jahrhundert," *Historische Zeitschrift* 206 (June 1968): 529–85.

126. Mosse, *Nationalization of the Masses*, 47.

127. Wolfgang Hardtwig and Harm-Hinrich Brandt, eds., *Deutschlands Weg in die Moderne: Politik, Gesellschaft und Kultur im 19. Jahrhundert* (Munich: Beck, 1993), 8. The book is a commemorative volume in honor of Nipperdey. Many of the collaborators were historians who had an interest in cultural history, including Fritz Stern, Peter Gay, Shulamit Volkov, Hermann Lübbe, Carl E. Schorske, and Mosse. Typically enough, few of them taught in Germany. In his *Deutsche Geschichte*, Nipperdey furthered an approach that took cultural history into consideration, in opposition to the historical methods of the dominating *Neue Sozialgeschichte*.

128. Nipperdey, "Nationalidee und Nationaldenkmal," 530, 532. This is a concept Mosse already knew and agreed with, which he had taken from Huizinga.

129. Ibid., 583.

130. Albert Speer, *Spandauer Tagebücher* (Frankfurt: Verlag Ullstein GmbH, 1975), 280.

131. Albert Speer, *Erinnerungen* (Berlin: Propyläen-Verlag, 1969).

132. George L. Mosse, "Albert Speer's Hitler," review of *Spandau: The Secret Diaries*, by Albert Speer (English translation of Speer's *Spandauer Tagebücher*), *Quadrant*, October 1976, 53–54.

133. Ibid., 54, 55.

134. See "Correspondence with Albert Speer," 1971–77, AR 25137, box 39, folder 36, George L. Mosse Collection, Leo Baeck Institute, New York.

135. Conversation with John Tortorice, April 2010. Sending Mosse a copy of his *Spandau Diaries*, Speer wrote: "Professor George L. Mosse, mit allen guten Wünschen, in Freundschaft. Albert Speer" (to Professor George L. Mosse, with best wishes, in friendship. Albert Speer). The book is in Mosse's private library in Madison.

136. George L. Mosse, letter to Martin Krygier, May 13, 1976, AR 25137, box 12, folder 25, George L. Mosse Collection, Leo Baeck Institute, New York.

137. Joan Ringelheim, "Interview with George Mosse," March 13, 1995, RG-50.030*0310, United States Holocaust Memorial Museum.

138. Conversation with Stanley Payne, October 2005.

139. Albert Speer, letter to Mosse, July 11, 1973, AR 25137, box 39, folder 36, George L. Mosse Collection, Leo Baeck Institute, New York.

140. Mosse, *Nationalization of the Masses*, viii.

141. Albert Speer, letter to Mosse, April 9, 1973, and George L. Mosse, letter to Speer, March 8, 1973, both AR 25137, box 39, folder 36, George L. Mosse Collection, Leo Baeck Institute, New York. In the 1981 edition of the book, Mosse had admitted that at the time he had not yet realized the importance of symbols and political liturgies.

142. Mosse interview, "Du Baroque au Nazisme," 250.

143. Symbols "give people their identity," Mosse wrote in *Nationalization of the Masses*, 7.

144. Aschheim, "George Mosse," xii.

145. In the late 1960s, as coeditor of the *Journal of Contemporary History*, Mosse showed on several occasions his interest in the "new methods now being applied to history" (George L. Mosse, letter to Allan Bogue, April 20, 1966, AR 25137, box 49, folder 23, George L. Mosse Collection, Leo Baeck Institute, New York). Ernest Hearst, the assistant editor, wrote that the journal "flavours the broad, interdisciplinary approach, which roughly speaking, would take in the entire flow of forces—political, sociological, cultural—resulting in 'historical events'" (Ernest Hearst, letter to Dr. Krister Wahlbäck, January 17, 1966, AR 25137, box 49, folder 23, George L. Mosse Collection, Leo Baeck Institute, New York). Mosse also tried, between 1967 and 1969, to edit an issue on the topic of psychology and history, but he was unable to find enough publishable essays. Mosse felt on that occasion that it may have been too early for such an attempt (see "Journal of Contemporary History—Psychology and History," 1967–69, AR 25137, box 50, folder 10, George L. Mosse Collection, Leo Baeck Institute, New York).

146. Eliade, *Myths, Dreams and Mysteries*, 8. The passage quoted here is in the foreword to the English edition.

147. Renzo De Felice, 1983 preface to *Le interpretazioni del fascismo* (1969; repr. Rome: Laterza, 1996), 7–25.

148. Eliade, *Myths, Dreams and Mysteries*, 8–10.

149. The expression is used by Emilio Gentile in his *Il fascino del persecutore*.

150. Mosse, *Toward the Final Solution*, xxv.

151. This is how Mosse came to define the Enlightenment's contribution to the creation of stereotypes and to racism. The expression "underside of the Enlightenment" can be found, for example, in Mosse's "European Cultural and Intellectual History, 1660–1870" lectures.

Chapter 4. The Dark Side of Modernity

1. Mosse, "Chapel Talks."

2. Mosse argued that "without the modern state there couldn't have been a holocaust" (Mosse interviewed by the *Auckland Star*, July 10, 1979).

3. Mosse, *Nazism*, 43.

4. George L. Mosse, "The Holocaust and Modern Manners and Morals," n.d., AR 25137, box 17, folder 36, George L. Mosse Collection, Leo Baeck Institute, New York.

5. George L. Mosse, *Nationalism and Sexuality: Respectability and Abnormal Sexuality in Modern Europe* (New York: Howard Fertig, 1985), 1. The book was later reprinted as *Nationalism and Sexuality: Middle-Class Morality and Sexual Norms in Modern Europe* (Madison: University of Wisconsin Press, 1988).

6. Respectability also represented, in Mosse's scheme of things, the defining element of the middle classes. He argued: "The middle classes can be only partially defined by their economic activity and even by their hostility to the aristocracy and the lower classes alike. For side by side with their economic activity was above all the ideal of respectability which came to characterize their style of life. Through respectability they sought to maintain their status and self-respect against both the lower classes and the aristocracy" (*Nationalism and Sexuality*, 4–5).

7. Mosse, *Confronting History*, 219.

8. Ibid., 185.

9. Lecturing at the Collège de France in the 1970s, Foucault explained how the "bourgeois revolution" of the turn of the nineteenth century examined not only state apparatuses or institutions, but it also invented a new technology of power that attempted to penetrate the social body in its totality. Medicine, for example, set standards of "normality" to which the whole body of the population ought to conform. Political control was thus exerted also through the establishment of social norms that drew a clear-cut line of demarcation between "normal" and "abnormal" behavior. Monstrosity, or simply "abnormalcy," was extensively translated on a judicial-moral plane that informed social behavior with much greater significance. See Michel Foucault, *Les Anormaux: Cours au Collège de France (1974–1975)* (Paris: Seuil/Gallimard, 1999). Like the French philosopher and historian, Mosse stressed the role played by physicians who took over from the Church the role of guardians of respectability. Though there seems

to be no direct influence of Foucault on Mosse's thought, the conclusions they reached are often very similar. Mosse mentions Foucault only once in his books, referring to the Frenchman's *History of Sexuality*, and partly criticizing his conclusions (Mosse, *Nationalism and Sexuality*, 21–22). Mosse was familiar with Foucault's work, and yet most of the books in his private library in Madison date to the late 1980s and 1990s. Many former colleagues and friends of Mosse's do not believe there was an influence.

10. Mosse, *Confronting History*, 178–79.

11. George L. Mosse, "Political Awakening: Berlin, Exile, and Anti-Fascist Movement," speech given at the University of Kentucky, 1998, AR 25137, box 18, folder 38, George L. Mosse Collection, Leo Baeck Institute, New York. To be sure, Mosse's attitude had at times been ambivalent; in his memoir, he recalls how he found heterosexuals' "normality" "attractive" (*Confronting History*, 118).

12. Breines, "Finding Oneself in History," 4, 11, 12–14.

13. Mosse, "Response by George Mosse," xxxi. "Reading the history of racism correctly means also pondering the history of Europe with which it is so closely intertwined" (Mosse, *Toward the Final Solution*, 236).

14. Mosse, *Toward the Final Solution*, xxviii.

15. George L. Mosse, "Modern Anti-Semitism: Failure of the Enlightenment," lecture, n.d., AR 25137, box 18, folder 15, George L. Mosse Collection, Leo Baeck Institute, New York. This lecture probably dates back to the late 1970s or 1980s.

16. Mosse, *Nazism*, 94–95.

17. Mosse, "The Significance of Nietzsche's Proposed Ethic of Masters."

18. Breines, "Finding Oneself in History," 12.

19. Mosse, "Political Awakening."

20. Mosse, "Modern Anti-Semitism."

21. Mosse, *Culture of Western Europe* (1988), 387.

22. Mosse interview, "Du Baroque au Nazisme," 249; Herf, "The Historian as Provocateur."

23. Theodor W. Adorno and Max Horkheimer, *Dialectic of the Enlightenment*, trans John Gumming (London: Verso, 1997), 3, xvii (originally published in German in 1944).

24. Ibid., 16, 13, 6, 24.

25. George Friedman, *The Political Philosophy of the Frankfurt School* (Ithaca, NY: Cornell University Press, 1981), 14, 134–35.

26. Mosse, "European Culture 1600 to 1800."

27. Mosse, "Culture, Civilization and German Antisemitism," as published in Mosse, *Germans and Jews*, 43–44.

28. Asa Briggs, review of *The Culture of Western Europe*, by George L. Mosse, *The Teacher*, June 7, 1963.

29. Mosse, *Culture of Western Europe* (1961), 8. The Enlightenment, according to Mosse, "had separated religion and life" (George L. Mosse, "Enlightenment to Romanticism," lecture notes, n.d., AR 25137, box 16, folder 37, George L. Mosse Collection, Leo Baeck Institute, New York).

30. Mosse, "European Cultural and Intellectual History, 1660–1870," lecture 03.

31. Ibid., lecture 02.

32. Adorno and Horkheimer, *Dialectic of the Enlightenment*, 13.

33. Mosse, "European Cultural and Intellectual History, 1660–1870," lecture 05.

34. Mosse, "European Culture 1815–1970—Enlightenment." The course probably dates back to the late 1970s or to the 1980s. Mosse argued that "a unanimous virtue can be quite repressive" ("European Cultural and Intellectual History, 1660–1870," lecture 05).

35. Mosse, "European Cultural and Intellectual History, 1660–1870," lecture 05.

36. Mosse, "Modern Anti-Semitism."

37. The reference is to Harold Nicolson's *Good Behaviour, Being a Study of Certain Types of Civility* (Gloucester, MA: Peter Smith, 1969), originally published in 1955. Mosse was influenced by the book's focus on how types function in society as powerful myths and its anticonformist élan, fiercely opposed to the subordination of the individual to the type.

38. Mosse, "Modern Anti-Semitism."

39. Mosse, *Nationalism and Sexuality*.

40. Mosse, "Modern Anti-Semitism."

41. Mosse, *Culture of Western Europe* (1961), 75–76, 83.

42. Mosse, *Culture of Western Europe* (1988), 85–86 (my italics).

43. Ibid., 97–98, 87.

44. The reviews of the book are collected in AR 25137, box 15, folder 16, George L. Mosse Collection, Leo Baeck Institute, New York.

45. Mosse, *Toward the Final Solution*, xi–xii.

46. Ibid., xiii–xiv.

47. A collection of reviews of and reactions to the book can be found in AR 25137, box 15, folder 1 and 2, George L. Mosse Collection, Leo Baeck Institute, New York.

48. Arthur Mitzman, "Fascism and Anti-Sex," *Stichtung Theoretische Geschiedenis* 12 (1986): 341 and 343.

49. Aschheim, "George Mosse," xv; Moro, "George L. Mosse, storico dell'irrazionalismo moderno," 33; Gentile, *Il fascino del persecutore*, 140.

50. Mosse, *Confronting History*, 180.

51. George L. Mosse, introduction to "Sexuality in History," special issue, *Journal of Contemporary History* 17, no. 2 (April 1982): 219. This special issue of the *Journal of Contemporary History* included an article of Mosse's by the title "Nationalism and Respectability: Normal and Abnormal Sexuality in the Nineteenth Century." Moreover, some previous and later unpublished seminars and lectures of Mosse's on the subject can be found in the Leo Baeck Archive, notably what he called a "Sexuality Course" held in Jerusalem in 1984, AR 25137, box 21, folder 26, George L. Mosse Collection, Leo Baeck Institute, New York; and a "Sexuality Seminar" held in 1987–88, AR 25137, box 21, folder 27, George L. Mosse Collection, Leo Baeck Institute, New York.

52. Mosse, *Confronting History*, 180.

53. George L. Mosse, "History of Anti-Semitism," notes for a seminar, 1978, AR 25137, box 17, folder 35, George L. Mosse Collection, Leo Baeck Institute, New York.

54. George L. Mosse, "Razzismo," in *Enciclopedia del Novecento* (Rome: Istituto dell'Enciclopedia Italiana, 1980), 1062. Mosse wrote: "To be sure, respectability eventually spread throughout Europe; a bourgeois movement at first, it soon encompassed all classes of the population" (*Nationalism and Sexuality*, 2). He also wrote: "What began as bourgeois morality in the eighteenth century in the end became everyone's morality" (191).

55. Mosse, *Nationalism and Sexuality*, 1–2.

56. Mosse, *Toward the Final Solution*, xiii–xiv. In that same 1978 book Mosse wrote that racism "made alliance with all those virtues that the modern age praised so much. Racism picked out such qualities as cleanliness, honesty, moral earnestness, hard work, and family life—virtues which during the nineteenth century came to symbolize the ideals of the middle class" (234).

57. Mosse, *Nationalism and Sexuality*, 3.

58. Ibid., 2, 9.

59. Here the connection Mosse makes is not with the aesthetics of the Baroque, which he considered to be essential to political liturgies. As far as bodily ideals are concerned, Mosse stressed the importance of the neoclassic ideals of Johann Joachim Winckelmann, immensely influential throughout the nineteenth century, highlighting the connection that was made between physical beauty and moral qualities and its importance for the characterization of outsiders.

60. Mosse, *Nationalism and Sexuality*, 13.

61. Ibid., 10.

62. Mosse wrote: "The ugly counter-image of the nervous, unstable homosexual and masturbator, whose physiognomy was ever more sharply delineated thanks to medical science's attribution of moral and aesthetic values, became an important symbol of the threat to nationalism and respectability posed by the rapid changes of modern age" (*Nationalism and Sexuality*, 31).

63. Mosse, *Confronting History*, 180–81. The outsider is a creation, said Mosse in a lecture, though an inevitable one since society needs not only respectability as a source of cohesion, but also the creation of an enemy, of a countertype to oppose to the type, the latter representing the ideal, moral man who embodies the positive features of the ideal, respectable bourgeois. See George L. Mosse, "Outsider," lecture, n.d., AR 25137, box 18, folder 34, George L. Mosse Collection, Leo Baeck Institute, New York.

64. Fussell, *The Great War*.

65. Mosse said this in an interview with Sandra Gereau, who wrote an MA thesis on him. See Sandra Gereau, "'Myth as Reality': George L. Mosse and the Cultural Interpretation of Nazism" (MA thesis, University of New Brunswick, 1986), 72.

66. See two special issues of the *Journal of Contemporary History*: "1914," 1, no. 3 (July 1966), and "1918–19: From War to Peace," 3, no. 4 (October 1968). Mosse's own contributions, which show his growing interest in the topic, are: *The Jews and the German War*

Experience 1914–1918, Leo Baeck Memorial Lecture 21 (New York: Leo Baeck Institute, 1977); "La sinistra europea e l'esperienza della guerra (Germania e Francia)," in *Rivoluzione e reazione in Europa 1917–1924: Convegno storico internazionale (Perugia 1978)*, vol. 2 (Rome: Mondo operaio-Avanti!, 1978), 151–67; "National Cemeteries and National Revival: The Cult of the Fallen Soldiers in Germany," *Journal of Contemporary History* 14, no. 1 (January 1979): 1–20; "Zum deutschen Soldatenlied," in *Kriegserlebnis: Der Erste Weltkrieg in der literarischen Gestaltung und symbolischen Deutung der Nationen*, ed. Klaus Vondung, 331–33 (Göttingen: Vandenhoeck and Ruprecht, 1980); "War and the Appropriation of Nature," in *Germany in the Age of Total War: Essays in Honour of Francis Carsten*, ed. Volker R. Berghahn and Martin Kitchen, 102–22 (London: Croom Helm; Totowa, NJ: Barnes and Noble Books, 1981); "Rushing to the Colors: On the History of Volunteers in War," in *Religion, Ideology and Nationalism in Europe and America: Essays Presented in Honour of Yehoshoua Arieli* (Jerusalem: Historical Society of Israel and Zalman Shazar Center for Jewish History, 1986), 173–84; "Two World Wars and the Myth of the War Experience," *Journal of Contemporary History* 21, no. 4 (October 1986): 491–513; "Der Erste Weltkrieg und die Brutalisierung der Politik. Betrachtungen über die politische Rechte, den Rassismus und den deutschen Sonderweg," in *Demokratie und Diktatur: Geist und Gestalt politischer Herrschaft in Deutschland und Europa. Festschrift für Karl Dietrich Bracher*, ed. Manfred Funke, Hans-Adolf Jacobsen, Hans-Helmuth Knütter, and Hans-Peter Schwarz (Düsseldorf: Droste, 1987), 127–39; "National Anthems: The Nation Militant," in *From Ode to Anthem: Problems of Lyric Poetry*, ed. Reinhold Grimm and Jost Hermand (Madison: University of Wisconsin Press, 1989), 86–100; "Über Kriegserinnerungen und Kriegsbegeisterung," in *Kriegsbegeisterung und mentale Kriegsvorbereitung: Interdisziplinäre Studien*, ed. Marcel van der Linden and Gottfried Mergner (Berlin: Duncker and Humblot, 1991), 27–36; "Souvenir de la guerre et place du monumentalisme dans l'identité culturelle du National-Socialisme," in *Guerre et Cultures 1914–1918*, ed. Jean-Jacques Becker, Jay Winter, Annette Becker, Gerd Krumeich, and Stéphane Audoin-Rouzeau (Paris: Armand Colin, 1994), 278–86; "The Knights of the Sky," in *War: A Cruel Necessity?* ed. R. A. Hinde (London: I. B. Tauris, 1994), 132–42; "La guerre et l'identité culturelle du National-Socialisme," *Vingtième Siècle* 41 (January–March, 1994): 51–59; "Männlichkeit und der Grosse Weltkrieg," in *So ist der Mensch: 80 Jahre Erster Weltkrieg* (Vienna: Eigenverlag der Museen der Stadt Wien, 1995), 57–69; "1915–18: La Madre di tutti gli stermini," *Panorama* 27 (May 25, 1995): 127–34; "Shellshock as a Social Disease," *Journal of Contemporary History* 35, no. 1 (January 2000): 101–08. In 1990 Mosse's book on the "myth of the war experience" was published: George L. Mosse, *Fallen Soldiers: Reshaping the Memory of the World Wars* (New York: Oxford University Press, 1990).

67. Marc Ferro, *The Great War 1914–1918* (1969; repr. London: Routledge & Kegan Paul, 1973), xii.

68. See Ferro, "Vers le renouvellement"; Kriegel, Ferro, and Besançon, "L'expérience de 'La Grande Guerre'"; and Ferro, "Société du XXe siècle."

69. Kriegel, Ferro, and Besançon, "L'expérience de 'La Grande Guerre.'"

70. See the already quoted "Journal of Contemporary History—Psychology and History," Mosse Collection, Leo Baeck Institute, and "Psychology and History—Acceptances," AR 25137, box 50, folder 11, George L. Mosse Collection, Leo Baeck Institute, New York.

71. Ernest Hearst, letter to Professor Dragovan Sepic, AR 25137, box 50, folder 6, George L. Mosse Collection, Leo Baeck Institute, New York.

72. George L. Mosse, letter to Mr. Richard Griffiths, March 16, 1967; George L. Mosse, letter to Dr. R. M. Griffiths, April 5, 1967; George L. Mosse, letter to Jane Degras, Assistent Editor, January 4, 1967; all in AR 25137, box 50, folder 6, George L. Mosse Collection, Leo Baeck Institute, New York (to Degras, Mosse wrote: "we should be very careful not merely to get a rehash of old approaches").

73. George L. Mosse, letter to Professor Hayden White, June 5, 1967, AR 25137, box 50, folder 6, George L. Mosse Collection, Leo Baeck Institute, New York; Ferro, "1917: History and Cinema."

74. Ferro, "1917: History and Cinema," 45.

75. Ibid., 49, 51.

76. William L. Langer, "The Well-Spring of Our Discontents," Patrick Renshaw, "The IWW and the Red Scare 1917–24," and Pewel Jasienica, "The Polish Experience," all in "1918–19: From War to Peace," ed. George Mosse and Walter Laqueur, special issue, *Journal of Contemporary History* 3, no. 4 (October 1968): 3–17, 63–72, 73–88.

77. Jay Winter and Antoine Prost, *The Great War in History: Debates and Controversies, 1914 to the Present* (New York: Cambridge University Press, 2005), 26.

78. Modris Eksteins, "Passage of *Rites*," *International Journal of Politics, Culture and Society* 12, no. 2 (1998): 247–52. Eksteins is the author of *Rites of Spring: The Great War and the Birth of the Modern Age* (Boston: Houghton Mifflin Company, 1989).

79. Fussell, *The Great War*; John Keegan, *The Face of Battle* (New York: Vintage Book, 1976). Mosse also knew Mario Isnenghi's *Il mito della grande guerra: Da Marinetti a Malaparte* (Rome: Laterza, 1973), which focused on literary sources and adopted a sociological and psychological approach to the myth of the Great War.

80. George L. Mosse, letter to the Connaught Fund, University of Toronto, December 7, 1978, AR 25137, box 34, folder 42, George L. Mosse Collection, Leo Baeck Institute, New York. Mosse wrote the letter in support of Modris Eksteins's project of writing a book on "The First World War and the Modern Imagination," which Eksteins himself defined, in his application, "an exercise in cultural history" aimed at analyzing the war from a different point of view, neither strategic nor political, a book "about the place of the first world war in modern consciousness." Eksteins's application is in the same folder of the archive, dated November 8, 1978. A year later, Mosse commented on Eksteins's project in another letter: "There is in fact nothing about the First World War quite like the kind of analysis he is proposing . . . Professor Eksteins is quite correct in saying that we must now start on an analysis of the First World War on a quite different level than most of the historical writing within the last decades. I think that what he proposes is such a new start" (George L. Mosse, letter to the Killam Program, The Canada

Council, October 12, 1979, same folder). Once Eksteins's book was published, Mosse admired the work and praised the "new twist" it had given to the historiography of the Great War by taking the discussion of the war "beyond the conventional" and giving it "new dimensions"; he regarded it as a "uniquely stimulating and exciting book which through locating the great war within the stream of European culture provides an entirely new perspective both on the war itself and on contemporary arts and letters" (George L. Mosse, letter to Mr. Nicolas Jackson, July 18, 1996; Mosse, letter to Peter Davison, December 30, 1988; same folder). Eksteins's book is *Rites of Spring*.

81. George L. Mosse, letter to Modris Eksteins, September 9, 1987, AR 25137, box 34, folder 42, George L. Mosse Collection, Leo Baeck Institute, New York.

82. Eric Leed, *No Man's Land: Combat and Identity in World War I* (Cambridge University Press, 1979); Eksteins, *Rites of Spring*. Mosse defined Leed's book as "one of the very best" on the First World War, "comparable only to the study of Paul Fussell"; *No Man's Land* had been, he wrote, a "pioneering" book that had been "indispensable for my own work, especially as far as the role of myth-making at the front was concerned. He combines very fine scholarship with a great deal of insight and empathy." See George L. Mosse, letter to Prof. Joyce Shaw Peterson, October 1, 1991; and Mosse, letter to Mr. Robert Scott, Center for Advanced Studies in the Behavioral Sciences, Stanford, July 22, 1994, AR 25137, box 37, folder 20, George L. Mosse Collection, Leo Baeck Institute, New York. As to the Historial in Péronne (strongly oriented toward a cultural approach to the Great War and inaugurated in 1992), see the correspondence in AR 25137, box 42, folder 37, George L. Mosse Collection, Leo Baeck Institute, New York, which includes a short paper by Mosse on the cultural historiography of the war.

83. See Joachim Whaley, ed., *Mirrors of Mortality: Studies in the Social History of Death* (New York: St. Martin's Press, 1981), particularly the essay by John McManners, "Death and the French Historians," 106–30.

84. The newspaper clippings he kept, as well as letters referring to his new interest, can be found in AR 25137, box 22, folder 9, George L. Mosse Collection, Leo Baeck Institute, New York.

85. Philippe Ariès, *Western Attitudes toward Death: From the Middle Ages to the Present* (Baltimore: John Hopkins University Press, 1974), 74–76.

86. David Cannadine, "War and Death, Grief and Mourning in Modern Britain," in Whaley, *Mirrors of Mortality*, 189.

87. Mosse, "National Cemeteries and National Revival," 1. Part of this essay was first given in 1977 as the Taft Lecture at the University of Cincinnati.

88. Michel Vovelle, *La mort et l'Occident: De 1300 à nos jours* (Paris: Gallimard, 1983), 646.

89. Mosse, *Fallen Soldiers*.

90. Kantorowicz, "Pro Patria Mori," 487.

91. Emilio Gentile, *L'apocalisse della modernità: La Grande Guerra per l'uomo nuovo* (Milan: Mondadori, 2008).

92. Fussell, *The Great War*.

93. Keegan, *Face of Battle*, 255–56.
94. Mosse, *Confronting History*, 180.

Chapter 5. From Machiavellism to the Holocaust

1. Meinecke, *Machiavellism*, 52.
2. Mosse, "The Significance of Nietzsche's Proposed Ethic of Masters."
3. Mosse, "National Socialist Morality."
4. Mosse, lecture notes for the Cultural History Course, 1946–47.
5. Mosse, "Puritanism and Reason of State," 71, 68.
6. Mosse, *Culture of Western Europe* (1961), 371–73.
7. It must be pointed out from the outset that Mosse's analysis of respectability relied mostly on German sources, an attitude that had slightly changed by the early 1990s but which is clearly connected to the connection he drew between respectability and National Socialism and to his vast knowledge of German political culture. Mosse had, as Stanley Payne pointed out, a tendency to overgeneralize from a German basis (conversation with Stanley Payne, July 2011).
8. Aschheim, "George Mosse at 80," 303.
9. Aschheim, "George Mosse," xv.
10. Gentile, *Il fascino del persecutore*, 139.
11. Mosse, *Confronting History*, 179.
12. Ibid., 179–80.
13. Mosse, *Culture of Western Europe* (1961), 47, 50–51 (my italics), 358.
14. Mosse, *Crisis of German Ideology*, 309–10.
15. Mosse, "The Genesis of Fascism," 19.
16. Mosse, *Culture of Western Europe* (1961), 352.
17. Mosse, "What Is Fascism?"
18. Mosse, *Culture of Western Europe* (1961), 352, 353.
19. Ibid., 353, 358.
20. Mosse, "National Socialist Morality."
21. Ibid.
22. Ibid. In the interview on Nazism, Mosse said that the Final Solution was in accordance with Hitler's taste, not at all with the taste of the German public, and not even of many SS. See Mosse, *Nazism*, 75.
23. Mosse, *Culture of Western Europe* (1961), 360. Neoromanticism, with its longing for an organic state, had furthered depersonalization and conformity within the community, Mosse wrote in 1961 (Mosse, *Culture of Western Europe* [1961], 353). Years later, he would highlight the other side of the coin and blame conformity on the Enlightenment.
24. Mosse, *Culture of Western Europe* (1961), 361. Men like Rudolf Höss exemplify the "danger of thinking about people in 'types'": "As a consequence, among men like Höss, morality was something not intrinsic to all men but only to Aryans" (374). This depersonalization of the outsider, Mosse argued, did not occur in Italian fascism.

25. Mosse, *Culture of Western Europe* (1961), 371–72.

26. Mosse, "Fascism and the Intellectuals," 225.

27. Gentile, "A Provisional Dwelling," 100–102. See also Gentile's "L'uomo nuovo' del fascismo: Riflessioni su un esperimento totalitario di rivoluzione antropologica," in Emilio Gentile, *Fascismo: Storia e interpretazione* (Rome: Laterza, 2002), 235–64.

28. Mosse, *Nazism*, 73 (my italics).

29. Mosse, "National Socialist Morality."

30. Mosse, *Nationalism and Sexuality*, 154, 157–59, 180.

31. Ibid., 191.

32. On Mosse and masculinity, see also Lorenzo Benadusi, "Una casa ben arredata: La storia della mascolinità," in *Sulle orme di George L. Mosse: Interpretazioni e fortuna dell'opera di un grande storico*, ed. Lorenzo Benadusi and Giorgio Caravale (Rome: Carocci, 2012), 59–79. The book originates from the conference "Sulle orme di George L. Mosse" ("On George L. Mosse's Traces"), held on May 11, 2010, in Rome.

33. George L. Mosse, *The Image of Man: The Creation of Modern Masculinity* (New York: Oxford University Press, 1996), 162.

34. Ibid., 180.

35. Ibid.

36. Reported by *Wisconsin Jewish Chronicle*, October 9, 1975.

37. George L. Mosse, "L'Olocausto, la morte e la memoria della guerra," in Staderini, Zani, and Magni, *La grande guerra*, 9–19.

38. Mosse, *Image of Man*, 155–62. For Mosse's view of the "new man," see particularly George L. Mosse, "Die Idee des 'neuen Mannes' in modernen revolutionären Bewegungen," *Mitteilungen der Magnus-Hirschfeld-Gesellschaft* 14 (December 1989): 9–13; Mosse, "New Man," lecture given at Cornell University, 1994–95, AR 25137, box 16, folder 27, George L. Mosse Collection, Leo Baeck Institute, New York; Mosse, "New Man," lecture, n.d., AR 25137, box 18, folder 29, George L. Mosse Collection, Leo Baeck Institute, New York; Mosse, *Image of Man*, 155–81.

39. Mosse, "New Man," Cornell lecture.

40. Mosse, "New Man," lecture, n.d.; Mosse, "New Man," Cornell lecture.

41. Mosse, *Image of Man*, 162–67.

42. See Mosse, "Die Idee des 'neuen Mannes,'" 9; and Mosse, "New Man," Cornell lecture.

43. Mosse, "New Man," Cornell lecture. Lorenzo Benadusi has hinted at fascism's difficulties at creating its "new man" according to the ideal of "respectability in uniform," arguing that this was due, at least in part, to the pervasiveness of bourgeois respectability. See Lorenzo Benadusi, *Il nemico dell'uomo nuovo: L'omosessualità nell'esperimento totalitario fascista* (Milan: Feltrinelli, 2005), 410, translated into English as *The Enemy of the New Man: Homosexuality in Fascist Italy* (Madison: University of Wisconsin Press, 2012), 273.

44. Mosse, "New Man," Cornell lecture. See particularly the lecture by the title "New Man, New Woman, and the Bourgeoisie."

45. Mosse, "New Man," Cornell lecture.

46. Mosse, "New Man," lecture, n.d.; and Mosse, "New Man," Cornell lecture.

47. Mosse, "New Man," lecture, n.d.. On this basis, I do not share Gentile's criticism that Mosse would have neglected the fact that *respectability in uniform* was incompatible with the private dimension of bourgeois culture. Instead, Mosse drew a clear distinction between the private and the public dimension of respectability, differentiating their concepts of manliness and their attitudes toward respectability. See Gentile, "L'uomo nuovo' del fascismo," 239.

48. Igor Golomstock has written about the claim that the ideal Nazi was the "ideal bourgeois": "This would indeed have been so but for the fact that under totalitarianism these universal values had acquired a new meaning: devotion meant blind faith in the Führer, optimism meant a thoughtless, uncritical attitude to the present, a readiness to make sacrifices meant murder or betrayal, love meant hatred, honor meant informing. The exceptional was put forward as the normal and typical. The 'new man' thus had many faces and was omnipresent. . . . If one is to say that he was the 'ideal bourgeois,' then one must add 'of the new type'" (Golomstock, *Totalitarian Art* [New York: IconEditions, 1990], quoted in Payne, *A History of Fascism*, 198–200).

49. Saul Friedländer, "Mosse's Influence on the Historiography of the Holocaust," in Payne, Sorkin, and Tortorice, *What History Tells*, 114–16.

50. Aschheim, "George Mosse at 80," 305–6.

51. Robert Jay Lifton, *The Nazi Doctors: Medical Killing and the Psychology of Genocide* (New York: Basic Books, 2000), 6, 427. Originally published in 1986, Mosse greatly admired the book and used it to better understand "the problem of how much memories of the First World War facilitated the killing process in the Second." See George L. Mosse, letter to Christopher Browning, July 16, 1991, AR 25137, box 33, folder 57, George L. Mosse Collection, Leo Baeck Institute, New York.

52. George L. Mosse, letter to Professor Daniel J. Boorstin, November 21, 1958, AR 25137, box 14, folder 29, George L. Mosse Collection, Leo Baeck Institute, New York.

53. Mosse, *Confronting History*, 180–81.

54. Mosse, *The Fascist Revolution*, 43.

55. Robert Nye, "Mosse, Masculinity, and the History of Sexuality," in Payne, Sorkin, and Tortorice, *What History Tells*, 197–98.

Chapter 6. The Missing Link

1. Gentile, "A Provisional Dwelling," 43; Gentile, letter to George L. Mosse, December 18, 1998, AR 25137, box 35, folder 9, George L. Mosse Collection, Leo Baeck Institute, New York.

2. Payne, *A History of Fascism*, dedication, 450–51.

3. Renzo De Felice, *Le interpretazioni del fascismo*, dedication, xviii–xix.

4. With the exception of the new introduction to *The Fascist Revolution*, a collection of his essays on fascism published in 1999.

5. Gentile, "A Provisional Dwelling," 93.

6. The most comprehensive analysis is Gentile, "A Provisional Dwelling." See also Gentile, *Il fascino del persecutore*; and Payne, *A History of Fascism*, 450–51, which contextualizes Mosse's interpretation into a wider frame.

7. Mosse, "What Is Fascism?"

8. Fritz Stern, *The Politics of Cultural Despair: A Study in the Rise of Germanic Ideology* (Berkeley: University of California Press, 1961); Ernst Nolte, *Three Faces of Fascism* (New York: Holt, Rinehart and Winston, 1966), 429. Stern's work focused on the thought of Paul de Lagarde, Julius Langbehn and Moeller van den Bruck. Nolte's book (originally published as *Der Faschismus in seiner Epoche* [Munich: Piper Verlag, 1963]) interpreted fascism as a resistance to "transcendence," transcendence being both "practical" (manifesting itself in material, technological, and social progress: in short, he saw fascism as a resistance to modernity) and "theoretical" (meaning humanity's urge for the divine, the infinite, the religious). This work tackled fascism from the perspective of the history of ideas, and fueled a debate on the possibility of a general concept of fascism. Mosse reviewed Nolte's book and praised the German historian's effort (George L. Mosse, "E. Nolte on *Three Faces of Fascism*," *Journal of the History of Ideas* 27, no. 4 [October–December 1966]: 621–25). Yet Mosse criticized Nolte's inclusion of the Action Française among fascist movements, and his reduction of fascism to anti-Marxism. Moreover, he disagreed with Nolte's view of fascism as a form of resistance to transcendence: he believed that "fascism worked with a transcendence of its own." This view is in line with Mosse's belief that fascism longed for a mythic past, that it had a religious nature, and that it sought to transcend the alienating reality of modernity to immerse humanity into a mythical dimension. In his book on the crisis of German ideology, Mosse had depicted the *Volk* as "idealized and transcendent," as seeking a way out of modernity "beyond contemporary reality" (*Crisis of German Ideology*, 15). According to Mosse, *Volk* "signified the union of a group of people with a transcendental 'essence'" (4). As Roger Griffin has noted, "while Nolte was developing his theory of fascism as 'resistance *to* transcendence,' Mosse was investigating the fascist impulse *toward* transcendence" ("Withstanding the Rush of Time," 122; Griffin also quotes from Mosse, "Fascism and the Intellectuals," 215, where it is stated that fascist intellectuals attempted to build a system of absolute values that "transcended reality"). There is also a little-known, and yet very interesting book written by Jean Neurohr (*Der Mythos vom dritten Reich: Zur Geistesgeschichte des Nationalsozialismus* [Stuttgart: Cotta, 1957]), which deals with National Socialism from the point of view of myth and ideology. Neurohr wrote of the "theology of nationalism" and faced the question of the "new man," all themes that captured Mosse's attention. A copy of the book is in Mosse's private library, though it is not possible to know if it influenced him, and if so to what extent, since he never quoted it in his works.

9. Mosse, "Pragmatism of the Freshman History Course," 289–90.

10. For a further examination of Croce and the importance of irrationality in history, see chap. 8; Meinecke had highlighted the irrational outburst, which, in his interpretation,

led to National Socialism in *The German Catastrophe*; for Lukàcs, see his *Die Zerstörung der Vernunft* (Berlin: Aufbau Verlag, 1954).

11. Mosse, *Nationalization of the Masses*, 214.

12. George L. Mosse, "Concepts of Democracy: The Liberal Inheritance and the National Socialist Public Sphere," unpublished speech, n.d., AR 25137, box 16, folder 14, George L. Mosse Collection, Leo Baeck Institute, New York. The paper, though undated, dates to no earlier than 1996, in that Mosse refers to Stuart Ewen's *PR! A Social History of Spin*, published in New York in that year.

13. George L. Mosse, "Fascism as a Cultural Movement," drafts, n.d. (1990s), AR 25137, box 17, folder 11, George L. Mosse Collection, Leo Baeck Institute, New York (the paper is a draft of the introduction to Mosse, *The Fascist Revolution*). The reference to Neumann is to his *Behemoth: The Structure and Practice of National Socialism, 1933–1944* (New York: Harper, 1944).

14. Mosse, *The Fascist Revolution*, ix.

15. Drescher, Sabean, and Sharlin, "George Mosse and Political Symbolism," 3.

16. Mosse, "What Is Fascism?"

17. Mosse, *Crisis of German Ideology*, 1–2.

18. Mosse, "The Genesis of Fascism," 19.

19. Mosse, *Nazism*, 50–51, 108.

20. Mosse, "What Is Fascism?" Mosse refers here to William Shirer, *The Rise and Fall of the Third Reich: A History of Nazi Germany* (New York: Fawcett Crest, 1960).

21. Mosse, "Adolf Hitler."

22. Mosse, "The Mystical Origins of National Socialism," 81.

23. A thorough analysis of Mosse's relation to the category of totalitarianism is in Gentile, *Il fascino del persecutore*, 41–56.

24. George L. Mosse, "Totalitarianism," lecture, n.d., AR 25137, box 19, folder 8, George L. Mosse Collection, Leo Baeck Institute, New York.

25. Mosse, *Nazism*, 77–78.

26. George L. Mosse, "Political Style and Political Theory: Totalitarian Democracy Revisited," in *Totalitarian Democracy and After*, ed. Yehoshua Arieli and Nathan Rotenstreich (Jerusalem: Magnes Press, 1984), 169. This article originates from a 1982 colloquium on the work of Jacob Talmon.

27. George L. Mosse, "Nationalism and War," notes for a seminar, n.d.; AR 25137, box 18, folder 24, George L. Mosse Collection, Leo Baeck Institute, New York. In this paper, Mosse deals mainly with the *Historikerstreit*, so it was not written before the late 1980s.

28. Mosse, "The Mystical Origins of National Socialism," 81; Mosse, *Crisis of German Ideology*, 1.

29. Mosse, *Crisis of German Ideology*, vi–vii.

30. Jürgen Kocka included Mosse's *The Crisis of German Ideology* among those books that are inclined toward a *Sonderweg* theory. See Jürgen Kocka, "German History before

Hitler: The Debate about the German *Sonderweg,*" *Journal of Contemporary History* 23, no. 1 (January 1988): 3–16.

31. Mosse, *Crisis of German Ideology*, 312–15. The difference is represented, Mosse wrote, by that uniquely German "ideological commitment" that made anti-Semitism a "primary concern" in that country (314).

32. Mosse, *Culture of Western Europe* (1961), 344.

33. Ibid., 345, 353, 354.

34. Mosse, "What Is Fascism?" In particular, Mosse referred to Ernst Nolte, who considered fascism as antibourgeois, antimarxist, and antimodern; see Nolte, *Three Faces.*

35. Mosse, "What Is Fascism?"

36. Ibid.

37. Mosse, *Crisis of German Ideology*, 312–13.

38. Mosse, "The Genesis of Fascism," 14.

39. Ibid., 15–25.

40. Mosse, introduction to *International Fascism*, 1, 25.

41. Ibid., 36.

42. Mosse, *Culture of Western Europe* (1961), 353; Mosse, "What Is Fascism?"; Mosse, *Crisis of German Ideology*, 8, 294–311; Mosse, "The Genesis of Fascism," 14, 19, 22 (Mosse restated that fascism was a "revolution of the spirit" in, for example, *Nazism*, 86); Mosse, *Nazism*, 99; and Mosse, *The Fascist Revolution*, xi.

43. Mosse, *The Fascist Revolution*, xii.

44. Fascism's psychological base consists, according to Mosse, in the longing for community, in ideological intolerance, and in the desire to destroy the enemy. See George L. Mosse, "Fascism as History," lecture, n.d., AR 25137, box 17, folder 9, George L. Mosse Collection, Leo Baeck Institute, New York. The lecture was surely given shortly after 1975.

45. George L. Mosse, "Il dibattito sul neonazismo," *Nuova Antologia* 569, no. 2186 (April–June 1993): 16–19.

46. Mosse, introduction to *International Fascism*, 37–38.

47. Mosse, *The Fascist Revolution*, xii.

48. Mosse, 1997 preface to *Crisis of German Ideology*, v, x.

49. For further discussion, see chap. 7.

50. Mosse, "Pragmatism of the Freshman History Course," 290.

51. To be sure, according to the changing contexts Mosse attributed many adjectives other than "integral." So this kind of nationalism could be defined as "cultural," "romantic," "racial," "irrational," "right-wing" or even "unjust." However, Mosse generally referred to that right-wing nationalism that at the turn of the nineteenth and twentieth centuries became radicalized, and after the First World War helped lay the ideological basis of the fascist movements.

52. Mosse, "Nationalism and Patriotism."

53. Mosse, *Culture of Western Europe* (1961), 69. Mosse also wrote that "in Europe the climax of this cultural nationalism came only with the totalitarian movements of the twentieth century" (57).

54. Mosse, *Culture of Western Europe* (1961), 71, 83.

55. Mosse, "Fascism Once More"; Mosse, *Culture of Western Europe* (1961), 366.

56. Mosse, *Nationalism and Sexuality*, 133.

57. Mosse, "Is Fascism Alive?"

58. Mosse, *Nazism*, 127; Mosse, introduction to *International Fascism*, 7, 20, 31.

59. Mosse, "Political Liturgy of Nationalism," 40.

60. Mosse, *Nationalization of the Masses*, 9.

61. Mosse, "Political Liturgy of Nationalism," 39.

62. Mosse, *Nationalization of the Masses*, 9–11.

63. George L. Mosse, "Caesarism, Circuses and Monuments," *Journal of Contemporary History* 6, no. 2 (1971): 170.

64. Mosse, "Political Liturgy of Nationalism," 39.

65. Ibid., 54; Mosse, *Nationalization of the Masses*, vii.

66. George L. Mosse, "Retreat to the Status Quo," *Society* 18, no. 4 (May–June 1981): 39. In 1980 Mosse collected some of his previous essays on fascism, preceded by a new introduction that focused almost entirely on the centrality of nationalism. See Mosse, *Masses and Men*.

67. George L. Mosse, "Fascism as a Nationalist Movement: The Missing Link," n.d., AR 25137, box 7, folder 21, George L. Mosse Collection, Leo Baeck Institute, New York.

68. Mosse, *Confronting History*, 182.

69. Mosse, *The Fascist Revolution*, xi.

70. Ibid.

71. Mosse, *Confronting History*, 53; Mosse, *The Fascist Revolution*, xi.

72. Mosse, "The Appeal of Nazi Culture."

73. Mosse, *The Fascist Revolution*, xi.

74. Mosse, introduction to *International Fascism*, 30. See also Mosse, "The Community in the Thought."

75. Mosse, "The Genesis of Fascism," 16.

76. Mosse, *Culture of Western Europe* (1961), 362. See also Mosse, introduction to *International Fascism*, 3.

77. George L. Mosse, "Anti-Democratic Thought and the Rise of National Socialism," n.d., AR 25137, box 16, folder 3, George L. Mosse Collection, Leo Baeck Institute, New York. Though undated, the speech is likely to have been given no earlier than the 1970s, since Mosse refers to the concept of Caesarism, which he first hinted at in the early 1970s.

78. Mosse, "Concepts of Democracy."

79. See George L. Mosse, "L'opera di Aldo Moro nella crisi della democrazia parlamentare in occidente," interview with Alfonso Alfonsi in Aldo Moro, *L'intelligenza e gli avvenimenti: Testi 1959–1978* (Milan: Fondazione Aldo Moro, Garzanti, 1979); Mosse, "Nationhood and Diaspora"; George L. Mosse, "Tel Aviv Lecture," n.d., AR 25137, box 19, folder 6, George L. Mosse Collection, Leo Baeck Institute, New York.

80. Mosse, "Adolf Hitler." It was exactly the NSDAP's organization that distinguished it from other *völkisch* parties, which remained elitist and refused mass politics. Mosse also stressed in a lecture how Hitler's *Mein Kampf* was divided into two halves, one dealing with ideology, and the other with organization, which was needed to rule in the age of the masses. In the same lecture, Mosse asserted that Adolf Eichmann symbolized "the product of the confluence of myth and organization" (Mosse, "Europe and the Modern World," lectures). In *The Crisis of German Ideology* (v) Mosse wrote that many of the *völkisch* prophets were individualists "who never united with the like-minded to form an effective political organization, and Adolf Hitler despised them for this very reason."

81. See in particular part 2 of *The Crisis of German Ideology*, "The Institutionalization of Ideology, 1873–1918," 149–236. What counts, Mosse wrote in 1961, is the "institutionalizing of a cultural atmosphere" (Mosse, "The Mystical Origins of National Socialism," 96). In a number of reviews, Mosse stressed the same ideas: see George L. Mosse, review of *European Positivism in the Nineteenth Century: An Essay in Intellectual History*, by W. M. Simon (George L. Mosse, "Reviews 1960s," AR 25137, box 11, folder 11, George L. Mosse Collection, Leo Baeck Institute, New York), and George L. Mosse, review of *Ideas in Cultural Perspective*, ed. Philip P. Wiener and Aaron Noland (*Journal of Modern History* 35, no. 4 [December 1963]: 289–90).

82. Mosse, *Nationalization of the Masses*, 214–15.

83. Mosse, *Crisis of German Ideology*, 316–17.

84. Mosse, "The Genesis of Fascism," 15.

85. Mosse, *Nazism*, 63.

86. Gentile, "A Provisional Dwelling," 103–4. Gentile makes clear in this passage that he, as the author of "several books on fascist ideology and culture that have drawn their inspiration from Mosse's work[,] . . . cannot be accused of being an adversary of the cultural approach or of underestimating the importance of ideology in fascism."

87. Mosse, *Confronting History*, 178.

88. Gentile, "A Provisional Dwelling," 102.

89. Mosse wrote that *The Nationalization of the Masses* "dealt with the sacralization of politics: the Nazi political liturgy and its consequences" (Mosse, *Confronting History*, 177), referring to Gentile, *Il culto del littorio*. The concept of "sacralization of politics" was devised by Gentile himself, and has become a major interpretive category in his analysis of political religions.

90. In Emilio Gentile's words: "For Mosse, the new politics is above all a phenomenon of aesthetic dramatization; for me, it is a phenomenon concerning the religious experience of politics" (Emilio Gentile interviewed by Lorenzo Benadusi and Giorgio Caravale: "Una lunga amicizia intellettuale: Intervista a Emilio Gentile," in Benadusi and Caravale, *Sulle orme di George L. Mosse*, 138).

91. Nipperdey, "Nationalidee und Nationaldenkmal"; Eliade, *The Sacred and the Profane*.

92. Mosse, *Nationalization of the Masses*, 50, 80; Mosse, "European Cultural and Intellectual History, 1660–1870," lecture 01.

93. Mosse, in his typical fashion, never elaborated much on a definition of religion: he used the term vaguely, mainly referring to the religious essence of fascism. Although he referred to fascism as *a religion* (see chap. 2), he probably meant a secular religion. For a general perspective, also on Mosse's contribution, see Didier Musiedlak, "Fascisme, religion politique et la religion de la politique. Généalogie d'un concept et des ses limites," *Vingtième siècle: Revue d'histoire* 108 (October–December 2010): 71–84.

Chapter 7. The "True Mission of Judaism"

1. Mosse, "Hillel Talk."
2. Mosse, *Confronting History*, 186.
3. Mosse, *Nazism*, 50.
4. Mosse, *German Jews beyond Judaism*, 12.
5. Mosse, *Confronting History*, 41–42.
6. Meinecke, *The German Catastrophe*, 10.
7. Mosse, *Confronting History*, 191.
8. Mosse, "Nationhood and Diaspora."
9. Ibid.
10. Runge and Stelbrink, *George Mosse*, 25.
11. Mosse, *Confronting History*, 27 and 42.
12. Runge and Stelbrink, *George Mosse*, 24. "My family, like most other Jewish families, considered themselves German without giving it another thought" (Mosse, *Confronting History*, 43).
13. Mosse, *Confronting History*, 44.
14. Ibid., 187. To be sure, Mosse had attended as a spectator the Zionist Congress of 1935 at Basel, driven by the continuous difficulties and humiliations of his refugee life and his stateless situation. However, he was at the time too engaged in socialist antifascism to turn to Zionism, he recalled. See Mosse, "Response by George Mosse," xxvi.
15. Mosse, *Confronting History*, 188.
16. George L. Mosse, speech given at the Hillel Foundation, reported by the *Daily Iowan*, November 14, 1947.
17. George L. Mosse, interview with the *Daily Cardinal*, October 30, 1972.
18. George L. Mosse, "Israel," Iowa lecture, n.d., AR 25137, box 17, folder 46, George L. Mosse Collection, Leo Baeck Institute, New York.
19. Mosse, *Confronting History*, 189.
20. Mosse mentioned such organizations as Habonim, Young Judaea, and the World Union of Jewish Students, to which he had been introduced by Steven Aschheim, a leading Habonim educator at the time.
21. Mosse, *Confronting History*, 192, 197.
22. Mosse, *Daily Cardinal* interview. In 1971 Mosse said that he was not an anti-Zionist: he just sought to keep a critical attitude; he loved to teach at the Hebrew University in Jerusalem because he saw it as a real scholarly community that deeply stimulated him intellectually (George L. Mosse, Modern Jewish History lectures, spring

1971). The lectures, edited under the supervision of John Tortorice, can be found along with the summaries on the Mosse Program website, University of Wisconsin–Madison, http://history.wisc.edu/mosse/george_mosse/modern_jewish_lectures.htm.

23. Runge and Stelbrink, *George Mosse*, 115. Menachem Begin (1913–92) was the leader of the Irgun, a militant Zionist group that operated in Palestine in the years before 1948. The group endorsed the use of force and violence to ensure the Jewish state, and was a political predecessor of the Likud Party, which in 1977, under the leadership of Begin, won the political elections in Israel after a long period of Labor Party government.

24. Mosse, *Confronting History*, 190. The stereotype Mosse had internalized was, in his own words, that of the "puny, weak, and ugly Jew," so he felt admiration for the "new Jew" he saw in Israel: "well built young Jews who carried their ethnicity openly and proudly without any of the mental contortions to which I was accustomed. Their looks and their normality seemed stunning in contrast to what I considered European Jewry" (198–99). See also other telling passages of the memoir, esp. 124–25.

25. Mosse, *Daily Cardinal* interview. Here Mosse expressed his approval of the Rogers Plan, which foresaw Israel's withdrawal from the areas occupied during the 1967 war (above all, the West Bank and the Gaza Strip) and the mutual recognition of the involved states' sovereignty and independence. The plan met with Israel's opposition and never became effective.

26. Ibid. Two years later Mosse defined the Likud Party as Israel's "greatest danger" (reported by *Wisconsin Jewish Chronicle*, December 26, 1974).

27. George L. Mosse, interview with the *Wisconsin Jewish Chronicle*, December 26, 1974; Mosse, interview with the *Capital Times*, August 27, 1979.

28. Mosse, *Wisconsin Jewish Chronicle* interview. Golda Meir (1898–1978) was prime minister of Israel from 1969 to 1974, first with the Mapai leftist party and then with the Israeli Labor Party.

29. *Capetown Argus* (Capetown), August 1, 1980; *Capital Times*, May 30, 1996. Begin's policies were, according to Mosse, based on hate (see *Jewish Chronicle*, October 1982); he had been elected by Jews coming from Arab countries who hated Arabs, Mosse said, hinting at the persecutions these Jews had experienced there (Mosse, *Capital Times* interview). Mosse also considered himself an "outspoken foe" of Begin's Lebanon policy: even though he approved of the annexation of southern Lebanon for security reasons, he denied its usefulness in combating the PLO, which could have regrouped anywhere else. Netanyahu (b. 1949) was prime minister with the Likud Party from 1996 to 1999, and since 2009.

30. *Capetown Argus*.

31. *Capital Times*, May 30, 1996. Mosse referred to Shimon Peres (b. 1923), a left-wing Israeli politician, twice prime minister of Israel and then president since 2007.

32. Volkov, "German Jewish History," 225.

33. Mosse, "The End Is Not Yet," 200.

34. Ibid., 197–99.

35. Mosse, *Confronting History*, 184, 182.

36. Ibid., 182–83.

37. Mosse, *German Jews beyond Judaism*, 81–82.

38. Jost Hermand, "German Jews beyond Judaism: The Gerhard/Israel/George L. Mosse Case," in *The German-Jewish Dialogue Reconsidered: A Symposium in Honor of George L. Mosse*, ed. Klaus Berghan (New York: Peter Lang, 1996), 242.

39. George L. Mosse, "The Heritage of Socialist Humanism," in *The Legacy of the German Refugee Intellectuals*, ed. Robert Boyers (New York Schoken, 1972), 124. The article originally appeared in *Salmagundi*, Fall 1969/Winter 1970, 123–39.

40. *Bildung* is, Mosse said, "the shaping of one's self in order to become a harmonious, fully formed personality"; it entails rationality and a "continuous quest for knowledge"; above all, it is an "educational principle" ("Central European Intellectuals in Palestine," *Judaism* 45, no.2 [Spring 1996]: 138). On this ideal, Mosse wrote "Jewish Emancipation between *Bildung* and *Respectability*," in *The Jewish Response to German Culture: From the Enlightenment to the Second World War*, ed. Jehuda Reinharz and Walter Schatzberg (Hanover, NH: University Press of New England, 1985), 1–16; Mosse, *German Jews beyond Judaism*; "Das deutsch-jüdische Bildungsbürgertum," in *Bildungsbürgertum im 19. Jahrhundert*, vol. 2, ed. Reinhart Kosselleck (Stuttgart: Ernst Klett, 1990), 168–80; "The Universal Meaning of the Concept of Bildung," *Zmanin* 16, no. 61 (1997–98): 6–10.

41. Rabinbach, "George L. Mosse 1919–1999," 333; Hermand, "German Jews beyond Judaism," 242–43.

42. Mosse, *Confronting History*, 184.

43. See Mosse, "Jewish Emancipation."

44. George L. Mosse, "German Jews and Liberalism in Retrospect," *Year Book XXXII* (London: Leo Baeck Institute, 1987).

45. Mosse, *German Jews beyond Judaism*, 62–63. Mosse references Herbert Marcuse, *One-Dimensional Man: Studies in the Ideology of Advanced Industrial Society* (Boston: Beacon Press, 1964).

46. Mosse, *German Jews beyond Judaism*, 63–64. It is worth remembering the influence that Harold Laski's attempt to balance Marxism and liberalism had on Mosse; see chap. 1.

47. Mosse, "The End Is Not Yet," 199–200.

48. Ibid., 200.

49. Mosse, *Confronting History*, 191.

50. Ibid., 200.

51. Mosse, *Capital Times* interview.

52. Mosse, "Nationalism and Patriotism." However, in 1961 he had stressed the liberal nature of English patriotism; see Mosse, *Culture of Western Europe* (1961), 61.

53. Mosse, "Nationhood and Diaspora"; Mosse, "Friendship and Nationhood: About the Promise and Failure of German Nationalism," *Journal of Contemporary History* 17, no. 2 (1982): 352.

54. George L. Mosse, "Can Nationalism be Saved? About Zionism, Rightful and Unjust Nationalism," 1995 Annual Chaim Weizmann Lecture in the Humanities, delivered November 29, 1995, 7, 8.

55. Ibid., 16. Among these intellectuals, Mosse mentioned Arthur Ruppin, Hugo Bergmann, Martin Buber, Gershom Scholem, Robert Weltsch, and Hans Kohn.

56. Ibid., 20, 24.

57. George L. Mosse, "The Influence of the Volkish Idea on German Jewry," in *Studies of the Leo Baeck Institute*, ed. Max Kreutzberger (New York: Frederick Ungar Publishing Co., 1967), 81–115.

58. George L. Mosse, "Max Nordau and his Degeneration," introduction to Max Nordau, *Degeneration* (1892; repr. New York: Howard Fertig, 1968); Mosse, "Max Nordau, Liberalism and the New Jew," *Journal of Contemporary History* 27 no. 4 (1992): 567.

59. Mosse, "Max Nordau, Liberalism and the New Jew," 575.

60. George L. Mosse, "Zionist Nationalism," lecture, n.d., AR 25137, box 19, folder 27, George L. Mosse Collection, Leo Baeck Institute, New York.

61. George L. Mosse, "Nationalism," lecture, 1988, AR 25137, box 18, folder 25, George L. Mosse Collection, Leo Baeck Institute, New York.

62. George L. Mosse, "The Jews and the Civic Religion of Nationalism," in *The Impact of Western Nationalisms*, ed. Jehuda Reinharz and George L. Mosse (London: Sage Publications, 1992), 322–23.

63. Mosse, "Nationalism." In Israel, according to Mosse, uniformity never won over individualism: even Israeli national monuments transmit no "aggressiveness, no glorification of the nation or hero-worship," and national cemeteries allow for individual decorations, thus adopting the cult of the fallen yet without depersonalizing the individual. See Mosse, "The Jews and the Civic Religion of Nationalism," 326–27.

64. Mosse, "Nationalism."

65. George L. Mosse, "Two States of Mind," *Jerusalem Post*, December 25, 1988.

66. George L. Mosse, "The End of an Epoch? The Leo Baeck Institute after the War," speech, 1995, AR 25137, box 16, folder 35, George L. Mosse Collection, Leo Baeck Institute, New York.

67. Mosse, *Confronting History*, 119.

68. George L. Mosse, "Hadassah Lecture," 1992, AR 25137, box 17, folder 28, George L. Mosse Collection, Leo Baeck Institute, New York.

69. George L. Mosse, "The Meaning of Zionism in 1897 and Its Future Today," speech, n.d., AR 25137, box 8, folder 32, George L. Mosse Collection, Leo Baeck Institute, New York; Mosse, "The End Is Not Yet," 200.

70. Mosse, "Nationhood and Diaspora."

71. George L. Mosse, "Gedanken zum deutsch-jüdischen Dialog," in *Chronik der Ludwig-Maximilians-Universität Munich 1982/83* (Munich: Munich University, 1982/83), 58; Mosse, *German Jews Beyond Judaism*, 81.

72. Mosse, "Hadassah Lecture."

73. George L. Mosse, "An Interdisciplinary Program in Jewish Studies (Draft for Discussion)," January 1989, George L. Mosse Archive, Memorial Library, University of Wisconsin–Madison, box 3, folder 5. Some papers and correspondence relative to Mosse's engagement in the establishment of Jewish studies at the University of Wisconsin–

Madison are in the George L. Mosse Archive, Memorial Library, University of Wisconsin–Madison, box 3, folders 4–9.

74. George L. Mosse, Modern Jewish History Lectures; Mosse, "The Meaning of Zionism."

75. Reported by *Jewish Chronicle*, October 1982.

76. George L. Mosse, "The Embourgeoisement of the Holocaust," Brandeis lecture, n.d., AR 25137, box 16, folder 12, George L. Mosse Collection, Leo Baeck Institute, New York. In this regard, see also "Holocaust Lectures," 1981–82, AR 25137, box 17, folder 38, George L. Mosse Collection, Leo Baeck Institute, New York.

77. *Jewish Chronicle*, October 1982; Mosse, "The Meaning of Zionism."

78. Mosse, "Hillel Talk."

79. Ibid.

80. George L. Mosse, "Manfred Swarsensky," commemorative speech, November 1981, AR 25137, box 18, folder 41, George L. Mosse Collection, Leo Baeck Institute, New York.

81. Mosse, "Nationhood and Diaspora."

82. Ibid.

83. Mosse, "The End Is Not Yet," 201.

84. Mosse, "The End of an Epoch?"; Mosse, "Gedanken," 57.

85. Mosse, *Confronting History*, 191.

86. Gentile, *Il fascino del persecutore*, 175.

87. Mosse, "L'opera di Aldo Moro."

88. Mosse, "Tel Aviv Lecture."

89. Mosse, *Confronting History*, 191, 192–93.

90. Mosse, "Does History Have Any Meaning?"; Mosse, "Europe and the Modern World—Final Lecture," 1969.

91. Steven Aschheim, "George Mosse and Jewish History," *German Politics and Society* 18, no. 4 (Winter 2000): 46, 51, 46, 47, 49. Mosse's works in question are "The Secularization of Jewish Theology," in Mosse, *Masses and Men*; Mosse, "Jewish Emancipation"; Mosse, "The Jews and the German War Experience"; Mosse, "The Influence of the Volkish Idea."

92. Volkov, "German Jewish History," 226. However, Anson Rabinbach has claimed that Mosse had no reverential attitude to *Bildung*, since he was fully aware that it had led to a lack of realism in politics, that it had "imprisoned German Jews in their own moral, aesthetic, and intellectual glass house" ("George L. Mosse 1919–1999," 333–34).

93. Volkov, "German Jewish History," 227, 234. Indeed, Mosse himself wrote that his commitment had him want to "hold the Jewish state to a higher standard of conduct than other nations" (*Confronting History*, 202).

94. Aschheim, "George Mosse and Jewish History," 52. Aschheim refers to his own book *Culture and Catastrophe: German and Jewish Confrontations with National Socialism and Other Crises* (New York: New York University Press, 1996).

95. Aschheim, "George Mosse and Jewish History," 52.

96. Ibid., 54.

97. Ibid. See the earlier discussion on Mosse's Machiavellism of democracy.

98. Mosse, "Response by George Mosse," xxxi.

Chapter 8. The Granitic Foundation of a Faith

1. Sabean, "George Mosse and *The Holy Pretence*," 17.

2. Aschheim, "George Mosse," xi.

3. Mosse, *Nazism*, 26–27.

4. Mosse, "Christian Statesman," 4; Mosse, *Confronting History*, 178, 175.

5. Mosse, *Nazism*, 27–28.

6. Mosse, *Confronting History*, 175.

7. Hurstfield, review of Mosse, *Struggle for Sovereignty*, 150.

8. The chapter on National Socialism was titled "National Socialism and the Deper-sonalization of Man" (Mosse, *Culture of Western Europe* [1961], 357–76).

9. Mosse, *Nationalization of the Masses*, vii.

10. Sabean, "George Mosse and *The Holy Pretence*," 19.

11. George L. Mosse, "Europe and the Modern World—Correspondence," 1956–1975, AR 25137, box 19, folder 29, George L. Mosse Collection, Leo Baeck Institute, New York.

12. "Mosse, "European Cultural and Intellectual History, 1660–1870," lecture 02.

13. Marina Cattaruzza, introduction to "Political Religions as a Characteristic of the 20th Century," special issue, *Totalitarian Movements and Political Religions* 6, no. 1 (June 2005): 12. The volume originated from a symposium Cattaruzza oversaw at Berne University in 2003, on the occasion of the presentation of the Hans Sigrist Award to Emilio Gentile for his works on political religions in the twentieth century.

14. Isabel V. Hull, "The Bourgeoisie and its Discontents: Reflections on 'Nationalism and Respectability,'" *Journal of Contemporary History* 17, no. 2 (April 1982): 248.

15. Eric Leed, letter to Mosse, November 10, 1988, AR 25137, box 15, folder 2, George L. Mosse Collection, Leo Baeck Institute, New York.

16. Mosse, *Confronting History*, 184.

17. Mosse, "Europe and the Modern World," lectures.

18. Mosse, *The Fascist Revolution*, xi.

19. George L. Mosse, letter to Professor Daniel J. Boorstin, November 21, 1958, AR 25137, box 14, folder 29, George L. Mosse Collection, Leo Baeck Institute, New York. In his memoir, referring to his participation in the activities of the Oratory of St. Mary and St. Michael in Cambridge, Mosse claimed to have been motivated also by "the attempt to enter Christian theology on a more profound level of understanding"; he wrote: "I thus became acquainted with the central Catholic rite, much to the benefit of my schol-arship" (*Confronting History*, 122).

20. Mosse, *Confronting History*, 5, 53, 172.

21. Mosse, "Europe and the Modern World—Final Lecture."

22. Aschheim, "George Mosse," xii.

23. Mosse, *Nazism*, 30.

24. Galasso, "Il Novecento," 51, 52–55.

25. Mosse, review of *The Political Philosophy of the Frankfurt School*, by George Friedman, *Clio* 12, no. 2 (1983): 188.

26. Mosse, "Response by George Mosse," xxviii–xxix.

27. Mosse, "Culture and Civilization."

28. Mosse, "Europe and the Modern World," lectures.

29. Benedetto Croce, *Teoria e storia della storiografia* (Milan: Adelphi, 1989), 14; Croce, "Antistoricismo," in Croce, *La mia filosofia*, 80.

30. Croce, *La storia come pensiero e come azione*, 5; Croce, *Teoria e storia della storiografia*, 34.

31. Croce, *La storia come pensiero e come azione*, 53, 254. The idea of myths represented through images was also recurrent in Huizinga; see chap. 3.

32. See Benedetto Croce, "Verità politica e mito popolare," in Croce, *La mia filosofia*, 231.

33. Croce, "Verità politica e mito popolare"; Croce, *Teoria e storia della storiografia*, 112–13.

34. Aschheim, "George Mosse at 80," 307.

35. Mosse, *Nazism*, 29; George L. Mosse, "Europe and the Modern World," lecture notes, 1956/75, AR 25137, box 19, folder 29, George L. Mosse Collection, Leo Baeck Institute, New York.

36. Wald, "Cultural History and Symbols," 183.

37. George L. Mosse, Phi Eta Sigma speech, n.d., AR 25137, box 19, folder 11, George L. Mosse Collection, Leo Baeck Institute, New York.

38. George L. Mosse, "European Cultural History: Old Lectures," n.d., AR 25137, box 19, folder 38, George L. Mosse Collection, Leo Baeck Institute, New York.

39. See Croce, *La storia come pensiero e come azione*.

40. George L. Mosse, "Old Lectures," n.d., AR 25137, box 18, folder 32, George L. Mosse Collection, Leo Baeck Institute, New York.

41. Mosse, "Response by George Mosse," xxviii.

42. George L. Mosse, "Europe and the Modern World—Soviet Revolution," n.d., AR 25137, box 19, folder 33, George L. Mosse Collection, Leo Baeck Institute, New York.

43. Mosse, "Does History Have Any Meaning?"

44. Drescher, Sabean, and Sharlin, "George Mosse and Political Symbolism," 3.

45. See Mosse, "Does History Have Any Meaning?"; Mosse, "European Culture—Old Lectures," n.d., AR 25137, box 19, folder 40, George L. Mosse Collection, Leo Baeck Institute, New York; Mosse, "Europe and the Modern World—Final Lecture."

46. See Mosse, "Europe and the Modern World," lecture notes; Mosse, "European Cultural History: Old Lectures."

47. George L. Mosse, "Freedom for What?," speech before students who were being graduated, 1946–52, AR 25137, box 17, folder 44, George L. Mosse Collection, Leo Baeck Institute, New York.

48. Ibid.

49. Mosse, "Europe and the Modern World—Final Lecture, 1969."

50. Mosse, *Confronting History*, 138, 172. The American historian Charles A. Beard, a noted supporter of cultural history in the first half of the twentieth century, had defined his discipline as an "act of faith" ("Written History as an Act of Faith").

51. Mankovitz, "George Mosse and Jewish History," xxiv.

52. Fishman, "GLM," 279; Gentile, *Il fascino del persecutore*, 189.

53. Mosse, "Fascism Once More."

54. Mosse, *Confronting History*, 120. Mosse recalled his experience at the Mommsen Gymnasium: "There I came into immediate conflict with its strict discipline, but what brought this schooling to an end after only one year was my encounter with the Latin irregular verb. The classics were still the core of the curriculum, but grammar had taken over what was once regarded as classical learning, confirming the victory of the philologist over the humanist. Learning these verbs by heart took more discipline than I could muster. I promptly flunked, and would have had to repeat the whole year over again" (50).

55. Ibid., 149.

56. Ibid., 115.

57. On the contrary, he admired historians who could merge extensive research and systematic treatment with definite theses. As he wrote to Emilio Gentile in 1990, "I know that we agree in approach and method but for me your method is much more concise and much more scholarly than my 'intuitions'" (letter to Emilio Gentile, October 15, 1990).

58. Laqueur, foreword to Mosse, *Confronting History*, xi.

59. Wald, "Cultural History and Symbols," 181–82.

60. Sabean, "George Mosse and *The Holy Pretence*," 17–18.

61. George L. Mosse, speech at the Graduate Club, n.d., AR 25137, box 17, folder 44, George L. Mosse Collection, Leo Baeck Institute, New York.

62. Ibid. Similar beliefs can be found expressed throughout his work: they related to his assertion that "the best results are achieved if the student has some personal or at least internal relationship to his historical work" (Mosse, "Response by George Mosse," xxviii); they are found again in his memoir, where he wrote: "I have always felt that history, in order to be absorbed, must be shown to have relevance to the students' lives, that it is more than just a good story of wars, adventures, and kings" (Mosse, *Confronting History*, 197).

63. Fishman, "GLM," 279; Rabinbach, "George L. Mosse 1919–1999," 331.

64. Herf, "The Historian as Provocateur." Emilio Gentile defined Mosse an "agent provocateur in the historiography of fascism," due to the "'subversive' character" of his works, which shattered common interpretations of the time. See Gentile, "A Provisional Dwelling," 52.

65. Mosse himself recalls this episode in his autobiography (*Confronting History*, 40). The episode is also stressed by Herf in "The Historian as Provocateur" (1) as characteristic of Mosse's personality.

66. Robert Nye, interview by Lauren Fairchild, *Oklahoma Daily*, November 6, 1979.

67. Mosse, letter to Professor Daniel J. Boorstin, November 21, 1958.

68. Fishman, "GLM," 281.

69. Breines, "Finding Oneself in History," 9–10.

70. Sabean, "George Mosse and *The Holy Pretence*," 19.

71. Mosse, *Nazism*, 29–30.

72. Mosse, *Reformation*, 1. Another significant passage is to be found in a 1954 article: "perhaps the crux of the assimilation of Machiavellian ideas lies not in the thought of this or that reformer, but in the general tension between religious presuppositions and political realities" (Mosse, "Assimilation of Machiavelli," 315). The "Hegelian" character of Mosse's earliest works has been highlighted particularly by Winter, "De l'histoire intellectuelle," 178.

73. Mosse, "Europe and the Modern World—Final Lecture"; Mosse, *Nazism*, 29–30. The Italian historian Giorgio Caravale has argued that three different kinds of dialectic appear in Mosse's work: in *The Struggle for Sovereignty in England*, the dialectic is traditionally Hegelian, materialistic in that it is intended as a dialectic between social forces; in *The Holy Pretence*, the dialectic is between moral principles and political reality; in later works, the dialectic becomes one between myth and social forces, between myth and objective reality. See Giorgio Caravale, "Una storia dimenticata: Gli studi sull'età moderna," in Benadusi and Caravale, *Sulle orme di George L. Mosse*, 19–39.

74. Mosse, "Europe and the Modern World," lecture notes. Another significant passage is: "Myth and symbol became an explanation for social life, a fact which functionally does not, however, rob life itself of importance. The 'objective reality,' as Marx would have called it, provides the setting and defines the limitations within which myth and symbol can operate. The actual political situation of Germany was in fact crucial in determining the content of myth and symbol and its linkage to nationalism. The workers' movement, while accepting much of the form of the new politics and even some of the nationalism involved, infused it with concepts of freedom which were directly relevant to the condition of the proletariat" (Mosse, *Nationalization of the Masses*, 210–11).

75. Mosse, *Confronting History*, 174.

76. Mosse, "European Culture 1815–1970—Enlightenment."

77. Mosse, *Culture of Western Europe* (1988), 46, 27.

78. Mosse, *Culture of Western Europe* (1961), 3.

79. Ibid., 5; Mosse, "History, Anthropology, and Mass Movements," 452.

80. Mosse, "Political Liturgy of Nationalism," 53.

81. Mosse, *Nationalization of the Masses*, 214–15 (my italics).

82. Mosse, *Culture of Western Europe* (1961), 2.

83. Mosse, *Reformation*, 112; Mosse, *Nazism*, 108.

84. Mosse, *Culture of Western Europe* (1961), 3–4; Mosse, *Culture of Western Europe* (1988), 4.

85. Mosse, *Nazism*, 27.

86. Mosse, "The Peasant and the Ideology"; Mosse, "Fascism Once More."

87. Mosse, *Culture of Western Europe* (1961), 5.

88. George L. Mosse, "Culture of Western Europe—Maastricht," notes for a course on Western Civilization, n.d., AR 25137, box 16, folder 32, George L. Mosse Collection, Leo Baeck Institute, New York. Though undated, the notes undoubtedly date to a recent period, in that Mosse criticizes his book, and particularly the little emphasis put on the positive sides of nationalism, the scarce attention devoted to respectability as the cement of society, the weight he had not given to the ideal of *Bildung*, and the neglect of the role played by the Great War. All these are themes Mosse did not deal with before the 1970s.

89. Mosse, *Culture of Western Europe* (1988), 5. However, it must be noted that Mosse's concept of the institutionalization of ideology was already developed in the early 1960s and fully elaborated in *The Crisis of German Ideology*, thus moving a first step toward that analysis of mass politics that came about in the late 1960s: "The importance of an ideology is how it was institutionalized," wrote Mosse in 1963, focusing then not only on individuals or groups or disciples, but also on movements that, he continues, ought to be studied with greater attention. See George L. Mosse, review of Simon, *European Positivism in the Nineteenth Century: An Essay in Intellectual History*. Reviewing another book, Mosse lamented the neglect of the "institutionalization of ideas. Surely the transmission of ideas becomes a more effective force in society when such ideas are embodied in social or educational institutions" (George L. Mosse, review of Wiener and Noland, *Ideas in Cultural Perspective*). "Ideas are 'important' only to the extent that they become popularized . . . and diffused across social boundaries and geographical and chronological distance" (Wald, "Cultural History and Symbols," 172).

90. Mosse, *Reformation*, 110, 112.

91. Mosse and Koenigsberger, *Sixteenth Century*, 10.

92. Mosse, "Europe and the Modern World," lectures.

93. Ringelheim, "Interview with George Mosse."

94. Mosse, "Europe and the Modern World," lectures.

95. Mosse, "Culture of Western Europe—Maastricht." "Mosse does not separate objective reality and the way it is perceived into two discrete analytic moments. Perception of a thing is as real as the thing itself. In such a process, myth, symbol, and value not only give form to perception, but become currency in themselves and the political system brought into action to valorize the dream" (Drescher, Sabean, and Sharlin, "George Mosse and Political Symbolism," 5).

96. As to the problem of choices, see the section "History and Psychology: Rationalizations, Motivations, Perceptions" in chap. 3, and also Mosse, "Europe and the Modern World," lectures.

97. See Mosse, *Masses and Men*, 14. Mosse gives a concrete example of this interplay between perception and reality with regard to the new politics: "I cannot list here all the factors which went into modern nation building such as war, social and in some nations rapid economic change. The 'objective conditions' (to quote Karl Marx) are always vital to any historical analysis, but they do not by themselves translate into human actions.

They must be mediated by people's perceptions, and these—in turn—can create new facts of great historical importance. Myths and symbols sway peoples' perceptions, especially in times of rapid movement and social and political disorientation. The new politics is both a product of objective reality and helps to create it." Mosse also argued that "to ignore the new politics as important in any explanation of the success of European fascism means to exclude most of the popular perceptions of fascism. The rejection of political liturgy as a serious and at times even decisive factor in the evolution of modern political movements lies in the unwillingness to acknowledge the importance of man's perceptions as an agent of politics" (Mosse, "Fascism as a Nationalist Movement").

98. Mosse, "European Cultural and Intellectual History, 1660–1870," lecture 01.

99. Mosse, "Europe and the Modern World," lectures.

100. Mosse, "Fascism as a Cultural Movement."

101. Mosse, "Culture of Western Europe—Maastricht."

102. Ringelheim, "Interview with George Mosse."

103. Mosse, "European Culture 1815–1970—Enlightenment."

104. Mosse, "History, Anthropology, and Mass Movements," 448.

105. Mosse, *Masses and Men*, 14. On myths and symbols viewed as images, see chap. 3.

106. Mosse, *Masses and Men*, 16–17. Mosse defined myths and symbols as the "mediating devices" of ideologies such as nationalism (Mosse, "Political Liturgy of Nationalism," 50). The general will of the people, Mosse wrote, is "mediated" by the nation (*Confronting the Nation*, 27); and he said that "the nation was the intermediary between the individual and a personal scheme of values and ethics. . . . National glory and the love for order expressed themselves through the symbols and myths mentioned earlier. They acted as a bridge between the people and government, for many taking the place of representative government itself" (*Culture of Western Europe* [1988], 68).

107. George L. Mosse, "European Culture 1815–1870—New Nationalism and Hegelianism," lectures, n.d., AR 25137, box 20, folder 6, George L. Mosse Collection, Leo Baeck Institute, New York.

108. Drescher, Sabean, and Sharlin, "George Mosse and Political Symbolism," 6.

109. Mosse, *Nazism*, 117.

110. In the drafts for a lecture, Mosse said that myth and ideology are what Marx called consciousness, though it is most likely that, in that context (he was speaking of the Eichmann myth), he was referring to "false" consciousness. See Mosse, "Europe and the Modern World," lectures.

Conclusion

1. Wald, "Cultural History and Symbols," 171; Winter, "De l'histoire intellectuelle," 178.

2. Aschheim, "George Mosse at 80," 296; Rabinbach, "George L. Mosse 1919–1999," 335.

3. Payne, "The Mosse Legacy," 9. In this article Payne mentioned Mosse's innovative contributions to the history of fascism, racism, mass movements, nationalism, sexuality, gender, and respectability.

4. Gentile, letter to George L. Mosse, December 18, 1998.

5. Aschheim, "George Mosse," xi.

6. The most significant recognitions he received include Doctor of Literature (honorary) from Carthage College, 1973; the Acqui-Storia Prize, 1975; the Premio Prezzolini, 1985; Doctor of Letters (honorary) from the Hebrew Union College—Jewish Institute of Religion, 1987; Doctor honoris causa from the Università Degli Studi di Camerino, Camerino, Italy 1995; Doctor honoris causa from the Universität-Gesamthochschule, Siegen 1998; American Historical Association's Award for Scholarly Distinction, 1998; Leo Baeck Medal for distinguished contributions to Jewish and European History, 1998. Important *Festschriften* in his honor are Drescher, Sabean, and Sharlin, *Political Symbolism in Modern Europe; George Mosse: On the Occasion of His Retirement, 17.6.8;* Staderini, Zani, and Magni, eds., *La grande guerra;* Berghan, ed., *The German-Jewish Dialogue Reconsidered;* Payne, Sorkin, and Tortorice, eds., *What History Tells;* Benadusi and Caravale, eds., *Sulle orme di George L. Mosse;* see also the special issue on Mosse of *German Politics and Society* 18, no. 4 (Winter 2000). Most of these *Festschriften* originate from symposia held in Mosse's honor. Furthermore, a George Mosse Foundation was created at the University of Amsterdam to further the advancement of gay and lesbian studies.

7. Ian Kershaw, *The Nazi Dictatorship: Problems and Perspectives of Interpretation* (1985; repr. London: Arnold, 1993); Klaus Hildebrand, *Das Dritte Reich* (1979; repr. Munich: Oldenbourg, 1989).

8. One exception is R. J. B. Bosworth, *Nationalism* (Pearson Education Limited, 2007), 123–24.

9. Peter Burke, *What Is Cultural History?* (Cambridge: Polity Press, 2004); Geoff Eley, *The Crooked Line: From Cultural History to the History of Society* (Ann Arbor: University of Michigan Press, 2005). Even Mosse's role as coeditor of the *Journal of Contemporary History,* the leading journal in the study of contemporary history and the stage upon which many pioneering trends in cultural history first surfaced, is hardly mentioned.

10. Herf, "Mosse's Recasting," 18.

11. Rabinbach, "George L. Mosse 1919–1999," 336.

12. Rudy Koshar, "George Mosse e gli interrogativi della storia tedesca," *Passato e presente* 21, no. 58 (2003): 104.

13. Moro, "George L. Mosse," 29.

14. Notably the booklet Mosse, *Reformation,* and Mosse and Koenigsberger, *Sixteenth Century.* For Mosse's contribution to early modern historiography, see also Sommerville, "George Mosse's Early Modern Scholarship," and Caravale, "Una storia dimenticata."

15. Herf, "Mosse's Recasting," 20.

16. Aschheim, "George Mosse at 80," 302.

17. Ibid., 296; Rabinbach, "George L. Mosse 1919–1999," 335.

18. Gentile, *Il fascino del persecutore,* 84.

19. Phyllis Cohen Albert and Alex Sagan, "George L. Mosse Memorial Symposium: Introduction," *German Politics and Society* 18, no. 4 (Winter 2000): 1.

20. Aschheim, "George Mosse at 80," 300. See also Rabinbach, "George L. Mosse 1919–1999," 335; Koshar, "George Mosse e gli interrogativi," 106; and Koshar, "Destination Culture."

21. Aschheim, "George Mosse at 80," 302.

22. Rabinbach, "George L. Mosse 1919–1999," 336; Gentile, "L'uomo nuovo' del fascismo."

23. Rabinbach, "George L. Mosse 1919–1999," 336.

24. Emilio Gentile, *The Sacralization of Politics in Fascist Italy* (Cambridge, MA: Harvard University Press, 1996); Emilio Gentile, *Politics as Religion* (Princeton, NJ: Princeton University Press, 2006), originally published in Italy as Gentile, *Il culto del littorio* and *Le religioni della politica: Fra democrazie e totalitarismi* (Rome: Laterza, 2001). For a debate on the concept of "political religions" see, among the many recent publications, "Political Religions as a Characteristic of the 20th Century," special issue, *Totalitarian Movements and Political Religions* 6, no. 1 (June 2005): 12.

25. Eric Voegelin, "The Political Religions," in *Modernity without Restraint: The Collected Works of Eric Voegelin*, vol. 5 (Columbia: University of Missouri Press, 2000); Hayes, "Nationalism as a Religion"; Hayes, *Nationalism: A Religion*; Hans Kohn, *The Idea of Nationalism: A Study in Its Origins and Background* (New York: Macmillan, 1944), 4, 23.

26. Emilio Gentile, letter to Mosse, October 14, 1982, AR 25137, box 35, folder 9, George L. Mosse Collection, Leo Baeck Institute, New York. It must be said that Mosse, in turn, praised Gentile's works on Italian fascism, stating that they had broadened his horizons (George Mosse, letter to Emilio Gentile, September 9, 1980, AR 25137, box 35, folder 9, George L. Mosse Collection, Leo Baeck Institute, New York). In 1990 Mosse wrote that "whatever little I know about Italian fascism I have gotten very largely from your recent work" (Mosse, letter to Emilio Gentile, October 15, 1990).

27. Donatello Aramini, *George L. Mosse: L'Italia e gli storici* (Milan: Franco Angeli, 2010).

28. The conference, by the title "Sulle orme di George L. Mosse" ("On George L. Mosse's Traces"), was held on May 11, 2010, and organized by a scientific board including Lorenzo Benadusi, Giorgio Caravale, Simona Colarizi, Renato Moro, and Luciano Zani with the support of the Faculty of Sociology of the Università di Roma La Sapienza and by the Faculty of Political Sciences of the Università degli Studi di Roma Tre. The contributors were Lorenzo Benadusi, Giorgio Caravale, Lutz Klinkhammer, Donatello Aramini, Merel Leeman, Simon Levis Sullam, Andrea Giardina, and Karel Plessini. Other participants were Luigi Frati, Mario Morcellini, Fabrizio Battistelli, Annunziata Nobile, Simona Colarizi, Luigi Goglia, Mario Toscano, and Vittorio Vidotto. From this conference originated the volume edited by Benadusi and Caravale, *Sulle orme di George L. Mosse.*

29. Aramini, *George L. Mosse*. See also Vittorio Vidotto, "La particolare fortuna di Mosse in Italia," in Benadusi and Caravale, *Sulle orme di George L. Mosse*, 109–20; and Giorgio Caravale, "'A mutual admiration society': Amicizie intellettuali alle origini del legame tra George L. Mosse e l'Italia," *Mondo contemporaneo* 3 (2011): 79–111.

30. Pier Francesco Listri, ed., *George Mosse*, Quaderni del 'Premio Prezzolini' 3 (Florence: Le Monnier, 1990), 15. As to the Italian reception of *The Nationalization of the Masses*, see Donatello Aramini, "George L. Mosse e gli storici italiani: il problema della 'nazionalizzazione delle masse,'" *Mondo Contemporaneo* 2 (2007): 129–59, and Aramini, *George L. Mosse*.

31. On the personal and professional relationship between Mosse and De Felice, see Emilio Gentile, "Renzo e George, anti-antifascisti," *Il Sole 24 Ore*, May 14, 2006; Gentile, *Il fascino del persecutore*; Emilio Gentile, *Renzo De Felice: Lo storico e il personaggio* (Rome: Laterza, 2003). See also Aramini, "George L. Mosse e gli storici italiani," and Aramini, *George L. Mosse*, 28–32. Aramini, together with Giovanni Mario Ceci, also edited the correspondence between Mosse and De Felice, publishing it for the first time: see their "Carteggio George L. Mosse—Renzo De Felice," *Mondo Contemporaneo* 3 (2007): 77–104.

32. In 1985 Mosse was also awarded the Premio Prezzolini. Emilio Gentile was on the jury. See Listri, *George Mosse*.

33. Emilio Gentile, "La nuova politica," *Il resto del Carlino*, May 24, 1975, quoted in Aramini, "George L. Mosse e gli storici italiani," 133–34. Aramini mentions the negative reactions to Mosse's book by Guido Quazza and Enzo Collotti, whose criticisms show how Italian historiography still regarded Mosse's work (as had been the case with De Felice) as close to an attempt to rehabilitate fascism (Aramini, "George L. Mosse e gli storici italiani," 136). The high esteem in which De Felice held Mosse's work was reciprocated. Both historians shared similar views on fascism, particularly those centering on the problem of consensus. What De Felice had said about consensus, Mosse asserted in a lecture, is painful but true: De Felice goes beyond illusions and "confronts us with historical reality." If Italy had such difficulties at accepting this view, it was because of its antifascist traditions and because Italy did not produce an Auschwitz; Mosse concluded, "Professor De Felice has taught us to understand fascism as a historical phenomenon, and painful though this may be, to understand is not to forgive. The contrary is true: to understand fascism without fear or favor means to be the anti-fascist of 1975" (Mosse, "Fascism as History").

34. See Aramini, "George L. Mosse e gli storici italiani," and Aramini, *George L. Mosse*.

35. Aramini shows Mosse's influence on Emilio Gentile's *Il mito dello Stato nuovo* (Rome: Laterza, 1982), and on Renzo De Felice's *Mussolini il Duce*, vol. 2, *Lo Stato totalitario 1936–1940* (Turin: Einaudi, 1981). Aramini also mentions De Felice's praise of Mosse's studies on racism (Aramini, "George L. Mosse e gli storici italiani," 138–40).

36. Aramini takes as a telling example Pier Giorgio Zunino's *L'ideologia del fascismo: Miti, credenze e valori nella stabilizzazione del regime* (Bologna: Il Mulino, 1985), which fully incorporated Mosse's influence. See Aramini, "George L. Mosse e gli storici italiani," 144–45.

37. Aramini, "George L. Mosse e gli storici italiani," 145. Among these Annales historians, Aramini mentions Maurice Agulhon, Pierre Nora, Mona Ozouf, and Michel Vovelle.

38. Important exceptions to this trend were, apart from Gentile, Renato Moro and Rudy Koshar (whose contribution on this subject was published by the Italian journal *Passato e presente*). See Aramini, "George L. Mosse e gli storici italiani," 146–51.

39. See Gentile, *Il culto del littorio*; Gentile, *Le religioni della politica*; Emilio Gentile, *La democrazia di Dio: La religione americana nell'era dell'impero e del terrore* (Rome: Laterza, 2006).

40. Moro, "George L. Mosse"; Galasso, "Il Novecento"; Gentile, "A Provisional Dwelling"; Gentile, *Il fascino del persecutore*. See also Karel Plessini, "The Nazi as the 'Ideal Bourgeois': Respectability and Nazism in the Work of George L. Mosse," *Totalitarian Movements and Political Religions* 5, no. 2 (Autumn 2004): 226–42.

41. Aramini, "George L. Mosse e gli storici italiani," 158–59; see also Aramini, *George L. Mosse*, 215–56.

42. Moshe Zimmermann, "Mosse and German Historiography," in *George Mosse: On the Occasion of His Retirement, 17.6.8*, xx.

43. Mosse, "Nationalism and War."

44. Zimmermann, "Mosse and German Historiography," xxi.

45. Aschheim, "George Mosse at 80," 296. On the Goethe-Medaille see the Award Certificate of the Goethe-Institut, March 22, 1988, AR 25137, box 1, folder 43, George L. Mosse Collection, Leo Baeck Institute, New York. It is significant that the University of Siegen is the home university of Professor Klaus Vondung, who was very receptive to Mosse's work, being himself a pioneer—rather in solitude in the German historiographical environment—of the study of the liturgical aspects of National Socialism in the late 1960s and early 1970s. See Vondung, ed., *Kriegserlebnis*, where Mosse published two of his first studies on the First World War. Vondung is also the author of *Magie und Manipulation: Ideologischer Kult und politische Religion des Nationalsozialismus* (Goettingen: Vandenhoeck and Ruprecht, 1971), a book that, in Roger Griffin's assessment, "achieved for the understanding of the cultic dimension of Nazism what Gentile's *Culto del littorio* has done for Fascism" (Roger Griffin, "'I Am No Longer Human. I Am A Titan. A God!' The Fascist Quest to Regenerate Time," http://www.history.ac.uk/eseminars/sem22tml#53t ("written-up version of a talk given in November 1998 at the Institute of Historical Research as part of the seminar series *Modern Italian History: 19th and 20th Centuries* organized by Carl Levy"). See also Vondung's "National Socialism as a Political Religion: Potentials and Limits of an Analytical Concept," *Totalitarian Movements and Political Religions* 6, no. 1 (June 2005): 87–95. Regarding Germany's recent favorable reception of Mosse, see also, for example, Friedländer, "Mosse's Influence." Another German historian who furthered a cultural approach was Thomas Nipperdey, whose influence on Mosse was discussed in chap. 3.

46. For example, *The Image of Man* and *Fallen Soldiers*, translated as *L'image de l'homme: L'invention de la virilité moderne* (Paris: Éditions Abbeville, 1997), and *De la Grande Guerre au totalitarisme* (Paris: Hachette-Littérature, 1999). Stéphane Audoin-Rouzeau has noted that only two articles on Mosse and one interview had appeared in French: Bruno Cabanes, "Les deux guerres de George Mosse," *L'Histoire* 199 (May 1996):

13–14, and Annette Becker, "Barbarie de la Grande Guerre," *L'Histoire* 241 (March 2000): 23; the interview is Mosse, "Du Baroque au Nazisme" (Stéphane Audoin-Rouzeau, "George L. Mosse: Réflexions sur une méconnaissance française," *Annales* 56, no. 1 [2001]: 183–86). There is one more contribution in French, written by an American historian: Winter, "De l'histoire intellectuelle." Recently, more works have been translated, such as *The Fascist Revolution* and *The Crisis of German Ideology*.

47. According to John Tortorice, Mosse's relationship with France was difficult because he had remained negatively impressed by the widespread anti-Semitism he perceived and experienced in the country in the 1930s, when he spent long periods of time there with his family. Conversation with John Tortorice, September 2010.

48. Audoin-Rouzeau, "George L. Mosse," 185–86.

49. Michele Nani, review of *Confronting History: A Memoir*, by George L. Mosse, *Chromos* 10 (2005): 1–3; see also François Cochet, "Pace e guerra nel ventesimo secolo: Un bilancio storiografico della ricerca francese," *Mondo contemporaneo* 1 (2005): 1–14. Mosse was also active, as it has been pointed out, as a founding advisor to the Historial de la Grande Guerre at Péronne, France.

50. In this regard, see Gentile, *Il fascino del persecutore*, 191–93, and also the correspondence between Mosse and Furet (but also with Emilio Gentile) in AR 25137, box 17, folder 21, George L. Mosse Collection, Leo Baeck Institute, New York. Mosse's article, which should have appeared in a volume on the legacy of the French Revolution edited by Vito Laterza, was eventually published in the *Journal of Contemporary History* 24 (January 1989): 5–26, due to Furet's opposition.

51. On the history of National Socialism, see also chap. 6; on Jewish history, see chap. 7.

52. See Drescher, Sabean, and Sharlin, eds., *Political Symbolism in Modern Europe*; Berghan, ed., *The German-Jewish Dialogue Reconsidered*; the "George L. Mosse Memorial Symposium" in *German Politics and Society*; and Payne, Sorkin, and Tortorice, eds., *What History Tells*.

53. Anson Rabinbach, "In Memoriam George L. Mosse," *Aufbau*, February 19, 1999.

54. Kenneth D. Barkin, "German Émigré Historians in America: The Fifties, Sixties, and Seventies" in *An Interrupted Past: German-Speaking Refugee Historians in the United States after 1933*, ed. Hartmut Lehmann and James Sheridan (Washington, D.C.: German Historical Institute, 1991), 147. Barkin argues that, though these historians were crucial for the establishment of German history, in some respects the greatest influence on the discipline of history was that of German Jewish social scientists like Hannah Arendt or Erich Fromm (165).

55. Barkin, "German Émigré Historians," 153–54. Telling in this regard are Mosse's recollections of anti-Semitism in the United States: see Mosse, *Confronting History*, 95, 119.

56. Barkin, "German Émigré Historians," 156–57.

57. Ibid., 158–59. Barkin mentions Hans Kohn, Hajo Holborn, Fritz Stern, Leonard Krieger, Klaus Epstein, and George Mosse, though emphasizing the differences between

their objects of study and methodology. Intellectual history was not new in the United States—Barkin mentions Lovejoy—and yet it must be kept in mind how Mosse deeply revolutionized such an approach. In this regard, see also Gentile, *Il fascino del persecutore,* 32–34.

58. Aschheim, *Beyond the Border.* Among prominent members of the "first generation," Aschheim lists Felix Gilbert, Hans Rothfels, and Arthur and Hans Rosenberg among others. The importance of "second-generation" scholars has been generally neglected by the vast literature on German Jewish émigré historians; see Jeremy Popkin, *History, Historians and Autobiography* (Chicago: University of Chicago Press, 2005), and Ethan Katz, "Displaced Historians, Dialectical Histories: George L. Mosse, Peter Gay and Germany's Multiple Paths in the Twentieth Century," *Journal of Modern Jewish Studies* 7, no. 2 (July 2008): 135–55, which focusses on the parallel between Mosse and Gay, and yet aims at a wider perspective.

59. Aschheim, *Beyond the Border,* 46.

60. Ibid., 47–48. To be sure, Mosse strongly distanced himself from such a view, despite his initial closeness to it in the 1960s.

61. Ibid., 48–49. This has been observed also by Friedländer, "Mosse's Influence," 137.

62. Aschheim, *Beyond the Border,* 62–63.

63. Ibid., 68. Similarly, Emilio Gentile argued that Mosse avoided accusations of furthering a revisionist approach (in the pejorative sense) only because he was a victim of National Socialism. See Gentile, *Il fascino del persecutore,* 193.

64. One rare exception to this rule was Gerald Reitlinger's *The Final Solution* (New York: Beechhurst Press, 1953).

65. Enzo Traverso, "To Brush against the Grain: The Holocaust and German-Jewish Culture in Exile," *Totalitarian Movements and Political Religions* 5, no. 2 (Autumn 2004): 243–70. Although Traverso focusses on Hannah Arendt, Günther Anders, Theodor Adorno, and Max Horkheimer, his conclusions fully apply, in my opinion, to other émigrés of the "second generation" like Mosse, who is also quoted by Traverso in his article.

66. Ibid., 254–55. On the connection between historiography and personal memory among German Jewish exiles, see Katz, "Displaced Historians," and Aschheim, *Beyond the Border.*

67. Traverso, "To Brush against the Grain," 255. As Mosse wrote in his memoir, one of the reasons that had pushed him into the study of the Holocaust had been that "finding an explanation has been vital not only for the understanding of modern history, but also for my own peace of mind" (*Confronting History,* 219).

68. Traverso, "To Brush against the Grain," 256.

69. Ibid., 257–58. Traverso asserts that these refugees (referring, to be sure, to those of the "first generation"), however, paid the high price of being stateless and politically powerless. If Mosse surely managed to integrate into American society, even adopting respectability, he perfectly fits Traverso's assertion that "the passport became the focal point of exile existence"; indeed, Mosse insisted on numerous occasions on his enduring

fear of separating from his passport. Speaking of his "built-in insecurity" due to exile and statelessness, he wrote that his father bought him a Luxembourg passport without an expiration date: "I have kept this passport to this day in case of emergency, for anxieties about passports have never left me, and I still refuse to hand my American passport over to hotels for overnight registration" (*Confronting History*, 90).

70. Traverso, "To Brush against the Grain," 263. The reference is to Mosse's contribution to *The German-Jewish Legacy in America 1933–1988*, ed. Abraham J. Peck (Detroit: Wayne State University Press, 1989), 17–24.

71. Moro, "George L. Mosse," 35; Herf, "Mosse's Recasting," 18.

72. Koshar, "George Mosse e gli interrogativi," 101–2.

73. Mosse, *Confronting History*, 182.

74. Mosse, *Crisis of German Ideology*, 8.

75. Wald, "Cultural History and Symbols," 172.

76. Mosse, *Crisis of German Ideology*, v–x.

77. Herf, "Mosse's Recasting," 26. See also Aschheim, "George Mosse," xii, and Aschheim, "George Mosse at 80," 298.

78. Breines, "Finding Oneself in History," 16.

79. Rabinbach, "George L. Mosse 1919–1999," 333, 336.

80. Aschheim, "George Mosse," xvii.

81. George L. Mosse, Unidentified Lectures—To Students, n.d., AR 25137, box 19, folder 12, George L. Mosse Collection, Leo Baeck Institute, New York. These lectures, though most of them are undated, were undoubtedly delivered during the 1960s, in that they bear references to the events of the time.

82. George L. Mosse, "Fraternity Talks," 1968, AR 25137, box 17, folder 19, George L. Mosse Collection, Leo Baeck Institute, New York.

83. Aschheim, "George Mosse," xi, xvi, xvii.

84. Mosse, *Holy Pretence*, 154.

85. Breines, "With George Mosse in the 1960s," 293.

86. George L. Mosse, "Discorso di ringraziamento," in Listri, *George Mosse*, 8.

87. Mosse, *The Fascist Revolution*, 44. The Italian political scientist Giovanni Sartori has used the term "homo videns" in his masterful analysis of the impact of television on human nature and behavior. See Giovanni Sartori, *Homo videns: Televisione e post-pensiero* (Rome: Laterza, 1997). On the relationship between knowledge based on the written word and knowledge based on television images, see also Neil Postman's classic study *Amusing Ourselves to Death: Public Discourse in the Age of Show Business* (New York: Penguin Books, 1985).

88. George L. Mosse, untitled speech on indoctrination in Mosse, "Is Fascism Alive?"

89. Mosse, *Reformation*, 1.

90. Mosse, *Confronting History*, 184.

91. George L. Mosse, "Commencement Address," 1960, AR 25137, box 16, folder 23, George L. Mosse Collection, Leo Baeck Institute, New York.

92. Mosse, "Manfred Swarsensky."

INDEX

George L. Mosse Series in Modern European Cultural and Intellectual History

STEVEN E. ASCHHEIM, STANLEY G. PAYNE,
MARY LOUISE ROBERTS, AND DAVID J. SORKIN

Series Editors

Of God and Gods: Egypt, Israel, and the Rise of Monotheism
JAN ASSMANN

The Enemy of the New Man: Homosexuality in Fascist Italy
LORENZO BENADUSI; translated by SUZANNE DINGEE and
JENNIFER PUDNEY

Collected Memories: Holocaust History and Postwar Testimony
CHRISTOPHER R. BROWNING

Cataclysms: A History of the Twentieth Century from Europe's Edge
DAN DINER; translated by WILLIAM TEMPLER with JOEL GOLB

La Grande Italia: The Myth of the Nation in the Twentieth Century
EMILIO GENTILE; translated by SUZANNE DINGEE and
JENNIFER PUDNEY

*Carl Schmitt and the Jews: The "Jewish Question," the Holocaust,
and German Legal Theory*
RAPHAEL GROSS; translated by JOEL GOLB

*Some Measure of Justice:
The Holocaust Era Restitution Campaign of the 1990s*
MICHAEL R. MARRUS

Confronting History: A Memoir
GEORGE L. MOSSE

Nazi Culture: Intellectual, Cultural, and Social Life in the Third Reich
GEORGE L. MOSSE

What History Tells: George L. Mosse and the Culture of Modern Europe
Edited by STANLEY G. PAYNE, DAVID J. SORKIN,
and JOHN S. TORTORICE

The Perils of Normalcy: George L. Mosse and the Remaking of Cultural History
KAREL PLESSINI

The Jews in Mussolini's Italy: From Equality to Persecution
MICHELE SARFATTI; translated by JOHN and ANNE C. TEDESCHI

*Jews and Other Germans: Civil Society, Religious Diversity, and
Urban Politics in Breslau, 1860–1925*
TILL VAN RAHDEN; translated by MARCUS BRAINARD

*An Uncompromising Generation:
The Nazi Leadership of the Reich Security Main Office*
MICHAEL WILDT; translated by TOM LAMPERT